Welcome

Welcome to part two of the in-depth examination of the engineers' wagon fleet of British Rail, this following on from the first volume which was released in December 2020. That initial instalment dealt with the ballast wagons and rail carriers that were purpose-built by BR from its creation in 1948 through to the early 1980s and which were predominately either unfitted or equipped with vacuum brakes. Many of the former revenue earning wagons that were taken on as the first wave of replacements were also covered, these also being vacuum-braked designs.

This second volume completes the story of the Civil Engineers wagon fleet up to the demise of British Rail in the mid-1990s as privatisation took effect. This period of roughly 15 years was marked by the modernisation of the fleet with many of the increasingly elderly and low capacity designs withdrawn and replaced by a variety of new types fitted with modern and efficient air brakes. As ever, the various engineering departments were at the back of the queue for investment so all-new wagon builds never progressed beyond a handful of prototypes. However, there were a number of conversion programmes put in place while the haemorrhaging of traffic by the Railfreight sector during the 1980s meant there were large numbers of nearly new wagons available to transfer across.

There was more to the Civil Engineers than just wagons though and this volume takes a look at the various cranes and track relayers that were available to the department over the same period. Again, there was great diversity to be found here with the last surviving steam cranes clinging to life and an array of diesel-powered types with different transmissions available as well.

The Civil Engineers were not the only department with its own wagon fleet and those belonging to the Signal and Telegraph Engineers are introduced here. This includes the department's own purpose-built designs along with transfers from the traditional BR wagon fleet before covering the colourful Satlink period of the early 1990s. Equally bright were the vehicles assigned to the Mercury telecommunications project, which are also included. Unfortunately, space precludes a full examination of the diverse wagon types employed by the Mechanical and Electrical Engineers, but the interesting Rail Stores fleet is covered in detail.

As ever, thanks are due to Trevor Mann and David Ratcliffe for their considerable input along with Terry Bendall, Mike Cubberley, Tim Easter, Steve Farmer, Mark Lambert, Hywel Thomas, Paul Wade and Carl White for their contributions on the modelling side. Further acknowledgements are due to Paul Bartlett, Mark Saunders, and Roger Silsbury for access to their photo collections along with the other photographers credited within.

Simon Bendall
Editor

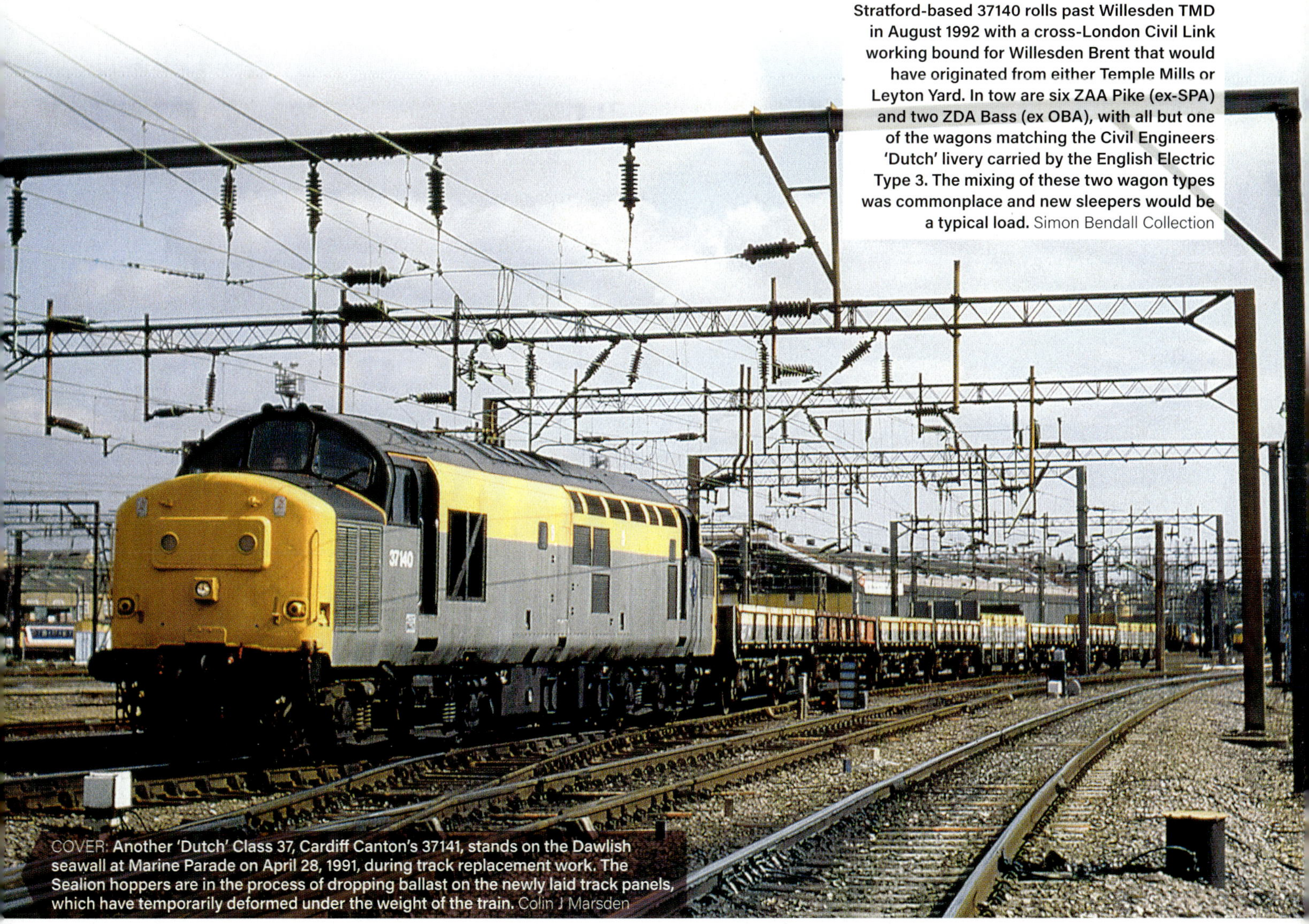

Stratford-based 37140 rolls past Willesden TMD in August 1992 with a cross-London Civil Link working bound for Willesden Brent that would have originated from either Temple Mills or Leyton Yard. In tow are six ZAA Pike (ex-SPA) and two ZDA Bass (ex OBA), with all but one of the wagons matching the Civil Engineers 'Dutch' livery carried by the English Electric Type 3. The mixing of these two wagon types was commonplace and new sleepers would be a typical load. Simon Bendall Collection

COVER: **Another 'Dutch' Class 37, Cardiff Canton's 37141, stands on the Dawlish seawall at Marine Parade on April 28, 1991, during track replacement work. The Sealion hoppers are in the process of dropping ballast on the newly laid track panels, which have temporarily deformed under the weight of the train.** Colin J Marsden

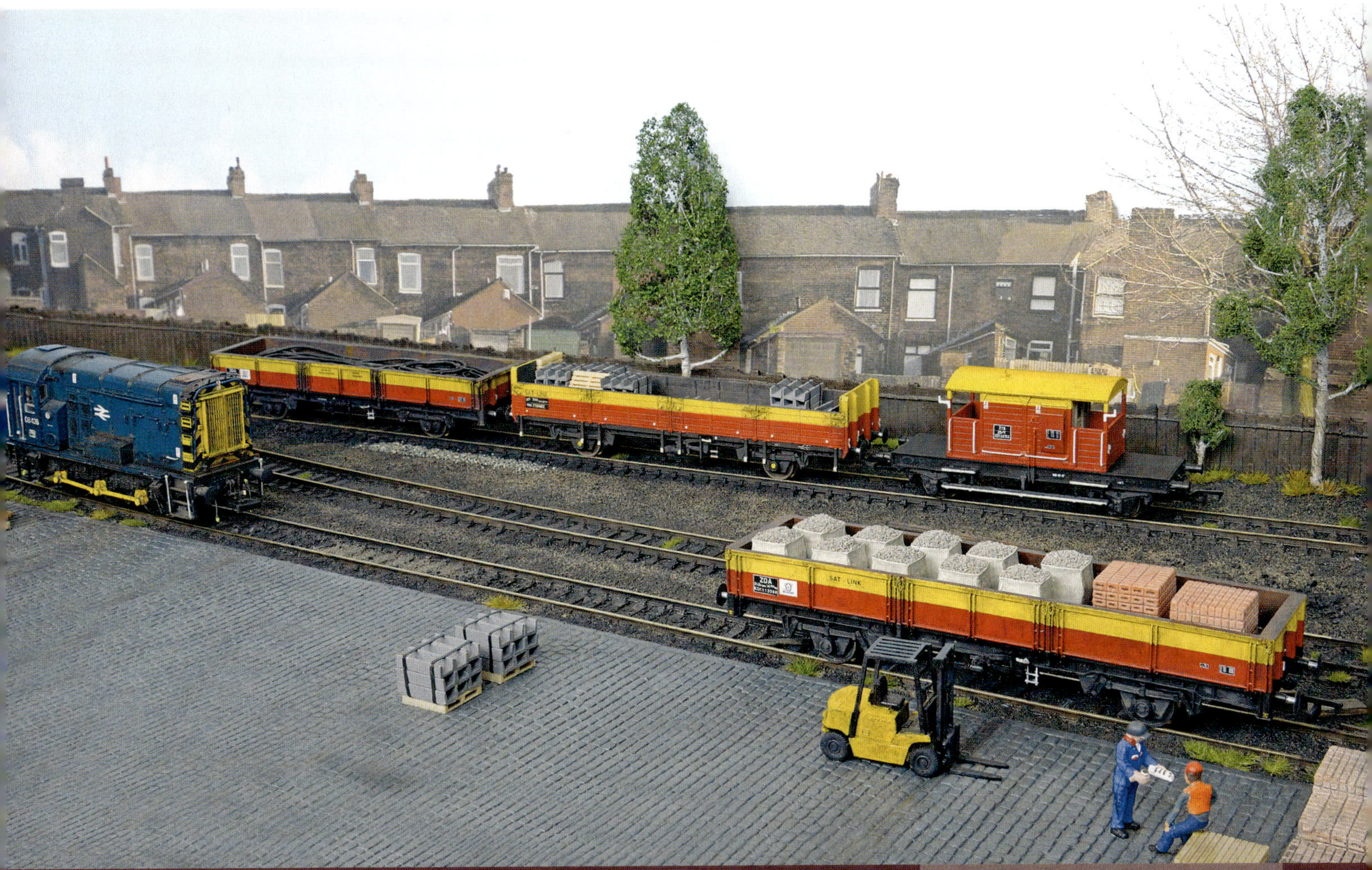

Contents

ABOVE: **Some engineering sidings could be quite compact in size, providing plenty of modelling inspiration for those with only a small amount of space available for a layout. Illustrating what can be achieved in a length of just 4ft and 13 inches at its widest point is Down Sidings, which is the work of Richard Coleman. The OO gauge layout provides further interest by focussing on the colourful Satlink fleet, which is less commonly modelled than the wagons of the Civil Engineers. In this scene, 08428 is marshalling ZDAs (former OBA and OCA opens) ready for weekend work with an ex-Southern Railway Pillbox brake van also in attendance for use as a personnel carrier.** Dennis Taylor

Editor: Simon Bendall
Main contributors: Trevor Mann, David Ratcliffe
Senior Editor Bookazines: Roger Mortimer
Email: roger.mortimer@keypublishing.com
Design: Julian Jefferson
Head Designer: Steve Donovan

Advertising Sales Manager: Brodie Baxter
Email: brodie.baxter@keypublishing.com

Advertising Production: Rebecca Antoniades
Email: rebecca.antoniades@keypublishing.com

Subscription/Mail Order
Key Publishing Ltd, PO Box 300, Stamford, Lincs, PE9 1NA
Tel: 01780 480404

Fax: 01780 757812
Subscriptions email: subs@keypublishing.com
Mail Order email: orders@keypublishing.com

PUBLISHING
Group CEO: Adrian Cox
Publisher: Mark Elliott
Head of Publishing: Finbarr O'Reilly
Chief Publishing Officer: Jonathan Jackson
Head of Production: Janet Watkins

Key Publishing Ltd, PO Box 100, Stamford, Lincs, PE9 1XP
Tel: 01780 755131 **Website:** www.keypublishing.com

Printing
Precision Colour Printing Ltd, Haldane, Halesfield 1, Telford, Shropshire. TF7 4QQ

Distribution
Seymour Distribution Ltd, 2 Poultry Avenue, London, EC1A 9PU **Enquiries Line:** 02074 294000.

Despite taking on much additional air and vacuum-braked stock, unfitted ballast wagons could still be found at the end of the 1980s. During April 1987, 31229 ambles through the outskirts of Cheltenham with a lightweight load of just two Grampus, the nearest being unfitted and the other vacuum-braked. As a result, a brake van is required, the example here being one of those modified with air pipes and given the yellow paintwork around the duckets. The leading wagon is carrying a hired-in Poclain tracked excavator, several Grampus being loaded with such a machine at this time. These remained in the wagon while working, being something of a bargain basement version of the excavators used for electrification work and similar where the machine body was fixed directly to the wagon floor. As the cab superstructure was out of gauge, this hinged forward to rest on the wagon floor when in transit and is out of sight behind the jib. Simon Bendall Collection

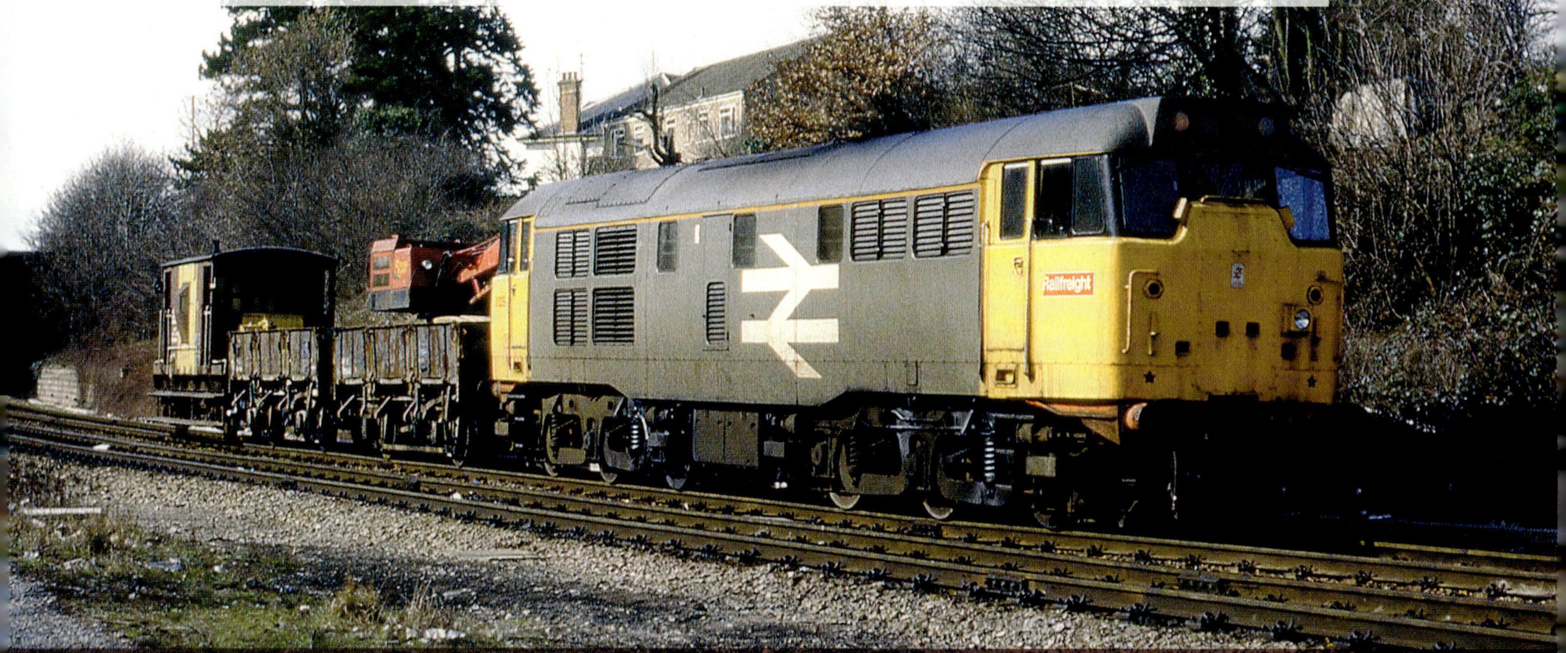

Modernising the fleet

With the late 1970s seeing British Rail strive for a leaner, faster network, the Civil Engineers' wagon fleet had to evolve to meet the demands. This meant taking on more modern stock or modifying existing wagons and working such assets more efficiently. Simon Bendall details the transition that took place in the final 20 or so years of BR's existence.

Railfreight original grey-liveried 37512 *Thornaby Demon* coasts through its namesake station on May 23, 1988, as it prepares to enter Tees Yard with a load of new concrete sleepers. These had originated from the Dowmac sleeper manufacturing plant at Tallington, near Peterborough, and are loaded in five ZAA Pike. The former SPA steel plate wagons were well suited to such a load as were the OAA, OBA and OCA opens that became Squid and Bass. Two of the Pike are carrying grey/yellow with the others still in Railfreight red. Simon Bendall Collection

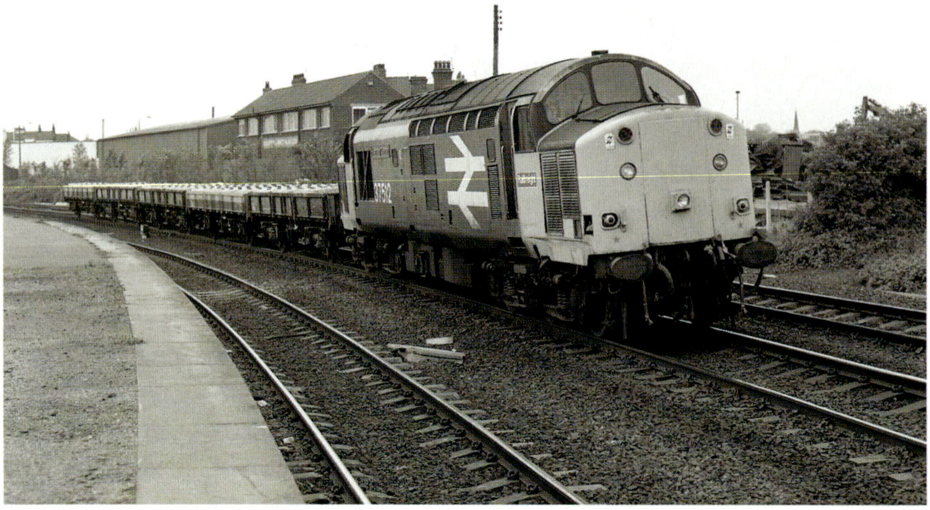

By the end of the 1970s, a large part of the Civil Engineers' wagon fleet was life expired, particularly amongst the ballast opens. Many of the latter were around 30 years old, or more in the case of pre-nationalisation designs, while their limited capacity and lack of train brakes made them inefficient and slow on a network looking to the future with the introduction of HSTs. The Railfreight sector was also in the process of receiving new wagons in the form of long-wheelbase air-braked vehicles that would greatly reduce transit times and increase payloads.

As ever, the Civil Engineers department had little in the way of finance available but it too desired to run fully-braked trains to speed up its operations. While a fleet consisting entirely of air-braked wagons was but a dream, it readily accepted vacuum braked stock made redundant from revenue-earning duties for use in carrying ballast. Such vehicles could be converted to make them suitable for this purpose, such as the Bogie Bolster E, which with drop-sides added became the YCV Turbots, or plate wagons which also gained new bodywork as ZCV Plaice. Other open wagon types could be used without alterations, such as the MSV tipplers and MTV sand wagons, which became Barbels and Zanders at the end of the 1980s, while the Shochood B were similarly re-tasked as Dace earlier in the decade. Detailed histories of all of these types were included in the previous volume.

While vacuum-braked stock was better than a train with no continuous brakes at all, it was still deemed an inferior system and one that BR was progressively looking to eliminate in favour of air brakes. As a result, there would only be one more substantial conversion programme for the Civil Engineers involving such wagons. The decline of the coal industry following the miners' strike had left large numbers of vacuum-braked 21-ton hoppers out of work, many of which still had good quality underframes and others with bodywork that also had some life remaining. This led to the appearance of the Topes, Clams and Rudds in the late 1980s of which the first two retained vacuum-brakes with the Topes also keeping their hopper bodies while the Clams received new box bodywork. In contrast, the Rudds underwent extensive work, gaining air-brakes and new dropside box bodies. Essentially a modernised version of the long-serving Grampus, the Rudds would serve with distinction into this century and some now earn a keep on preserved lines.

Nearly new

The rapid decline of general freight traffic, particularly the need for open wagons, in the early 1980s presented the Civil Engineers with an unexpected opportunity to acquire some of the aforementioned air-braked stock from Railfreight, many of these recently built vehicles such as the wooden-bodied OBAs having seen comparatively little use. Like the OAA and OCA types that would later join them in the engineers' fleet, these were not for ballast carrying but were well suited to moving sleepers, be they wooden or concrete, and could also carry the longer lengths needed for pointwork. Designated as general materials carriers, they also transported anything else that was bulky, including light machinery.

In the early 1990s, these open wagons served as conversion fodder for a new generation of ballast opens as their bodywork began to tire. Ultimately culminating in the Sea Urchin design, of which there were several different styles, they helped see off the Grampus and many of the other vacuum-braked types. Around the same time, the opportunity to acquire two-axle POA aggregates boxes from the private owner fleet arose, these being modified into the Limpets, which again brought the withdrawal of older designs.

The tradition of giving wagons allocated to the Civil Engineers aquatic-themed names continued with this new influx of types, even if some started to veer into the obscure! Worthy of mention is the number prefix given to air-braked wagons transferred from revenue to engineers' use, this being 'DC'. Previously 'DB' had been used but to apply this to the newcomers risked creating number clashes on the TOPS computer system with older wagons still in use so the next letter along was adopted to avoid this. As would be expected, new three letter TOPS codes were given to each type as well with the Y series for bogie wagons and Z for two-axle designs.

In terms of liveries with so many wagons transferring across in a relatively short time, large numbers retained their previous colour scheme for some years, such as the short-lived Railfreight maroon scheme or its red/grey replacement. Invariably the Railfreight lettering would be painted out and the new TOPS code, number prefix and fish name added on in numerous styles. Sometimes specific lettering would also appear, such as the circuits to be worked by stores wagons. By the start of the 1990s, the grey and yellow Civil Engineers livery was increasingly prevalent, although the style of application and lettering still varied widely. The livery also spread to the locomotive fleet from the summer of 1990 and within a couple of years, matching locos and rakes of stock were not uncommon, which was a far cry from the dirty blue locos and wagons in varying shades of rust seen a decade earlier.

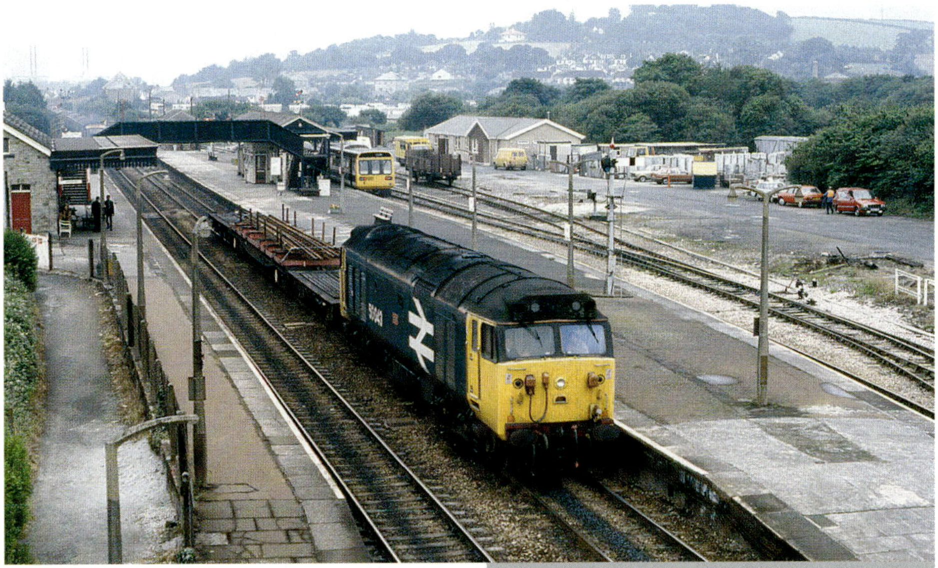

ABOVE: **The load behind 50043 *Eagle* was hardly one to tax the English Electric Type 4 as it heads through Par while working from Truro to Tavistock Junction on July 14, 1987. In tow is a YLA Mullet carrying four switch assemblies, this still retaining Railfreight red after transfer from the revenue fleet and recoding from BRA. With the load overhanging the borail at both ends, runner wagons have been provided, both being ex VDA vans; in this case with their bodywork removed and recoded as ZEA Bream. In the background, a Class 142 Skipper, as the railbuses were known in the West Country, awaits departure to Newquay.** Simon Bendall Collection

Fewer changes

If the ballast opens needed large scale renewal, the opposite was true of the ballast hoppers, where the air-braked Seacows built in 1981/82 and the decade-older and predominately dual-braked Sealions were more than sufficient to cope with requirements. These were supported by the vacuum-braked Dogfish and Catfish hoppers throughout the 1980s and early

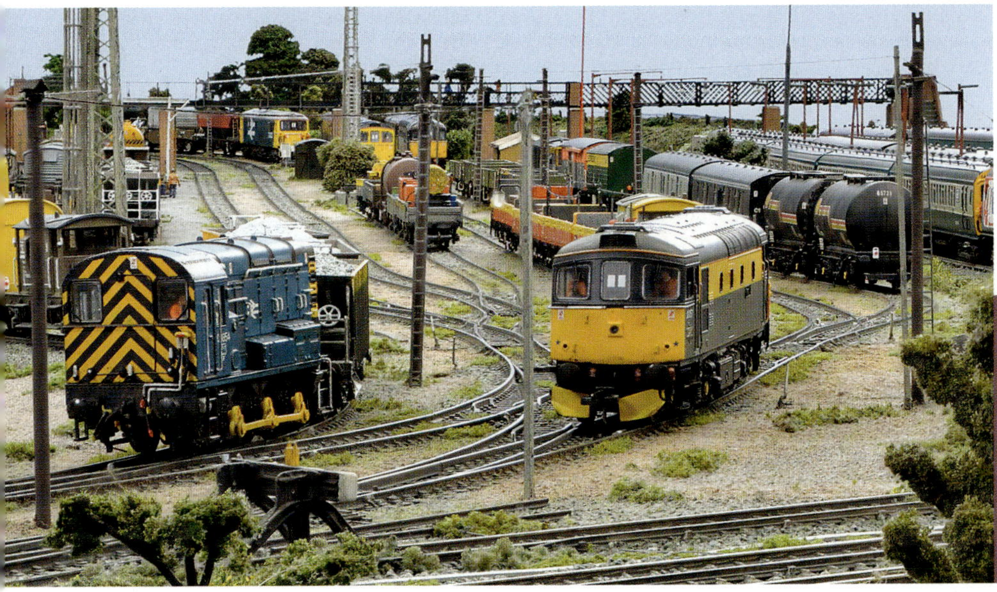

LEFT: **The Civil Engineers' fleet of the late 1980s and particularly the early 1990s was full of colour, a far cry from the drabness of previous eras. With air and vacuum braked stock operating alongside each other and with vehicles from other departments, it is a fascinating period to model. The sheer variety on offer can be glimpsed in this view of Paul Wade's popular OO gauge recreation of Tonbridge West Yard with 08854 and 33057 *Seagull* prominent.** Trevor Jones/Hornby Magazine

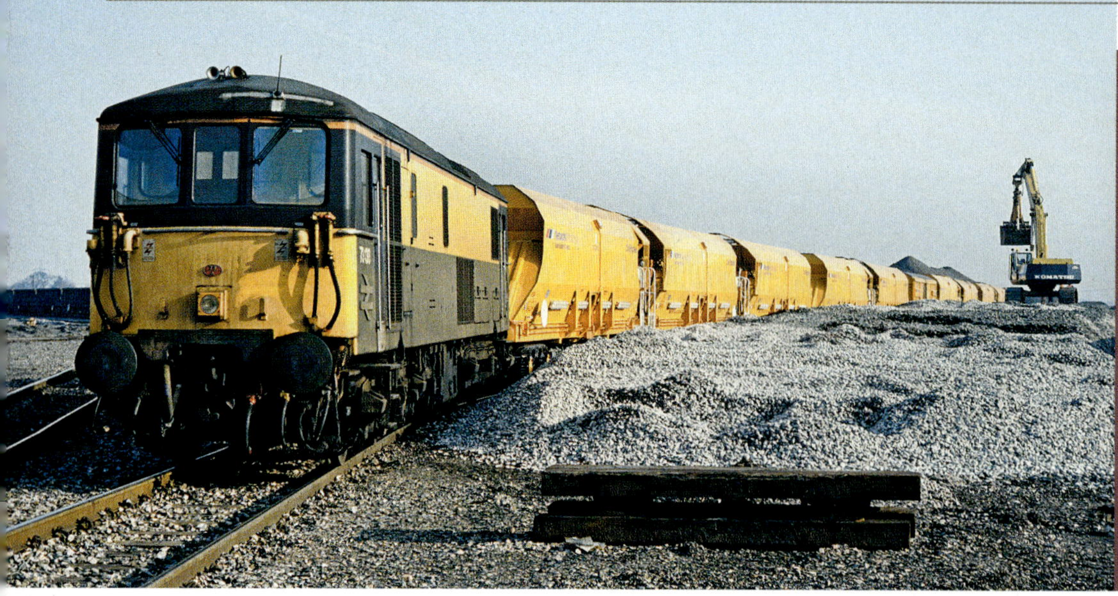

LEFT: **Network SouthEast's Skako auto-ballasting train is seen at Hoo Junction on February 1, 1993, with 73138 on the front during a demonstration of the set's capabilities following delivery. The ten YDA Octopus hoppers, numbered DR92213-22, were built on the frames of Clyde Cement presflos, while the generator van DC210306 was extensively altered from a VDA and can be seen in the middle of the formation. The train was highly innovative for its time and allowed for remote-controlled discharge of new ballast and also precision laying around conductor rails, something that was difficult to achieve using manually-controlled hopper doors. Today, the Skako is owned by DB Cargo and based at Carlisle Yard.**
Colin J Marsden

1990s along with the side-tipping Mermaids as the other elderly and lower-capacity types were condemned. Only in the early 1990s were additional hoppers taken on with the repurposing of PGA aggregate hoppers, many of which had previously worked for Foster Yeoman. Coded Gunnell, the railway spelling used two 'Ls' whereas the eel-like fish only has one.

The fleet of wagons used to carry track components was similarly in little need of outright renewal, the preferred option being to fit air brakes to the sturdily-constructed Salmons and Sturgeons so they could continue for years to come. However, to again replace the older types of rail carriers, BDA bolsters, BPA boplates and BRA borails were transferred across from the air-braked revenue fleet in varying quantities to become YAA, YNA and YLA/YQA, respectively. While these were in some cases too short to carry 60ft track panels, they came in handy to transfer lengths of rail, switch and crossing assemblies and, in the case of the YQA Parr, new concrete sleepers. A diverse range of compatible runner wagons was assembled to go with the rail carriers, these allowing overhanging rail loads to be carried regularly.

As a result of these various acquisitions, the Civil Engineers department had a mix of air brake and vacuum brake wagons on its books, both being incompatible with each other unless a brake van was added. Only the YGH Sealion ballast hoppers could operate on either system, while the later YGB Seacows were vacuum-piped so could run un-braked in vacuum formations. Other piped vehicles, be it air or vacuum, were largely limited to the fleet of specially-constructed wagons, for example Lowmacs, Flatrols, Weltrols and the like, which still had a role to play in carrying bulldozers and excavators to worksites along with other specialist equipment.

Such a mix would have been operationally challenging, especially in the first half of the 1980s when not all locos were equipped with air brakes, such as those scheduled for withdrawal or which had not seen a works overhaul for a while. Such scenarios can easily be recreated on a layout to give some operational interest by ensuring trains are marshalled prototypically and suitable locos assigned to them.

Into privatisation

During 1992, the various engineering departments were reorganised with their responsibilities and assets largely passed to the control of the three passenger sectors: InterCity, Network SouthEast, and Regional Railways. This arrangement only lasted for a couple of years until the locomotives and rolling stock were re-distributed again as part of the newly-created regional freight companies in preparation for privatisation. However, within this two year period, the passenger sectors were responsible for the upkeep of the wagon fleets, which lead to some vehicles incongruously carrying InterCity logos after repainting.

Network SouthEast was also responsible for introducing one of the first sets of automatic ballast discharge trains in 1993. This consisted of ten 90-tonne GLW hoppers built by Powell Duffryn and a generator van in a fixed formation, the wagons having swivelling conveyor belt systems mounted underneath to deliver the ballast to between the rails or onto the track shoulders. Dubbed the Skako after the manufacturer of the conveyors, the train helped pave the way for the Railtrack/Network Rail autoballasters. In a similar fashion, BR would sometimes hire the Redland self-discharge trains at weekends, where the on-board conveyor belt system and discharge boom could unload ballast to create trackbeds.

In 1993/94, the use of high capacity box wagons previously used for aggregates traffic was also trialled by BR for possession work as they offered considerable capacity advantages. However, the temptation to overload these with often sodden spoil and earth due to their size was sometimes taken, particularly by inexperienced contractors during the early years of privatisation. This led to several incidents and their use on such work came to an end under EWS.

So, as British Rail faded from existence in the mid-1990s, the Civil Engineers fleet was largely split between Mainline Freight, Transrail and Loadhaul, only to be reunified under EWS. All the unfitted ballast wagons had been withdrawn and the vacuum-braked types were down to the core types, such as Dogfish, Turbot, Barbel, Clam, Tope, and the rest. These too would be all but gone by the end of the decade as EWS decimated its ex-BR traction in favour of air-braked only Class 66s. This left the air-braked types to continue into the 21st century. ●

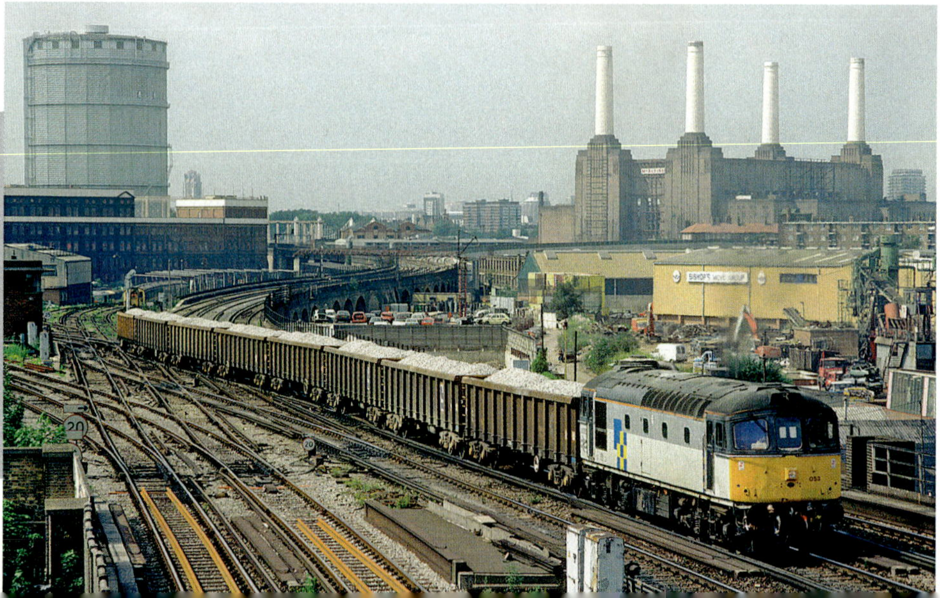

RIGHT: **An early deployment of the high capacity bogie box wagons was to deliver the vast quantities of ballast needed for the construction of the Channel Tunnel terminal at Cheriton, Dollands Moor freight yard and all the new connecting lines. On July 16, 1992, 33053 approaches Wandsworth Road with the 6O68 Temple Mills-Hoo Junction for onward transfer, this featuring eight JNA and KEA boxes. Such wagons would be trialled on possession work by BR and later Mainline Freight during the middle of the decade, but they proved unsuitable.**
Anthony Kay

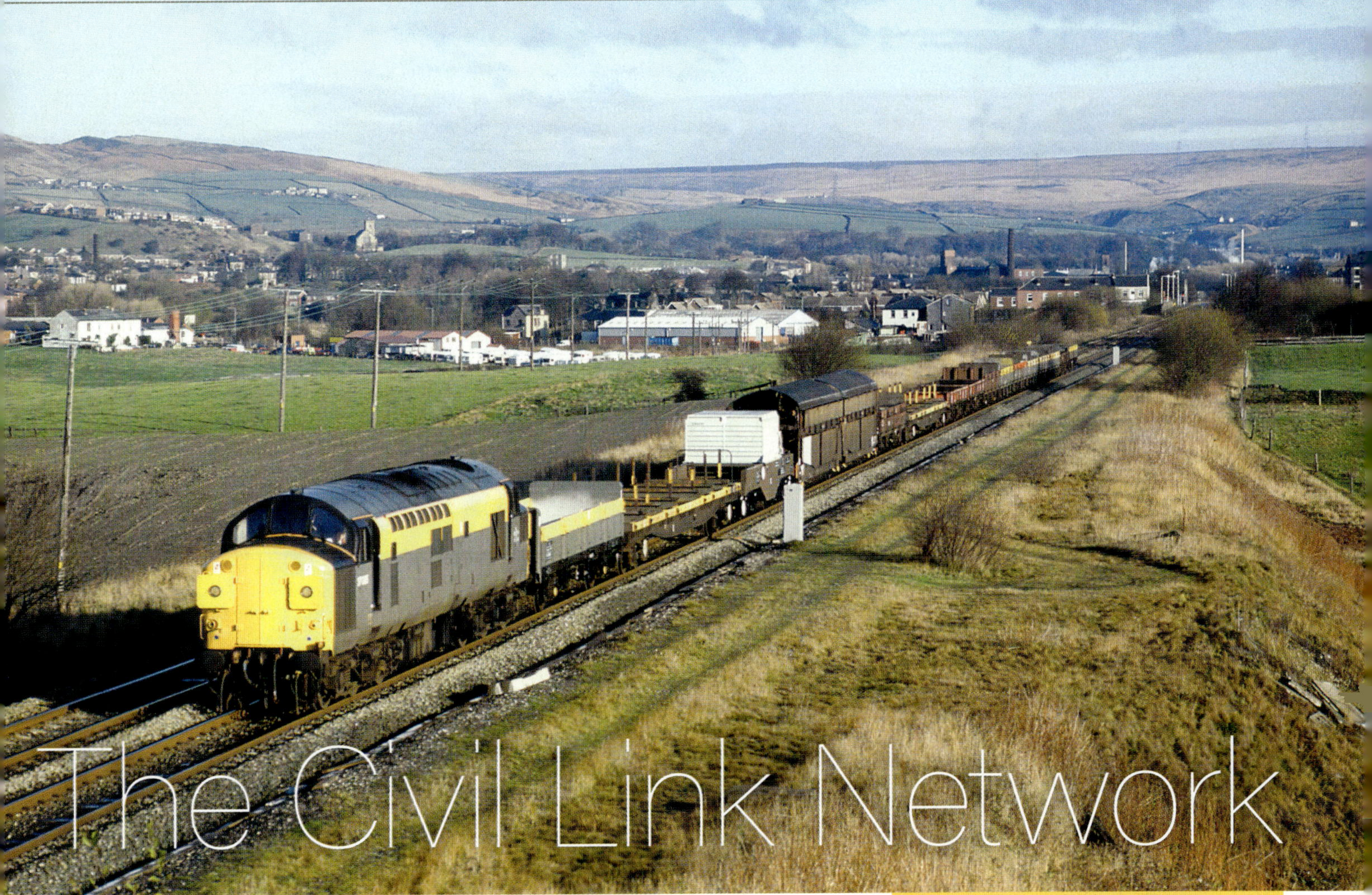

The Civil Link Network

Created at the end of the 1980s, this was the Civil Engineers' answer to Speedlink, designed to move departmental stock quickly between yards, as David Ratcliffe explains.

ABOVE: **In fine autumn light, 37095 powers along with the 6M87 07.53 Healey Mills to Warrington Arpley Civil Link service at Clegg Hall, to the northeast of Rochdale, on November 20, 1991. The diverse collection of air-braked engineers' stock includes ZDA Bass (ex OBA) in grey/yellow, original maroon and one in Railfreight red/grey, three ZAA Pike (ex-SPA) in faded Railfreight red, two YLA Mullet borails and a solitary ZDA Squid (ex OAA) on the rear. The consist is enhanced by a FNA nuclear flask and Railease Autic car carrier, both returning from attention at the Procor works at Horbury Junction.** Simon Bendall Collection

Following sectorisation in 1986, the various bulk Railfreight sub-sectors, such as Construction and Metals, began transferring their remaining wagonload traffic away from the Speedlink network to their own less-than-trainload services. From 1988, a number of Civil Link trunk and trip workings were similarly introduced to expedite the movement of engineers' traffic, which had previously been regarded as something of a poor relation when compared to revenue-earning loads.

Some existing Speedlink feeder services which were already conveying mainly departmental traffic, such as the daily train from Warrington to the Long-Welded Rail (LWR) and Central Materials Depot (CMD) at Castleton, were transferred to the Civil Engineers' account, while new trunk Civil Link services began running between some of the main yards on behalf of the department. Locations served included the likes of Healey Mills, Millerhill and Tonbridge, which were already important centres for engineers' traffic, along with others such as Bescot, Doncaster, Mossend, Newport Alexandra Dock Junction, and Warrington Arpley, where capacity had become available as the Speedlink network declined.

However, in contrast to trunk Speedlink workings, where the majority ran overnight to meet the needs of private business customers, most Civil Link services operated in daylight hours. Furthermore, greater flexibility was built into the train plan in order to meet the differing needs of the engineering sector, while each main yard also remained as a base for local engineers' workings. For instance, Tonbridge West Yard despatched trips to the pre-assembly depots (PAD) at Ashford and Hither Green, as well as to the yards at Hoo Junction and Three Bridges, while Warrington Arpley was the originating point for workings to engineers' yards and depots across northwest England (see Tables 1 and 2).

During 1988, some of the OAA open wagons were transferred to the Civil Engineers' fleet, being recoded ZDA and given the name of Squid. The first five examples to be transferred, DC100010/18/36/56/65, were repainted with full Civil Link branding and allocated to the movement of stores from Swindon Works. DC100010 is pictured at Radyr engineers' sidings on October 21, 1990. Hywel Thomas

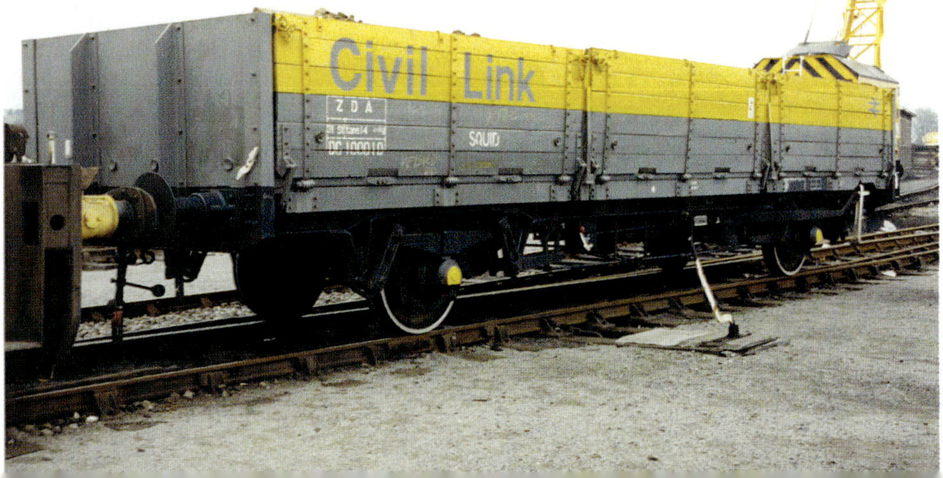

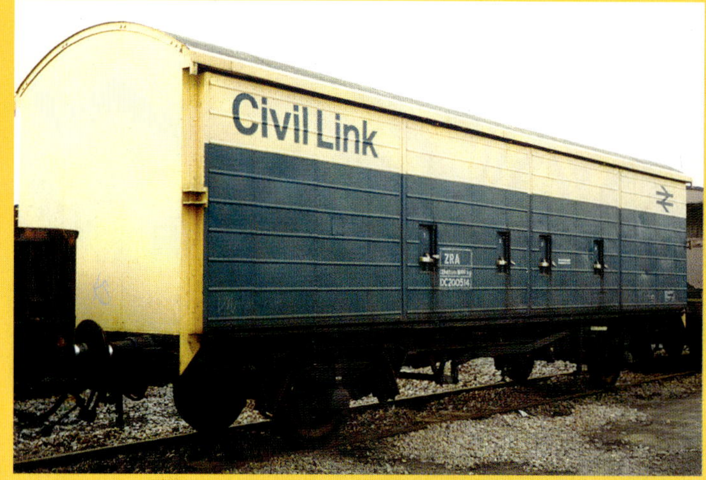

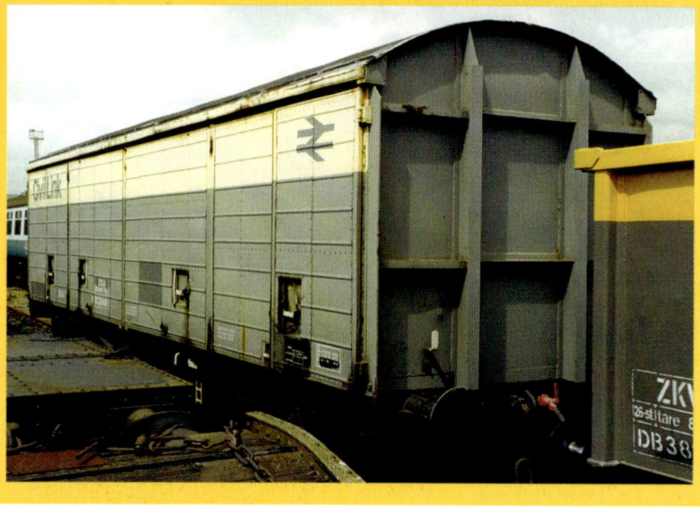

LEFT AND BELOW: **A number of air-braked vans transferred from revenue use were also fully repainted and given Civil Link lettering. These included ZRAs DC200514, originally coded VCA, which is seen at Radyr Yard on February 16, 1992, and DC200660, previously a VDA, which was at the same South Wales location on June 9, 1991, and with its paintwork already heavily faded in comparison to the adjacent ZKV Barbel. Such vans were used to carry miscellaneous Civil Engineers' stores and ancillary equipment, while they were also recorded operating between BREL workshops and Traction Maintenance Depots loaded with locomotive parts on behalf of the Mechanical & Electrical Engineers department.** Hywel Thomas

Civil Link trunk services - Warrington Arpley May 1992	
Departures	**Note**
6C09 09.07 Arpley-Workington	1
6E32 12.43 Arpley-Healey Mills	2
6C09 12.52 Arpley-Workington	1
6G55 14.53 Arpley-Bescot	3
6S44 20.21 Arpley-Mossend	4
Arrivals	
6F87 19.22 Workington-Arpley, arriving 00.32 or 03.02	5
6M87 07.53 Healey Mills-Arpley, arriving 10.21	2
6F15 09.43 Bescot-Arpley, arriving 12.57	6

Notes

1 6C09 would either run directly up the West Coast Main Line or alternatively first visit the Manchester area to serve Castleton CMD. When heading to Castleton, the train would depart Arpley at 09.07 running via the Chat Moss line to the Manchester area and back before re-joining the WCML at Golborne Junction.

2 6M87 ran via Castleton CMD where it might, depending on traffic requirements, be terminated and then return as the 6E02 11.05 Castleton to Healey Mills. When this occurred, 6E32 would not run.

3 On Tuesdays to Fridays, this train was replaced by the 6M65 07.20 Mossend-Bescot, which would call at Warrington Arpley from 14.00 to 14.53. Both 6G55 and 6M65 then called at Crewe Basford Hall.

4 Called at Carlisle Kingmoor yard.

5 6F87 called at Carlisle Kingmoor and could then run either directly up the WCML to Warrington or alternatively take the Bolton line at Euxton Junction to serve Castleton CMD before heading for Arpley via Eccles and Earlestown. When running via Castleton, 6F87 was booked to arrive at Arpley at 03.02.

6 Called at Crewe Basford Hall.

Timetabled engineers trip workings - Warrington Arpley May 1992
Departures
8D33 12.18 Arpley-Chester Yard
8C28 18.09 Arpley-Carnforth F&M Junction
8F43 19.18 Arpley-Liverpool Tuebrook Sidings
8H27 20.07 Arpley-Guide Bridge Brookside Sidings
Arrivals
8F37 23.17 Guide Bridge Brookside Sidings-Arpley, arriving 01.06
8F26 22.50 Carnforth F&M Junction-Arpley, arriving 01.10
8F16 14.30 Chester Yard-Arpley, arriving 15.16
8F33 21.12 Liverpool Tuebrook Sidings to Arpley, arriving 22.17

Following the closure of Speedlink in July 1991, some Civil Link services would occasionally convey a limited amount of revenue freight where no other workings were available. For instance, the Warrington to Mossend Civil Link train could include covered hoppers carrying granulated limestone from Hindlow to Mossend, which had reached Warrington in a Construction sub-sector service from Peak Forest. The movement of new wagons along with that of empty wagons to and from works for repair could also result in the inclusion of non-departmental stock in a Civil Link working. However, with the creation of the three shadow freight companies in 1994, Civil Link was gradually absorbed by the new and expanding Enterprise wagonload network.

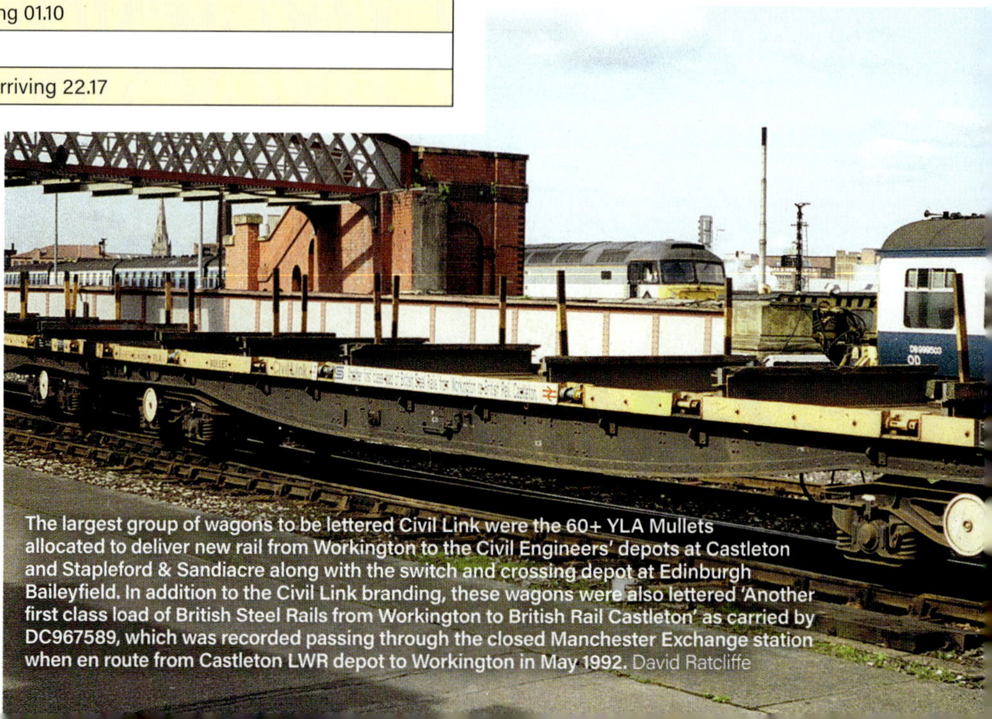

The largest group of wagons to be lettered Civil Link were the 60+ YLA Mullets allocated to deliver new rail from Workington to the Civil Engineers' depots at Castleton and Stapleford & Sandiacre along with the switch and crossing depot at Edinburgh Baileyfield. In addition to the Civil Link branding, these wagons were also lettered 'Another first class load of British Steel Rails from Workington to British Rail Castleton' as carried by DC967589, which was recorded passing through the closed Manchester Exchange station when en route from Castleton LWR depot to Workington in May 1992. David Ratcliffe

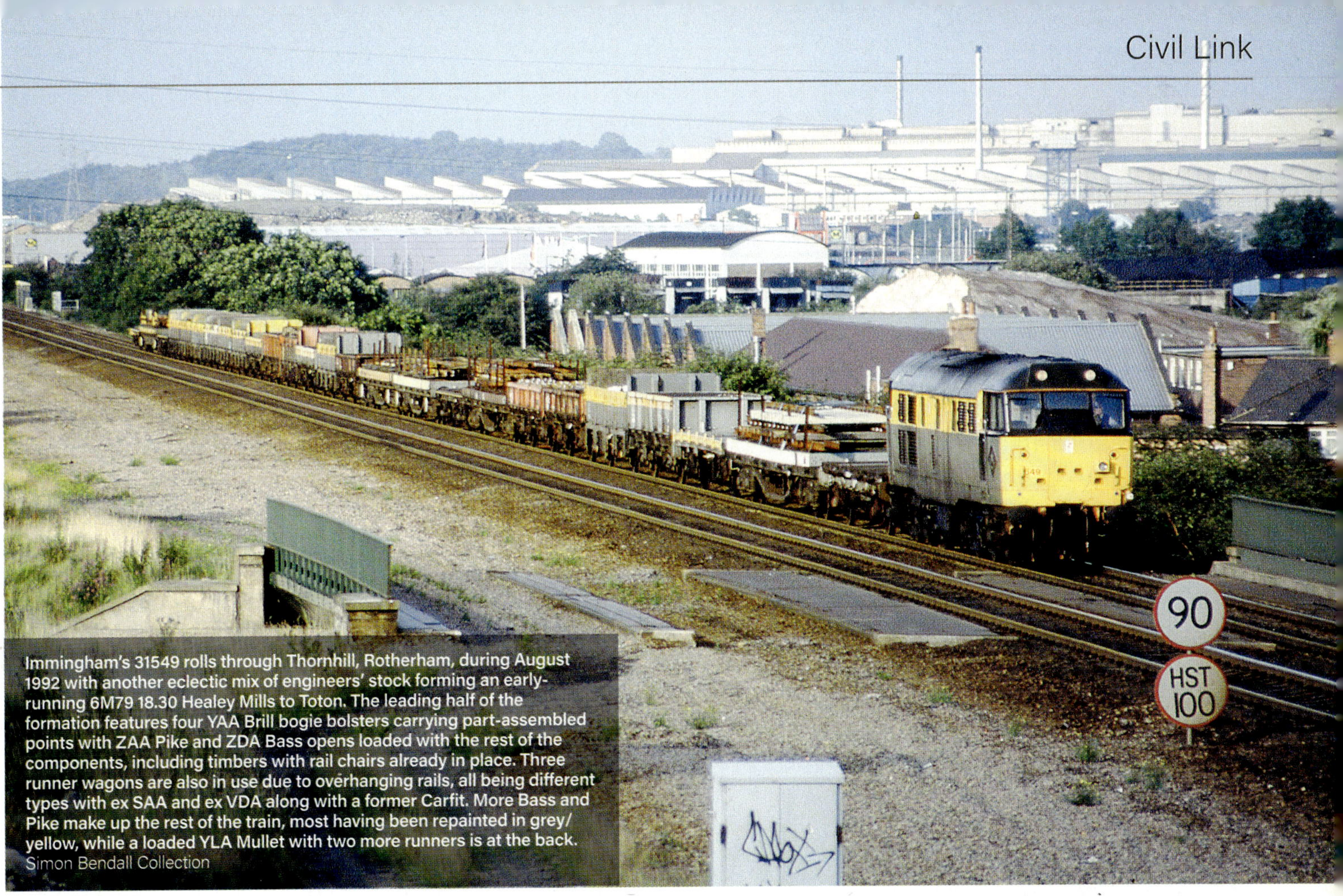

Immingham's 31549 rolls through Thornhill, Rotherham, during August 1992 with another eclectic mix of engineers' stock forming an early-running 6M79 18.30 Healey Mills to Toton. The leading half of the formation features four YAA Brill bogie bolsters carrying part-assembled points with ZAA Pike and ZDA Bass opens loaded with the rest of the components, including timbers with rail chairs already in place. Three runner wagons are also in use due to overhanging rails, all being different types with ex SAA and ex VDA along with a former Carfit. More Bass and Pike make up the rest of the train, most having been repainted in grey/yellow, while a loaded YLA Mullet with two more runners is at the back. Simon Bendall Collection

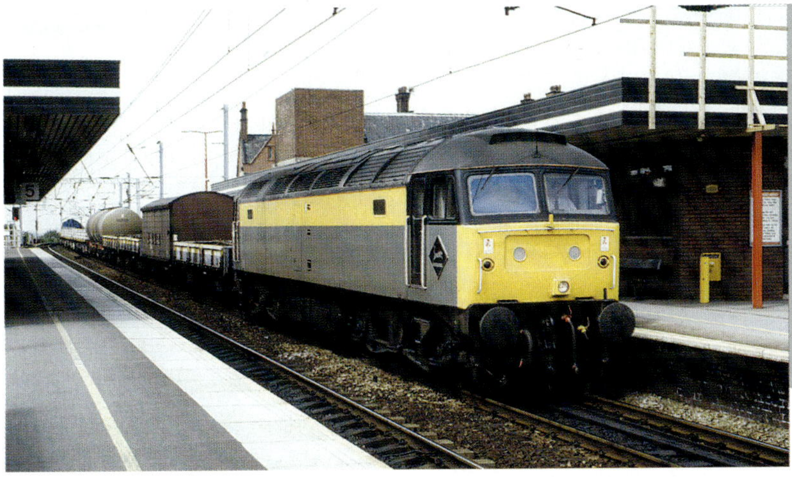

LEFT: **Part of the Crewe Diesel allocation, 47339 rumbles through Wigan North Western during 1991 with the 6M65 07.20 Mossend-Bescot, which had already called at Carlisle Kingmoor and still had stops to make at Warrington Arpley and Crewe Basford Hall before reaching the West Midlands. Departmental traffic on show includes YQA Parr carrying new concrete sleepers from the Costain works at Coltness while three Pike and a ZRA stores van are also included. The two Esso Class A TTA tanks were likely returning from the terminal at Bowling, on the outskirts of Glasgow, while at least one Cargowaggon van is also in the formation.** Simon Bendall Collection

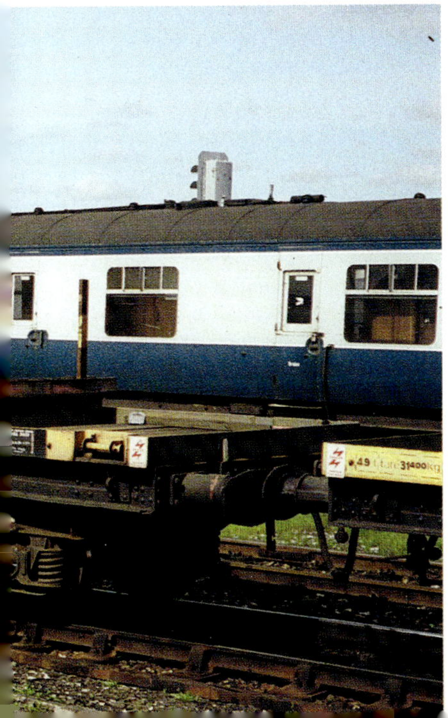

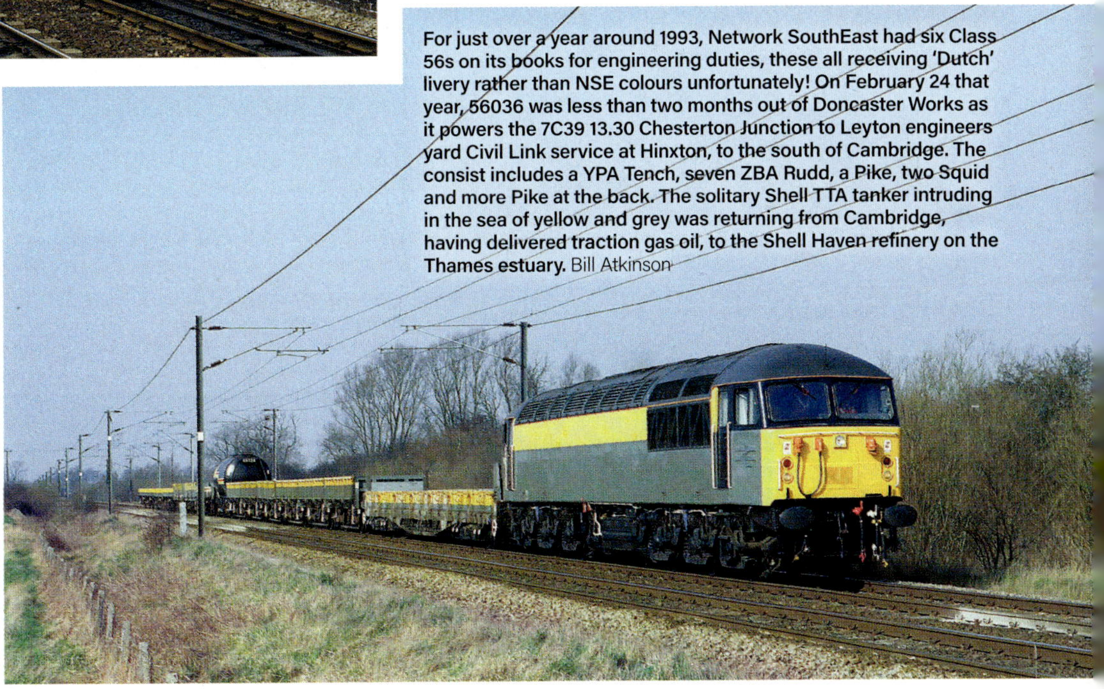

For just over a year around 1993, Network SouthEast had six Class 56s on its books for engineering duties, these all receiving 'Dutch' livery rather than NSE colours unfortunately! On February 24 that year, 56036 was less than two months out of Doncaster Works as it powers the 7C39 13.30 Chesterton Junction to Leyton engineers yard Civil Link service at Hinxton, to the south of Cambridge. The consist includes a YPA Tench, seven ZBA Rudd, a Pike, two Squid and more Pike at the back. The solitary Shell TTA tanker intruding in the sea of yellow and grey was returning from Cambridge, having delivered traction gas oil, to the Shell Haven refinery on the Thames estuary. Bill Atkinson

Early experiments

The first half of the 1980s saw a handful of prototype air-braked engineers' wagons appear for evaluation, these either being completely new or substantial rebuilds using the frames of existing vehicles. However, none progressed to a production build, largely on the grounds of cost as cheaper alternatives were available. Simon Bendall takes a look at these interesting curios, many of which lasted to the turn of the century.

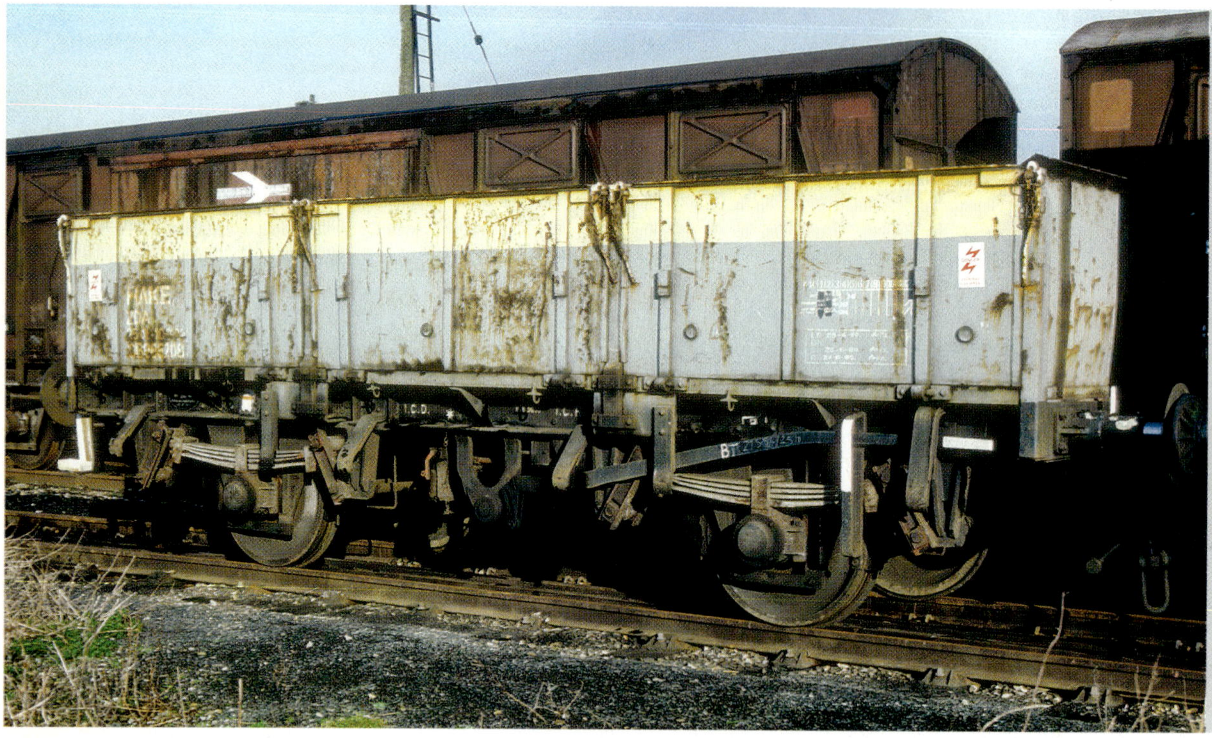

LEFT: **The three Hake were built in 1981 using the frames of unfitted Grampus dating from 1956, these receiving new bodywork on top and similarly modernised air brakes and suspension below. On February 6, 1988, DB986208, then coded ZDA, was recorded at Hoo Junction, shortly before it was transferred away from the former Southern Region to work in Scotland.** Paul Bartlett

The first of the air-braked prototypes appeared in mid-1981, these, like most of the others, being intended as a new design of open ballast wagon. With a huge number of unfitted Grampus still in use, this was a trial to examine re-using the underframe and adding a new body, suspension, and brakes. Three ZBOs, DB986147, DB968208 and DB986251, were duly selected for the project and are believed to have been rebuilt at Bristol East carriage and wagon depot, although some accounts differ. The new body consisted of three drop-doors per side along with fixed ends, all of which were higher than on the Grampus wagons and consequently gave a revised carrying capacity of 25-tonnes.

The chassis received BR friction link suspension and leaf springs along with clasp air brake equipment, roller bearings and hydraulic buffers. While the three wagons were not renumbered, they were given the new name of Hake and initially coded ZBA. The latter was changed to ZDA in 1983 after the trio were reclassified as general materials carriers. After seven years working in the south, the Hake were transferred to Perth by the middle of 1988 for ballast duties on the Highland lines, this seeing them revert to ZBA. Although they passed to EWS ownership, they were stored by 1998.

In an amended version of the engineers' grey/yellow livery, DB986147 stands in its new Scottish surroundings at Perth on August 1, 1989. The TOPS code has reverted to the original ZBA after the three Hake resumed use on ballast workings. Paul Bartlett

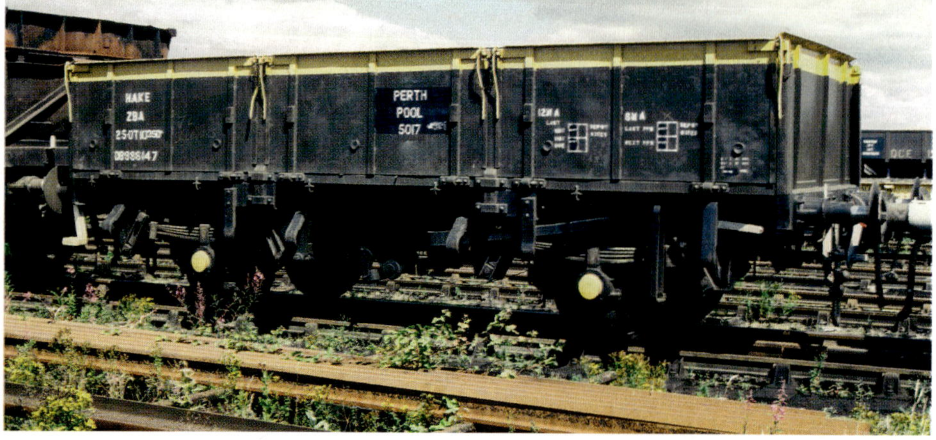

The next two-axle ballast open prototype was of entirely new construction, DB988600 emerging from Shildon Works in 1983. Christened as a Carp, this followed the Hake in having three doors per side and fixed ends with a capacity of 27-tonnes thanks to its longer length of 28ft. Built with air brakes, it also had parabolic springs and friction link suspension, allowing 60mph operation. Coded ZBA, it too transferred from ballast carrying to general materials use early in its career but initially without the TOPS code altering. By 1992, it was carrying all over yellow and had become a ZDA, going on to survive Mainline Freight ownership, where

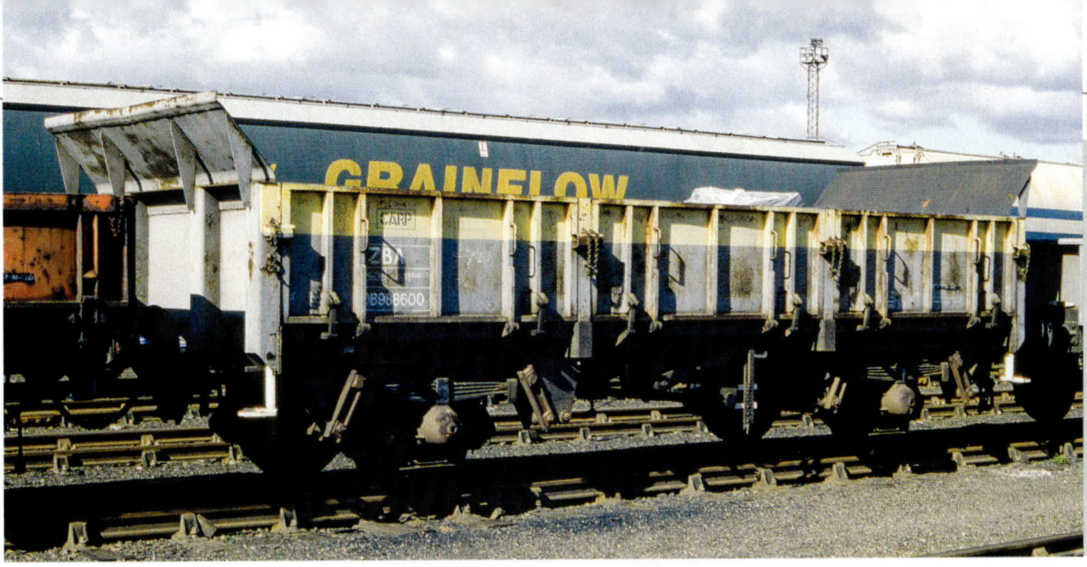

LEFT: **The unique Carp DB988600 is seen in as-built condition at Millerhill on March 28, 1989. Although still coded as a ZBA, indicating a ballast wagon, the polythene-covered load protruding above the sides shows it was now in general materials traffic.** Trevor Mann

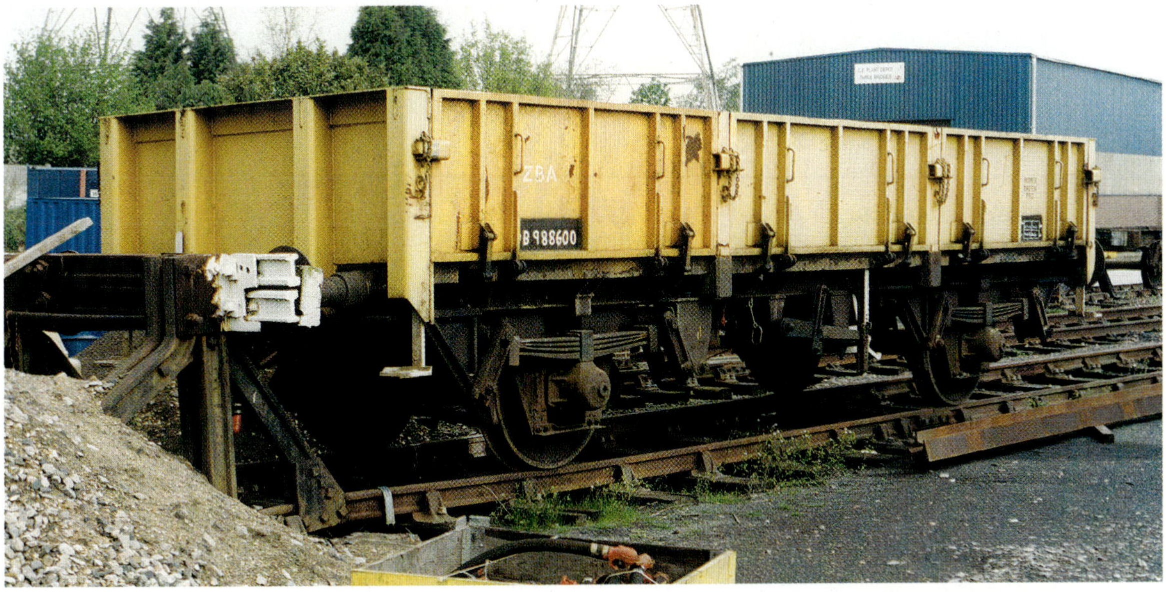

RIGHT: **Seen back on more familiar Southern territory, DB988600 displays the all-over yellow livery it had received earlier in the 1990s. The Carp name had gone as had the sizeable, angled spill plates atop the ends when recorded at Three Bridges in May 1994. Under Mainline Freight ownership, the number panel would be redone with a blue background and ZDA code applied, only for EWS to overpaint the blue with yellow once again later in the decade.** Colin Wright/David Ratcliffe Collection

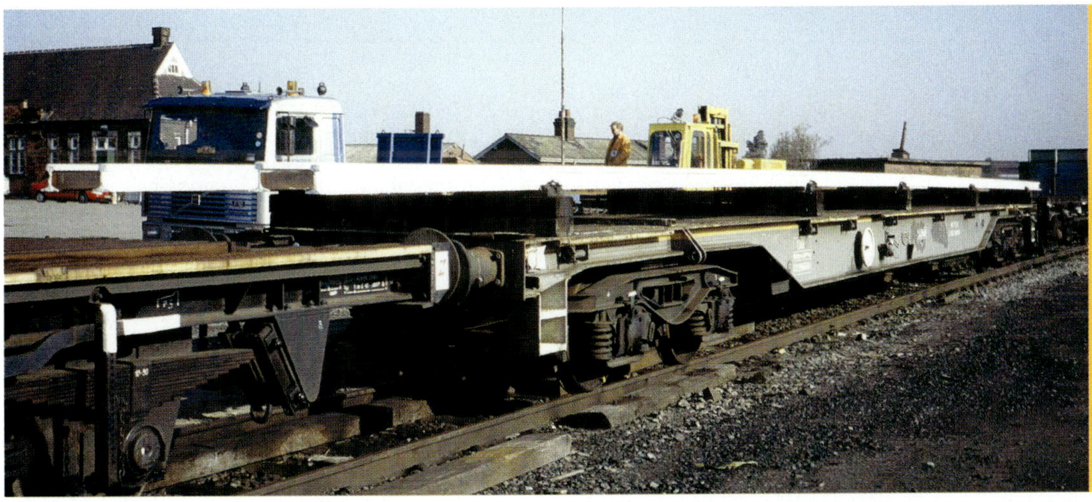

LEFT: **Salmon prototype DB996699 is seen at Scunthorpe freight depot on October 9, 1995, while being loaded with sections of point and crossing rail. As these are over-length, runners are present at both ends while the new rails are notably painted white in an effort to help with heat deflection during hot weather. The livery is the original engineers' grey and yellow, although the latter is restricted to a thin stripe along the top edge. During 1998, its TOPS code would briefly become YLA before the new FZA identity was adopted.** David Ratcliffe

it was lettered for scrap traffic relating to engineering duties, and on into the EWS era.

Bogie designs

Sharing some design characteristics with the Carp but altogether more monstrous were the two YCA Halibut wagons constructed at Shildon Works in 1980. This immense design was rated to carry 56-tonnes, measured 54ft over buffers and had seven doors per side. Riding on fabricated Y25C bogies, the fish-belly underframe design was reminiscent of the BBA steel wagons while the pair were numbered DB98100 and DB981001.

Like the other prototypes described above, the Halibut tended to inhabit the Southern Region and for a time in 1984, the pair formed an interesting train for moving engineers' stores between Redbridge Works (Southampton) and New Cross Gate pre-assembly depot. This also included the solitary Carp, the three Pollock (see overleaf) and a trio of air-piped ZBQ Grampus, DB986291, DB986320 and DB986331.

However, in later years, the Halibut saw reduced use as they were just too big for most purposes but were retained for those times when their capacity was a bonus. As such they passed to Mainline Freight and then EWS, the latter having plans to use them as part of a revamped Fort Bridge maintenance train in the early 2000s, but they ultimately went for scrap.

Moving away from ballast wagons, the last experimental wagon was DB996699, which was the prototype for a new generation of air-braked Salmon rail carriers. Built at Shildon Works in 1983, its design was largely identical to the Perch wagons then being constructed for British Rail's new long-welded rail trains. Coded YMA, it could carry 53-tonnes and featured five bolsters. While no further examples were built, the wagon was retained as its length made it suitable for carrying switch and crossing rails, a role it still performs today with DB Cargo, albeithaving been renumbered and recoded as FZA 600500. ●

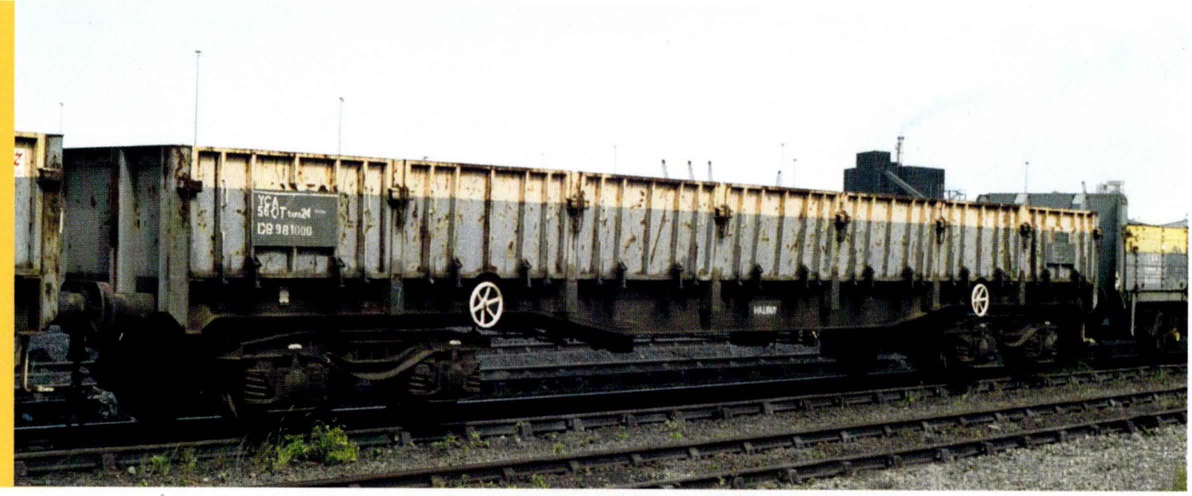

RIGHT: **Far away from the Southern, not to mention the territory of new owner Mainline Freight, both YCA Halibut could be found at Immingham in June 1994 with DB98100 illustrated and its sister to the left. When new, they had angled spill plates fitted to the ends like the Carp, but these were removed after a few years.** David Ratcliffe

A Halibut in N gauge by Carl White

In N gauge, the only available option for a recreation of the YCA Halibut wagons was a 3D printed model that was designed by Rail 3D and available on Shapeways.com. Unfortunately, this user has now closed their shop, citing technical difficulties with the changing 3D printing service. When it was available to buy, it arrived as a one-piece body that required only a pair of Taylor Precision Models Y25 bogies to complete.

The first step when working on 3D printed models is to clean off any residue left over from the printing process; for this a soft scrub with a toothbrush and a cream cleaner in warm water will suffice. Normally, a 3D printed model has slightly tiered lines visible on the surface as the printing process is unable to produce smooth curves, these requiring a light sanding to flatten them out. Thankfully, with the Halibut just having horizontal and vertical surfaces, there was no need for any of this sanding, especially as working around all the ribs would have been difficult.

This allowed the model to progress straight to the painting stage, which began with an initial coat of white primer from an aerosol can. Once this was fully dry, I

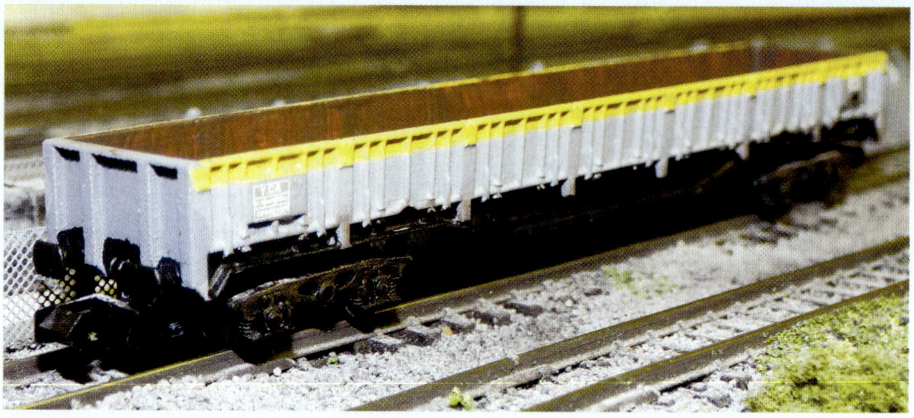

brush painted the outside of the wagon with two coats of warning yellow from the Phoenix Precision Paints range. To be able to paint a straight joint between the grey and yellow but avoid a difficult masking job over the ribs, I instead lightly laid a strip of thicker masking tape on the wagon in a slightly higher position than I wanted the line to be. Then at a 45 degree angle to the top of the wagon, I sprayed from a can of Halfords grey primer, which is a close enough match to engineers' grey. Any touching up was done with a paintbrush using some paint that I sprayed on a piece of card.

The inside of the wagon was given a coat of Humbrol brown (No. 26) before dry brushing with various other browns to give an authentic worn appearance. As the wagon only required a few transfers, I only applied gloss varnish in the areas where these would be applied. For the TOPS panel and numbering, I used Fox transfers and the wagon repair markings were from Railtec.

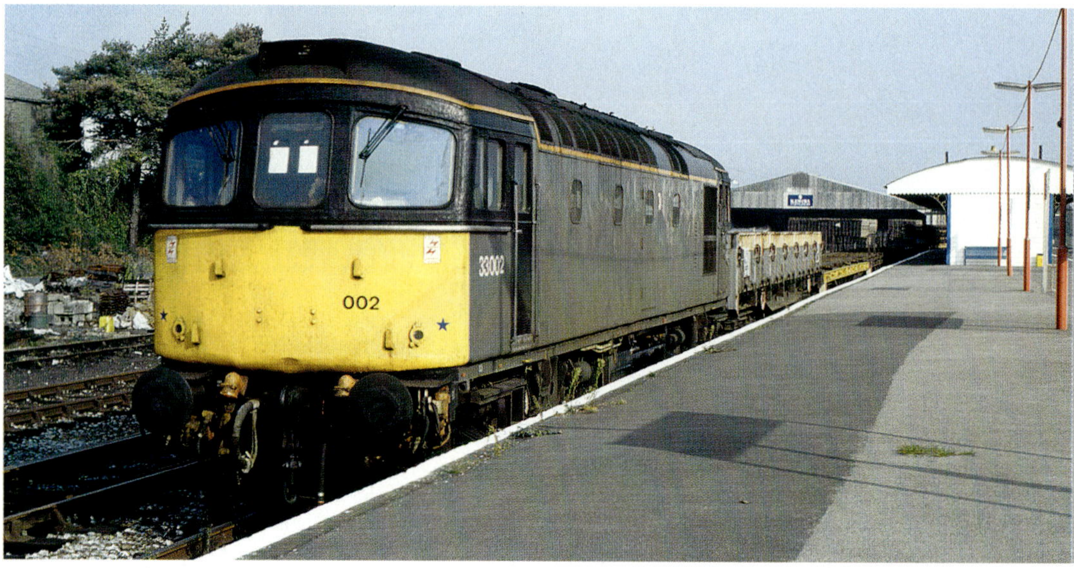

LEFT: **With a YCA Halibut directly behind the loco, 33002 arrives at Andover with an engineers' working during October 1990. Also visible in the consist are three Salmon with a Tench largely hidden in the shadows and a further Salmon loaded with track panels. The loco is carrying the much dis-liked Departmental/General Grey livery, which first appeared in February 1989 and would go on to modify into the 'Dutch' grey/yellow scheme in most cases.** Simon Bendall Collection

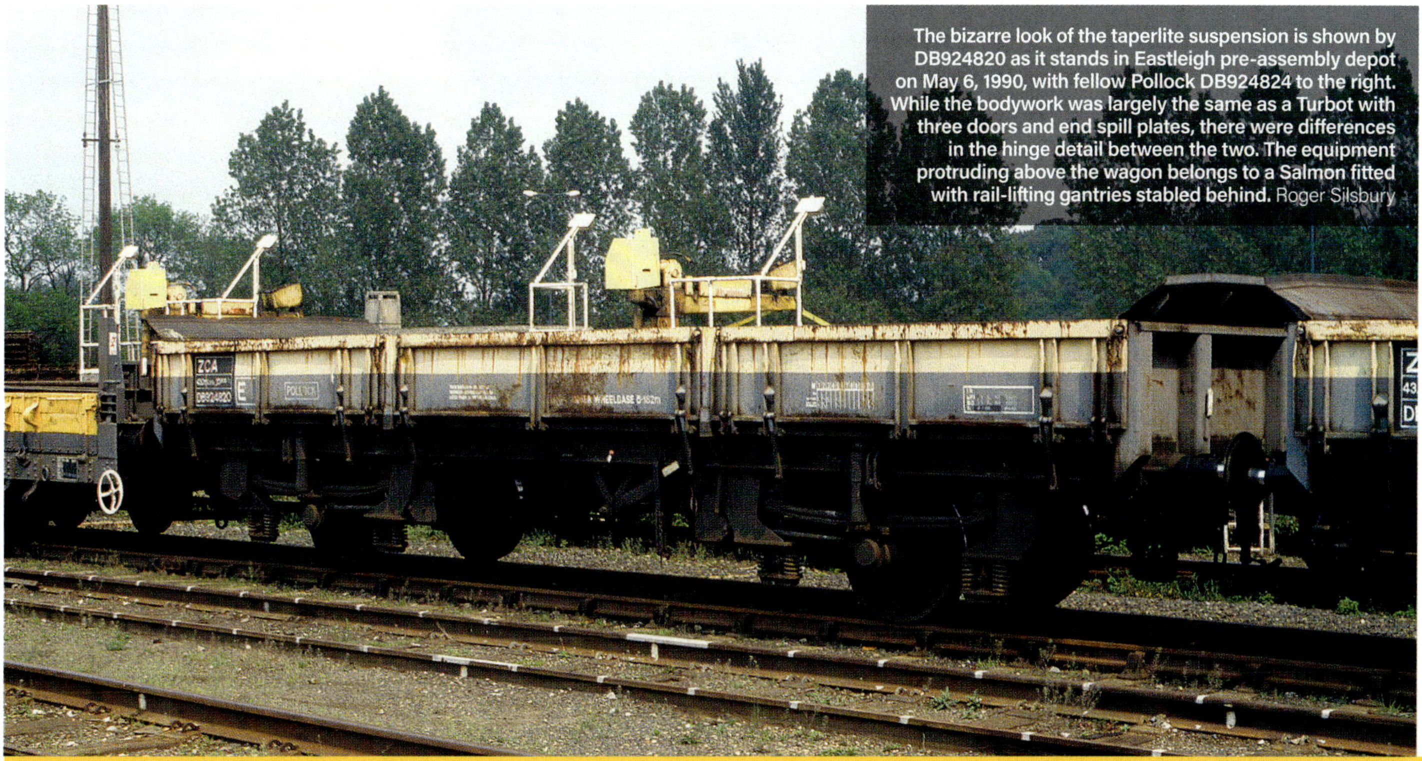

The bizarre look of the taperlite suspension is shown by DB924820 as it stands in Eastleigh pre-assembly depot on May 6, 1990, with fellow Pollock DB924824 to the right. While the bodywork was largely the same as a Turbot with three doors and end spill plates, there were differences in the hinge detail between the two. The equipment protruding above the wagon belongs to a Salmon fitted with rail-lifting gantries stabled behind. Roger Silsbury

ZCA Pollock

This last trio of prototype ballast open wagons were perhaps the most interesting thanks to their convoluted origin. During 1979, five vacuum-braked Bogie Bolster E wagons were set aside to be converted into air-braked steel wagons that would have been coded SEA and numbered 410000-04. This work included removing the Davis & Lloyd bogies and fitting the wagons with the experimental taperlite suspension, thereby converting them into two-axle vehicles.

This conversion was partially completed at Shildon when the SEA project was cancelled. Two of the five were eventually completed in 1983, DB924807 and DB924860 becoming ZSA runner wagons for use with ballast cleaning equipment on the Eastern Region. While both had air brakes and the new suspension, the body remained as built except for the removal of the bolsters.

The Civil Engineers also took on the other three wagons, which appeared in 1984 as ballast opens and were amongst the last wagons to be outshopped from Shildon Works. As well as the new brakes and suspension, DB924820, DB924824 and DB924848 were also given new bodywork that was very similar in style to the YCV Turbots. The latter wagons were also former Bogie Bolster Es that had been converted for ballast use, but these retained their original vacuum-braked underframes and were covered in the first volume of *Modelling British Railways - Engineers' Wagons*.

The three converted wagons were coded ZCA, painted in grey/yellow and given the fish name of Pollock. The latter caused some consternation amongst senior management over the possibility of the spelling being 'modified' and the name was reported as officially cancelled. Nonetheless, Pollock made it onto the sides of the wagons and the inevitable duly occurred!

Like the other prototypes, they initially found their way to the Southern for use on non-ballast traffic and DB924820 and DB942824 were still there under Network SouthEast ownership in 1992 for the same purpose. Around the same time, DB924848 was modified for use as a drain cleaning wagon, the sides were removed in order to accommodate a water tank while it was also altered to work in between the two halves of a GP-TRAMM maintenance vehicle. The two unmodified Pollock passed to EWS ownership with one lasting until 2002 or so, while DB924848 came under Balfour Beatty's control and gained the company's blue livery. It later found its way to the Dartmoor Railway, from where it was for sale in May 2021.

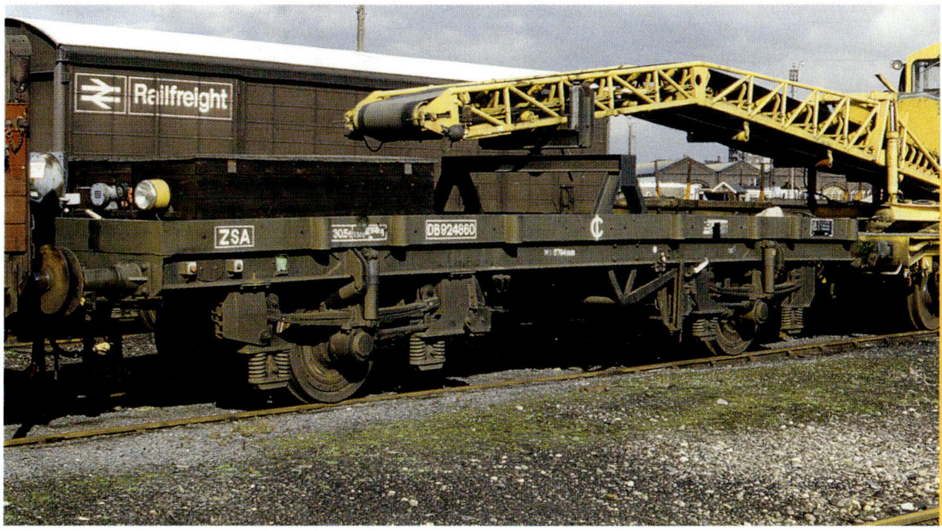

LEFT: **The other two Bogie Bolster E wagons rebuilt as part of the project did not qualify for the Pollock name, these becoming runner wagons instead. ZSA DB924860 is seen at York Leeman Road on August 20, 1985, when in use as a support wagon for the conveyor of Plasser & Theurer unloading station DR88201. This machine worked with a ballast cleaner and the Skate skip-carrying wagons as a spoil handling system. Notably, the wagon still retains its stanchion pockets down the sides and the leading end is fitted with headlights and a warning klaxon. It was condemned in August 1994 and scrapped the following year.** Trevor Mann

Netting a Pollock by Mark Lambert

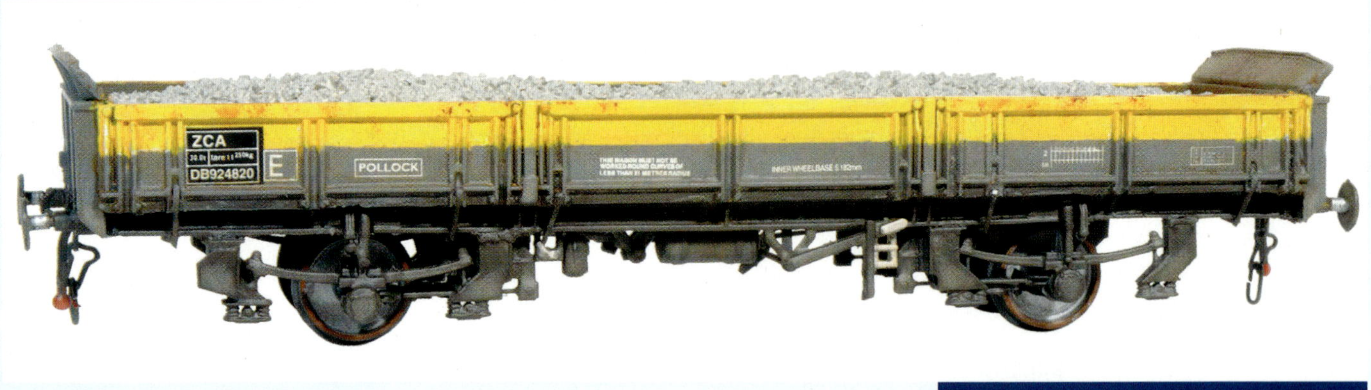

ABOVE: The Pollock may be near identical to a Turbot above the solebars, but it is completely different below, offering a welcome bit of variation and interest thanks to the taperlite suspension.

This project began with the purchase of a set of 3D printed taperlite suspension and brake frame parts with no particular conversion in mind, these coming directly from the designer at the time but now available from Shapeways. However, once I had seen a picture of a Pollock and realised that I had all the transfers required on an Appleby Model Engineering sheet, I knew I had to do the conversion.

As the Pollock shared much with the Turbot, I purchased an old 4mm scale Cambrian kit for the latter and set to work. Taking the bodywork first, the ends would not fit the sides and floor properly so in the end, I re-profiled some Parkside Rudd ends (from the PC72 Grampus kit) and used these instead, including the plastic Parkside bufferheads. The chassis members were then modified to remove the unwanted underframe trussing but not the V hangers, while the sides received new hinge strengtheners just inboard of the existing ones at each end. For some reason, the hinges were repositioned in comparison to a Turbot, but the unused parts were not removed.

Initially, I could not get the 3D printed suspension units to line up with the original bogie centres and only then realised that the Pollock had a wheelbase that did not match anything else! As a result, I fitted the suspension units using photos and the bodyside features as reference points since I had no accurate wheelbase measurement to hand or a properly dimensioned drawing. The wheels are held in MJT internal W-iron etches that I had in the spares box, while the wheels themselves are 11mm plain disc wheels with no pinpoints.

Underframe detailing

The distinctive brake frames were fitted to pads positioned on the underside of the floor and were lined up by eye. I had to file the top of the 3D printed frames in order to glue them in place as they are designed for the Bachmann VDA. The inner brake shoes also had to be removed as they are a very tight fit round the wheelsets. The suspension units are not quite the same design as the taperlites fitted to VDA vans, but the differences are limited to plates bolted to the castings for some reason, so I made the plates from 20 thou sheet and superglued them to the prints.

The brake equipment is a mixture of Cambrian and Parkside parts from the spares box while the handbrake levers are the original Cambrian parts. I added door controller arms between the body and solebars towards the end of the build, these being made from square-section 20x30 thou plastic strip. The last job was to add the Turbot spill plates, these fitting nicely atop the Parkside ends once I had flattened the bottom of the mouldings.

Painting began by undercoating the underframe with Games Workshop 'Chaos Black' while the body received the same company's 'Corax White' (which is actually a very light grey) before brush painting the yellow top edge of the wagon. I masked the sides and painted the bottom part of the body with a slightly faded grey, while the underframe received a coat of Army Painter 'Hardened Carapace'. Following a coat of gloss varnish, the transfers were added. The centre doors fitted to the Pollock were clearly already prepared for Turbots as they featured incorrect wheelbase markings on them!

Lastly, the wagon was given another coat of gloss varnish to seal the transfers in and then a covering of matt varnish to flatten it all out. The last touch was to add a Make Your Mark Models Turbot load, this being the version supplied in grey primer, which received some dry brushing with a light stone colour.

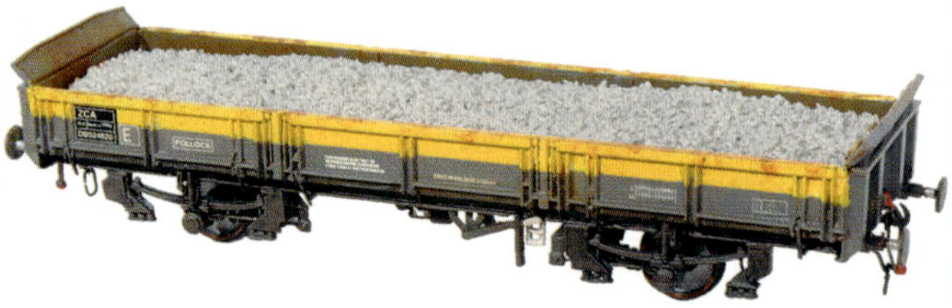

RIGHT: While the Cambrian Turbot kit is the basis of the model, plenty of other components are needed to complete the job, which is where a well-stocked spares box comes in handy!

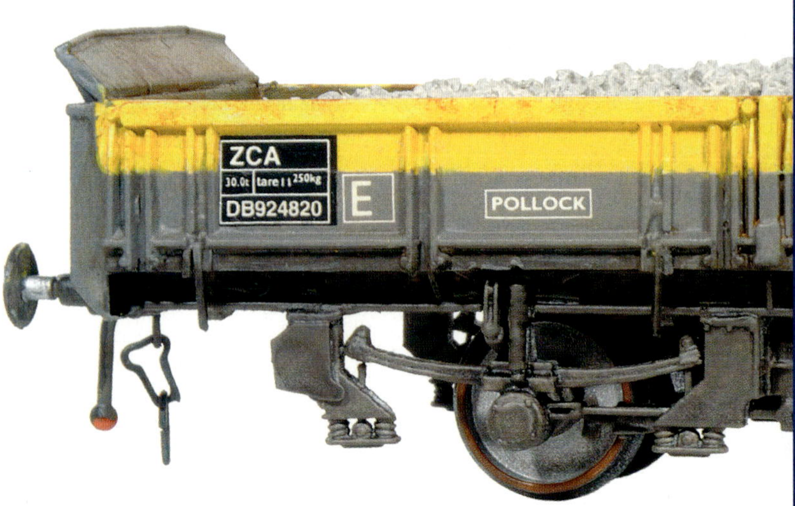

LEFT: The advent of 3D printing has allowed the production of components that were previously all but impossible to produce with the required finesse. While somewhat fragile, the suspension and brake frames, which are largely obscured behind, look superb.

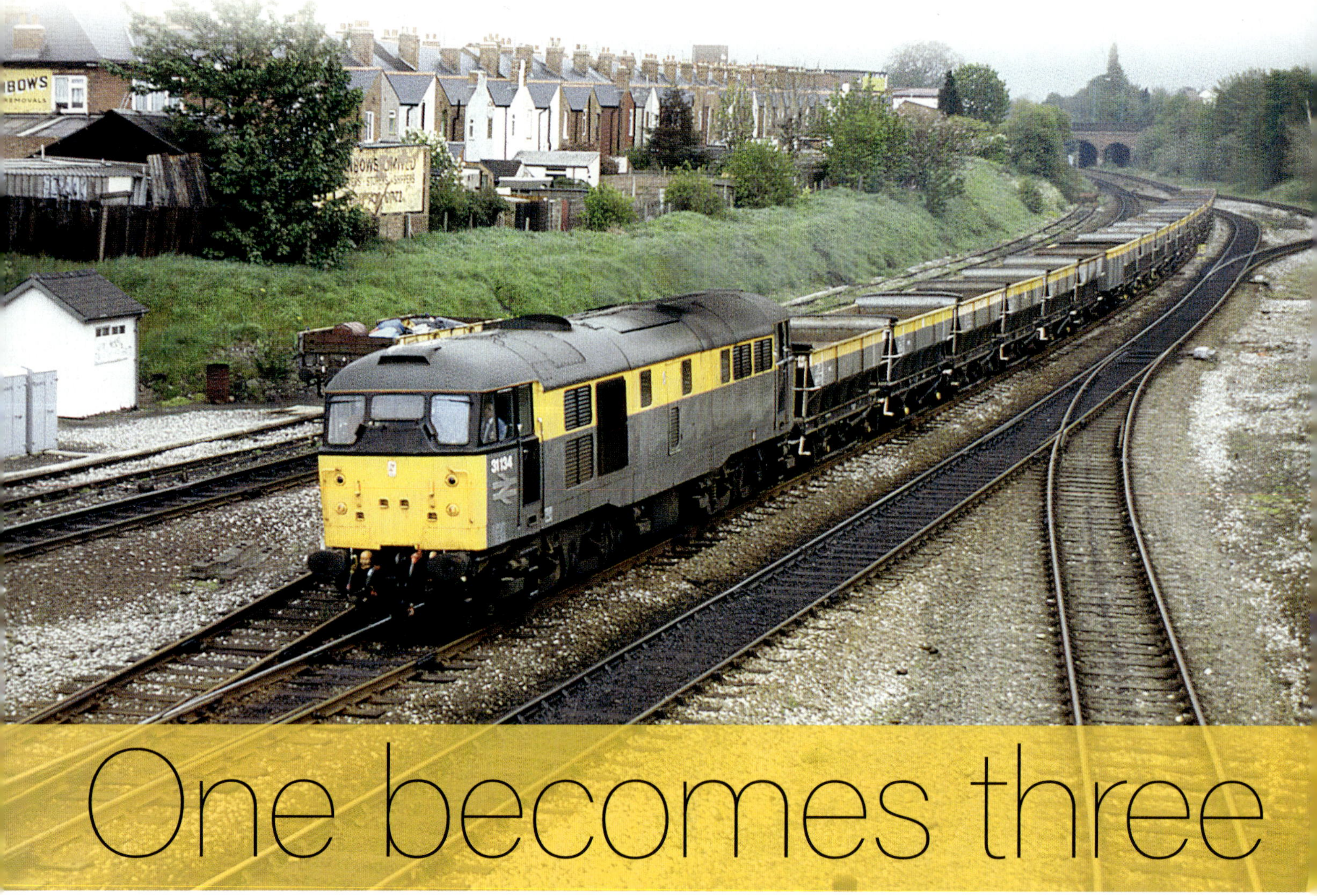

One becomes three

The end of the 1980s saw the last substantial conversion programme involving vacuum-braked wagons as redundant coal hoppers were converted into three different types of ballast and spoil wagon, As Trevor Mann explains, the results were the Tope, Clam and Rudd.

Somewhat fortuitously, the 1980s saw large numbers of HTV 21-ton hoppers withdrawn from revenue-earning service, having been made redundant from power station coal traffic by the spread of merry-go-round operation and the closure of smaller power stations. In addition, movements to coal concentration depots had been modernised by the introduction of the HEA hoppers while it was a similar story in aggregates traffic with the arrival of additional private-owner hoppers. Consequently, it was this hopper fleet that was to become the basis of a rebuilding programme that would provide the Civil Engineers with a fleet of ballast, spoil and general materials wagons that would last into the privatisation era.

In 1984, three HTVs were converted to carry spoil and ballast at BREL Doncaster under BR lot number 4051. Coded ZDV and named Tope, they retained their original numbers, with a new prefix, of DB423760, DB425994 and DB426194. In an attempt to prevent overloading, and to ease loading and discharge using mechanical excavators, the height of the bodywork was reduced by 460mm before a new top capping was

ABOVE: **'Skinhead' 31134 rumbles across Tyseley South Junction in May 1991 with a lengthy rake of empty ZCV Tope in tow. Converted from HTV hoppers, 813 of these wagons were taken on by the Civil Engineers and were a mainstay on spoil workings throughout the 1990s. Notably the train also contains an interloper in the form of a solitary ZKV Barbel ex tippler as the seventh wagon.** Simon Bendall Collection

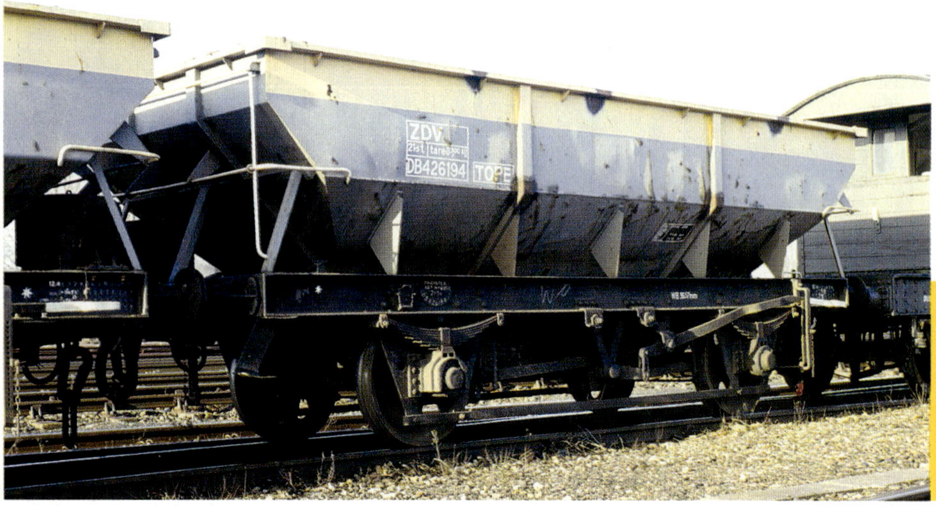

LEFT: **One of the three prototype Tope, DB426194, is seen at Three Bridges on December 14, 1986, it is carrying the original ZDV TOPS code. Just two years after conversion at Doncaster, the wagon is sporting noticeable scorch marks along the top capping, no doubt the result of welding work made necessary by an ill-directed excavator grab!** Andy Prime

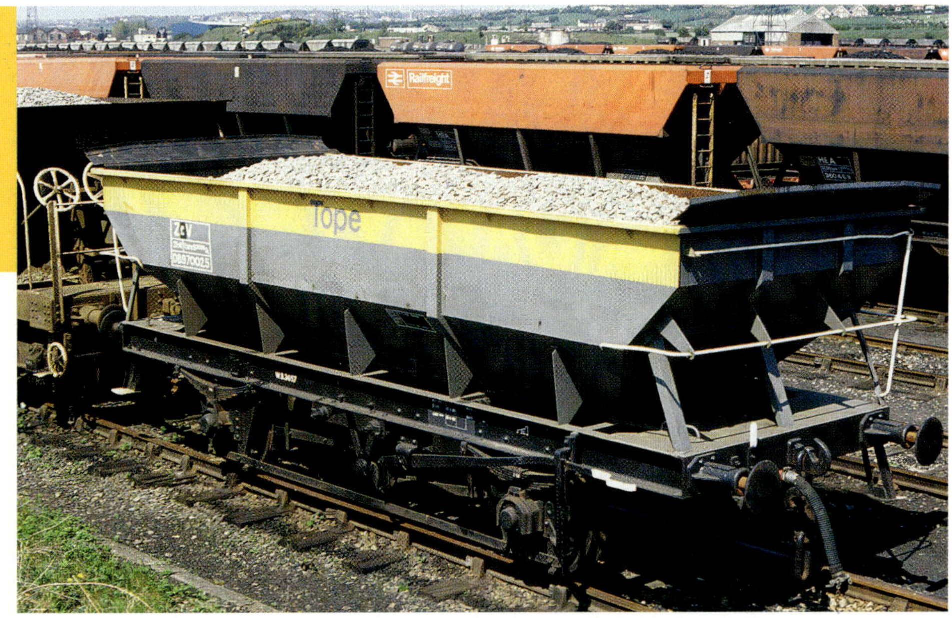

RIGHT: **The first production batch of Tope conversions is illustrated by DB970025, which was rebuilt by RFS from B428263. Seen at Healey Mills on May 7, 1989, the wagon displays the deeper yellow band and larger Tope lettering found on this batch while the TOPS code has been obviously altered from ZDV to ZCV. This batch also saw the introduction of the end spill plates while the wagon was carrying fresh ballast, a less common load for the type.** Trevor Mann

welded into place. Less obvious but more important to the function of the wagon, a plate floor was fitted, this being supported by transverse steel sections that rested on the upper face of the underframe. The redundant hopper chutes were left in situ and, although the door operating handles were removed, their backplates remained. The underframe remained unmodified, so the wagons retained vacuum brakes and they were finished in the engineers' grey and yellow scheme. The three wagons evidently proved a success as three additional batches eventually followed between 1987-90.

The first production batch was again rebuilt at Doncaster in 1987/88 but this time by the privatised RFS Engineering. The only significant improvement was the addition of angled spill plates to the ends while the hopper chutes and the baseplates for the door handles were again left intact. They were painted in a modified version of grey/yellow with the yellow band being broader than usual in order to accommodate larger and grey Tope lettering. Numbered DB970000-059, they were initially coded ZDV, but this was altered to ZCV during construction.

Split order

Although the vehicles in the next batch, converted by Powell Duffryn in Cardiff between 1988-90, retained the spill plates, there were subtle changes to the design. The door handles were removed in their entirety and on most, possibly all, of DB970100-399, the hopper chutes were cut away. The livery specification returned to the arrangement seen on the prototypes with a narrower yellow band with the Tope code applied in white lettering on the grey lower bodywork. Prominent vertical white lines were applied to the bodysides in order to reveal the maximum extent of the flat floor, this assisting excavator drivers during loading and unloading.

For the third production batch of 450 wagons, for which BR returned to RFS Engineering in 1988/89, further minor variations in both construction and livery were introduced. The spill plates were retained but, in contrast with previous RFS batches, the door handles were completely removed. The hopper chutes seem to have been retained on most of DB970400-849 but some did have them cut away. In terms of livery, the Tope name was now applied in small grey lettering within a box on a narrow yellow band while the vertical white lines showing the ends of the wagon floor were retained.

What was essentially an add-on to the final RFS production batch saw an additional six Tope conversions completed for use by the Electrification Engineer in 1989, presumably to move spoil excavated during the installation of overhead electrification masts or the laying of foundations for sub-stations. Numbered LDB970850-855, they were not fitted with spill plates but were otherwise identical to the rest of this build. All were finished in the rather drab olive green scheme still favoured by the Mechanical & Electrical Engineers and were branded 'Electrification Engineer (Construction)'. Initially based at Kings Norton for use on the Birmingham cross-city line, they also saw use on the East Coast Main Line electrification and by the winter of 1993/94, at least one had migrated to the Western Region, working from Southall. All six survived into the new millennium but had been condemned by the end of 2001.

The Tope were primarily utilised in the movement of spoil from the site of re-ballasting work to tips and ballast recycling facilities. Occasionally, they were used for new ballast while they could be seen across much of the rail network. In a seemingly unlikely development, a rake was returned ➤

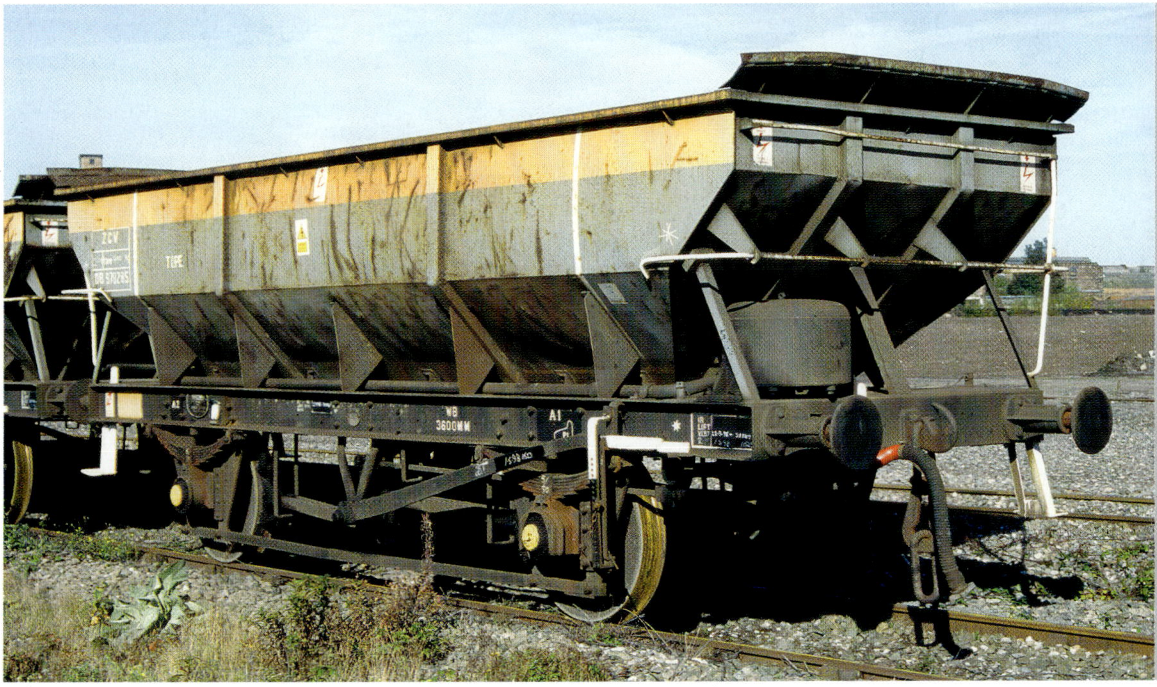

LEFT: **From the Powell Duffryn batch of conversions, DB970285 (ex B340543) is seen at the ballast recycling plant at Cockshute Sidings, Stoke, following privatisation on October 10, 1998. This batch generally saw the hopper chutes removed, as evidenced by the daylight visible through the underframe, along with the fittings for the door handles. The slightly narrower nature of the yellow band is evident with the Tope lettering repositioned onto the grey. The two vertical white lines indicated the extent of the horizontal floor and were intended to assist excavator operators during unloading.** Trevor Mann

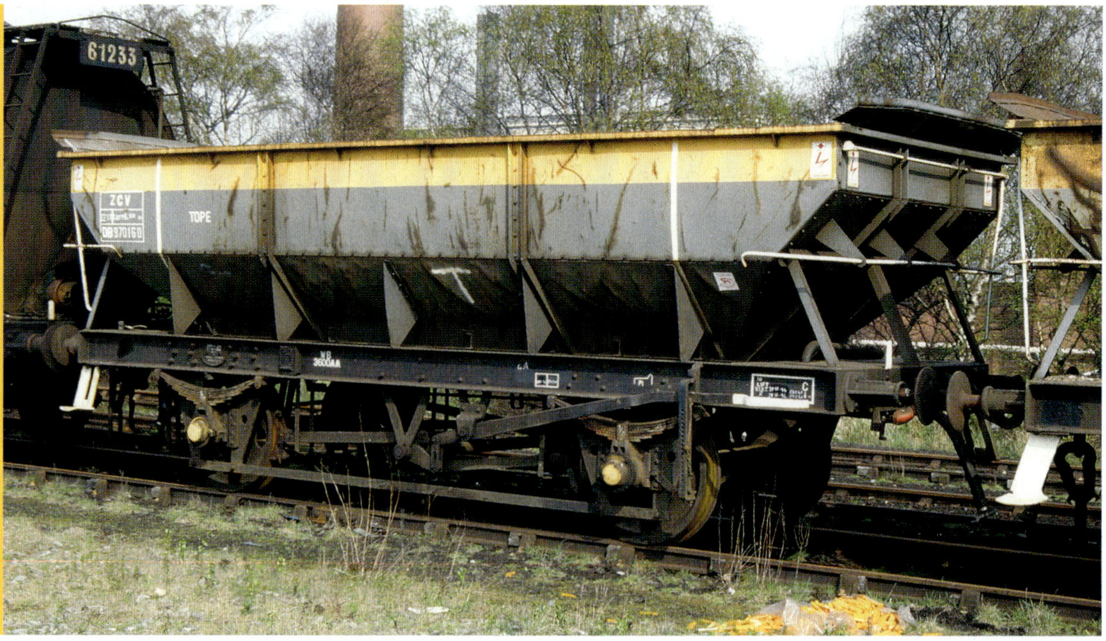

RIGHT: **All of the Tope conversions retained the bodywork fitted during the 1970s, when large numbers of the 21-ton hoppers had passed through BR workshops for refurbishment. For a comparatively small number of wagons this had involved the use of 'huck-bolt' rather than welded construction, this giving a distinctive appearance to any Tope that were subsequently converted from such vehicles. The body plates were bolted together and the side and end ribs, which were of 'U' channel construction, were 'huck-bolted' to the body plating. An example was DB970160, seen at Ellesmere Port on April 10, 1995, which was rebuilt from B340405 by Powell Duffryn and again lost its hopper doors.** Trevor Mann

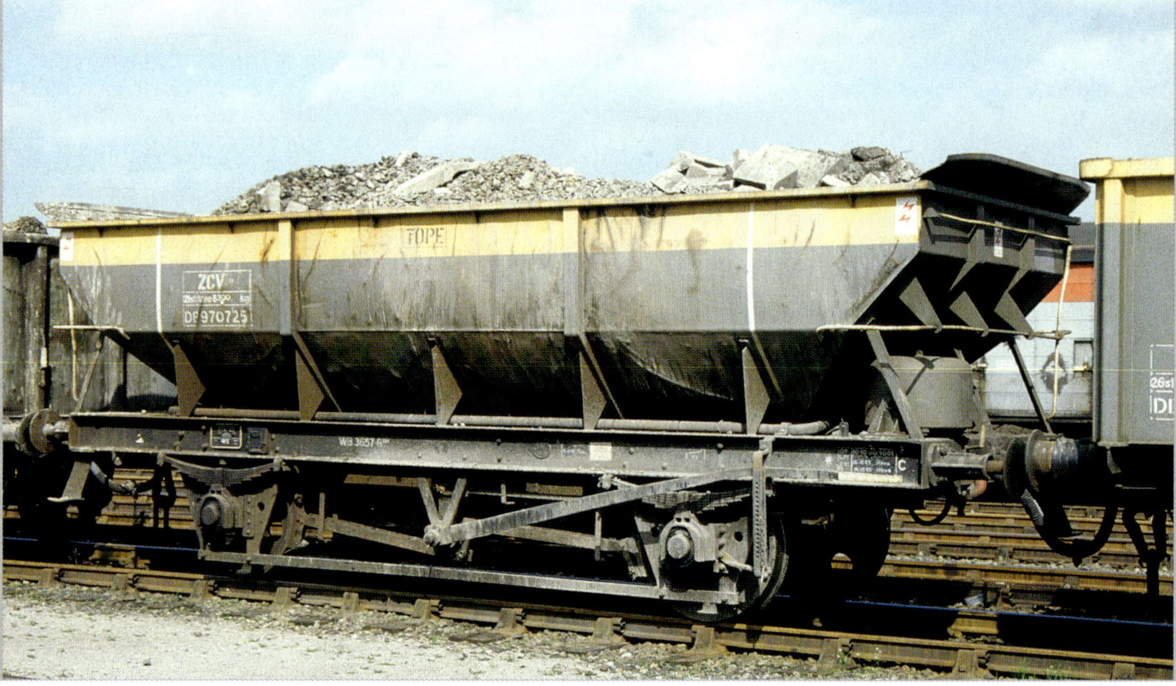

LEFT: **The final production batch of Tope conversions by RFS introduced further variety. The spill plates were retained, and the door operating handles were completely removed but, while some examples kept their hopper chutes, others had them removed. The livery featured a centrally-positioned Tope code with grey lettering and surrounding box on a narrow yellow band. DB970725, which had been converted from B435444, was loaded with demolition spoil at Tees Yard on May 1, 1994.** Trevor Mann

to revenue traffic in 1999 for conveying coal to the Renishaw blending site. Most survived into privatisation, any withdrawals probably being the result of body damage, but condemnations accelerated in the late-1990s and the type became extinct during the early 2000s. One curiosity was the renumbering of prototype DB423760 as T970060 by Transrail around 1995, although the other two examples were never altered.

Enter the Clam

The second rebuild of the HTV hoppers, coded Clam, was an altogether more comprehensive conversion and utilised donor wagons with life-expired or damaged bodies. The hopper bodywork, including the chutes, was completely removed, and replaced by a robustly-constructed box body that was clearly designed to withstand the rigours of loading and unloading by mechanical grab.

Below a sturdy top capping, the sides featured 13 vertical ribs which, at the base of the sides, tucked underneath to run across

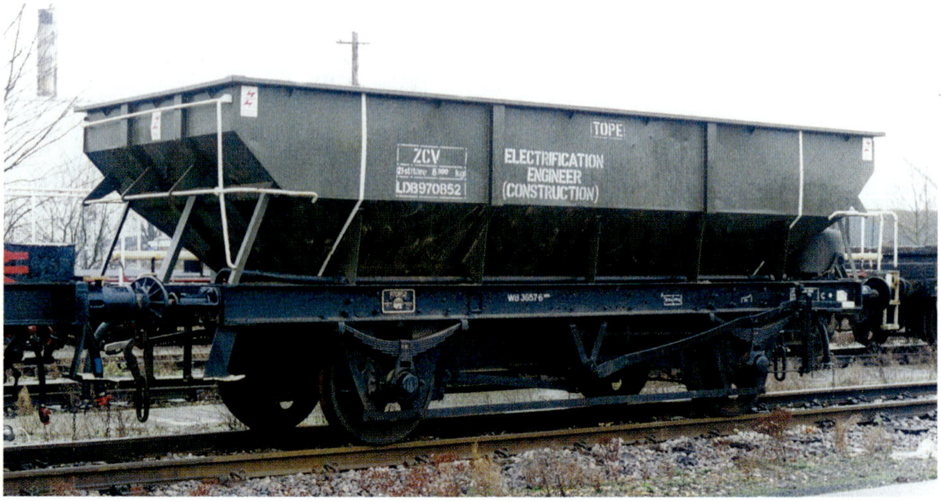

ABOVE: **The six Tope allocated to the M&EE Electrification Department were built as an add-on to the final RFS batch, the only difference being the absence of the spill plates. Reflecting their different ownership, they carried olive green with white lettering. LDB970852, which had been rebuilt from B426754, was recorded at Southall in December 1993.** Colin Wright/David Ratcliffe Collection

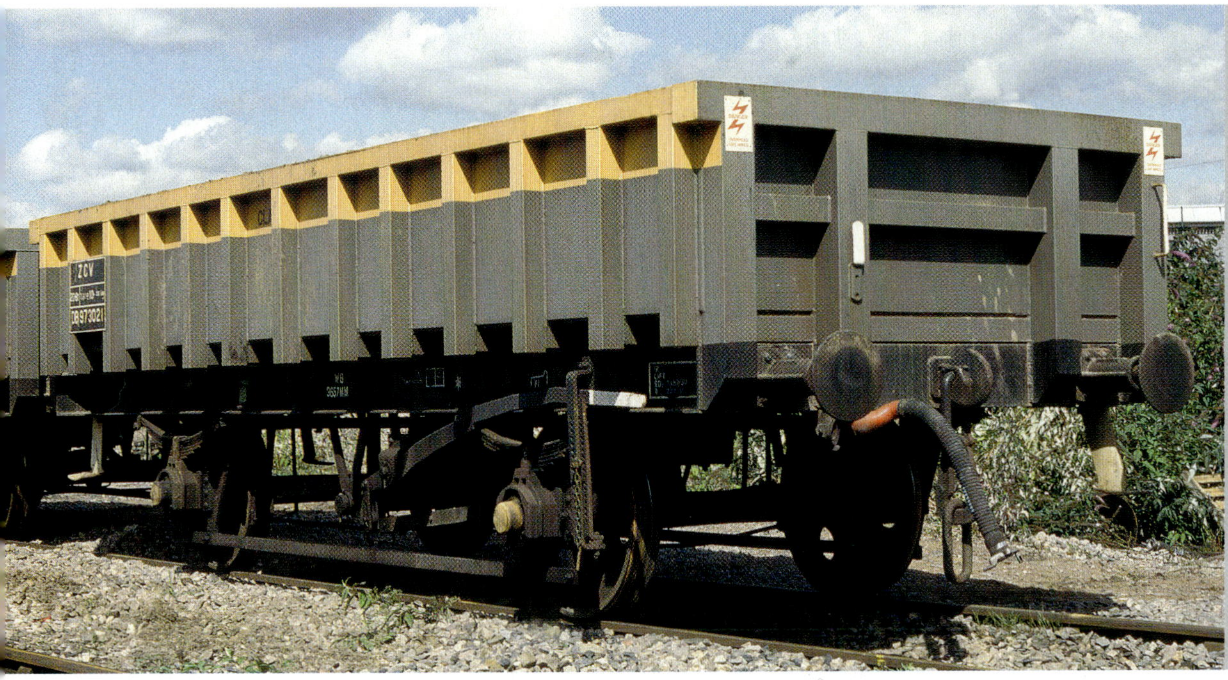

LEFT: **The ZCV Clam conversions saw a new box body added to the existing vacuum-braked underframe. DB973021, which was rebuilt from B432845 by Powell Duffryn, is seen at Radyr on August 25, 1991, and shows the separate number plate employed on the wagons converted by the company.** Trevor Mann

the wagon, these ribs resting on the upper surface of the underframe and supporting the floor. The ends were equally well strengthened with a top capping and four vertical ribs made from noticeably larger steel section than used on the sides, together with a horizontal stiffener. The void beneath the floor was blanked off using steel plate while the basic underframe and brake rigging was retained. However, the vacuum cylinder was by necessity moved from the former hopper end platform to a more conventional position between the solebars.

Two batches of Clam were built but, in contrast with the Tope, there appear to have been no design or constructional differences between them. All were converted in 1989/90 with Powell Duffryn outshopping DB973000-149 from its Cardiff workshops and RFS Engineering contributing DB973150-449 from Doncaster, all appearing in the standard engineers' grey and yellow livery. The lettering was the only significant variation between the two batches with Powell Duffryn examples having the Clam code painted in solid script grey lettering and applied centrally towards the top of the sides, while the other lettering was on a plate attached to the second and third bodyside ribs. In contrast, those rebuilt by RFS had the Clam code in the same position and colour but applied with a stencil and with a box surround, while the number, ZCV TOPS code and other data were painted along the solebars.

With the exception of the Southern Region, the Clam saw service across the entire network, being primarily used for the movement of spoil between worksites and either tips or ballast recycling facilities. The

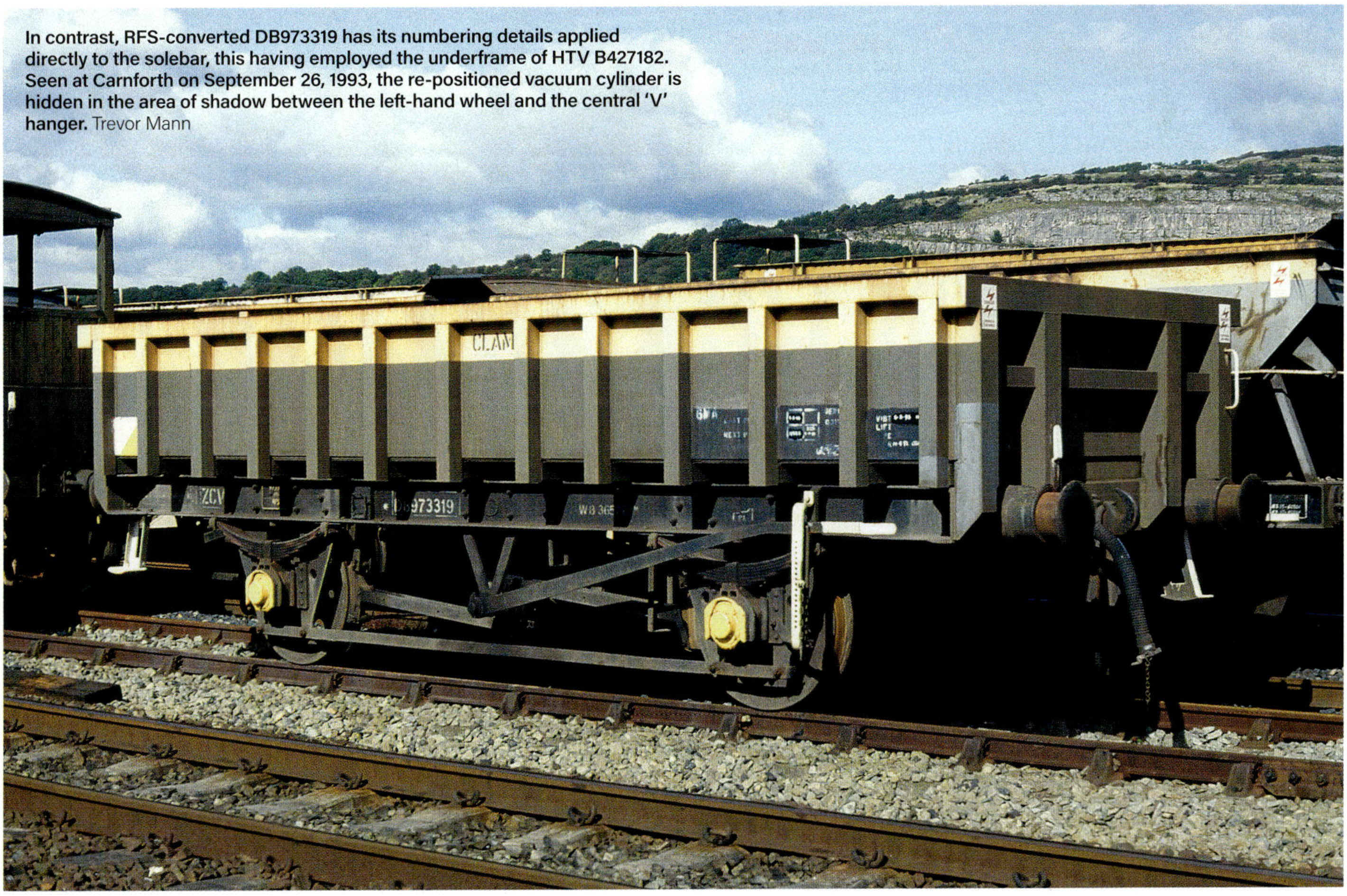

In contrast, RFS-converted DB973319 has its numbering details applied directly to the solebar, this having employed the underframe of HTV B427182. Seen at Carnforth on September 26, 1993, the re-positioned vacuum cylinder is hidden in the area of shadow between the left-hand wheel and the central 'V' hanger. Trevor Mann

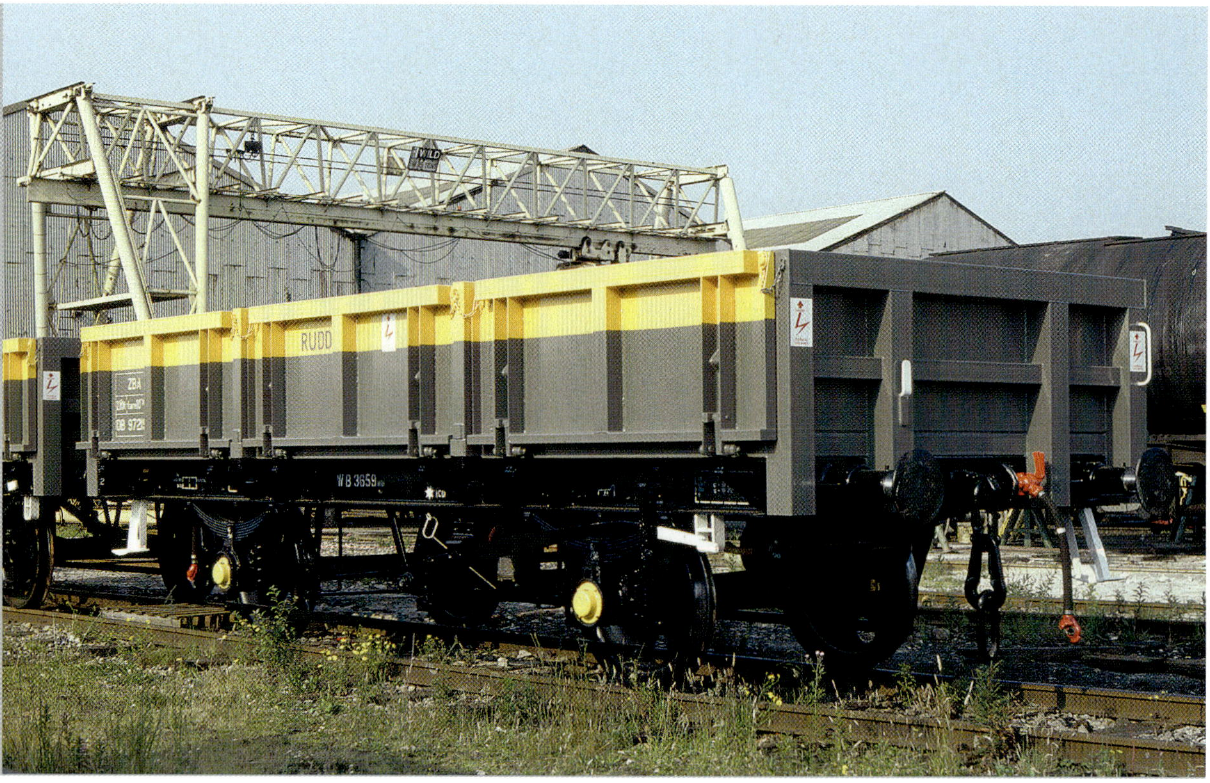

RIGHT: **Fresh out of the paint shop at the Stoke workshops of Marcroft Engineering on July 7, 1990, DB972198 exemplifies the first batch of Rudd conversions, in this case from B427448. The door springs had yet to be fitted while the corner posts and end ribs show off their square section appearance. The white number panel is also evident.** Trevor Mann

entire fleet survived into privatisation and all but a handful into the new millennium. The majority were recoded MGV by EWS from 2000 onwards but this was unrelated to any change in use. The elimination of vacuum-braked locos saw the wagons go the same way within a couple of years.

Rudd rebuilds

The third and final conversion of the HTV hoppers was the most involved, resulting in the appearance of an air-braked wagon that may genuinely be regarded as the late 20th century equivalent of the Grampus. Coded ZBA Rudd, a total of 800 wagons were rebuilt between 1989 and 1991 with DB972000-399 coming from Marcroft Engineering at Stoke while CC Crump of Connah's Quay contributed DB972400-799.

The donor wagons not only lost their hopper bodywork and chutes but also had the vacuum brake equipment removed, leaving a stripped down chassis on which to add the new bodies. The replacement sides featured three reinforced drop doors with two intermediate door posts, which could be lifted out to make the entire length of the side available for loading and unloading. Door springs were also fitted above each of the hinges to ease the task of lifting and lowering the doors.

The new ends were similar to those on the Clam, being reinforced by a sturdy framework consisting of top capping, corner posts, vertical ribs, and a horizontal stiffener. The ends were also the main difference between the two batches, specifically the appearance of the corner posts and vertical ribs. On wagons rebuilt by CC Crump, the bottom of these four verticals was chamfered upwards at about 45 degrees but on those converted by Marcroft, the four pillars lacked this,

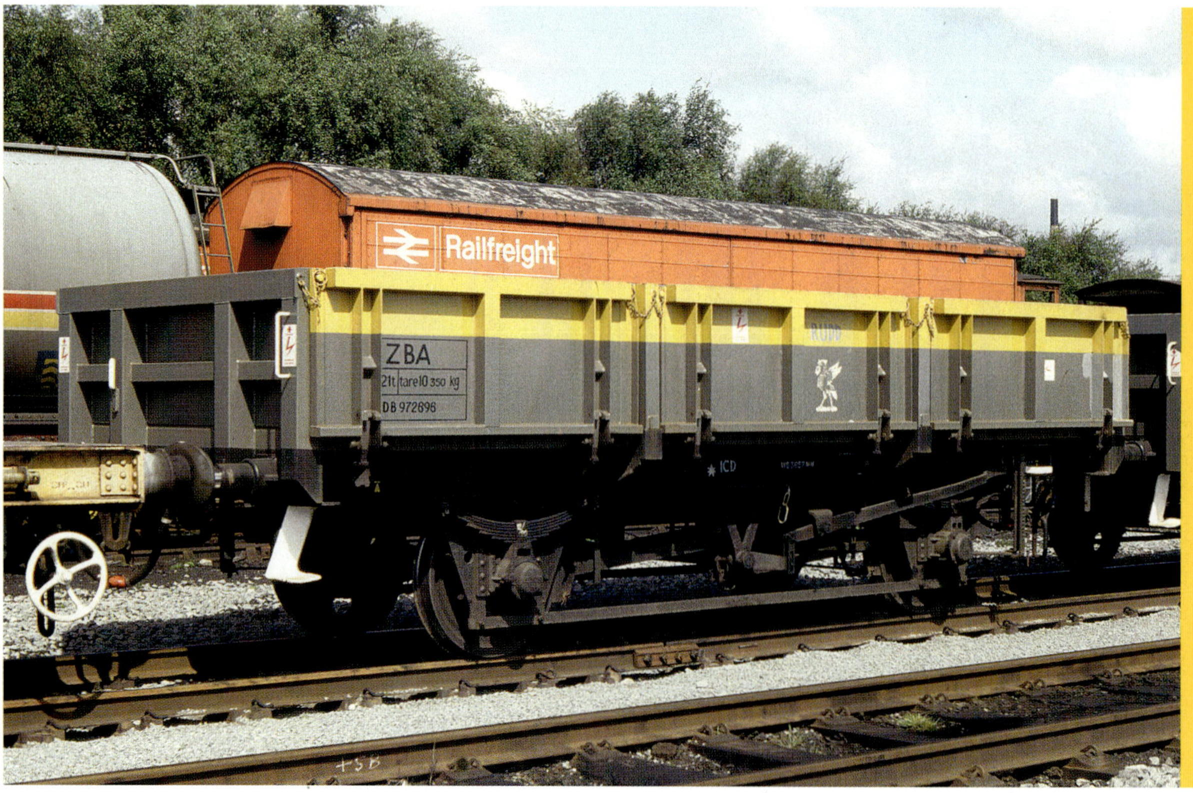

LEFT: **Photographed at Ellesmere Port on May 2, 1992, DB972696 (ex B427668) shows the specifics of a CC Crump Rudd conversion. The black number panel is the most obvious, but the adjacent corner post also shows the angled chamfer given to all eight end posts and ribs. In addition, the bottom edges are all painted black whereas they are grey on the Marcroft example. Worthy of note is the Liver Bird logo, indicating allocation to the Merseyside area.** Trevor Mann

RIGHT: **Only recently rebuilt by Marcroft Engineering on the underframe of B423282, Rudd DB972214 is seen at Ashford Crane Repair Depot on March 27, 1991, having been fitted out as a tunnel ventilation unit, complete with generator, heavy duty fan and control gear. It is understood that this was a temporary modification, utilising hired-in equipment, for a specific tunnel maintenance job with the wagon being returned to standard condition following the completion of the work.** Andy Prime

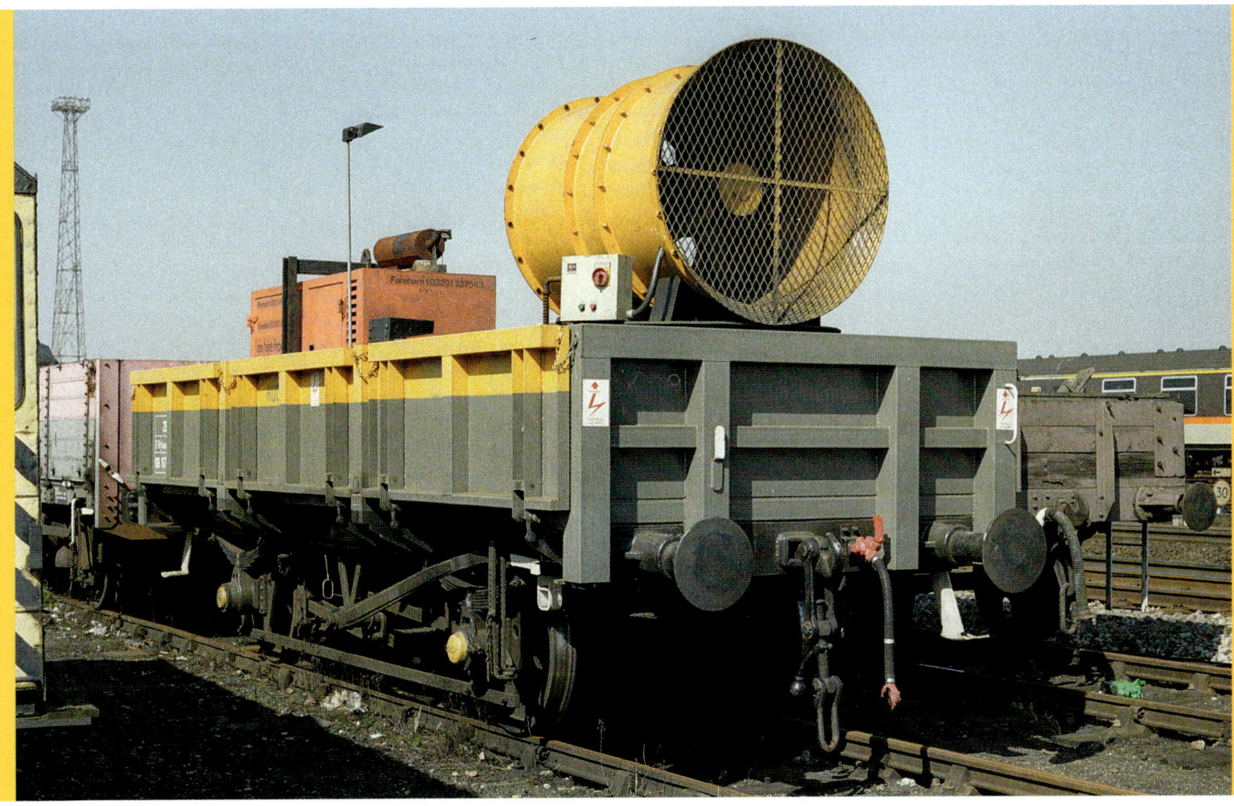

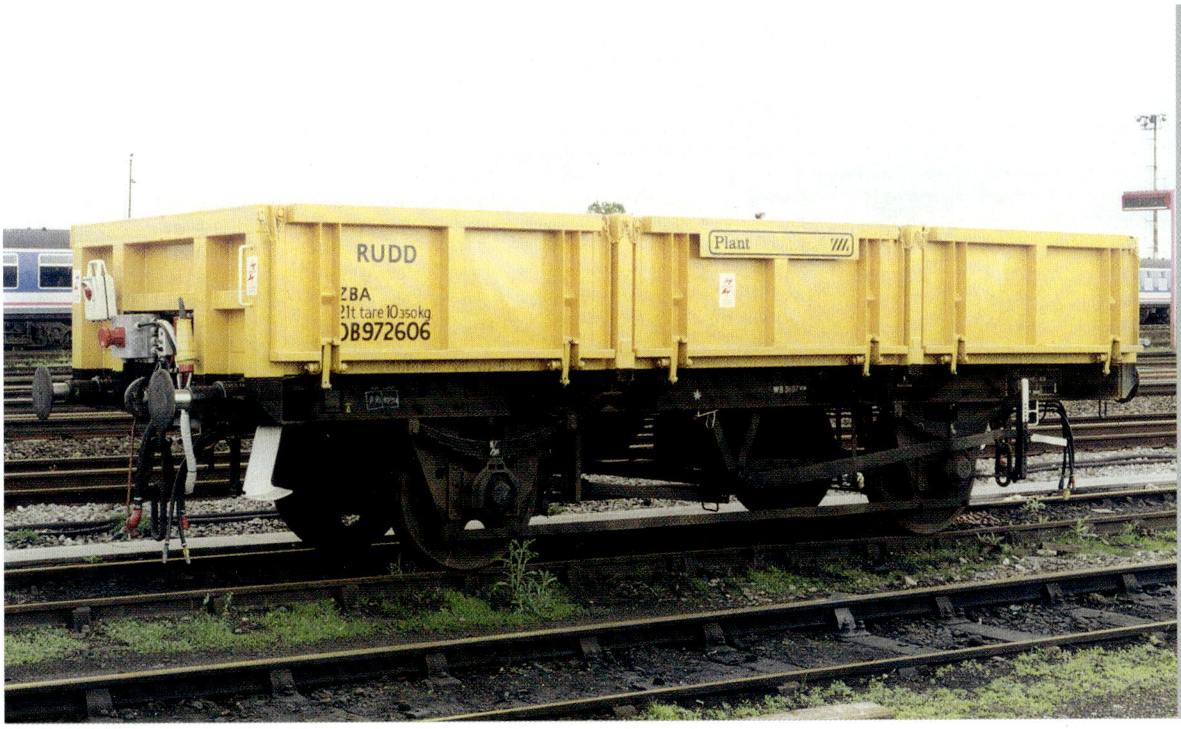

LEFT: **In another demonstration of the versatility of the Rudd design, two examples - DB972208 and DB972606 - were converted at Ashford Crane Repair Depot as intermediate vehicles to work between the two halves of GP-TRAMM light maintenance vehicles. Both carried stone for spot re-ballasting work with DB972606 displaying the through cabling that had to be fitted to allow this new role at Ashford in May 1994. The yellow livery with Plant South East logos would later be replaced by Balfour Beatty blue.** Colin Wright/David Ratcliffe Collection

remaining square section throughout.

The basic underframe and brake rigging was unaltered, but air brake equipment was fitted, this acting on the existing push rods. Oleo buffers and roller bearing axleboxes were also given to any vehicles like the JNA Falcons not already equipped while grey and yellow was again all encompassing. The Rudd lettering was applied in grey on the yellow band of the centre door in all cases but Marcroft examples had the number panels applied in white, stencilled script, whereas those constructed by Crump had black, hand-painted ones.

The Rudd was a highly versatile design, examples seeing use across the entire network carrying loads such as sleepers and crossing timbers, track components, drainage pipes and sumps, hand tools and small items of plant and equipment in addition to new ballast and spoil. A handful were modified for more specialised use during the 1990s as shown in the photos.

As relatively modern, air-braked wagons, the vast majority of Rudd survived into privatisation minus a small handful which had been lost to accidents. Most continued in service until the mid-2000s, by when high-capacity bogie vehicles were increasingly used for spoil and new ballast, and OBA and OCA opens were available for general materials such as drainage pipes or bagged track components.

Grampus conversions

In 1988, 30 Grampus ballast opens, which had already seen some three decades of service, were dispatched to RFS Engineering at Doncaster for overhaul and conversion to air-brakes. When they emerged, they were the first wagons to carry the Rudd name.

Rather surprisingly, given the small number of wagons involved, there were two distinct design variations. The more common saw the side doors of the Grampus retained but the original ends, with their combination of hinged lower flap and lift out top planks, were completely replaced. The new reinforced steel ends were very similar to what would appear on the ➤

ex-HTV Rudd but without the horizontal stiffener. Numbers of this style included DB984194/788/896, DB985300/561/683/728/774/828/879, DB986250/446/450/465.and DB990109/371/770.

A handful of the wagons were fully re-bodied, these receiving the new ends but also completely new drop doors as well. These again bore a strong resemblance to what would appear on the ex-HTV Rudd the following year but, as door controller arms were not fitted, the vertical strengthening ribs above each hinge were of box construction instead of the 'U' channel later employed. Known examples of this style are DB984849, DB985336/544 and DB986552/689/933/946. The other Grampus that were modified as Rudd by RFS but where the body style is unknown were DB984075/629/837 and DB990393/630/687.

Turning to the underframe, which was the same beneath both body variants, the air brake equipment was coupled to the existing rigging. Vehicles not already so equipped received wheelsets with roller bearing axleboxes but, rather surprisingly, the spindle buffers were not upgraded to the modern Oleo design. The original Grampus door bangers were also retained to protect the underframe from damage when the heavy doors dropped open. All were turned out in grey/yellow with the Rudd name applied in large grey letters onto the yellow band and the revised TOPS code of ZBA and other lettering added in white using the standard 'boxed' style.

All of these rebuilds were initially allocated to the Scottish Region, with a number branded 'To work between Perth and Highland Line Locations'. As deliveries of the ex-HTV Rudd conversions gathered pace, many of these former Grampus migrated south of the border and the type eventually saw use across the BR network. In operation, they were often mixed indiscriminately with the other Rudd while one example, DB990109, was also modified as an intermediate vehicle for a GP-TRAMM. Many lasted into the early 2000s with EWS, DB984788 even receiving a coat of maroon with a thin, yellow solebar stripe.

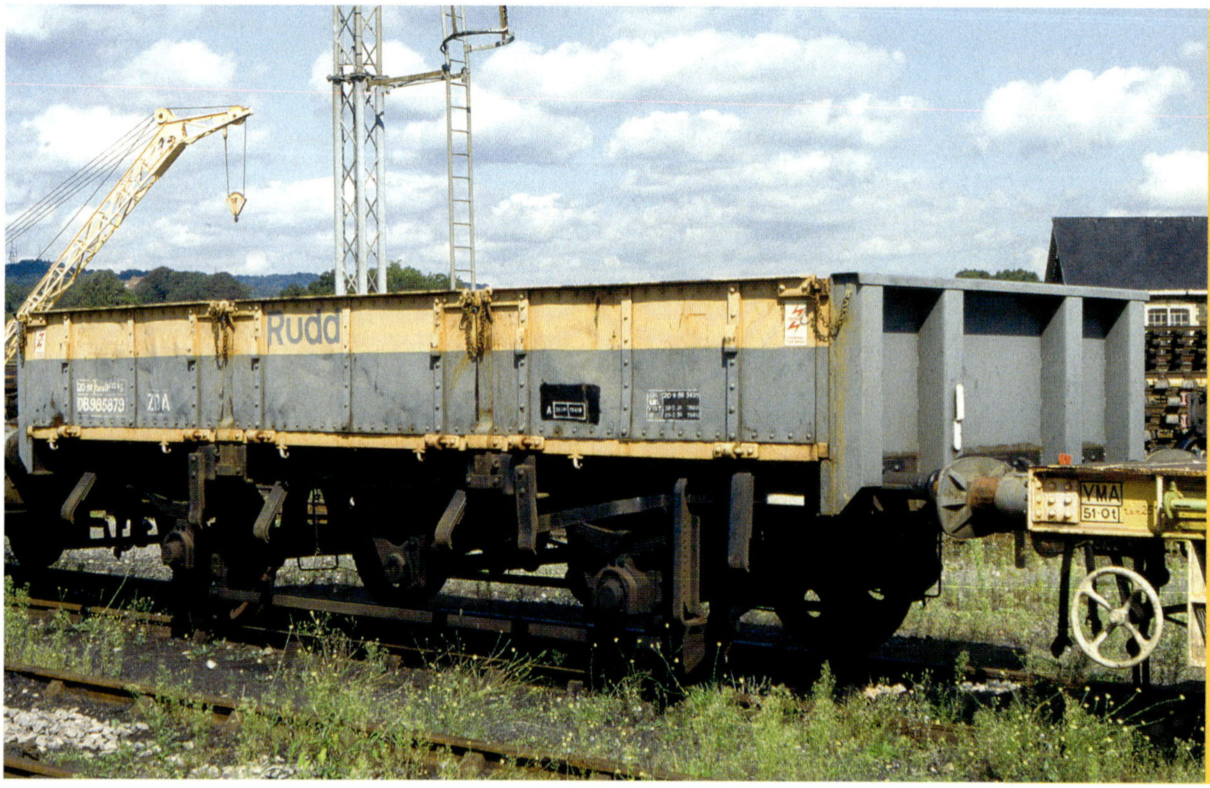

LEFT: **The most common version of the Grampus to Rudd conversion just saw the ends rebuilt and air brakes fitted. On August 25, 1991, DB985978 was found residing in Radyr Yard. The thin yellow stripe along the solebar was a common feature of the conversions and may have been a form of visual identification.** Trevor Mann

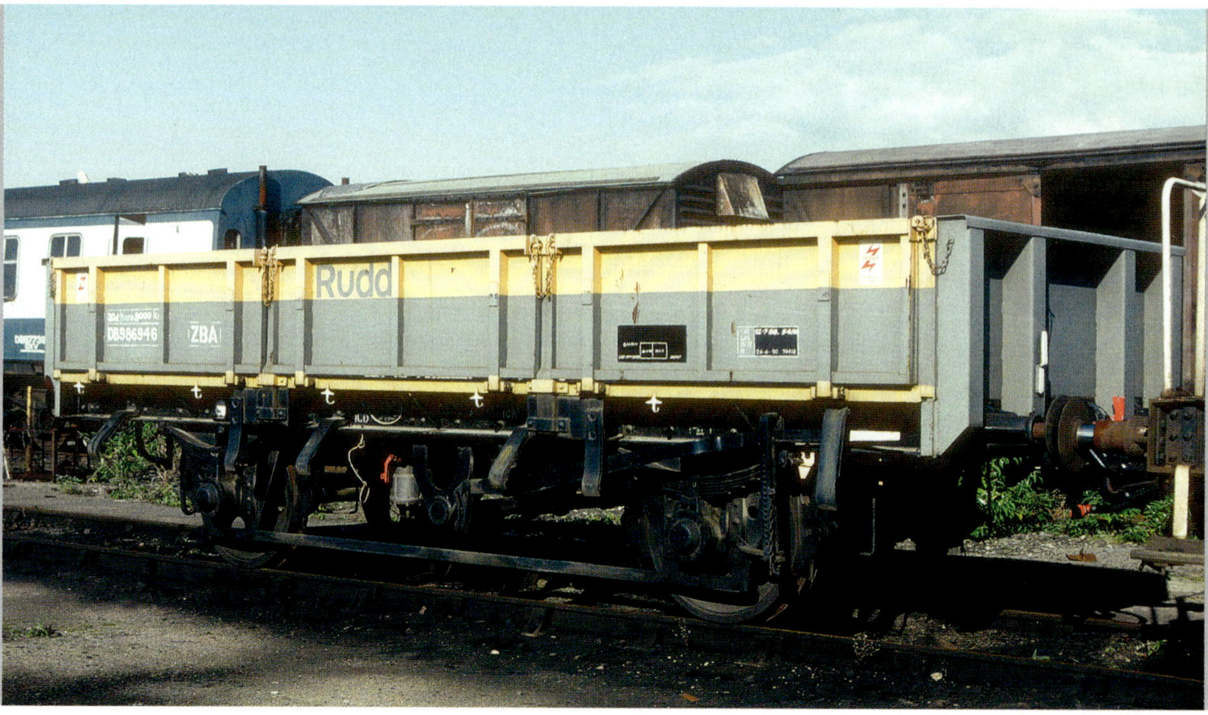

RIGHT: **At least seven of the Grampus received the full re-body with new doors, On September 30, 1990, DB986946 was also to be found at Radyr, looking for all the world like a production Rudd. However, subtle differences in the door ribs and presence of the Grampus-style door bangers help give the game away.** Paul Bartlett

An alternative Tope by Tim Easter

There has been a model of the ZCV Tope in the Hornby range since 2011. Unfortunately, this is rather let down by the hopper moulding being of an inaccurate shape and height, so I opted for a different way of making a batch of these wagons in 4mm. My starting point was the excellent Parkside kit for the re-bodied HTV 21-ton hoppers, this allowing me to create a Tope in a similar fashion to how they were rebuilt by BR. This also gave an opportunity to add some of the detail missing on the Hornby model, such as the ends of the floor support brackets along the sides of the hopper body.

The kit instructions were generally followed as written with the addition of the vacuum pipe run above the chassis framework, which was made from 1mm diameter brass rod. Depending on which batch of conversions is being modelled, the mounts for the former hopper door release handles can be carefully removed from the solebars. Once the lower parts of the hopper were in place, the ends of the support beams for the new floor were added using eight short pieces of 'C' channel section. These were only fitted on the side without the vacuum pipe as this largely obscures them on the other. For wagons with self-contained buffers, I used the excellent ones from Lanarkshire Models and Supplies but, otherwise, replacement turned metal heads were fitted to the existing housings, these coming from Wizard Models/51L.

The sides and ends of the hopper all need to be reduced in height by about 5.5mm to match the modification made to the Tope. This is best done with a steel rule and a Stanley knife and by making several light passes with the blade until the pieces part company. Also, the small horizontal brackets on the inside faces of the vertical sides need to be removed. Once fully assembled, the top of the hopper can be squared off with a large file to ensure all the parts are level. New top capping was then added using 60 by 30 thou plastic strip.

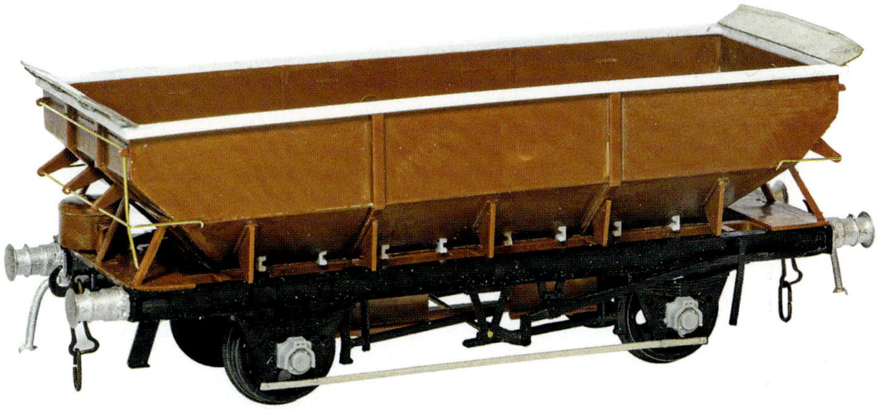

ABOVE: **With the model ready for painting, the Tope shows off the alterations and enhancements made to the Parkside HTV kit. The white 'C' sections representing the floor support ends can be seen along the hopper side as can the new top capping. On the end, the way the two handrails meet is also shown.**

Internal alterations

The new flat floor inside the hopper was made from 30 thou plasticard measuring 62mm by 16mm but before gluing this in place, lead sheet was cut to size and fitted underneath to provide some weight. It is also best to chamfer the underside of the floor so that it fits better inside the hopper. To represent the witness marks of where the sloped dividing sections have been cut away, I would recommend using some 10 by 20 thou plastic strip in a vee arrangement, although some flattened 0.5mm rod would also do the job. These marks were not always visible on the Tope, so it is an optional task.

The handrails were made from 0.33mm wire instead of the slightly thicker wire supplied with the kit. The long L-shaped handrail that goes across from the top left of the end and then down to the bottom right end support is very fiddly. I found the best solution was to drill a hole downwards through the top right bracket and have a continuous length of wire (48mm long) to do it in a single hit. In reality, they are two separate handrails. The vertical part of this handrail goes inside the waist-height horizontal one and the two can be fixed together for rigidity using a tiny blob of solder paste and a touch with a hot iron.

The spill plates were the final job, being made from 12thou scrap brass etch and carefully formed to the correct curved shape using a set of plain nose pliers. The gussets to mount each spill plate onto the ends were also made from brass scrap and were soldered onto the undersides before filing to the right shape. The assemblies were then glued on using a contact adhesive.

With my Tope portraying a mid-1990s condition, the paint was required to have a faded look to assist with the weathering. I used Railfreight flint grey and added a bit of white to some warning panel yellow as I did not have anything lighter. Early warning panel yellow would probably give the same effect though. The underframes were painted black although, depending on where the wagons were converted, the vacuum cylinder could either be grey or black. Finally, transfers came from the Appleby range, but Railtec also offers a similar sheet.

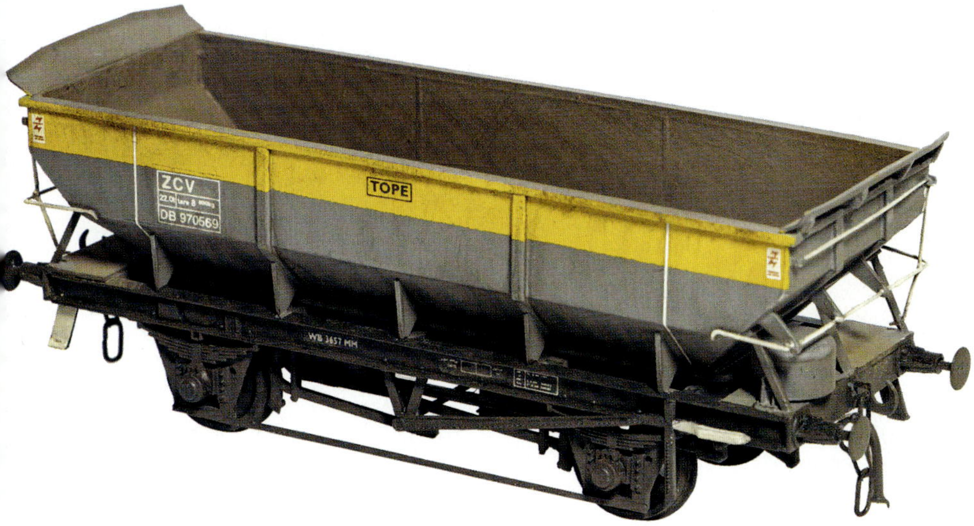

LEFT: **The Tope shows off its faded and weathered finish from the vacuum pipe side. In this instance, Appleby transfers were used as they were to hand but the Railtec ones are more readily available. The wagon certainly looks the part and makes the more involved conversion process worthwhile.**

Modelling Rudd and Clam by Mark Lambert and Mike Cubberley

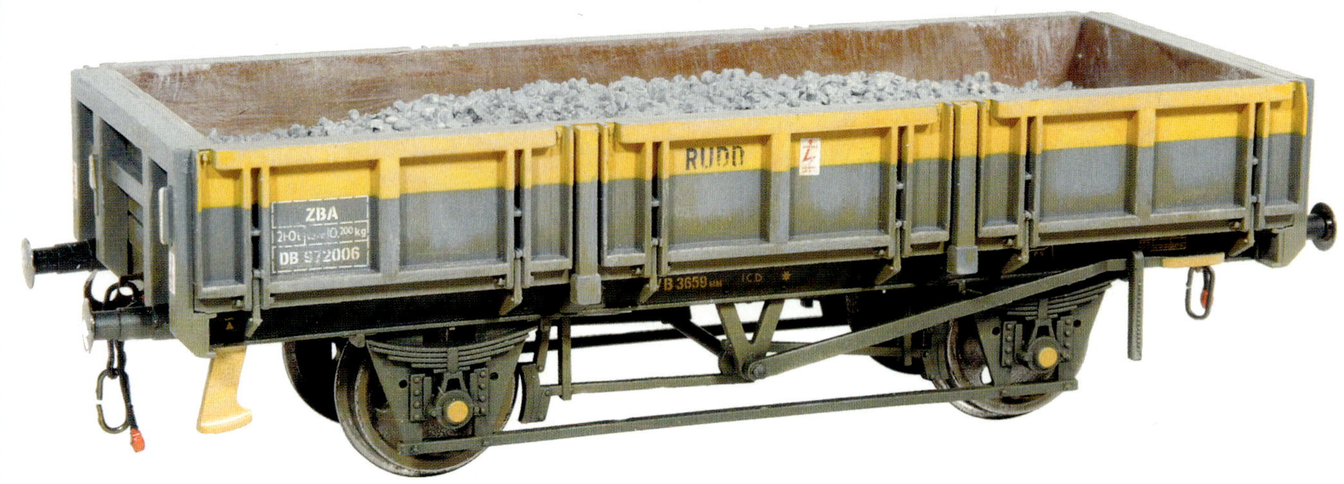

ABOVE: In 4mm scale, there are two options for modelling the ZBA Rudd, these being the ready-to-run model produced by Hornby and the plastic kit offered by Parkside, of which the latter is the older route. Both have their faults, most notably the thickness of the sides and ends on the Hornby offering to prevent warping while the plastic kit is 2mm too narrow in width. Neither is easy to correct but the RTR Rudd has the advantage of not having to paint the yellow stripe on yourself, which is difficult over all the door ribs. Opting for the Hornby model, these have been produced in both pristine and weathered forms over the years. Those supplied with factory dirt are best avoided though as the all-over grot finish and colour leaves a lot to be desired. However, if these are all you can source, the good news is that the weathering is easy to remove with cotton buds and isopropyl alcohol (IPA) or white spirit and comes off long before the tampo-printed lettering does. The underlying colours are quite good, although the grey may be a little dark.

I removed the weathering from the body but not the underframe and then gave the whole wagon a coat of the dark brown wash from the Ammo by Mig Jimenez range. On the underframe, this corrected the tone and gave the wagon a used look but, on the body, I used a large flat brush to remove much of the wash, leaving it on the bottom of the doors and in crevices, which darkened any residual factory weathering. The pre-primed ballast load came from Make Your Mark Models and was dry-brushed with a light stone acrylic colour. For pristine Hornby Rudd, these can be air-brushed on the underframe with Railmatch frame dirt, and the body washed as before. Finally, Smiths Instanter couplings were fitted along with air pipes from a loco detailing pack.

Of note is that the Hornby model represents a Rudd with CC Crump ends, these having the chamfered bottoms to the corner posts and ribs. If a Marcroft bodied wagon is desired, S Kits produces replacement whitemetal ends with the square section ribs. Mark Lambert

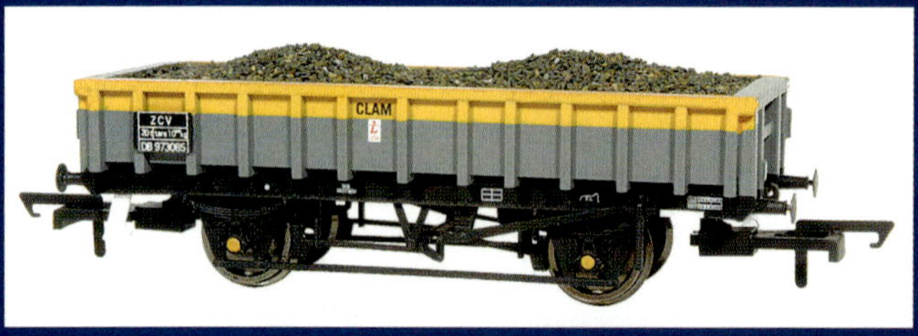

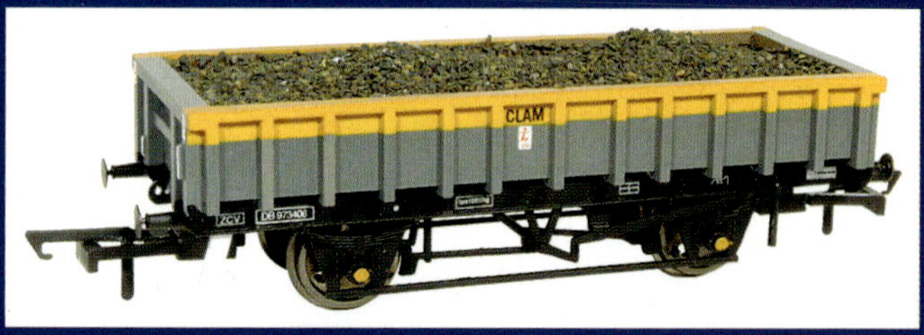

Hornby and Parkside are again the source of ZCV Clam in 4mm but this time, it is the RTR model that has the dimensional error as it is just over 2mm too wide. This, combined with the chunky sides and ends should make the Parkside kit the easy favourite but, again, the sheer difficulty of painting the yellow stripe over all the ribs comes into play.

It was therefore decided to modify the Hornby model, first by removing the ends and then using a razor saw to cut both bodysides completely away from the floor. The sides of the remaining body tub then each have to be carefully sanded down by around 1-1.5mm before reattaching the bodysides. The ends of the body also need to be modified to match, this seeing the corner posts cut off, the adjacent recessed bodywork trimmed down, and the corner posts then glued back on. Any slight gaps can be filled and sanded down afterwards.

The paint was touched up where necessary with RAF Harrier grey from Hannants, which is a direct match for the Hornby grey. The top of the bodysides should also be finished in yellow rather than grey as Hornby always does. Finally, the spoil load was the Meldon Quarry mix produced by Attwood Aggregates. Hornby has tended to produce Clam with the Powell Duffryn-style separate number plates but has done the odd RFS example with solebar lettering as well. It is easy enough to change one to the other by removing the glued-on plate. Mike Cubberley

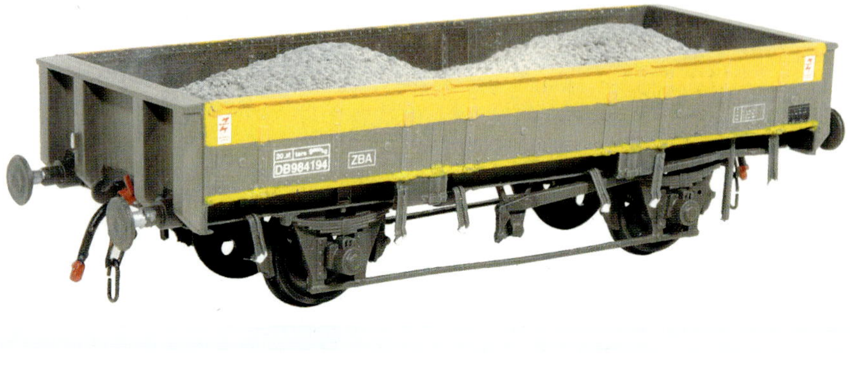

LEFT: Parkside produces a 4mm scale kit for the vacuum-braked Grampus (ref no. PC72) and this includes additional parts to model the wagons that were converted to ZBA Rudd by fitting air brakes and new ends. The kit does not cater for those wagons that also received new sides though. The one pictured here was built as per the instructions with no deviations or additional parts and goes together very nicely. As part of the conversion, the underframe baskets that could hold the removable end sections were also dispensed with so there is no need to fit those parts from the kit. One potential modification would be to fit the etched door bangers produced by Rumney Models, these being finer and also less vulnerable to falling off! Mike Cubberley

While the earliest OAA transfers to engineers' stock were treated to a smart repaint into grey and yellow, this was not the case when the bulk of the fleet followed in 1990. With so many transferring at once, many were left in their previous Railfreight colours with just the logo removed. DC100021 is seen at Hoo Junction on April 28, 1993, with the top half of the number panel having been over-painted in grey and ZDA and Squid added, while the DC prefix is squeezed in either side of the hinge strap. The wagon has also been lettered 'For RCE (SR) Inter Depot Use Only', a role that many Squid came to perform. David Ratcliffe

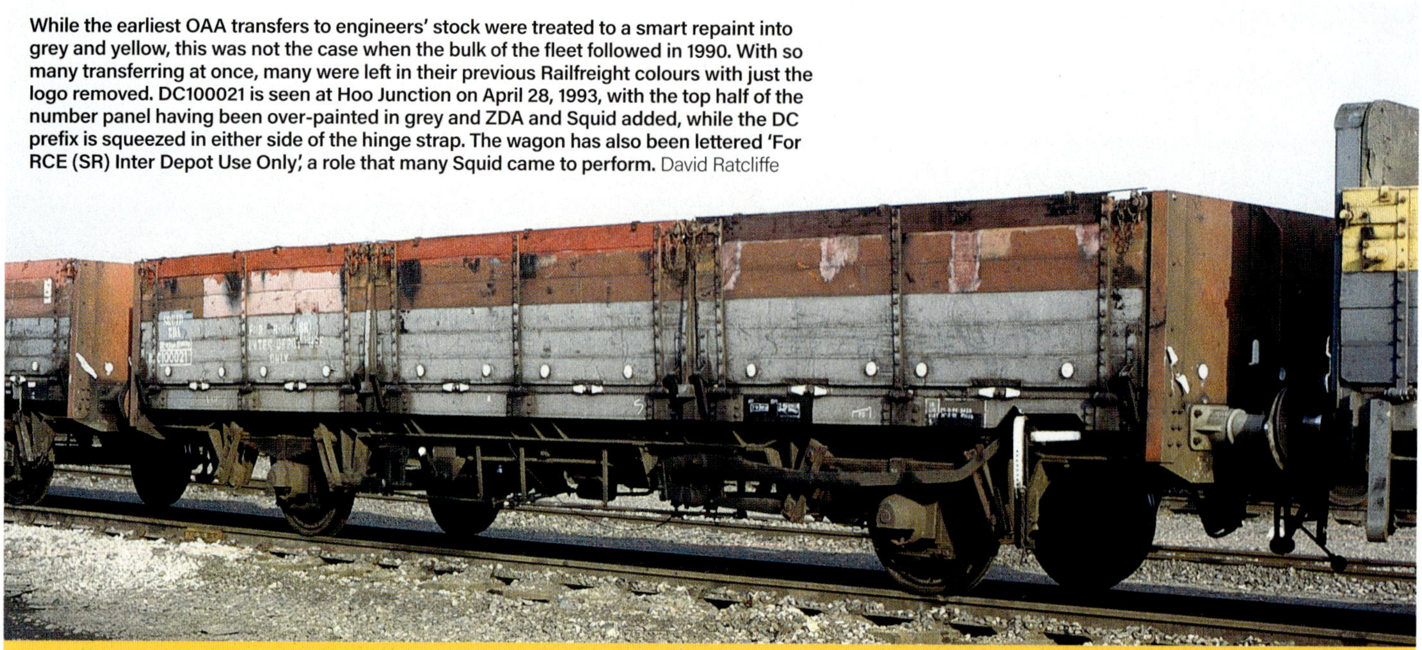

ZDA Squid

With new builds ruled out, the majority of the air-braked stock for the Civil Engineers was provided by transferring vehicles that were no longer required for revenue earning duties. Simon Bendall examines each type in turn, beginning with the many different designs of open wagon before looking at bogie flats and other assorted types.

The first type to be considered is the oldest of the air-braked open wagon designs, the OAA or as they were originally known the Open AB, given they were delivered from Ashford Works in late 1971 before TOPS codes had been introduced. Numbered 100000-099, they measured 33ft 6in over headstocks with a wheelbase of 20ft 9in and capacity of 32-tonnes, while they were air-braked only from new, eschewing any provision of a through vacuum pipe. Three wooden drop-doors featured on each side, these being six planks high and rather heavy as a result. The steel ends were the same height as the sides while, despite the weighty doors, no bangers were provided on the solebars to protect the underframe when they were opened.

Like other open wagons, the OAAs were short of work by 1984, their primary revenue role at the time being to move newsprint reels from the paper mill at Corpach, Fort William, to Plumstead in East London. As a result many were temporarily loaned to the engineers for a year or so, ten going to the Mechanical & Electrical Engineers at Warrington to carry lubricating oil and another 68 to the Civil Engineers. Despite this only being a loan, at least one wagon, 100051, managed to gain a DC prefix, ZDA code and Bass name by mistake after a repaint into freight brown.

Permanent transfers to the Civil Engineers did not start until 1988, somewhat late in comparison to other types and, as pictured on page 9, the first five were deployed on Civil Link services with a fresh coat of paint and took the codename of Squid. It was another two years before mass transfers commenced with two-thirds of the fleet having become ZDAs by mid-1991. Many were to be found on the Southern as general materials carriers in the early 1990s, working between various engineering depots but they could also be deployed to worksites when required. EWS took ownership of the fleet in 1996, many being recoded back to OAA for revenue work, such as the Mendip block traffic, while numerous others were re-bodied to become Sea Urchin ballast wagons.

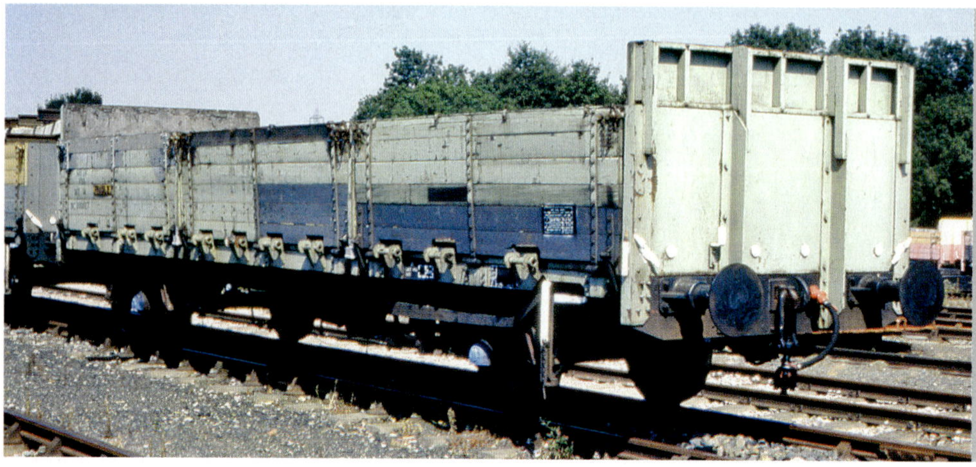

LEFT: During the second half of the 1980s, 15 OAAs were hired to Redland for use in carrying roofing tiles across the country in Speedlink services, these receiving end extensions and the company's light green livery. When the traffic ended in July 1990 on economic grounds, the wagons were transferred to the Civil Engineers' fleet, again on the Southern. Apart from the removal of the Redland logo, they initially retained all of their previous features, including the yellow 'Fragile' board, as demonstrated by DC100027 at Eastleigh on August 16, 1995. This has received the ZDA Squid coding in black above the number panel along with some planking repairs. Some would gain grey/yellow in due course and retained the extended ends. Roger Silsbury

New chassis for a Squid by Mark Lambert

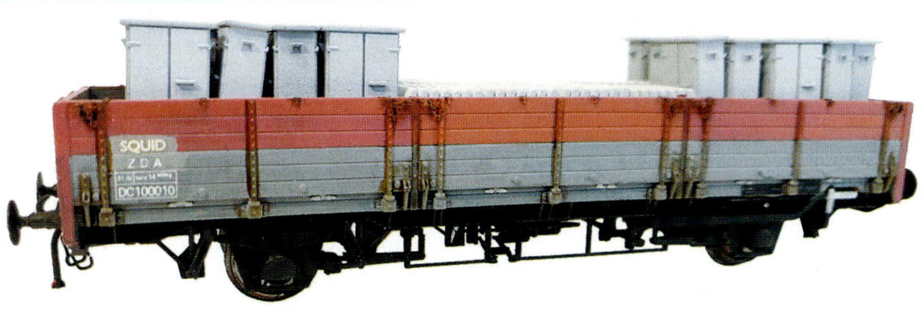

For those wanting to model an OAA or its departmental equivalent in 4mm scale, the only option is the Hornby RTR model. Released decades ago, this is very much a trainset model of its time when accuracy was largely unimportant. As such it suffers from a number of compromises, particularly the poor underframe and swivelling axles to get the wagon around first radius curves.

While an all new model is desperately needed, the relatively recent release of a complete 3D printed underframe goes some way to curing the OAA's ills, although it creates a new problem of where to put the weight! This print has been produced by the same designer as the taperlite suspension used on my ZCA Pollock and is nicely done but fragile in places. Before fitting it, I gave the print a covering of black undercoat and a topcoat or Army Painter 'Hardened Carapace' for a weathered look. Whatever resin the underframe is printed in does not take glue particularly well but superglue grips the painted finish superbly.

The Hornby body fits over the underframe perfectly but this is not quite the end of the modifications. Internally, 10thou strip was added to replicate the uprights between the doors while 60x60 thou strip was glued to the bottom of the ends, which was then profiled to complete the bufferbeams; these being only partially moulded by Hornby. The holes for the buffers should be filled in as the buffers need to be moved upwards to line up with the underframe.

For the buffers, I used the 2ft ½in Oleos with 18in heads produced by Lanarkshire Models and Supplies, these castings helping to add a little weight to the wagon. The new wheels were some old Jackson 12mm disc-braked ones while the top-hat bearings dropped straight into the holes provided in the 3D print, allowing the wheels to fit with barely any adjustment. I did remove the inner brake shoes though as, like on the Pollock, they were tight.

As I was planning to fit a load in the wagon, I did not sand the inside of the ends flush, instead just giving the interior a spray of light grey Tamiya Fine Surface Primer. The body I used was already in Railfreight red and grey, so the factory-printed lettering was removed with a fibreglass pencil followed by a good wash to remove stray fibres. The grey was repainted using Games Workshop's 'Dawnstone' mixed with a little 'Celestra Grey' from the same source to lighten it further. For the faded red paint, I used two other Games Workshop colours, 'Pink Horrors' and 'Squig Orange' being dry-brushed over the original red to give a patchy and aged appearance.

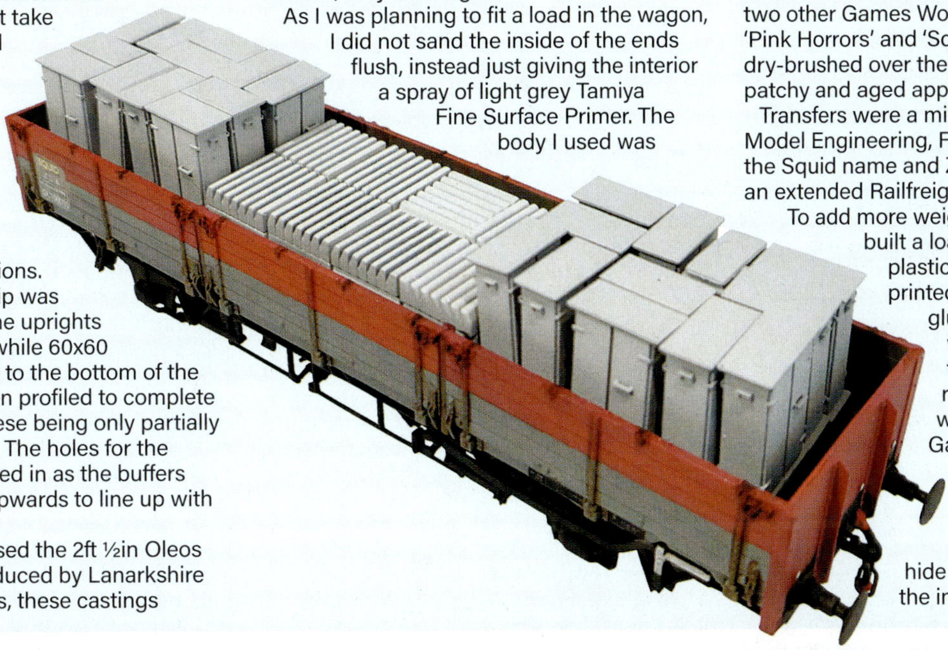

Transfers were a mixture of Appleby Model Engineering, Fox and Railtec with the Squid name and ZDA code applied on an extended Railfreight grey background.

To add more weight to the wagon, I built a load on a base sheet of plasticard, this featuring 3D printed trackside cabinets glued in place along with palletised slabs from the Base Toys range. The cabinets were sprayed with Games Workshop's 'Corax White' over a coat of 'Chaos Black' primer and once in place, they neatly hide the shortcomings of the interior.

Upgrading the Hornby model by Mike Cubberley

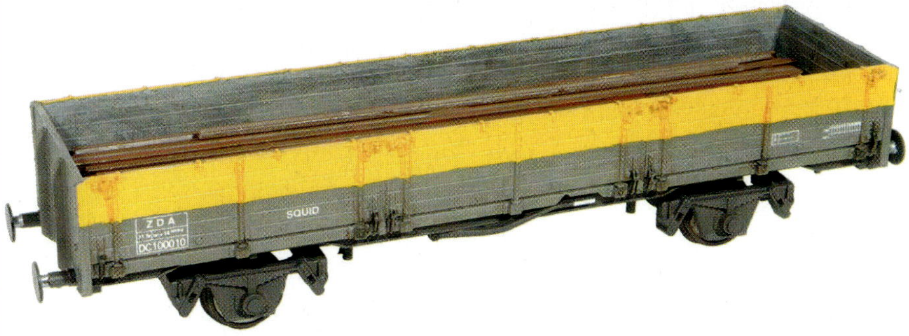

If you just want to use the venerable Hornby OAA as supplied, it can be made more presentable with a fresh coat of paint and an appropriate load. The body was given a coat of grey primer from a Halfords spray can and then painted with Games Workshop acrylics, namely 'Dawnstone grey' and 'Averland Sunset yellow', with the latter being given a final topcoat of Railmatch acrylic warning panel yellow. The underframe was also undercoated with the grey primer and then given a coat of Games Workshop 'Charadon granite grey' to give a slightly in-service look.

The transfers came from Appleby sheet 4T37 and everything was sealed in by a couple of coats of Army Painter flat varnish spray. The ends of the wagon were fitted with a Smiths screw coupling along with an Intercity Models lost-wax cast air brake pipe. The wheels were also changed for Romford ones and fitted with MJT disc brake inserts. An old rail load was made up from sections of Peco Code 100 rail that were cut up and stuck to a separate floor then painted with Tamiya XF-64 red brown to give them a track-weathered appearance.

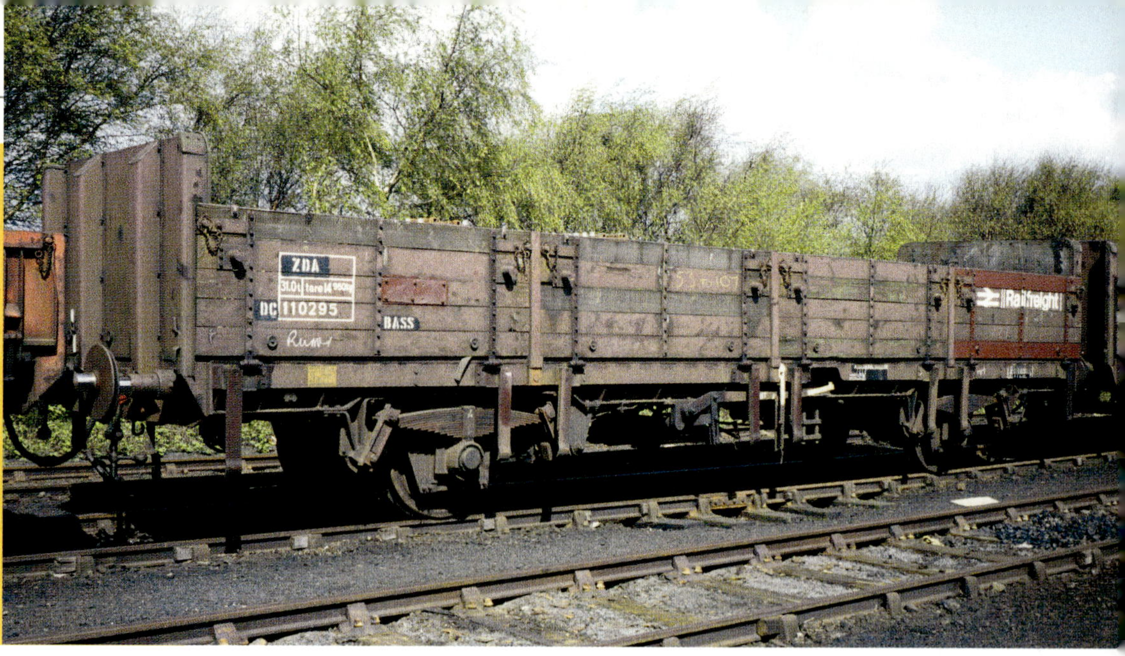

RIGHT: **When pictured at Ellesmere Port in April 1985, DC110295 was still fitted with its original leaf springs and, as such, was something of a late survivor. The number panel has been modified in a common fashion, but the Bass lettering applied to the bodywork without a yellow background was more unusual. The Railfreight lettering is also just about hanging in there while the wagon was carrying chaired sleepers.** David Ratcliffe

ZDA Bass (Wooden)

Following experience with the OAAs, BR opted to implement a number of design changes for its next batch of air-braked open wagons. These were first tried out on a prototype with OAA 100043 being rebuilt at Shildon Works in mid-1974 to have four doors of five planks instead of three of six planks, thereby making them lighter to use. The ends were also given a height extension to help with load retention, although the new section was hinged so could be lowered if required. After some 16 months of trials, the wagon became OBA 110000 early in 1976 and would pass to the Civil Engineers in 1982.

With the modifications having proven a success, 800 production OBAs followed between 1977-79 with Ashford building 110001-500 and Shildon contributing 110501-800. These retained the four doors of the prototype along with the extended height ends but the latter were fully fixed with no hinged part. The length over headstocks increased by nine inches while eight protective door bangers were added to each solebar, and short pull-up stanchions were included in the removable door posts. When built, the Ashford wagons had leaf springs but, in contrast, the Shildon wagons were fitted with modern Bruninghaus parabolic springs while they also had minor alterations to the layout of the door furniture. A programme to re-spring 110001-500 to the same type commenced in 1980, this taking until 1985 to complete.

Surplus stock

However, with the UK in recession in the early 1980s, the demand for general freight traffic declined, leaving BR with a large surplus of open wagons. Thus, in 1982, almost all of the initial 500 OBAs were transferred en masse to the Civil Engineers, despite them being no more than five years old. These became ZDA Bass while a handful also found their way to the Mechanical and Electrical Engineers. As the programme to fit Bruninghaus springs was still ongoing at this time, both types of spring could be found under the Bass for three years or so.

Livery-wise, the OBAs were by and large still in Railfreight maroon upon becoming Bass but the odd example already repainted in Railfreight red/grey also transferred across. The Railfreight lettering was typically removed, with the fish name added in black on a yellow background of varying size. Repaints in grey/yellow were underway by 1983 with numerous different styles of lettering appearing depending on where the work was done, although some tatty maroon examples could still be found in the 1990s.

Of the remaining 300 or so OBAs, all from the Shildon batch, these were largely retained for revenue work into the 1990s, although the odd example here and there found its way across to the Civil Engineers in the intervening period. Designated as general material carriers, the Bass could carry pretty much anything from sleepers, rail chairs and short rail lengths to relay cabinets and lightweight equipment, although typically not ballast or spoil. With privatisation and EWS ownership, many reverted back to being OBAs while others were rebuilt into Sea Urchins.

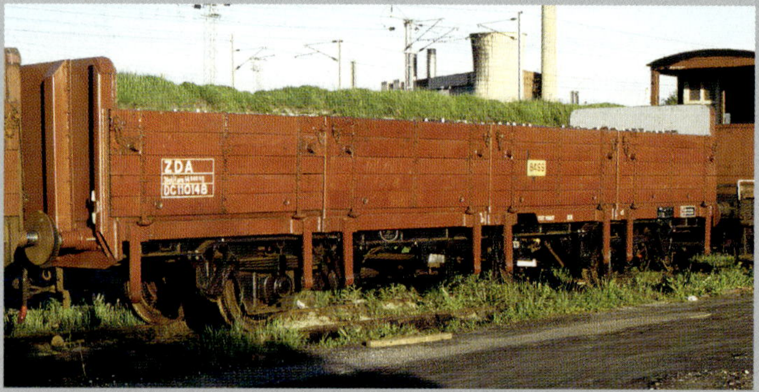

ABOVE: **Also carrying new sleepers at Warrington Arpley carriage and wagon sidings on June 15, 1985, was DC110148, this displaying the yellow background to the Bass name and revised Bruninghaus springs. Far less common was the freight brown livery, which had been applied at Doncaster Works during overhaul six months earlier. This colour was occasionally applied to Civil Engineers' stock despite the grey and yellow livery being well established by this time.** Trevor Mann

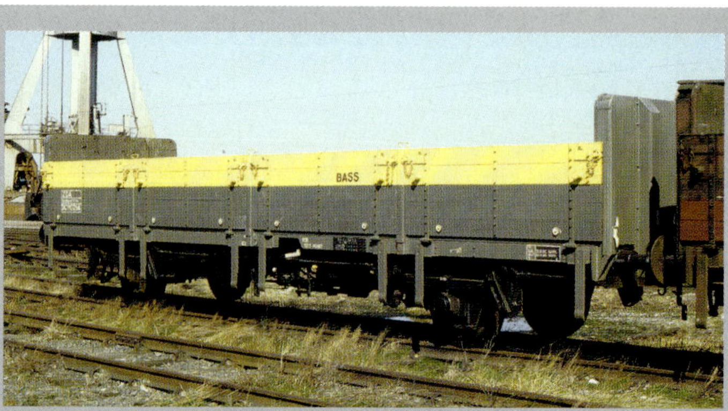

ABOVE: **A typical application of engineers' grey/yellow is displayed by DC110264 at Birkenhead on April 4, 1986, with the Bass code applied in black on the yellow band. The Civil Link branding was not common on the Bass, partly because many wagons were repainted before the network was created. Known examples though were DC110271 and ex Shildon batch DC110669.** Trevor Mann

Bass for the early 1980s by Terry Bendall

Like many of Bachmann's 4mm scale BR air-braked wagon models, the OBAs are a very solid offering as supplied with little in the way of extra detailing required. The main limiting factor is that the model portrays the batch built by Ashford between 1977-79 as 110001-500. The 300 extra wagons that followed from Shildon, 110501-800, had more noticeable square doorstops, some of which were in different positions along with the corresponding underframe door bangers.

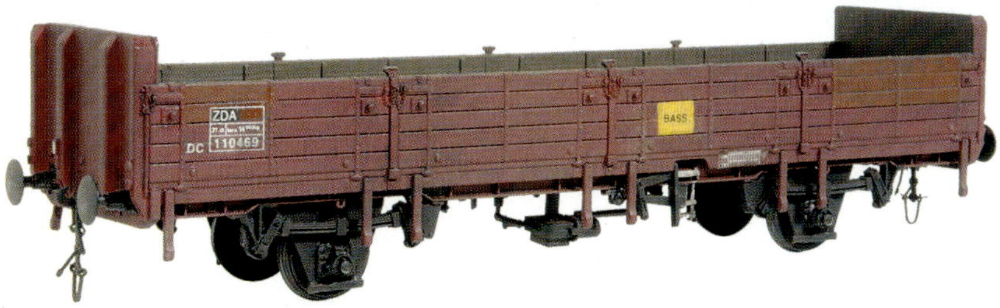

The Bachmann model is also fitted with the revised Bruninghaus parabolic springs that were given to the Ashford wagons between 1980-85. If the older leaf type springs are desired, these are now available as castings from Stenson Models. With all this in mind, the Bachmann OBA is the most accurate starting point for the vast majority of Bass as the Cambrian plastic kit portrays the Shildon-built wagons.

With the wagons required for use on a layout built to P4 gauge, the first job was to dispense with the swivelling axle assemblies and replace them with suitable compensation units, in this case BR heavy duty W-irons from MJT. Employing these requires the wagon floor to undergo some modifications so they can be recessed to obtain the correct ride height. With Alan Gibson 12mm wheels utilised, these received stainless steel brake discs from Stenson Models while new BR hooded style axleboxes came from Wizard Models

Maroon dip

For the Railfreight maroon livery, no specific paint is available, so Railmatch BR maroon (No. 306) was utilised with a small amount of black added. This range also provided the Railfreight grey (No. 226) for the Civil Engineers scheme, while the yellow was applied using an airbrush after masking off the required area.

Initially, Humbrol yellow was employed, this having better covering properties, before switching to Railmatch warning yellow for the top coat. The yellow background for the Bass lettering on the maroon ZDA was applied by hand after first masking out the dimensions of the panel. The inside of the wagons were painted by hand using a variety of browns from the Humbrol range, mixing them together in varying amounts to give different tones.

Even by 1983, the wagons had begun to receive replacement planks so, using photos as a guide, these were represented with an assortment of Humbrol colours mixed together as required. On the maroon Bass, particular attention needs to be given to the right hand door to represent the over-painted Railfreight lettering.

Final finishing

Transfers were mostly taken from a stash of Appleby sheets and supplemented by Modelmaster decals where required. On the maroon wagon, the number panels first had to be applied and then black paint added over the top to represent the painted out OBA code before applying the replacement ZDA and DC prefix.

After varnishing the transfers, the body weathering began with a wash of thinned down Railmatch track colour, this being worked into the planks and other recesses, and applied and wiped off again in varying amounts on other areas. The same colour was then applied with an airbrush, mostly to the underframe but also allowing it to waft over the body.

Finally, a sleeper load was made using 1.5mm plywood, this being cut into strips to represent both standard 8ft 6in sleepers and longer point timbers. Once treated with wood stain, the sleepers were glued together in stacks and loaded into the Bass as shown in the photographs.

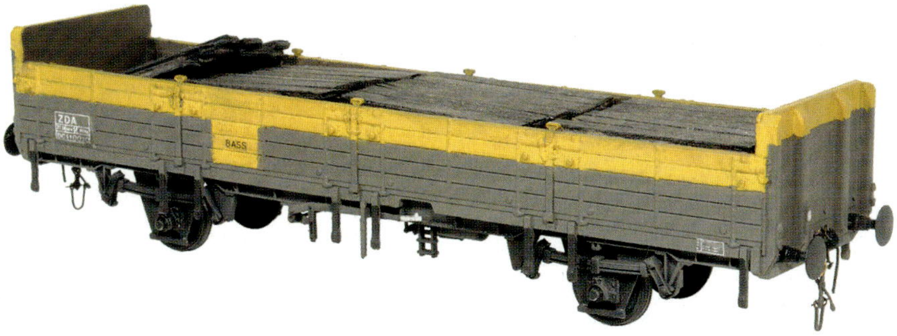

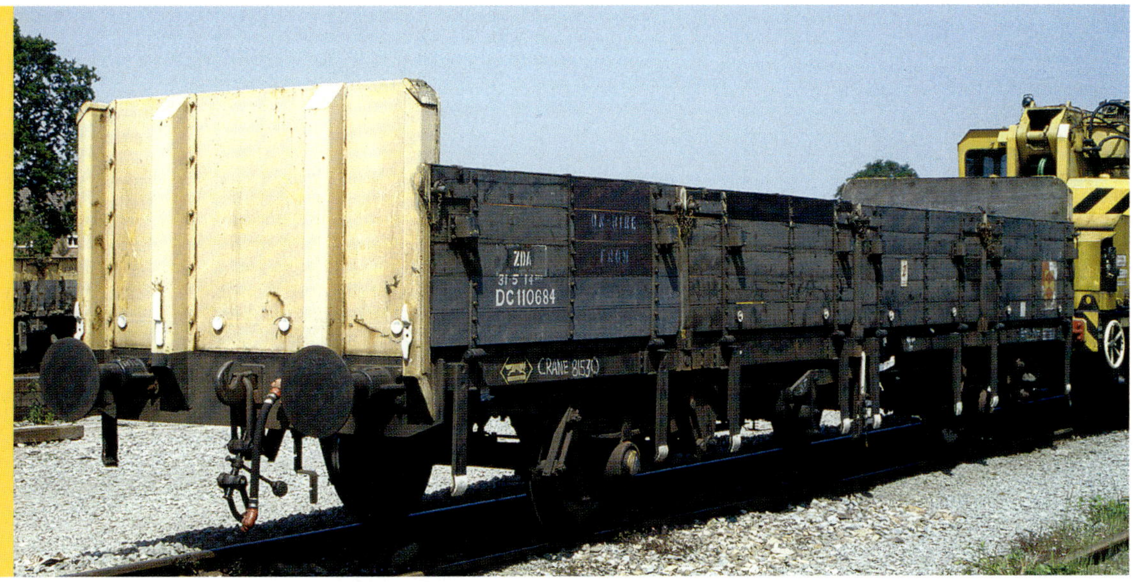

RIGHT: **Wagons carrying the Railfreight grey and yellow sub-sector livery were not immune to transferring to the engineers' fleet, as illustrated by Shildon-built DC110684. Although captured after privatisation at Crewe on May 31, 1997, the transfer had occurred prior to EWS ownership. Still with its Railfreight Distribution logo and Carlisle Currock depot sticker, the ZDA is marked up to work with Plasser & Theurer GPC-72 crane DRP81530 as a support wagon. The lettering next to the number reads 'On hire from' but nothing more as the planks beneath have been renewed.** Trevor Mann

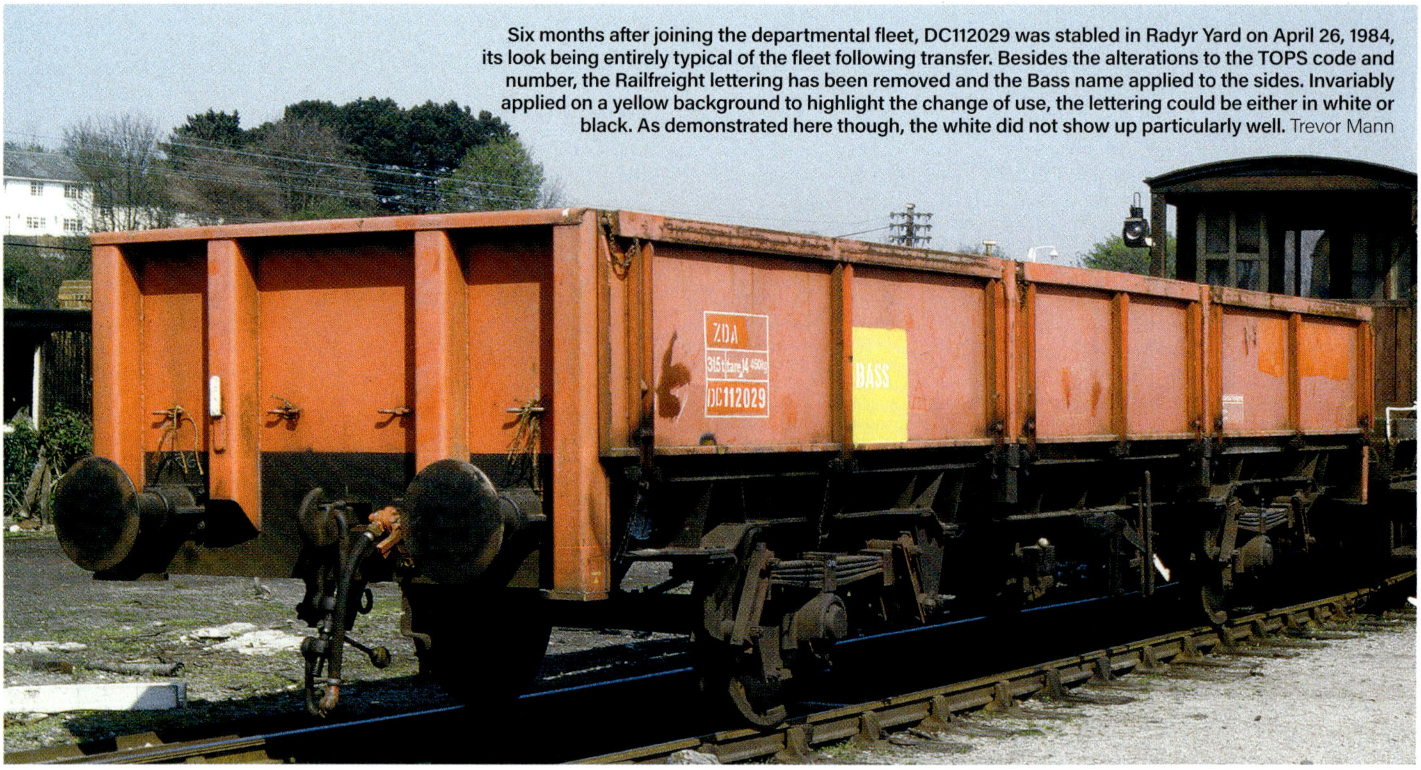

Six months after joining the departmental fleet, DC112029 was stabled in Radyr Yard on April 26, 1984, its look being entirely typical of the fleet following transfer. Besides the alterations to the TOPS code and number, the Railfreight lettering has been removed and the Bass name applied to the sides. Invariably applied on a yellow background to highlight the change of use, the lettering could be either in white or black. As demonstrated here though, the white did not show up particularly well. Trevor Mann

ZDA Bass (steel)

For its final purpose-built general merchandise open wagon design, BR dropped the wooden bodysides in favour of all-steel construction. Coded OCA, the wagons were to the same dimensions as the OBA, but the bodywork was essentially an enlarged version of that given to the SPA steel plate carriers (see overleaf) with higher sides and ends. The number of drop doors reverted to three while the extended ends of the OBA were also abandoned. Shildon built 400 of the wagons during 1981 and 1982, these being numbered 112000-399, and all were delivered in all-over Railfreight red.

Inevitably, the same fate befell the OCAs as their predecessors with underemployment seeing the earliest examples removed from the revenue fleet after just two years. The first 26 wagons were offloaded onto the Mechanical and Electrical Engineers

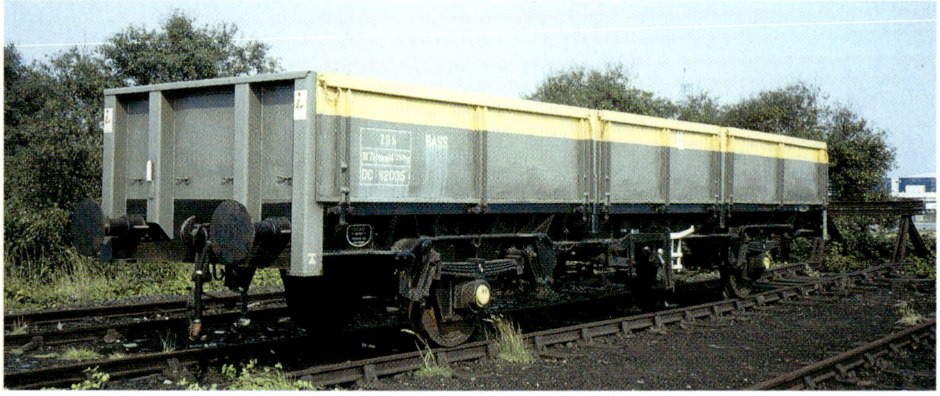

ABOVE: **Equally typical in its appearance was DC112035 at Ellesmere Port in September 1991. The Bass lettering could either be applied in white next to the number or in black on the yellow band and positioned on the middle door. The rainwater streaking of the white paint used for the lettering was quite a common feature on engineers' stock and would be interesting to recreate in model form!** David Ratcliffe

ZCA Seahorse conversions

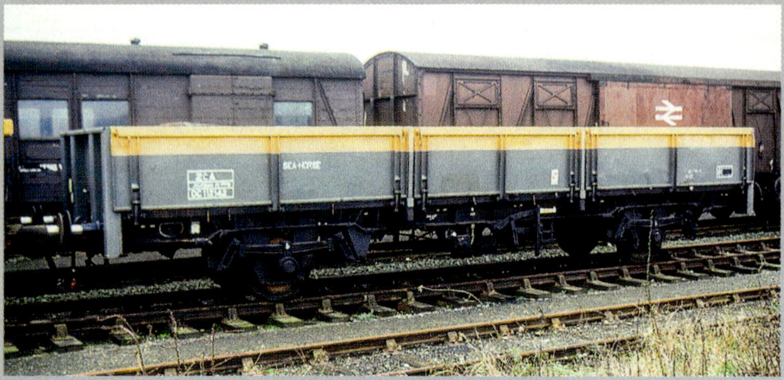

During the spring of 1988, 15 Bass were transferred from the West Country to Kent for modifications to allow them to carry new ballast. The work included welding shut the doors while the wooden floor was also replaced by steel. All appear to have received a fresh coat of engineers' grey/yellow as part of the work with the resulting wagons being re-coded ZCA and given the new aquatic name of Seahorse. Their identities were DC112029/39/59/64/68/76/78/82/94/95 and DC112132/42/51/54/57 with DC112142 pictured at Hoo Junction on January 15, 1989, by Paul Bartlett. The Seahorse lasted for just over a year in this condition before the unsuitably of the OCA sides for ballast traffic triggered a more distinctive conversion, the results of which are covered on p37.

Two ways to a Bass by Mike Cubberley and Mark Lambert

This model is from the 4mm scale Cambrian kit, having been refurbished after originally being built in the mid-1990s! The body is painted with the now discontinued Evenmatch 'Weathered Rail red' acrylic paint to give the characteristic salmon pink washed-out look and it was then originally given a wash of black and dirty white spirit to enhance the decrepit look further.

As part of the model's overhaul, Games Workshop 'Evil Sunz Scarlet' has been used to create the 'new' patched red paint and the yellow panel was masked off with Tamiya low-tac masking tape and painted with Games Workshop 'Averland Sunset' with the transfers coming from Appleby Model Engineering. The buffers were changed out for S Kits Oleos while Smiths screw couplings and lost wax cast air pipes from Intercity Models were also added. Meanwhile, the wheels were upgraded by adding etched disc brakes from MJT and the chassis was repainted with Games Workshop 'Charadon granite grey' to give it an in-service look.

The old sleeper load is from Skytrex Models, namely 4A/010A Assorted piles of sleepers, and was spray undercoated in Games Workshop 'Chaos Black' and then given a dry-brushing with light greys to highlight the grain effect of the castings. The area where the rail chairs have been removed was given a dash of dark brown ink to bring out the detail. A couple of light coats of Army Painter flat varnish were then sprayed over the model to seal everything in. Mike Cubberley

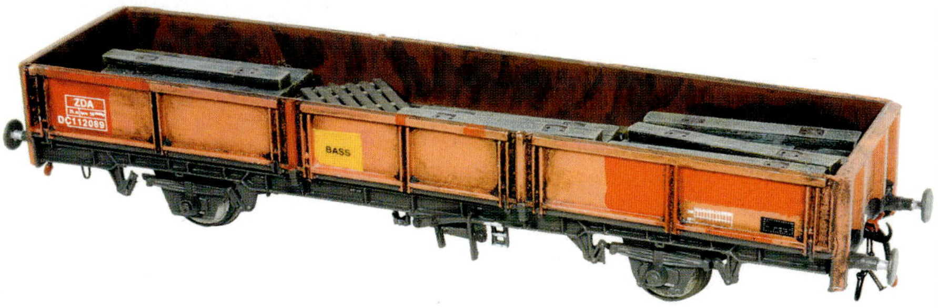

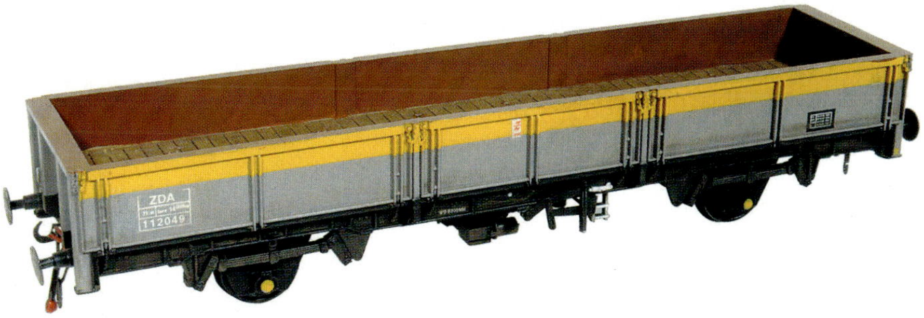

ABOVE: **Bachmann's ready-to-run version of the OCA was released in OO gauge back in 2007 and has subsequently appeared as a Bass in engineers' grey/yellow amongst other liveries. While it is a nice model in many ways, the sides and particularly the ends are overly thick to help with rigidity. While many are happy to overlook this issue, the visual impact is difficult to ignore for others and means the Cambrian kit still has a role to play. Illustrated is the Bachmann Bass in largely as supplied condition but with the number changed and the modern overhead wire flashes removed and replaced by a reduced number of 1980s style red/white ones. The axlebox covers have also been repainted to remove the more modern yellow/blue identification colours in favour of the traditional all yellow appearance. Otherwise, the model has received a light coat of weathering inside and out to represent a recently-repainted wagon running in the early 1990s.** Mark Lambert

department during November 1983 for transporting stores and became ADC112000-025 (see page 80). At the same time, all of the OCAs in the 112026-158 range, with four exceptions, became part of the Civil Engineers fleet, receiving DC number prefixes and the classification of ZDA Bass. Although of different construction to the wooden-bodied ex OBAs, the two types shared the same capacity and characteristics, meaning they were treated as one overall fleet of Bass. With the paint barely aged, the re-branding initially amounted to altered number panels, removed Railfreight lettering and the Bass name on a yellow panel.

Unsurprisingly, their use mirrored the other type of Bass in carrying all manner of fittings, parts and equipment but not ballast or spoil in everyday use, as the wooden floor of the wagons would have been vulnerable to damage by the excavators during unloading. Repaints in grey/yellow had commenced by 1987 with only one example noted as receiving Civil Link lettering, this being squashed in on the narrower yellow band. Some wagons numbered above DC112158 would also transfer to engineers' use in later years, but these were few in number, especially as many had been converted into OTA timber carriers. From 1996, it was the usual story under EWS; a return to being coded OCA or conversion fodder.

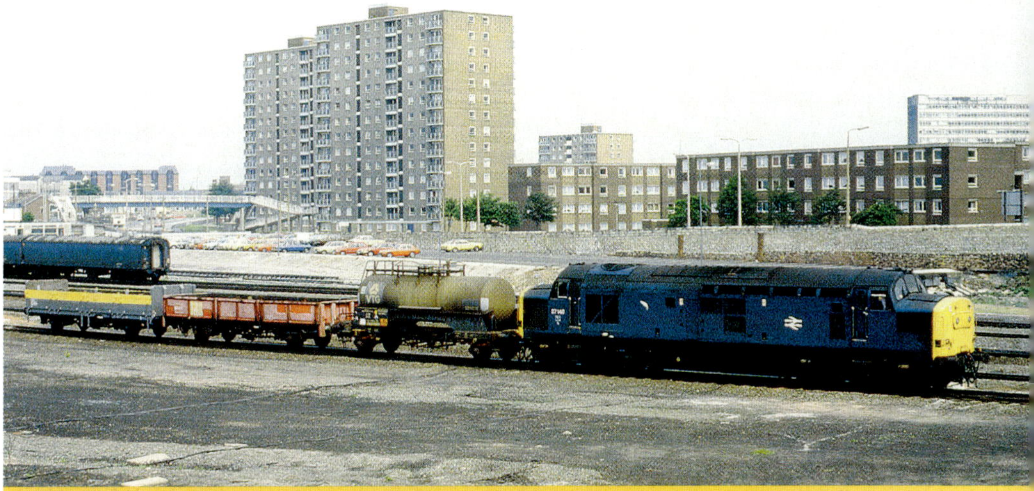

ABOVE: **Although carrying a Motherwell salmon depot logo, 37146 was Inverness-based when recorded at Doncaster in July 1986. Either way, the Type 3 was far from home as it departs to the south with one of each type of Bass along with a VTG ferry tank forming the 6D84 15.07 Healey Mills to Doncaster Belmont. Built in 1977, the tanker was TOPS-coded ICB and was in use transporting hydrogen peroxide from the continent to Dewsbury freight depot, from where it was distributed by road to local textiles companies. In the background is the Doncaster Works test train, then formed of blue-painted Mk.1 coaches in departmental stock.** Simon Bendall Collection

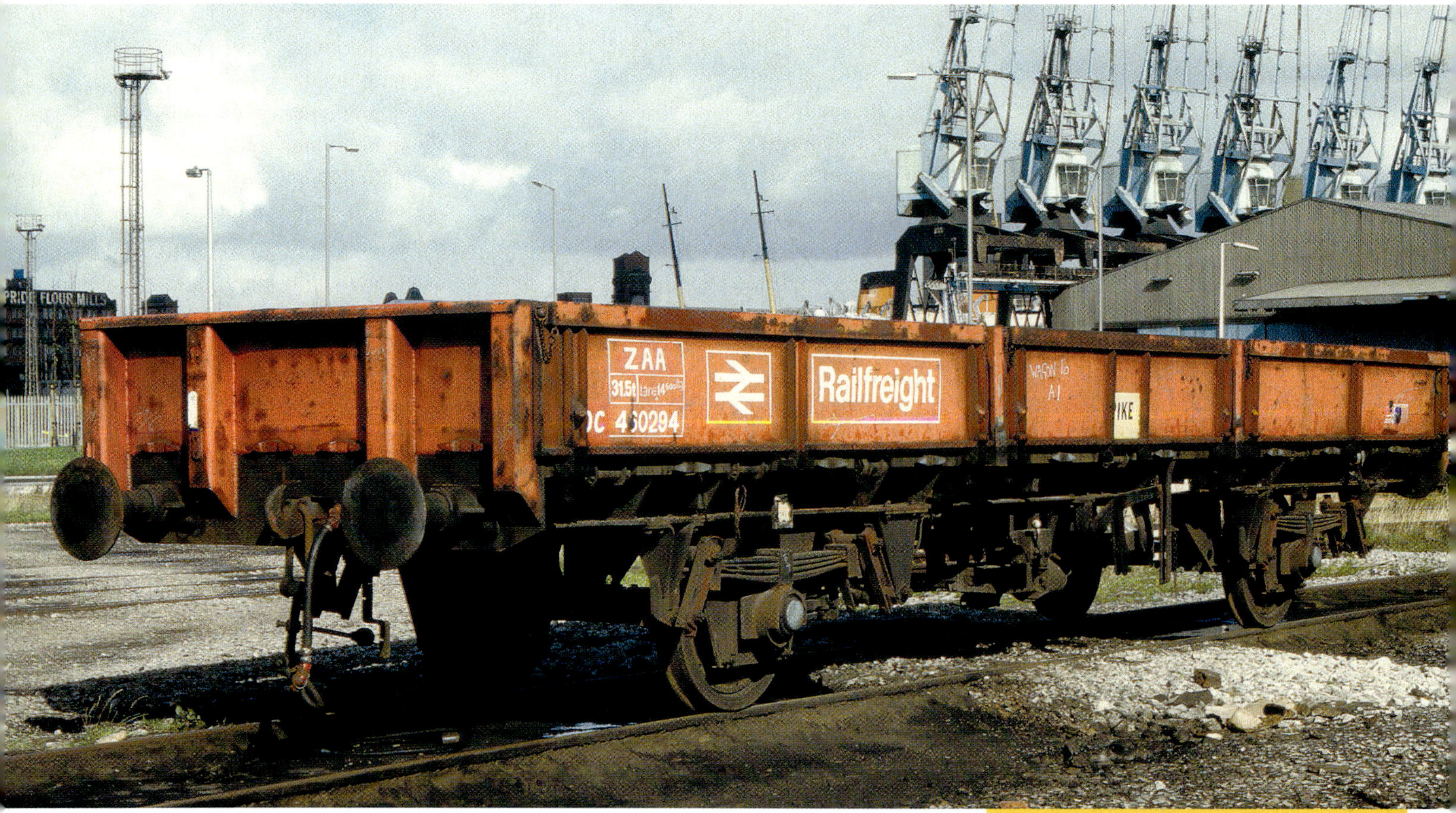

ABOVE: **A year after becoming a Pike, DC460294 was recorded at Birkenhead Docks on September 22, 1984. Still carrying its Railfreight lettering, the fish name has been added in black on a yellow panel. The TOPS code has also been properly replaced rather than just painted over as was often the case.** Trevor Mann

ZAA Pike

Although looking like general merchandise open wagons, the SPA was designated as a steel plate carrier, consequently taking numbers and a TOPS code in the range used for two-axle steel wagons. Built by Shildon Works once again, 1,100 examples were delivered between 1979-81 and numbered 460002 to 461101. Two prototypes had been built in 1977 to a design that would be altered before the production batch was authorised, these accounting for the missing numbers of 460000 and 460001.

Despite finding wide-ranging employment in both steel traffic and beyond, the fleet was not fully employed as the 1980s progressed, despite the cancellation of another 400 examples before they could be built. Inevitably, 1983 saw 320 SPAs transferred to the Civil Engineers from the 460002-331 range, these becoming ZAA Pike with the addition of the DC prefix to the numbers. Another 40 examples would be taken by the Mechanical and Electrical Engineers, but these were spread randomly throughout the remaining number range. The application of the new ZAA code initially brought some errors with several Pike noted running with ZZA instead, as used on snowploughs!

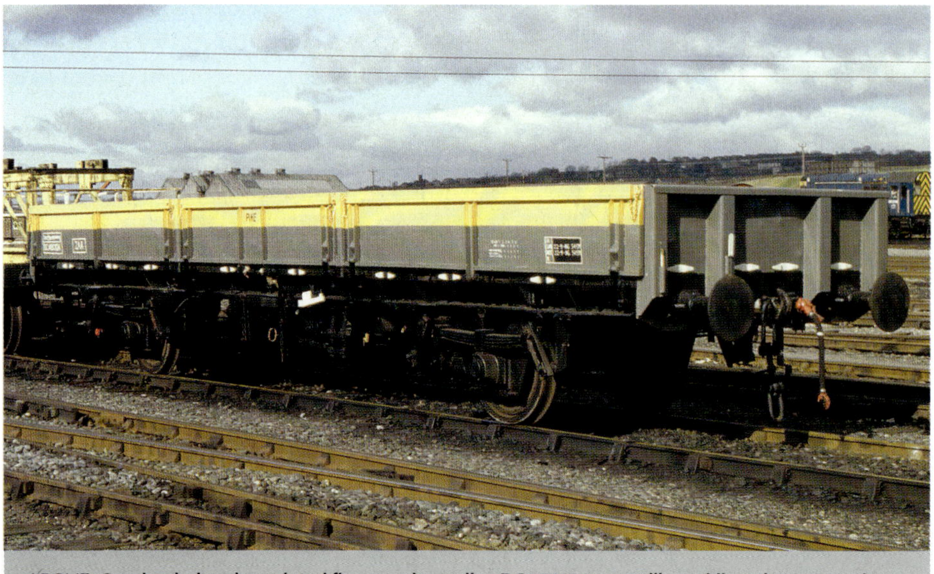

ABOVE: **Overhauled and repainted five months earlier, DC460124 was still sparkling clean at Healey Mills on February 22, 1987. The central position for the Pike lettering was very common, although the white style next to the number panel could also be seen.** Trevor Mann

As the SPAs had been built with a steel floor, the Pike could be used for ballast and spoil duties, although the comparatively lightweight doors were not ideal for such work as they were vulnerable to damage. They could also carry other materials as needed and during the early 1990s became useful for moving lightweight track machinery. Like the ex OCA Bass, initially the Railfreight red livery was retained with the addition of Pike lettering. Repaints into grey and yellow were noted as early as 1985 with the odd example appearing with small Civil Link lettering later in the decade.

As described in the next section, the door weakness would be dealt with in some cases by the Seahare conversions, but numerous Pike still made it into EWS ownership, where it was once more either back to the revenue fleet or rebuilding as Sea Urchins.

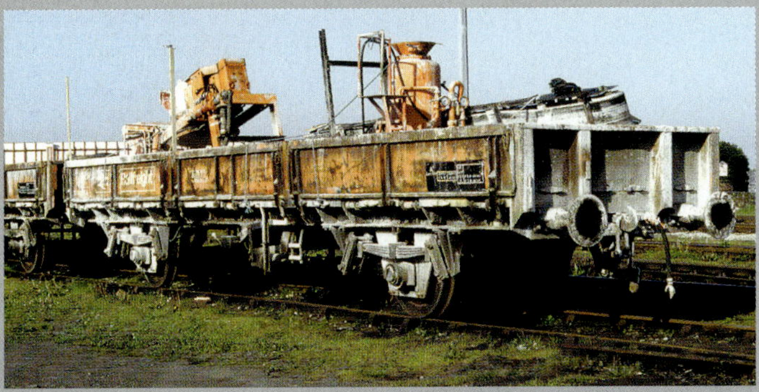

ABOVE: **A filthy DC460164 was the centrepiece of what was seemingly a cement mixing train at Blackburn on May 17, 1992, the wagon still being in Railfreight red with yellow-backed Pike lettering. Of note are the wooden poles to allow rudimentary electric lights to be strung up. Accompanying it were three more Pike, DC460089/278/327, these all being in the same livery but slightly cleaner and with lighting poles also fitted. These were variously carrying un-sheeted gravel, what was likely sand and cement bags under tarpaulins and a rectangular tank, doubtless as a water supply.** Trevor Mann

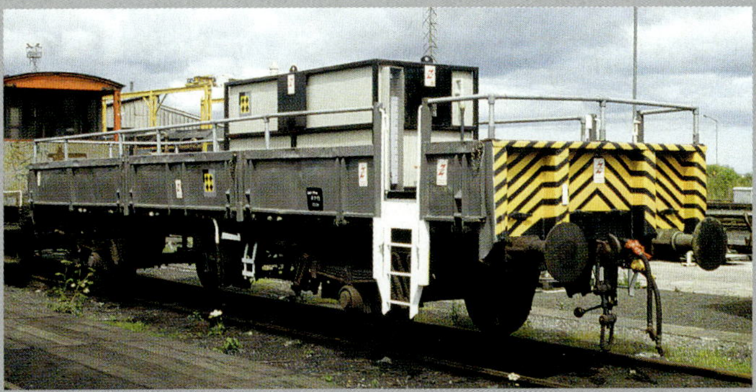

ABOVE: **SPA 460717 stands at Blyth Cambois TMD in July 1993 following conversion to a weedkilling wagon for use on the freight-only Blyth & Tyne route. With the conversion having been funded by Trainload Coal, it was still officially a revenue earning wagon even if its purpose was not. At this stage, its number panel had yet to be applied to the smart sub-sector colours.** Mark Saunders

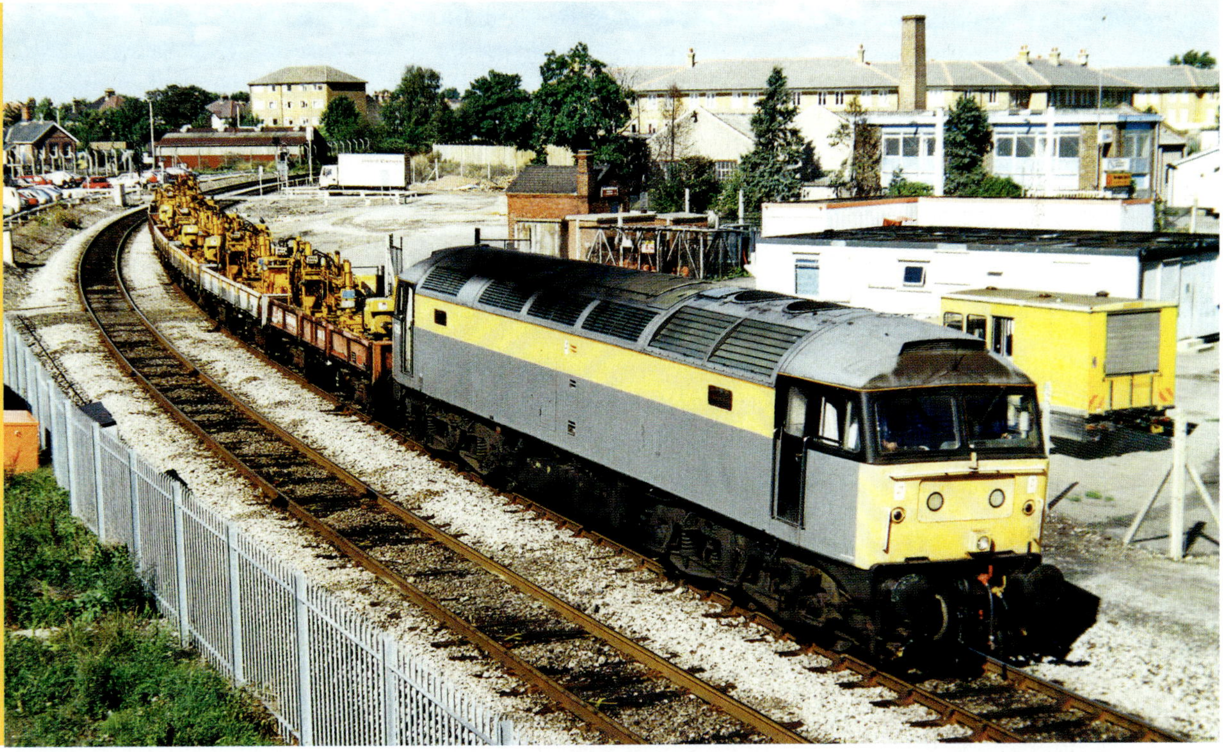

RIGHT: **Illustrating the plant carrying role of the Pike, 47315 runs off the Greenford branch at West Ealing on September 17, 1991, with seven or so ZAAs in tow. These are carrying Geismar PUM machines in their retracted transit form. At worksites, these machines operated in sizeable groups to lift and position pre-fabricated track assemblies, being particularly useful to move large sections of pointwork.** Steve Stubbs

Angling for a Pike by Mark Lambert

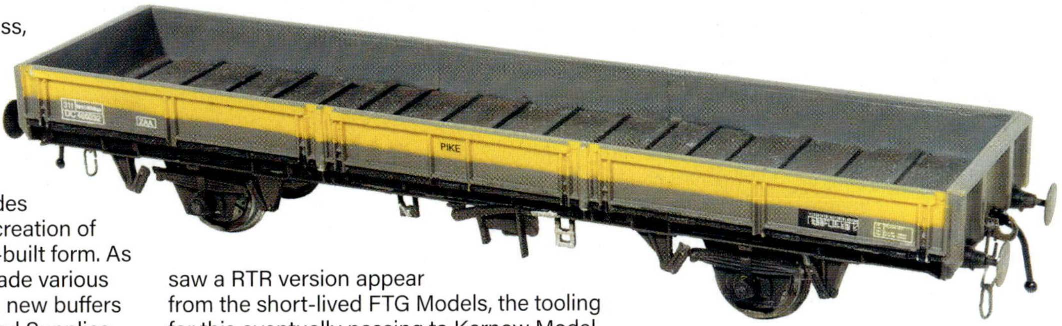

As with the two types of Bass, there are both ready-to-run and kit options for the Pike in 4mm scale. Pictured here is the venerable Cambrian plastic kit, which has been around for over three decades and builds up into a fine recreation of the SPA wagons in their as-built form. As ever, there is scope to upgrade various aspects of the kit, including new buffers from Lanarkshire Models and Supplies along with stainless steel brake discs from various sources. December 2014 saw a RTR version appear from the short-lived FTG Models, the tooling for this eventually passing to Kernow Model Rail Centre. While not without its issues, the wagon has proven to be popular with Kernow still having stock of the four grey/yellow Pike it released a few years ago.

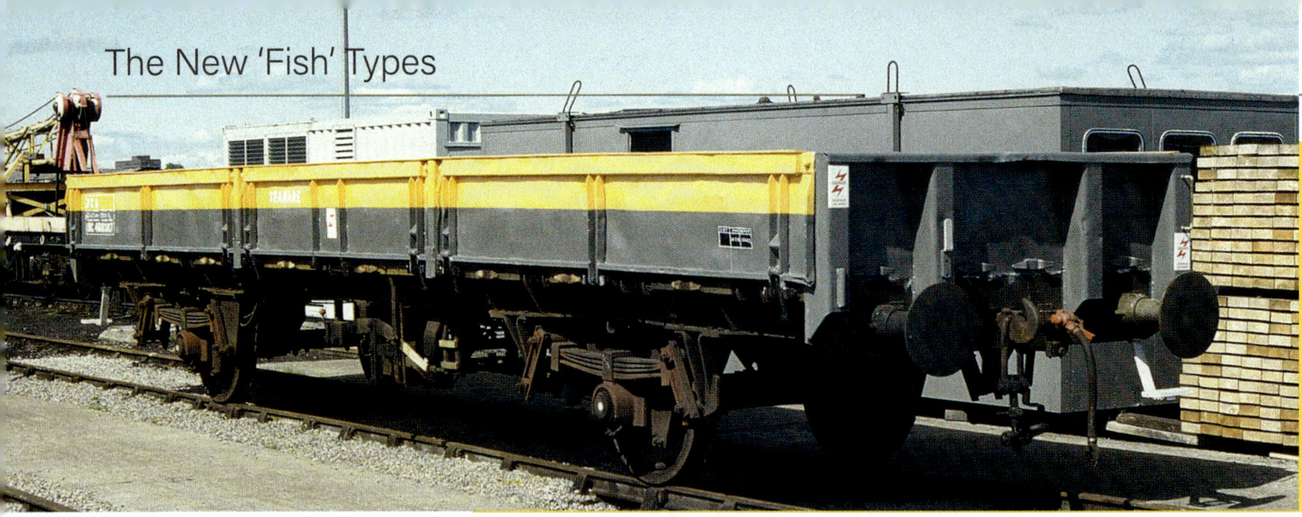

LEFT: **The Seahare fleet had become quite significant in the final years of BR with considerable inroads made into the number of ZAA Pike. The steel strips along the top of the sealed doors can be seen on DC460387 at Tees Yard on May 4, 1993.** Trevor Mann

ZCA Seahare

The comparatively low sides of the ZAA Pike meant that they were useful for carrying ballast and spoil, but the drop doors were vulnerable to damage from excavators as was the steel bolster floor. These limitations were overcome from late 1990 with the introduction of a new modification programme. An initial 68 Pike were put through York wagon shops to have their doors welded shut and then reinforced by the addition of steel strips along the top edge, while the floor was also replaced with flat steel sheeting.

These altered wagons were duly given the new designation of ZCA Seahare. The modifications proved to be worthwhile with several hundred wagons attended to over the next three years, Network SouthEast alone taking 99 Seahare for use on renewals in East Anglia. The wagons also received a repaint into grey/yellow as part of the work with some variation in branding style. Ultimately though, the full Sea Urchin re-bodies would win out as privatisation took effect.

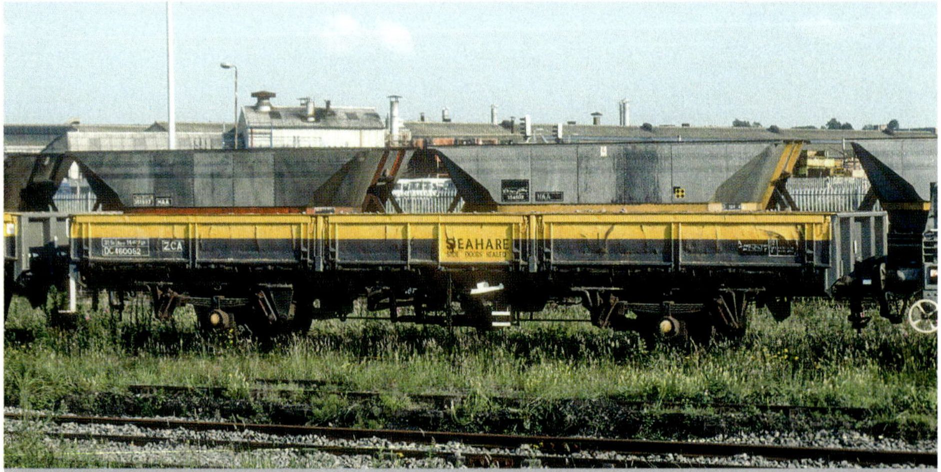

ABOVE: **The initial Seahare conversions were very obviously marked up as to the status of their doors, DC460082 displaying a large version of the name at Washwood Heath on July 6, 1991, along with 'Side doors sealed' underneath. This style of branding could still be seen for years afterwards as the wagons were typically not repainted again, the branding just getting lost under rust.** Paul Bartlett

A speedy conversion by Mike Cubberley

The Seahare had their doors sealed up by the simple expedience of welding a section of angle iron along the length of the top and inside of the three doors and adding a triangular-shaped strengthening section of plate to the back of the two door posts and the floor on each side. A new, plain, floor replaced the fixed bolsters and chequer plate original and also allowed the covering of the ratchet tensioner holes to stop ballast falling through them.

On some early conversions, the whole of the ratchet section of the doors was removed and a pre-made section welded in to the floor strap holes, giving the bottom of the doors a 'gapped tooth' look to them. Later conversions lost none of the ratchets, these just relying on the new floor to cover the holes, while they also gained a footstep and grab rail on the left hand end of the wagon to assist staff who needed to access the interior from ground level.

Using a 4mm scale Cambrian kit as the basis, I represented the sealed up doors by adding some sections of .10x.40 thou plastic strip. One went along the top of the doors on each side with a couple of millimetres extra on either end to overlap onto the top of the ends. Another strip was added to the inside top of the doors each side, this butting up to the edge of first one to create the angle iron section of the prototype. The rest of the kit was largely built as per the instructions.

Other improvements included using Romford disc brake wheels, these having the rims painted to remove the shiny look but retaining the bright discs. The moulded buffer bases were removed from the ends and S Kits whitemetal Oleo buffers added for robustness. Once undercoated, the model was painted with Railfreight/Engineers grey and a line was then gently scored across the doors with a new knife blade and steel edge. Warning panel yellow was then carefully hand-painted up to the line. The chassis was painted with Army Painter 'Hardened Carapace' to give a slightly in-traffic look.

The transfers are mainly from the now unavailable Appleby Model Engineering sheet 4T48 although the Seahare and 'Side doors sealed' lettering came from a homemade set of laser printed markings produced by a friend.

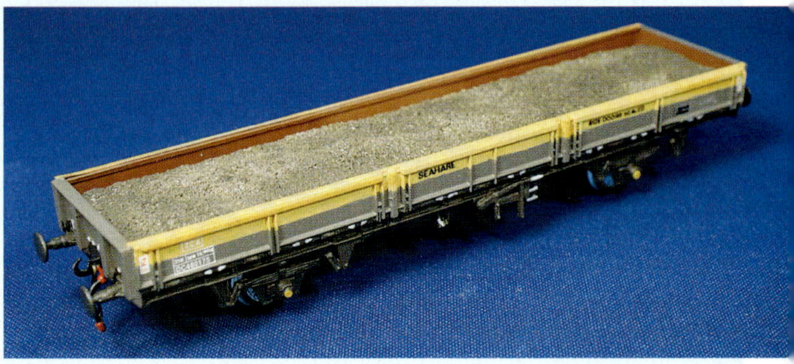

ZCA Seahorse

As detailed on page 33, 15 steel-bodied Bass (ex OCA) had their doors welded shut and a new metal floor fitted in the spring of 1988 to allow them to carry ballast, becoming ZCA Seahorse. While they ran in this form for a year or so, the doors remained an issue, partly because they were higher than most other ballast opens so got in the way during loading and unloading. Additionally, as they had only been welded up rather than reinforced, strikes by excavator buckets caused damage and deformation.

Consequently, the late spring of 1989 saw further conversion work carried out with the OCA doors and all associated fittings removed in favour of new fixed sides. These were significantly lower than before and were strengthened by ten ribs. The ends were left unmodified though so consequently were now taller than the sides. All of the wagons were finished in engineers' grey/yellow once again with the TOPS code and Seahorse name being retained as all 15 examples, DC112029/39/59/64/68/76/78/82/94/95 and DC112132/42/51/54/57, were rebuilt in this manner.

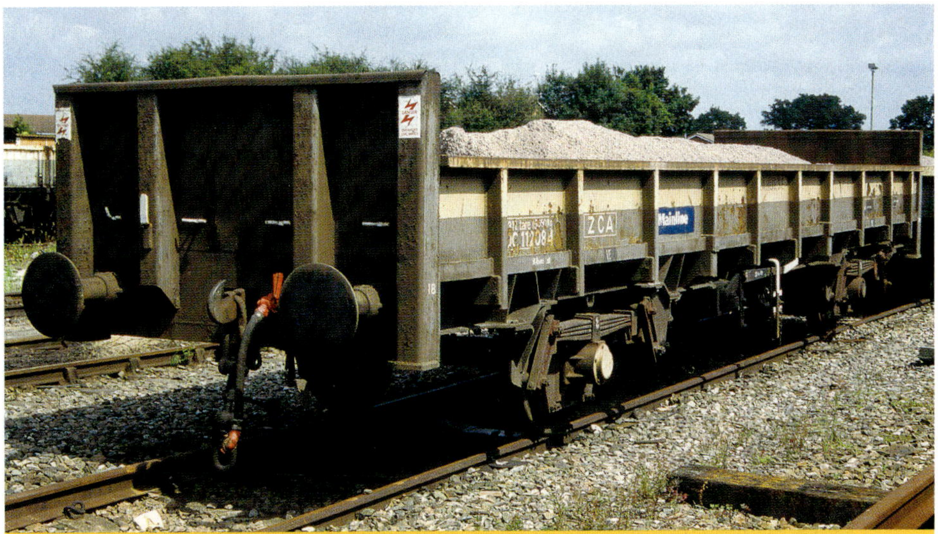

Seahorse DC112084 was a long way from its traditional haunts when recorded at Crewe Gresty Lane on August 1, 1998. Once rarely seen outside of the southeast, EWS ownership allowed the type to roam more freely as they were effectively treated as Sea Urchins in a nationwide pool. With its livery battered and rusting, the ZCA also still displays its Mainline logo applied three or four years previously. Trevor Mann

This new look Seahorse fleet was expanded further during 1989 and early 1990 with the conversion of 15 more Bass, namely DC112040/42/50/70/73/80/84/98 and DC112108/10/13/40/43/47/49. These were again based in Kent with the entire fleet of 30 wagons coming under NSE control following the break-up of the engineers' fleet in 1992. Mainly used for new ballast, they could carry other material when needed and travelled widely across the sector's patch.

As the first of the various air-braked open wagons to be rebuilt with new bodywork specifically for carrying ballast, they were the forerunners of the similar but much more expansive Sea Urchin programme that would soon follow. The Seahorse wagons all passed to Mainline Freight in 1994 and EWS two years later, this second change of ownership allowing the type to spread further afield. Most remained in service until the mid-2000s but were withdrawn as new, higher-capacity stock arrived.

Breaking in a horse by Mike Cubberley

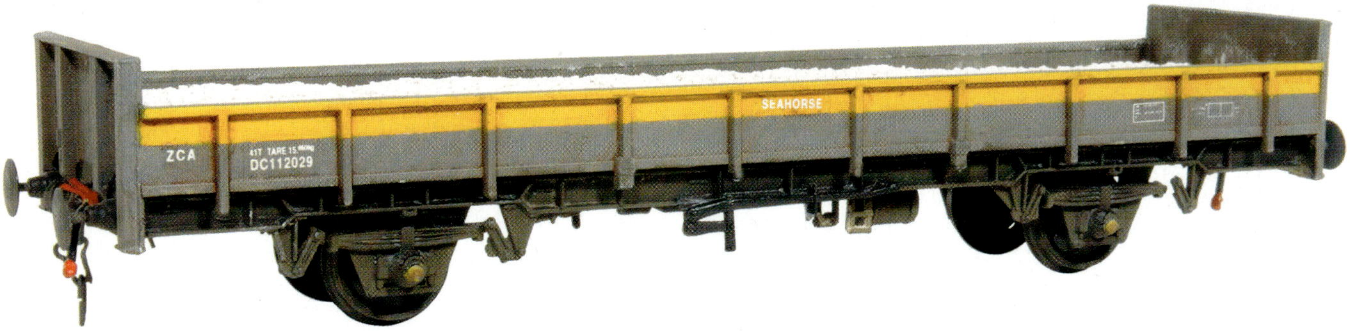

With Cambrian already making an OCA, it was a simple enough task for the company to tool up a new pair of sides to create a variant of the 4mm plastic kit for the Seahorse, this appearing early in the 1990s. Naturally enough then, the same comments apply to this wagon as similar types in the range, being straightforward enough to build and capable of being upgraded in terms of buffers and brake gear as desired. This example is largely as supplied and is finished with Appleby transfers along with a one-piece cast load from Ten Commandments, this simply dropping in.

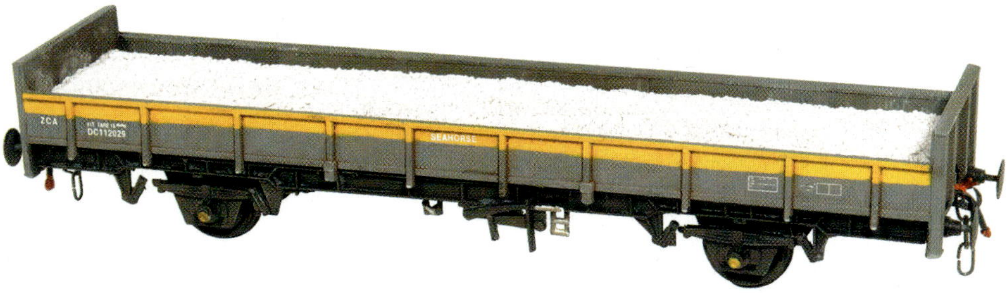

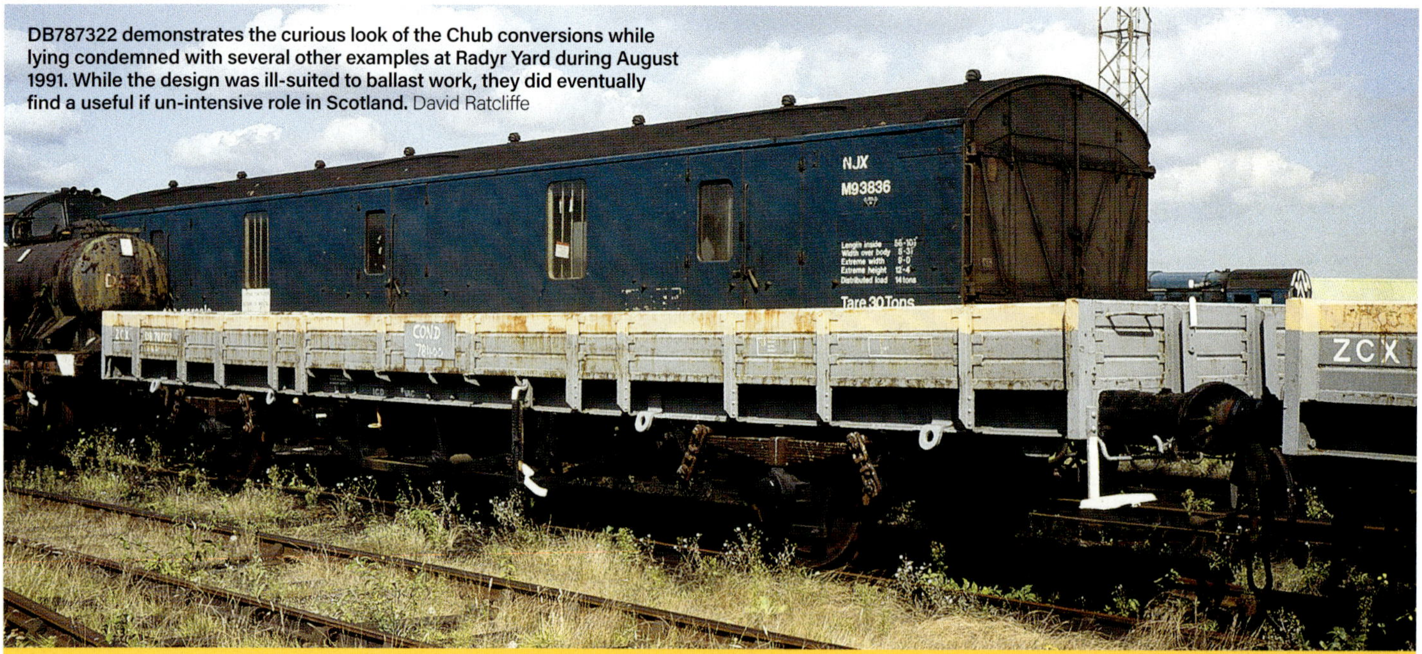

DB787322 demonstrates the curious look of the Chub conversions while lying condemned with several other examples at Radyr Yard during August 1991. While the design was ill-suited to ballast work, they did eventually find a useful if un-intensive role in Scotland. David Ratcliffe

ZCX Chub

First sighted in mid-1988, the Chub was an attempt to re-purpose the numerous 20-ton ferry vans that BR had languishing in store. With the van bodywork completely removed, the highly-useful dual-braked underframe then received low bodywork and a steel floor for the purpose of carrying ballast and spoil. The fixed sides were just three planks high with short metal strengthening ribs all the way along.

First to emerge from Cardiff Cathays was DB787301, this carrying the TOPS code of ZCX and finished in grey/yellow. By the end of the year, it was on trial on the Southern Region and rated to carry 25 tonnes, while 1989 saw 12 further examples converted, namely DB787117/27/63/84/98/99, DB787241/44/60/87, and DB787316/22.

The low sides were intended to encourage the even distribution of the ballast or spoil load along the full 41ft length of the wagons and also prevent overloading. However, this was operationally inconvenient, and the Chub offered little capacity advantage over shorter ballast wagons that could be loaded higher. As such, the concept was abandoned, and some Chub withdrawn in 1990/91.

However, around half of the fleet was retained into the 1990s for use as miscellaneous maintenance wagons, finding their way to Scotland, where some Chub were formed into the Tay Bridge maintenance train based at Dundee. With privatisation, they remained with the Scottish infrastructure units and came under the ownership of First Engineering, being withdrawn around 2000.

Creating a Chub by Steve Farmer

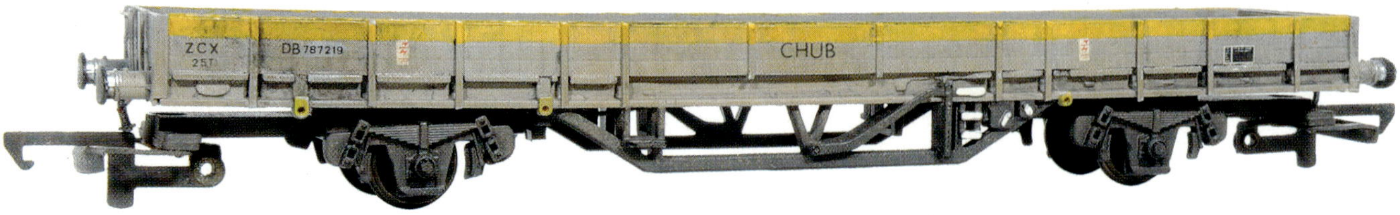

This OO gauge Chub was built over 20 years ago and currently forms part of the Tonbridge West Yard fleet. The basis of the model was the same as the full-size version, it utilises the chassis of the Hornby ferry van. This was left as supplied except for changing the wheelsets for Romford ones; the need for it to negotiate tight curves on my layout of the time meaning the swivelling axle assemblies and tension lock couplings were best left alone.

The sides and ends were made from Slater's embossed planks plastic sheet cut to a width of three planks and with two pieces laminated together back to back to give an inner face. The floor is slightly raised from the underframe due to the weight and plastic mouldings that exist on top of the chassis. Once the basic box body was in place, the ribs were added using plastic strip and photos as a guide while the grab handles were made using brass wire. Despite the tension locks, there was still room to add coupling hooks and both air and vacuum pipes on the bufferbeams.

The model was primed in white, and the top plank painted with Humbrol yellow (No.24). This was masked off and the grey, which is Humbrol No.64, painted onto the lower two planks along with the solebars, ends and internal planking. Finally, the floor received a coat of brown (Humbrol No.110) with the rest of the underframe finished in matt black. The transfers all came from the Fox range with the number, weight and TOPS code being the individual number panel characters and the Chub lettering from an alphabet sheet. The whole wagon then received a spray with varnish.

ZGA Seal

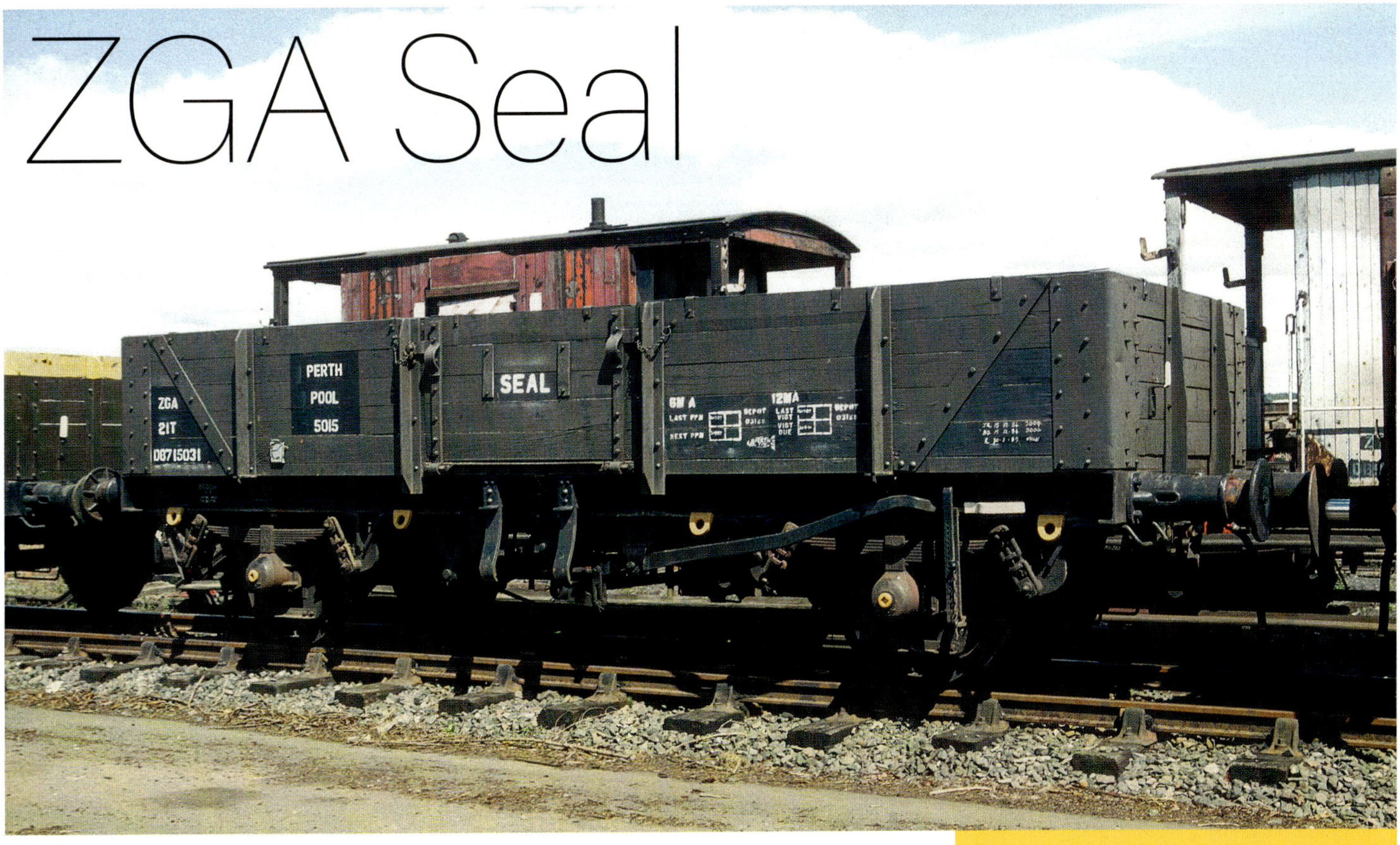

Arguably less well known than the 22-ton Ferry Tubes were the 40-strong fleet of 21-ton Ferry High open wagons built to diagram 1/055, these being numbered B715000-039. Built in 1957/58, they featured eight plank-high wooden bodies with one door per side and a wagon sheet support bar. Later modifications saw virtually all of the type become dual-braked with many also receiving roller bearing axleboxes. Their use on train ferry traffic finished in the mid-1970s.

By the mid-1980s, the type was split between revenue traffic and departmental use. Of the latter, ten had lost their bodywork to become either cable drum carriers or tunnel inspection wagons and ADB715030 was assigned to the M&EE on the Southern to carry coke. Two wagons had been withdrawn, leaving 27 coded OJX or OJA as their vacuum brakes were in the process of removal. These were either assigned for use as barrier wagons or for carrying agricultural lime in Scotland.

Some of the OJA/OJX had previously seen their bodywork reduced in height from eight planks to five to make loading and unloading easier. At the end of 1987, five of these cut down examples were transferred to ballast and spoil duties in Scotland, particularly on the Highland routes, being recoded as ZGA and taking the name Seal. Their identities were DB715009/16/25/31/37, some if not all of which were repainted in olive green upon transfer with at least DB715009 being recorded as lettered 'West Highland Engineer'. In this guise, the Seal worked alongside the three Hake. Four remained on EWS' books in 2000 with at least DB715037 working in the northwest but all were withdrawn from traffic soon after.

ABOVE: **Finished in olive green, DB715031 is seen at Perth on August 1, 1989, this carrying not only its Seal name but also its pool allocation. Built with eight-plank bodywork, there is no particular sign of the height reduction with all of the strengthening struts having been re-profiled.** Paul Bartlett

Adjacent to DB715031 on the same day was DB715037, this having received the welcome addition of a yellow stripe to enliven its olive green. The lettering style was otherwise identical to its fellow Seal. This ZGA was still in use with EWS 11 years later when recorded at Warrington and remained in this livery, albeit which much of the lettering painted out. Paul Bartlett

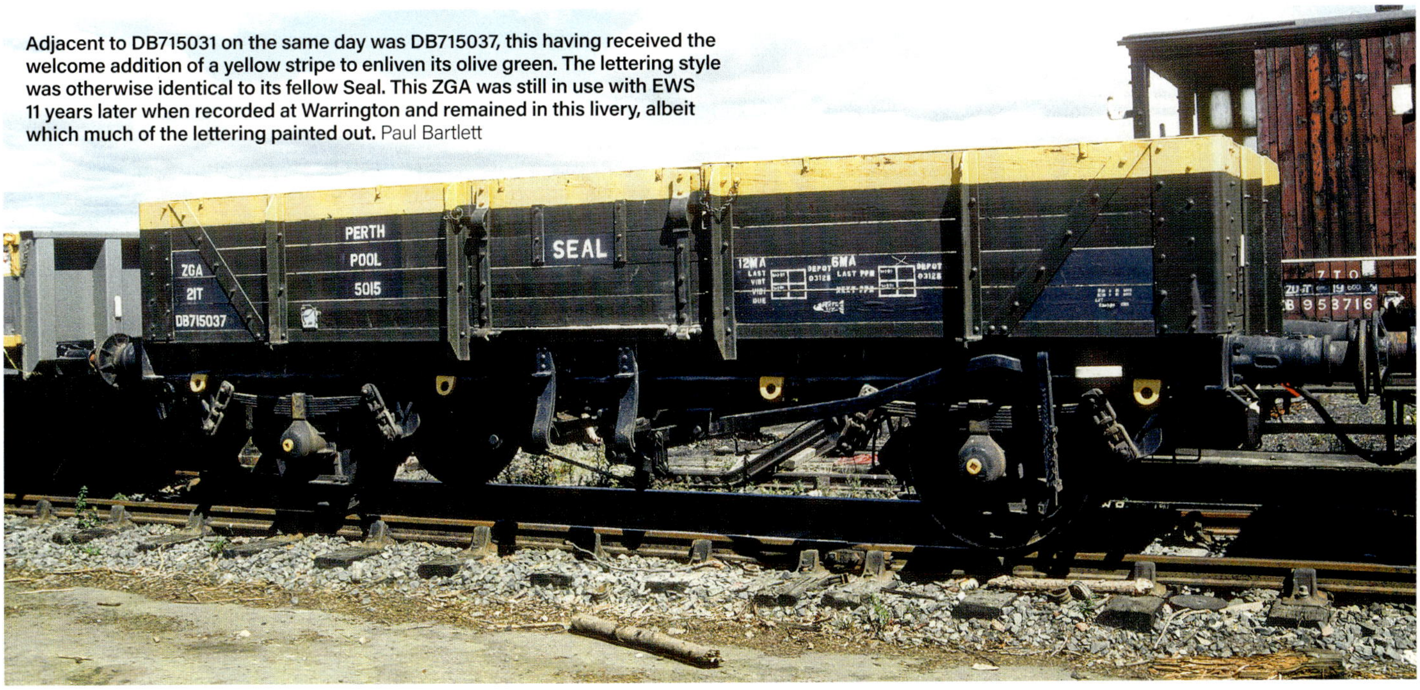

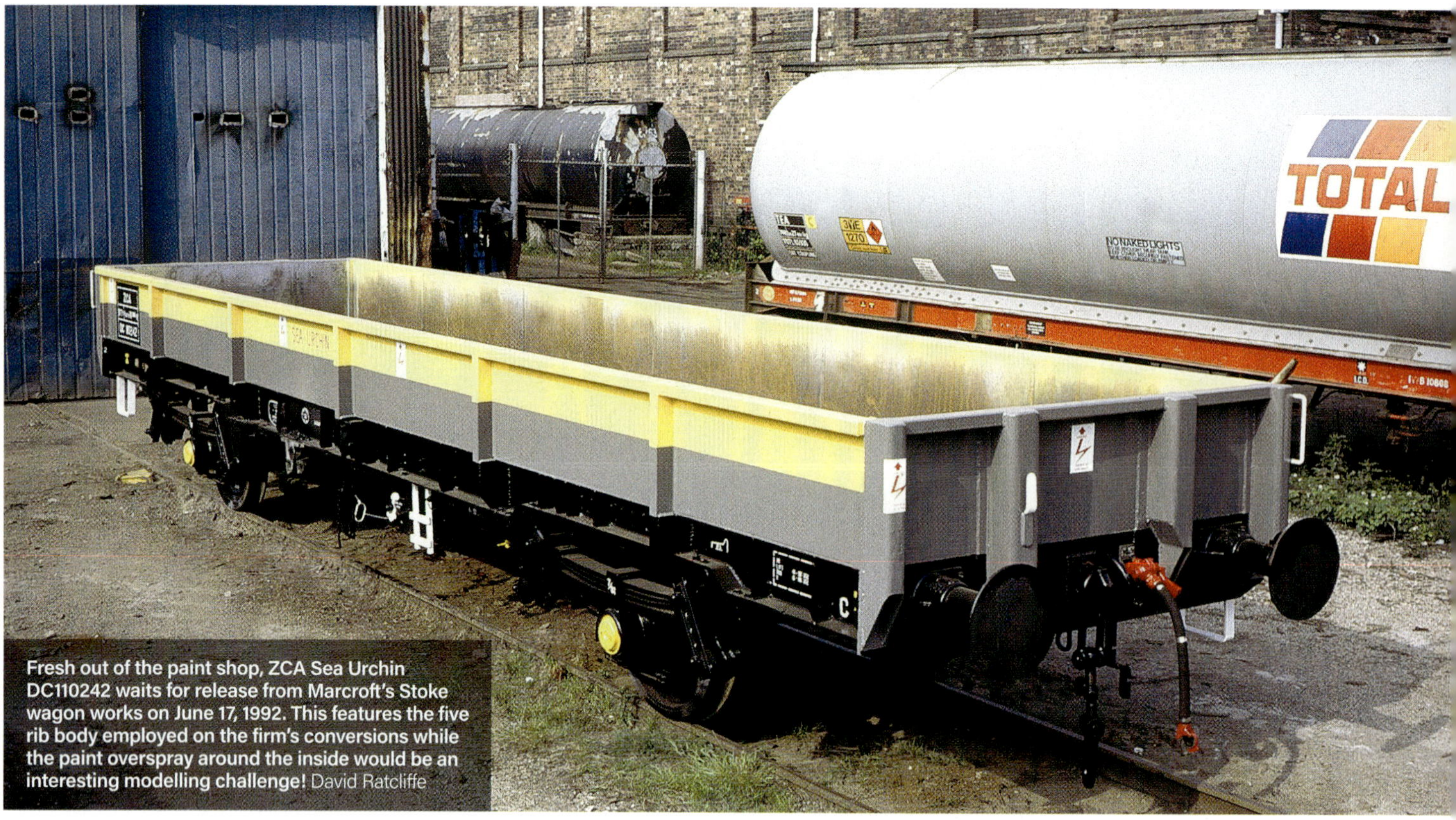

Fresh out of the paint shop, ZCA Sea Urchin DC110242 waits for release from Marcroft's Stoke wagon works on June 17, 1992. This features the five rib body employed on the firm's conversions while the paint overspray around the inside would be an interesting modelling challenge! David Ratcliffe

ZCA Sea Urchin

With the Seahorse having demonstrated that the air-braked open wagons could be successfully rebuilt for carrying ballast, 1991 saw the first steps taken towards expanding the concept. By now, there was a need to replace the purpose-built vacuum-braked ballast opens that had made it through the 1980s, particularly the Grampus, while even the conversions and transfers undertaken during that decade were approaching retirement, especially with vacuum-braked locos diminishing in number. Another aim of this new rebuilding programme was to end the constant cycle of repairs to the wooden bodies of the ex-OBA Bass, which was becoming increasingly uneconomic.

Completed early in 1991 were two trial conversions utilising Bass as donors, both losing their wooden sides in favour of reinforced steel ones while the floor was similarly upgraded to metal. Of these, DC110066 was converted by RFS and retained its original OBA ends, albeit these were cut down to the same height as the sides with new top capping. Its sides were reinforced by ten ribs with the sheeting extending down over the solebars, so much so that a cut-out was required for the handbrake lever.

Meanwhile, DC110108 was rebuilt by Marcroft Engineering, this also having ten ribs per side but without the sheeting encroaching on the solebars. The ends may have been new as well or just modified more extensively than on DC110066; they certainly retained none of the OBA features that its fellow wagon kept. The two prototypes were recoded as ZCA Sea Urchin, painted in grey/yellow and initially deployed from Mountsorrel.

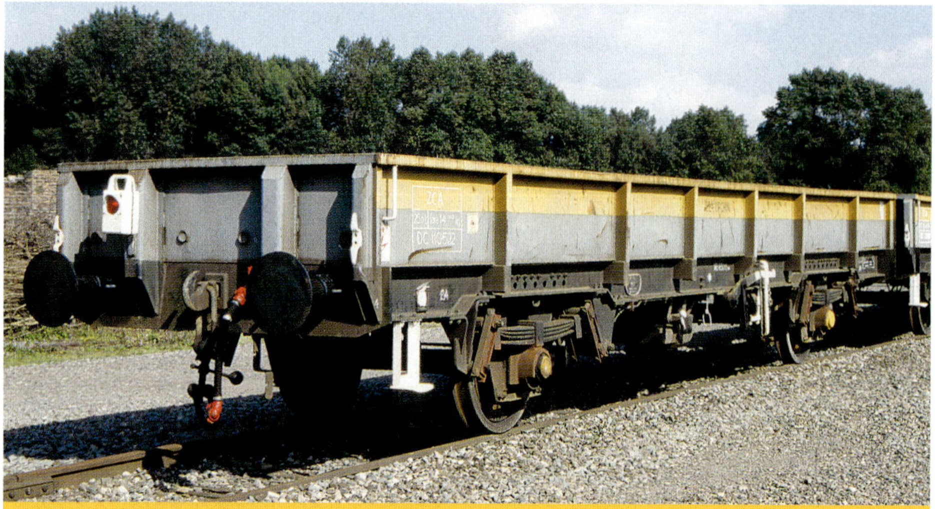

ABOVE: **The six rib body preferred by RFS Engineering is illustrated by DC110522 at Cockshute Sidings, Stoke, on August 1, 1998, it being in EWS ownership by this date. The end fittings clearly show that this was the original OBA end cut down and modified.** Trevor Mann

Production batch

Following evaluation, both Marcroft and RFS were awarded contracts for further conversions from wooden-bodied Bass, the two builds commencing concurrently in the summer of 1991. However, some alterations were made to the design for this 43-strong production batch, most noticeably a reduction in the number of reinforcing ribs. Those converted by Marcroft emerged with five bodyside ribs while the corner posts and end ribs had a square profile at the top, examples being DC110033/121/129/181/188/190/213/215/230/242/265/276/305/528/619/630/677/712/728/765.

Meanwhile, the RFS examples were given six ribs along the sides and the four verticals on the ends all had sloping tops. The ends were clearly the originals re-profiled once again as the lashing cleats were retained and, in some cases, the circular fittings as well. Examples were DC110075/208/ 221/258/273/321/356/365/389/408/449/517/522/523/ 525/594/623/672/686/710/729. The body

A tale of three Urchins by Mark Lambert

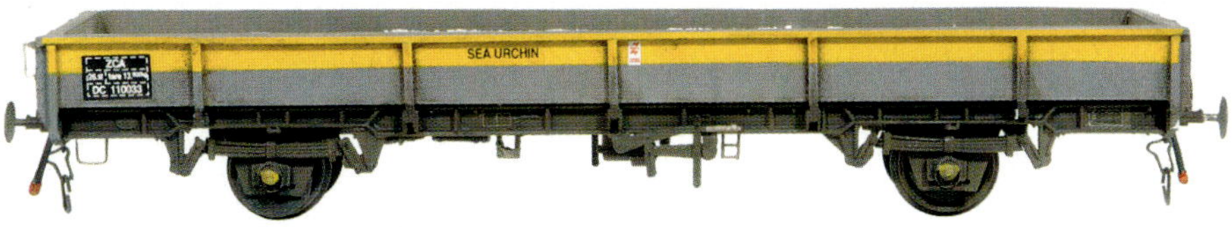
The Cambrian Sea Urchin kit in its as-supplied five-rib form.

Cambrian was the first to release a 4mm scale kit for a Sea Urchin, this using the OBA/OCA underframe mouldings. Like all Cambrian kits, with a little bit of care and filing, it all fits together very nicely but lacks some of the finesse of a more modern offering. The swivelling axle assemblies do work well though and with a little bit of weight under the wagon and a substantial load of ballast (in this case a Ten Commandments plaster cast), it holds the track well.

I have fitted turned brass buffer heads as the Cambrian versions are prone to breaking off in a heavy shunt. MJT supply 18in heads and springs on a 1mm shank, which is a little fine but acceptable with a coat of paint on; I have switched to using Lanarkshire Models and Supplies Oleo buffers on more recent models, they add a bit more weight and they are very well cast. Painted with Railmatch paints and finished off with transfers by Appleby Model Engineering, there is not much more to say about this wagon.

These days I would source 3D-printed brake frames from Shapeways and add a rudimentary representation of all the underframe equipment, but this is still a relatively cheap and easy way to build a good representation of a Sea Urchin. It is also easy to convert the five-rib bodysides into a six-rib version by filing off the moulded ribs (but not the top capping) from the sides before assembly and replacing them with Evergreen strip. I used dimensions from articles and photos in DEMU's Update magazine to get the revised rib spacing correct.

The resin route

The S Kits Sea Urchin portrays the ex VDA van conversions, this 4mm scale mixed-media kit employing resin, brass and whitemetal castings. The main body and underframe are cast as one piece in resin and requires some cleaning up before assembly; the ends are whitemetal castings and the suspension is made up from etched W-irons and cast springs and axleboxes. There is also a representation of the brake gear to make the underframe look busier. Cast buffers are also supplied and these are more than adequate so there is no need for aftermarket bits at all.

The assembly is straightforward and mostly uses superglue as the parts grab the resin almost immediately and stay on. The side ribs are 'T' or 'I' beam and each outer face is a small etched part. Getting them to stay parallel when fixing them on turned out to be the trickiest part of the construction but it just requires a bit of patience. The next tricky job is painting the engineers' grey and yellow livery. Depending on the body style, Sea Urchins can be difficult to paint well, even with an airbrush.

In this case, I painted the yellow first as I thought it would be easier to mask the yellow and spray the grey from an angle to minimise the risk of paint bleeding under the tape. In hindsight, it would be even easier to paint the body before fitting the etched rib parts. Painting the underframe was also complicated by the number of brackets and supports cast in but there is no easy fix here, just perseverance and a steady hand with a paintbrush. As with the Cambrian kit, I used Railmatch paints and Appleby transfers with a plaster-cast load.

It is relatively straightforward to create a six-rib ZCA by filing off the ribs and adding new ones made from plastic strip in the revised positions.
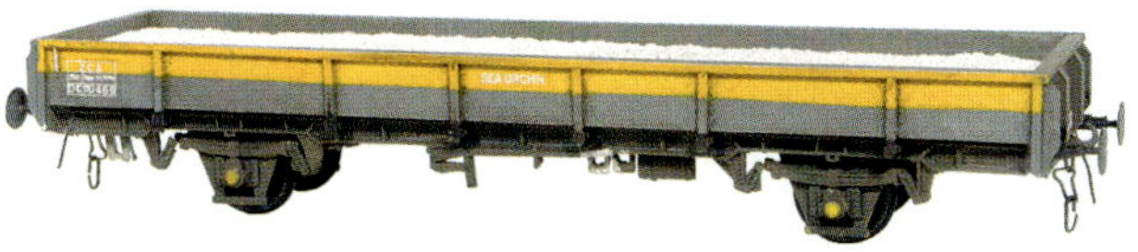

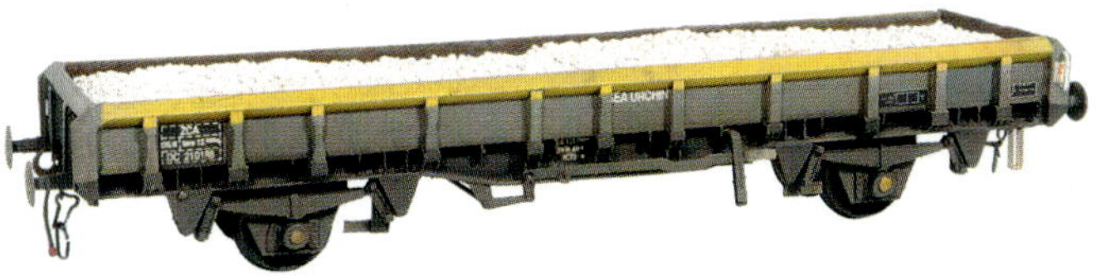
The S kits offering captures the chunky look of the ex van Sea Urchins very well and it is a type you rarely see modelled.

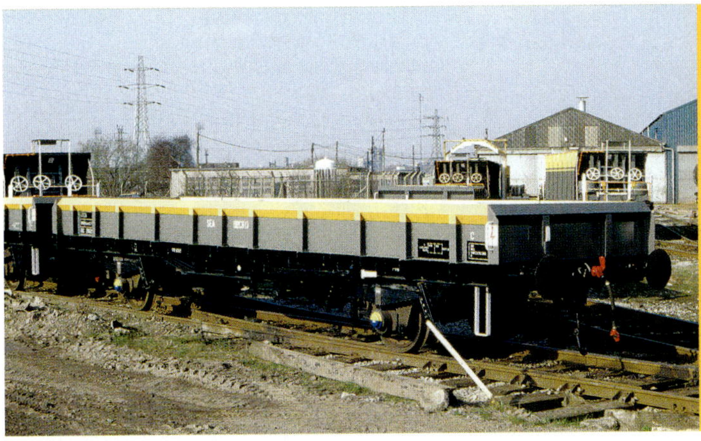
LEFT: An early example of an ex VDA Sea Urchin was also to be found at Marcroft, Stoke, on March 13, 1993, soon after the second phase rebuilds got underway. DC210292 shows the altogether more rugged style of body adopted for the van conversions. Trevor Mann

style of the remaining two wagons, DC110257 and DC110318, is sadly unknown.

With most, if not all, of these Sea Urchins completed by the end of 1992, a much more extensive second phase of conversions commenced at the start of the following year. The donors for this batch were initially VDA vans, including examples that had been in departmental stores traffic as ZRAs. The bodywork design was significantly altered for these Sea Urchins, having a bulkier appearance with 11 side ribs, while the side and end capping was angled to prevent ballast pick-up.

A total of 400 wagons was initially ordered, this being equally divided between Marcroft, ABB Transportation, Prorail Bombardier and RFS. With four companies involved, there were differences between the builds, most notably in how the end ribs joined the capping. By the end of 1993, some VBA vans were also becoming Sea Urchins, albeit far fewer were involved. These also had an earlier style of underframe with a much less pronounced 'fish-belly', making them easy to distinguish. Irrespective of the donor, all these Sea Urchins were again finished in grey/yellow, albeit with some variation in branding layout.

Over 300 of the wagons were despatched straight to Network SouthEast, where, amongst other work, they saw use on upgrading the Kent main line ahead of Eurostar services commencing. The remainder headed to the West Coast Main Line, where many of the ex-OBA Sea Urchins were also to be found. By 1995, the van-based conversions had spread to the Midlands, Yorkshire and northeast as privatisation took effect. Under Transrail, Mainline Freight and then EWS, many more Sea Urchins would appear in a variety of styles and using new donors such as OAA and SPA opens along with VCA vans but that falls outside the scope of this volume.

ZKA Limpet

By late 1991, the Civil Engineers department was actively examining the acquisition of surplus private owner wagons to carry out another round of fleet replacement. With the UK in recession once again, comparatively modern air-braked aggregates wagons were standing idle while BR staff were struggling to maintain elderly vacuum-braked ballast wagons of limited capacity.

The Civil Engineers department was already hiring 22 Tiger Rail PNA and POA two-axle box opens that year, the so-called Tiger 'cubs' being deployed on ballast duties between East Usk, Newport, and Acton in connection with the building of the rail link to Heathrow Airport. However, it was not until the start of 1993 that a deal was done for InterCity to purchase around 190 PNA/POA from CAIB which had acquired the fleet after Tiger Rail collapsed.

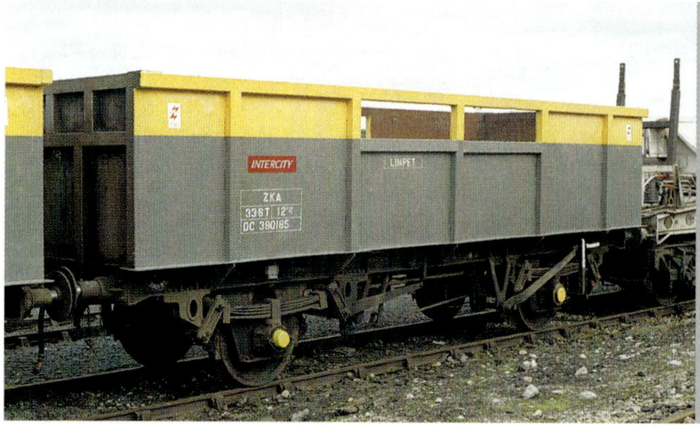

LEFT: **The initial Limpet were quite presentable when first converted with the sides fully repainted, although even then the ends were not touched. DC390185 displays its InterCity lettering at Carlisle Currock during September 1993 with the unlikely bedfellow of Ministry of Defence nuclear flask wagon MODA95780 off to the right.** David Ratcliffe

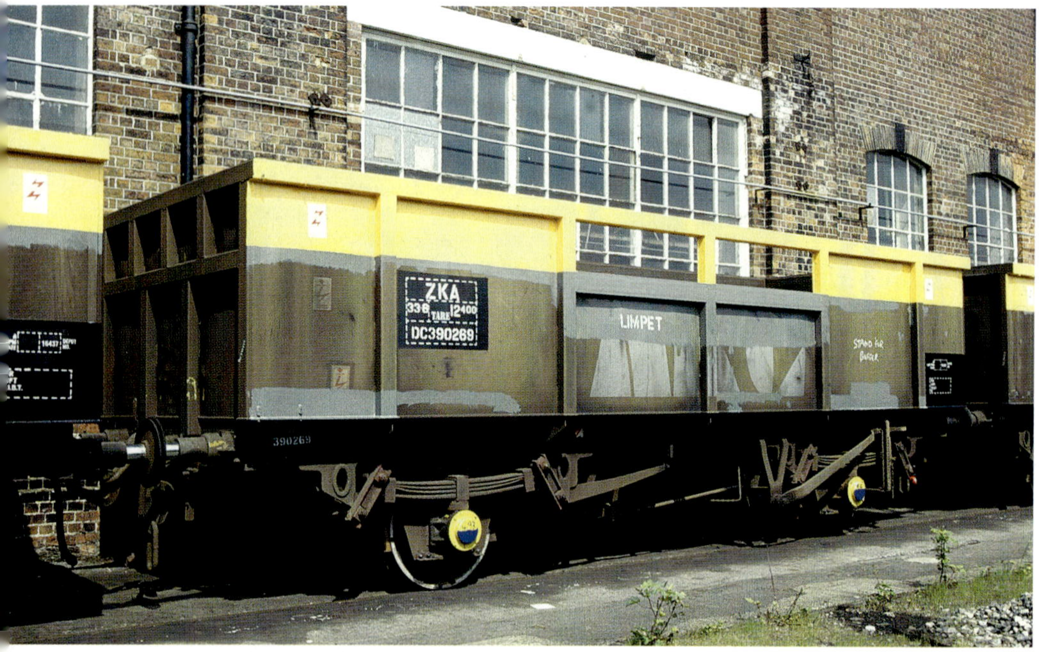

ABOVE: **When the budget got tight so did the painting with DC390269 displaying the result at York wagon repair depot in June 1993. The original ARC lettering is still clear to see, the associated mustard livery not so much!** Mark Saunders

Conversion work started immediately at both York and Carlisle Currock with bodyside cut-outs being created on both sides to prevent over-loading. The modified wagons were renumbered into the BR air-braked series and coded ZKA Limpet, initial conversions seeing their bodysides repainted into grey and yellow and, amusingly, claret-backed italic InterCity lettering applied. As befitted the company paying for them, the first Limpet wagons were deployed onto West Coast Main Line ballast duties from Northampton in April 1993 with others going to the East Coast over the following months.

Limited money

The conversion programme was not generously funded though and the fully repainted bodysides soon gave way to a patchwork appearance with the grey only applied where absolutely necessary, although the yellow band was always added in full. As a result, Limpet were released to traffic

Doorand conversions

September 1993 saw a new conversion emerge from York in the form of the Doorand. Whereas the Limpet largely prevented over-loading by having the cut-outs in the side, this was not a perfect solution as the ballast could still build up at either end. The Doorand was the natural conclusion to this process and saw all of the extraneous bodywork cut away above the safe loading limit, creating a low-sided ballast wagon with fixed sides.

DC390256 was the first to be completed, it receiving a full repaint into grey and yellow with the name applied in black. The ZKA TOPS code was retained with it being allocated to the InterCity ECML fleet at Tyne Yard. This wagon was photographed at York in October 1994 by Mark Saunders, its positioning between two Limpets showing the amount of bodywork removed as well as the angled top capping added to the sides. Following evaluation, 11 more Limpets were cut down in the same manner and similarly renamed during mid-1994, these being DC390197, DC390248/50/52/55/61/63/71/95/99 and DC390304. These also passed to EWS and were re-numbered and reclassified as MTA 395001-012 around 2002, going on to serve until the mid-2010s in some cases and working alongside the MFA and MHA.

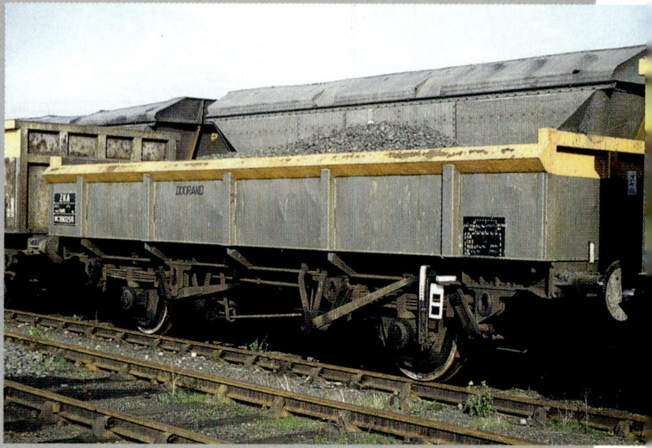

Re-springing a Limpet by Terry Bendall

The RTR Bachmann model is the obvious starting point to model a Limpet in 4mm scale, this having been produced over the years in grey/yellow, Transrail grey and Loadhaul black/orange. However, as one of the manufacturer's older models, it does suffer from the production compromise of using an underframe with the wrong type of springs, something that also affects many of the TTA tanker models as well.

The moulded springs therefore need to be replaced, in this case with the whitemetal parabolic ones available from S Kits, these also featuring the correct type of suspension linkage. With the model stripped down, the tension lock coupling mounts were cut off along with the moulded coupling hooks on the bufferbeams. The separate handbrake levers also needed to be carefully prised off and set aside for re-use as they are in the way. Not wishing to replace the W-irons or axleboxes, the springs were cut through by the hangers using a cutting disc in a mini-drill and the remainder carefully trimmed away with a scalpel

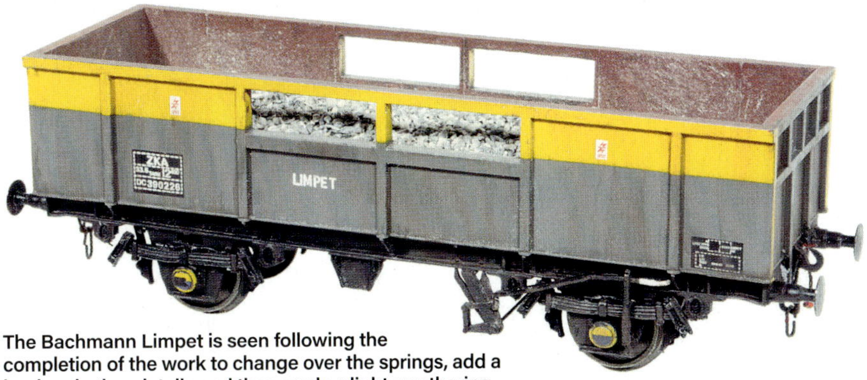

The Bachmann Limpet is seen following the completion of the work to change over the springs, add a load and other details and then apply a light weathering.

The new springs were then cleaned up with a file where needed and glued in place using superglue, ensuring they were level and aligning with the hangers. Instanter coupling hooks from the Smiths range were glued into slots cut in the bufferbeams with brake pipes made from 0.5mm brass wire also added. The model was then re-assembled, and the new parts painted using Humbrol black with a touch of red added to the brake pipe taps.

The inside of the Limpet was painted using Railmatch No.405 dark rust and weathered by giving it a thin wash of Railmatch No.406 sleeper grime. Additionally, some new ballast was placed inside, the top covered with a piece of card and the wagon then given a vigorous shake. Sufficient ballast dust adhered to the insides to give an effective finish.

The start of the ballast load was a piece of 40 thou thick white styrene with small rectangles glued on top to form the basis of the 'humps'. The edges of these were then bevelled off and supports added underneath to get the base at a suitable height in relation to the cut-outs. The edges of the base were next painted with Humbrol light grey with PVA glue then painted onto the surface and new ballast sprinkled over it and pressed into the glue. When the glue was dry, the loose ballast was shaken off and more glue and ballast applied where needed. Finally, the wagon was given a wash with thinned shades of brown to tone down the factory paintwork.

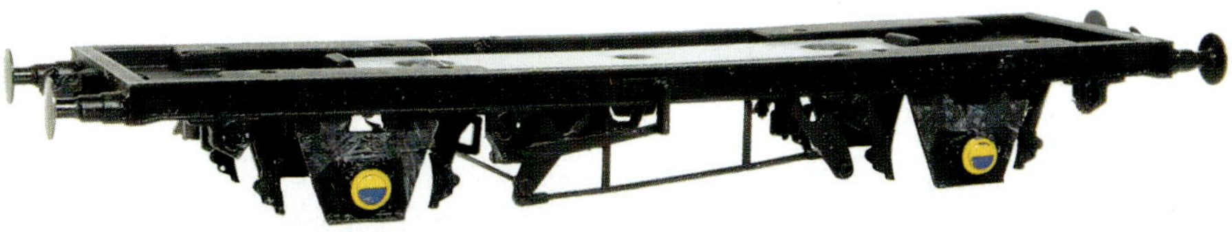

The Bachmann chassis is pictured following the removal of the moulded springs. While initially messy, the scars will be covered by the new castings.

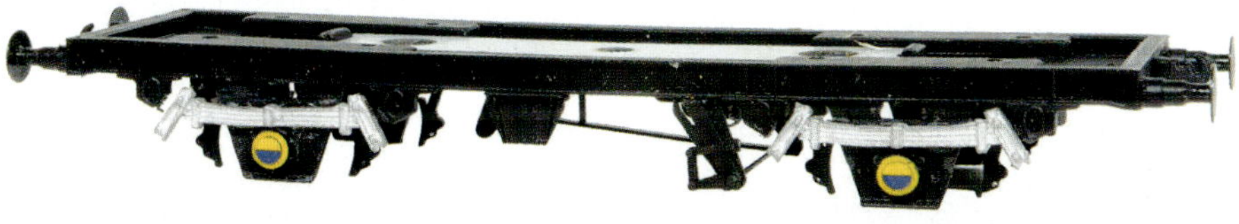

The new S Kits parabolic springs are seen glued in position and awaiting a coat of paint.

still displaying parts of their previous liveries, most commonly ARC, although the original mustard colour had long since dirtied and faded to a grotty brown. Unsurprisingly, the InterCity lettering did not appear on these!

With privatisation bringing the reallocation of engineers' stock from the passenger sectors to the three newly-created regional freight companies, the Limpet conversions were not fully completed. As they had not been renumbered consecutively following conversion either, the ZKA were in the DC390150-331 range but with gaps.

The conversions did initially continue under Loadhaul, but the project was re-tasked to produce MKA, these lacking the side cut-outs as they were intended for coal blending traffic rather than ballast. A total of 36 of these emerged from York in late 1994 numbered 393000-036, the earliest examples carrying Loadhaul black and orange. In most cases, no repaint was involved and this again left the old liveries discernible, including the odd Foster Yeoman example. All of the Limpets passed to EWS and were gradually withdrawn, some making it to the early 2010s.

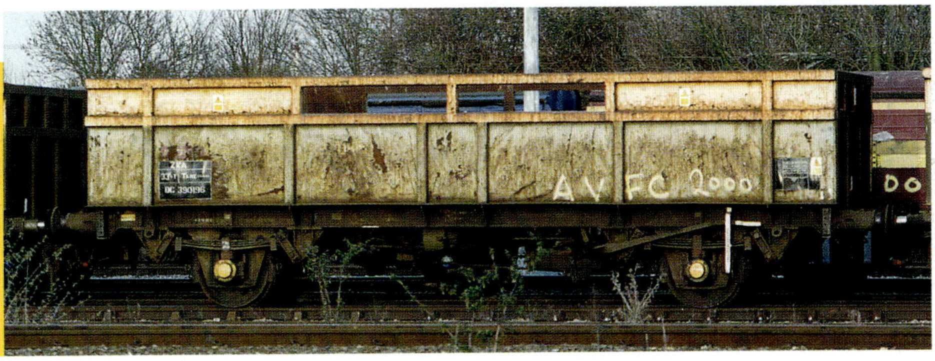

RIGHT: **All of the PNA/POA box wagons were built on recovered tank wagon underframes, leading to various detail differences. This carried through to the Limpet where DC390195 and DC390196 were noticeably longer than the rest of the fleet due to the origins of their donor wagons. While DC390195 would gain Transrail grey in the mid-1990s, its sister would retain engineers' grey/yellow until withdrawal. Looking rather scruffy, DC390196 is pictured at Didcot on February 20, 2001.** Simon Bendall

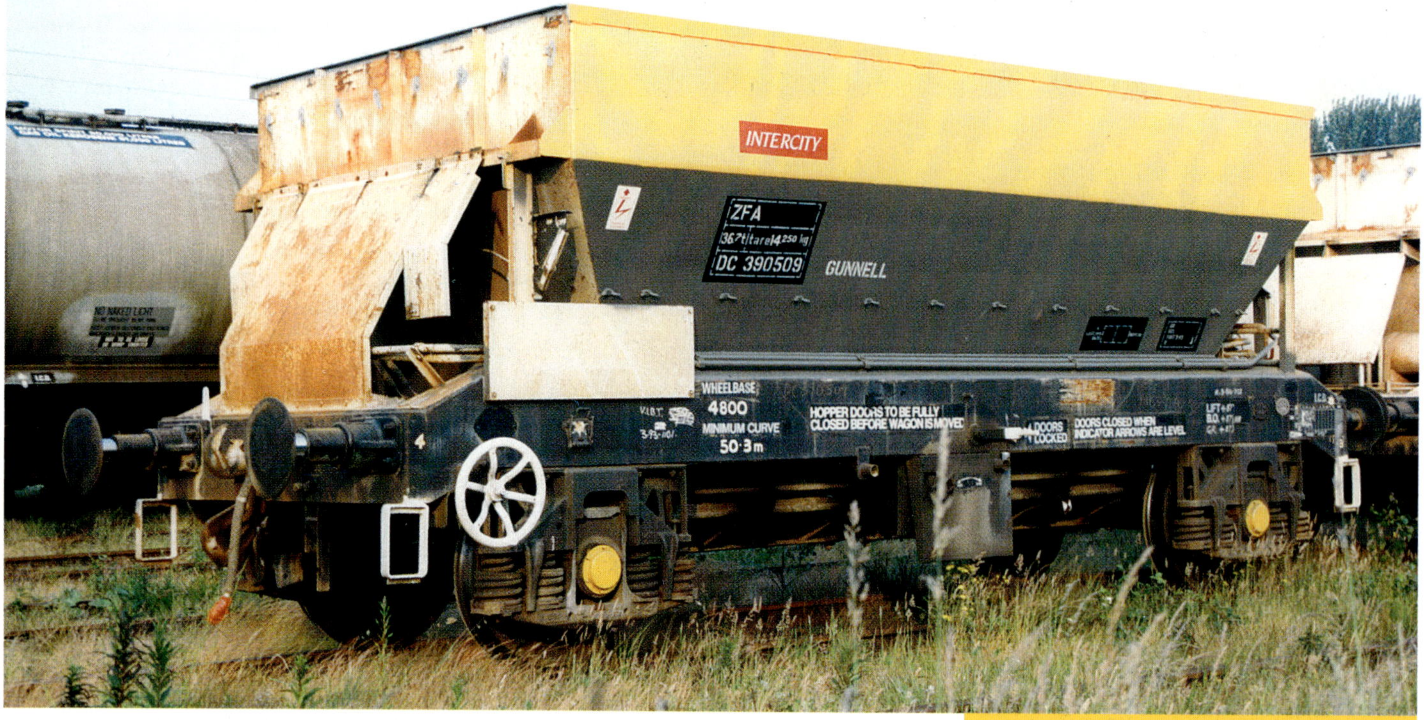

ZFA Gunnell

ABOVE: **DC390509 was modified from ex Yeoman PGA PR14009 and is seen at Longport on June 30, 1993, soon after conversion at Marcroft Engineering. This shows the original look of the Gunnell with unaltered and unpainted ends. The solebars rarely saw any attention either but at least no ZFAs received the patchwork body treatment given to the Limpets.** Colin Wright/David Ratcliffe Collection

At the same time as InterCity was purchasing the PNA/POA Tiger 'cubs' from CAIB in early 1993, it also reached agreement to buy 147 two-axle PGA hoppers from the PR14000-151 series. These were the former Procor hoppers that had worked for Foster Yeoman for many years but had been returned off hire following the arrival of the JHA bogie design. Notably, these were the first hoppers to join the engineers' fleet in over a decade.

Again, modifications to the PGAs started immediately at Marcroft Engineering, this initially involving reducing the height of the hopper sides and removing the end walkways and access ladders. Completed wagons were painted in grey and yellow, which was confined to the sides only; the ends typically remaining in rusty Yeoman light grey The InterCity logos once again appeared with the wagons given new BR numbers and the designation of ZFA Gunnell. The spelling of the latter initially caused some confusion, but double 'l' is what appeared on the wagons so is used here.

By the spring of 1993, 26 wagons were at work on the Great Western, being based at East Usk. However, deliveries were suspended after 50 wagons had been released from Stoke due to an issue with the hopper shape. As shown in the photo of DC390509 above, the hopper of a PGA was squared off with no angled extension out over the brake gear and headstocks. Thus, when a train of Gunnell were formed up, there was a large gap between each hopper and the next. It was found that during loading, from a ballast cleaner conveyor for example, a large amount of ballast was falling between the gaps and ending up on the track.

Modifications

The solution to this was to extend the hopper body at both ends with newly-fabricated angled sections being welded on. It also meant that the yellow paint now extended around the ends over the new parts, although

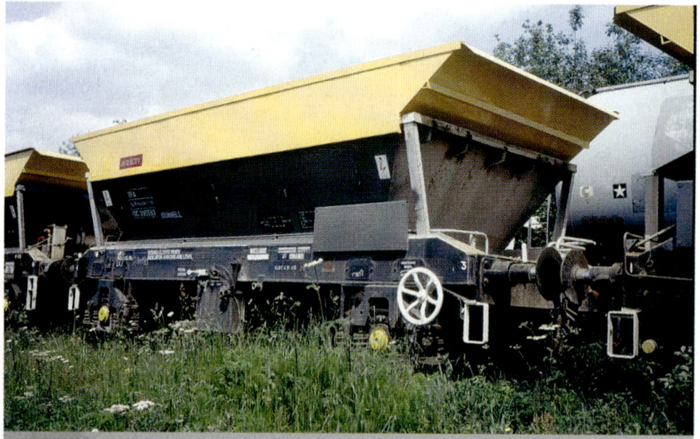

ABOVE: **Also seen in June 1993 at Stoke, DC390593 displays the angled hopper extensions that were quickly devised and welded in place to reduce ballast spillage. These end pieces were reinforced with a horizontal strengthening rib and yellow paint applied all over, greatly reducing the visual impact of the remaining rusty and faded end panels.** David Ratcliffe

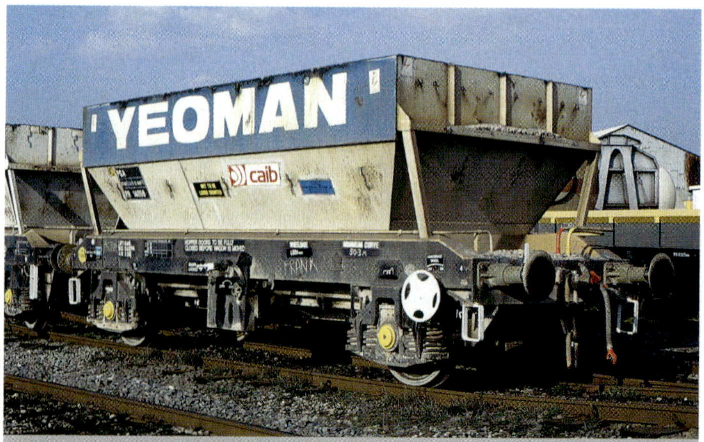

ABOVE: **PGA PR14059 is seen in the initial stage of Gunnell conversion at Marcroft Engineering in March 1993. Burn marks are visible around the hopper lip where the body has been cut down while the end walkways and ladders have also gone. It would soon be completed and repainted to become DC390619.** David Ratcliffe

New look for Lima PGA by Mike Cubberley

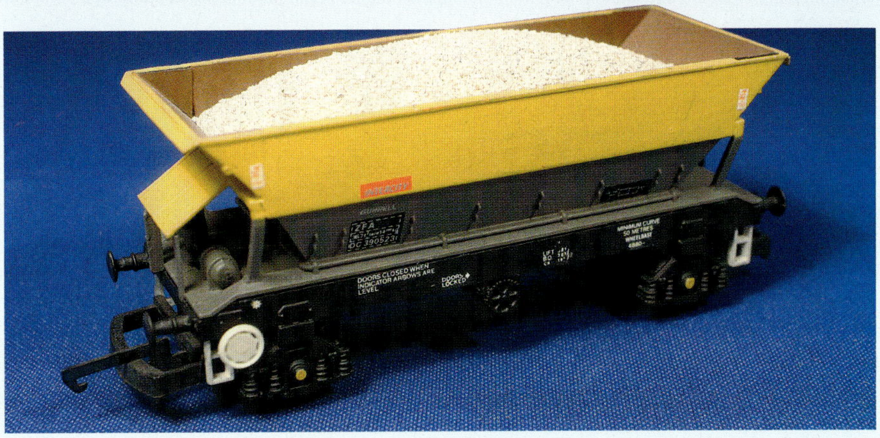

A Lima Yeoman PGA was used for this 4mm scale conversion dating from the mid-1990s. This saw the hopper ends removed and the sides reduced in height by carefully sanding them down by the appropriate amount. The angled hopper extensions were formed from 30 thou plastic sheet and grafted onto the rest of the body with the joints then being filled. Slaters strip was then overlaid to form new top capping and the small, angled spill plates. The protective cover over the air brake equipment was made up from a square of 10 thou sheet with two supporting legs from strip of the same thickness and some five thou strip detailing on the top.

The model was brush painted with Railmatch Railfreight grey and Humbrol 'Trainer yellow' to give a good depth of colour coverage, followed by Humbrol matt black on the chassis. The mould lines on the Lima buffer heads were carefully filed off, with transfers coming from the Fox range, including pack F4101 for the small PGA lettering and sheet F4273 for the InterCity infrastructure fleet brandings.

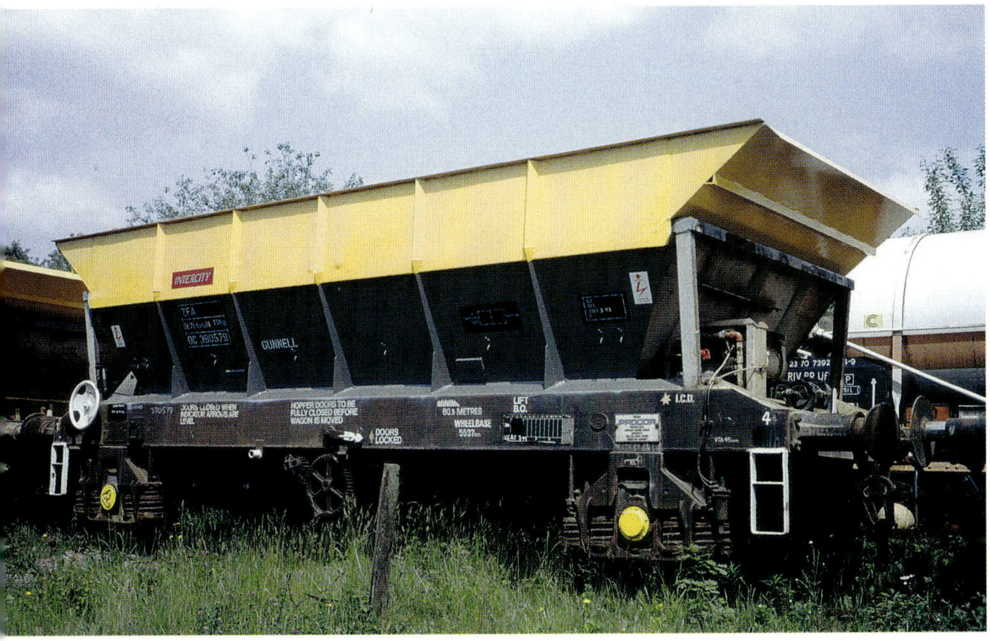

LEFT: **Not all of the Gunnell were converted from Procor/Yeoman PGAs, 13 using former salt hoppers as their basis. These remained visually distinctive due to the bodyside ribbing, although they were not the only ZFAs to have ribs of some form. Once again seen at Stoke in June 1993 awaiting delivery to InterCity, DC390579 was previously PR8275. The weld lines of the end extensions are clearly visible beneath the paint.** David Ratcliffe

BELOW: **Previously PR14135, DC390543 was converted to a standard ZFA Gunnel in 1993. However, the following year saw it modified into a prototype for air operation of the hopper doors. This involved the removal of the manual door-operating gear and its replacement by a pneumatic door control motor, this being fed by the air pipe running diagonally down from the other end. A platform, steps, and safety screen were provided to allow staff to check the hopper interior, these modifications meaning the end extensions also had to be removed. Notably recoded as a ZCA, the wagon never progressed beyond the testing phase and was an early withdrawal. It is seen at Marcroft Engineering on October 31, 1995.** Trevor Mann

the grey rarely did. This alteration was quickly put in place and deliveries restarted by early summer while the initial wagons were recalled to be modified.

At the same time, the pool of PGA donor wagons was expanded with the addition of a small number of former salt hoppers in the PR8258-PR8300 and PR8902-11 series. As these had been built with ribbed bodysides, this feature was carried over to the Gunnell so DC390576-585 and DC30656-658 were always distinctive. A small number of PGAs previously used by ARC in the PR14688-703 range were also converted, becoming DC390660-671. By the time the programme was completed, there were 171 Gunnell wagons numbered consecutively as DC390502-672

Following their brief tenure with the regional freight companies, EWS acquired all but one of the fleet, eventually deeming them more useful as aggregates wagons. Apart from a handful of defective examples, the Gunnell were recoded as HGA very early in the 2000s to give service for another five or six years.

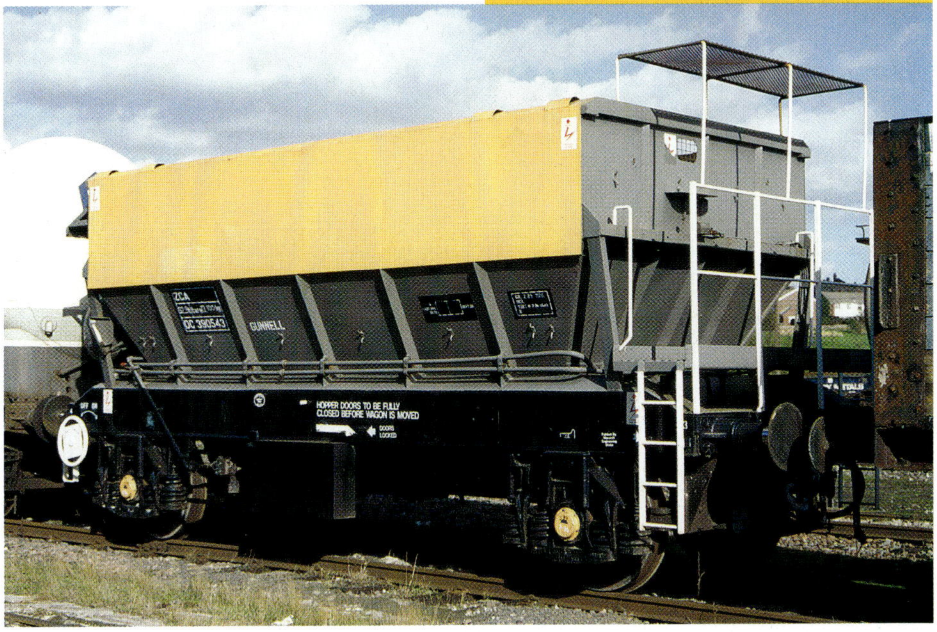

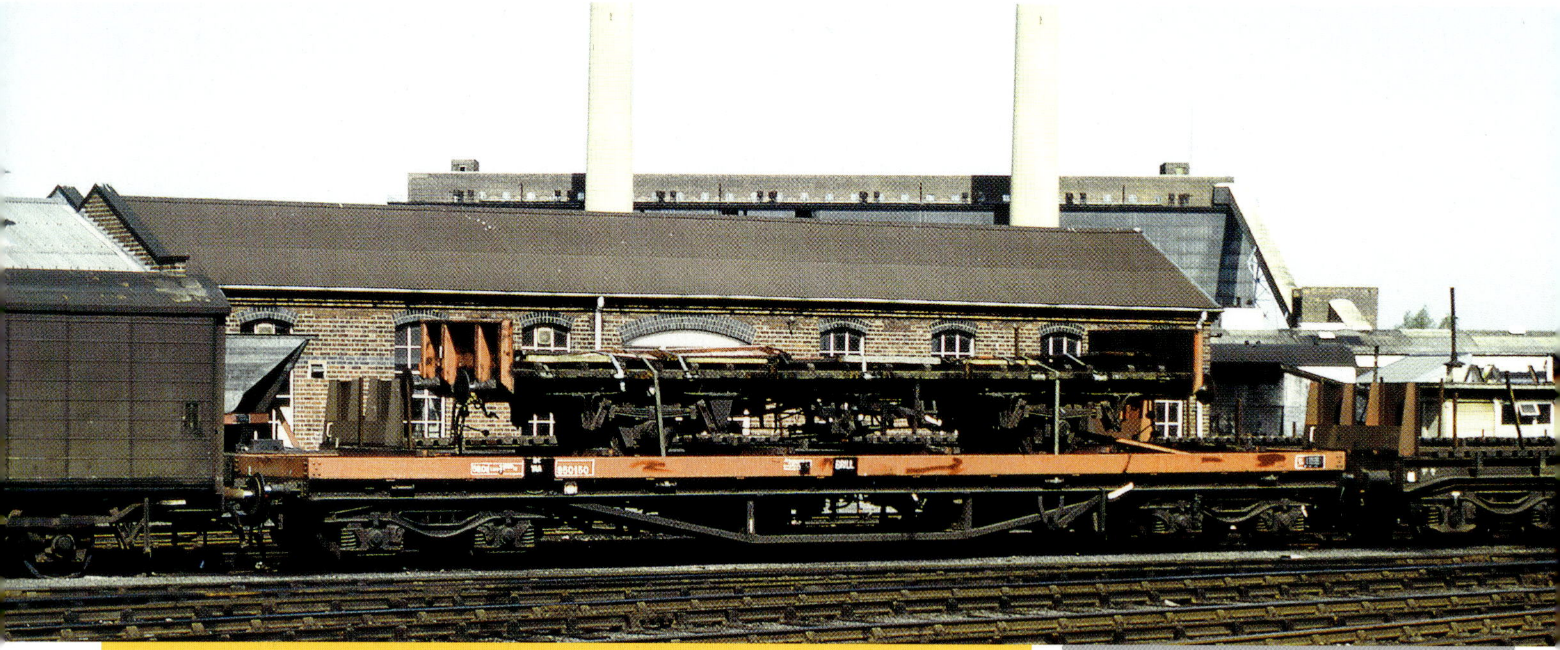

YAA Brill

ABOVE: **An unusual load for DC950150 at Doncaster on May 13, 1984, with the Brill having arrived carrying an accident-damaged SPA for repair at the works. The plate wagon has the majority of its doors strapped to its deck but at least one is loaded on the bogie bolster at the right hand end. The branding changes to the YAA are minimal with the TOPS code and DC prefix squeezed in next to the number and fish name painted on a black patch.** 53A Models of Hull Collection/the late David R Vickers

With BR's desire to move to an air-braked network, it faced a decision with its extensive fleet of bogie bolster wagons. Unlike with the open and van fleets, where new builds offered a clear advantage in providing extra capacity, there was little to be gained in building new bolster wagons, especially as the existing sturdily-constructed types had plenty of life in them.

The decision was therefore taken to experimentally convert two Bogie Bolster C and a single Bogie Bolster D to air brakes for evaluation, this taking place at Swindon Works in 1975. The former emerged renumbered as 960000 and 960001, coded BCA and riding on Y25C bogies. However, despite the type being BR's most numerous bogie bolster design, no more were modernised. This was quite likely due to their length being only 45ft over headstocks, which meant they were too short for long girders and rail loads and limited to carrying 30-tons. In contrast, the Bogie Bolster D were 52ft over headstocks and could take up to 42-tons, it making sense to modernise the bolster type that was the most versatile.

As a result, the two BCA were duly deemed non-standard and had found their way into departmental use by 1980, being part of the Mechanical and Electrical Engineers' fleet. Initially, they were based on the Eastern Region, recoded YNA and retained their bolsters and stanchions. Later in the decade, both had moved to the M&EE's Southern-

The most common load for Brill, certainly during the 1980s, was a stack of new rails, as demonstrated by DC950095 at Workington on April 22, 1984. Having been loaded at the British Steel plant, the rails would be taken to a pre-assembly depot and track panels put together. The YAA retains a weathered and patchy coat of freight brown and has a Bream runner wagon at each end. Trevor Mann

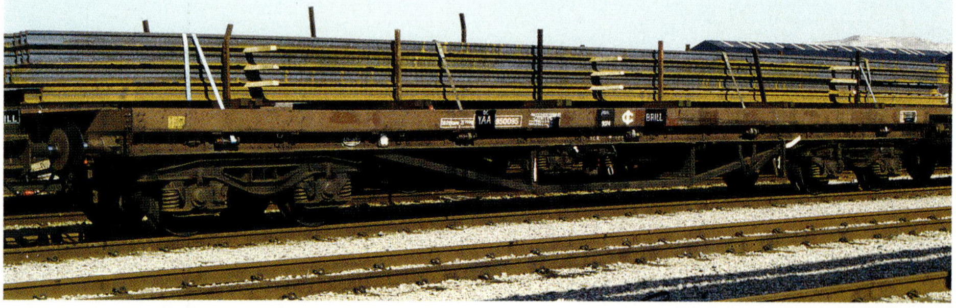

The prototype Eel

The Brill were not used for 60ft track panel loads due to their length, although examples could occasionally be seen carrying recovered panels that had been broken up into shorter sections. These rested on the bolsters and were lashed in place with the intermediate stanchions removed if they were in the way. It was therefore surprising that late 1987 brought the appearance of a prototype conversion with this load in mind. DC950181 saw its bolsters and low sides removed and a steel floor fitted in place

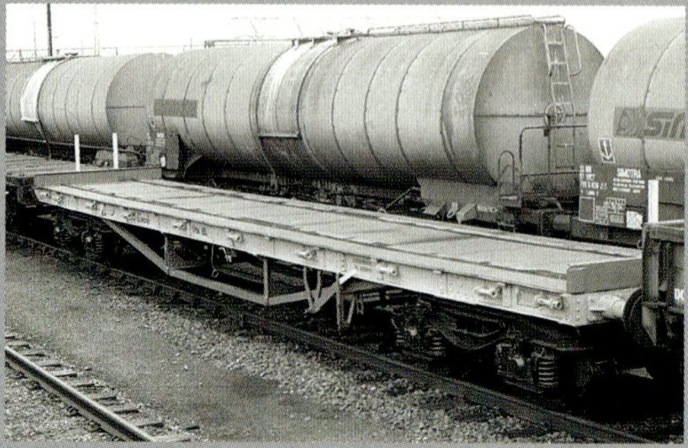

of the wooden planks, while a piece of 'C' section steel was fitted across the ends along with two short stanchions. Finished in yellow, the wagon was recoded YMA and coded Eel. Even in this form, regular 60ft panels were still too long so it may have been intended to carry shorter track sections destined for a specific application. Seen fresh from conversion, DC950187 was captured at Hoo Junction on November 15, 1987, by Bob Wallace. No more followed and by 1991 it was at York carriage and wagon works with the bogies removed.

Buffing up some Brill by Mark Lambert

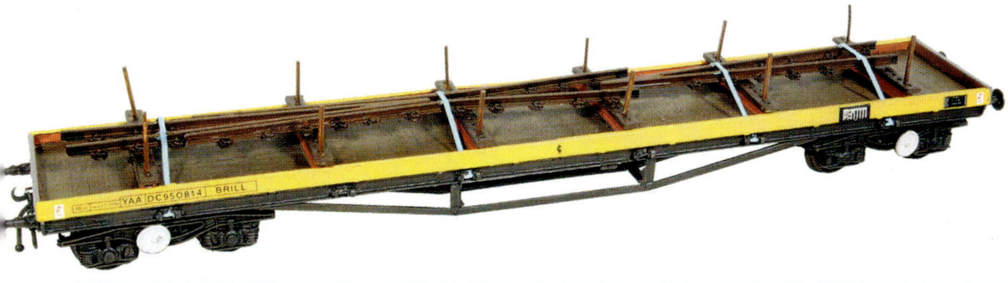

I first built my Brill about 25 years ago from the 4mm scale Cambrian kits, these being finished as BDA wagons at the time and with the original three-piece Y25C bogie mouldings. Over the years, the buffers were damaged and repaired more than once and the bolster pins replaced with plastic strip more times than I can remember. By the mid-2010s, the models were looking a bit sorry for themselves and not a patch on the ready-to-run Bachmann version that had appeared in the interim.

Loath to throw them out, I decided to refurbish them as YAA Brill, this being triggered by a DEMU society member making an etch available to replace the plastic core of the Y25C bogies. I duly disassembled the bogies, actually they fell apart as I chopped the securing pins off and soldered up the etched inner frames. Although this etch was a private project, Stenson Models now provides something similar. The plastic Cambrian frames fitted well and the improvement in running was instant.

Buoyed up by this, I replaced the buffers with Lanarkshire Modes and Supplies castings, stripped the paint off the bodies and set to work. The side panels were a poor fit, so I prised them off, sanded them down and re-fitted them. While I was at it, I built new bolsters from the spares box to replace some of my early efforts and fitted new pins into them, drilling holes through the bolster this time rather than relying on the moulded dimple.

I came across plenty of photos online that showed a variety of loads and painting differences, so I loaded one of my pair with 60ft lengths of rail, which now has to operate with runner wagons as a YAA is several feet shorter than the rail. The second received some switch rail parts, which were soldered up from spare lengths of C&L rail left over from layout building, with chairs from the same source slid on and secured with superglue.

I painted the wagons using Games Workshop paints, mixing my own shades of yellow for variety and fading. Most YAA seem to have retained Railfreight red bases to the bolsters; painting these was a little trying as it is easy to get paint from the bolster on the wagon sides and vice versa. If doing these from scratch, I would paint the bolsters off the model and apply them later.

The loads were painted with rust-coloured acrylics after a good undercoat and then glued to the bolsters. I secured them with retaining straps made from phosphor bronze strip. This is not cheap, but it is particularly good for replicating the straps used to hold down loads on modern wagons. I painted the straps with a light blue paint, although real ones are only this colour when new as they tend to fade to a light grey-blue quite quickly. Most transfers came from the Appleby Model Engineering sheet for BDA wagons and conversions (sheet 4T42) including the centreline marking, with overhead warning flashes from Replica.

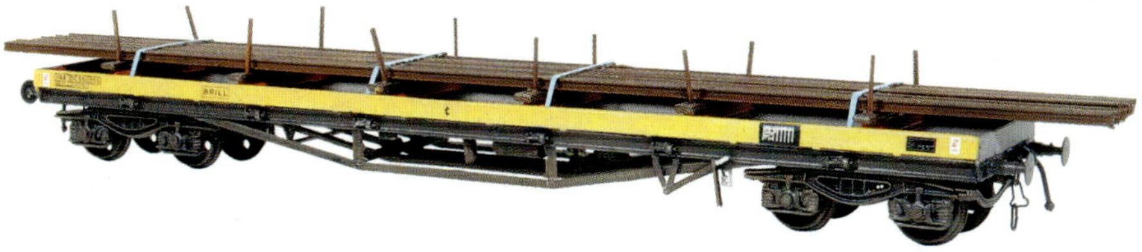

based Rolling Stock Engineers fleet and had their bolsters and stanchions removed to become YVA. In this form, they were commonly used to carry bogies between depots and works. ADC960000 duly survived into EWS ownership and was last heard of in internal use at Stewarts Lane carrying bogies for the Pullman stock based there.

Mass conversions

Returning to Swindon Works in 1975, the first air-braked Bogie Bolster D emerged as 950000 with the new code of BDA and again fitted with Y25C bogies. An extensive modernisation programme duly commenced two years later at Ashford with 200 more wagons receiving air brakes and another 600 following from Shildon at the end of the decade. These were renumbered 950001-800 and featured body-mounted handbrake levers. A final group of 450 wagons, 950801 to 951250, were completed at Shildon between 1979 and 1981, the most obvious difference on these being the fitting of disc handbrake wheels on the bogies in place of the handbrake levers.

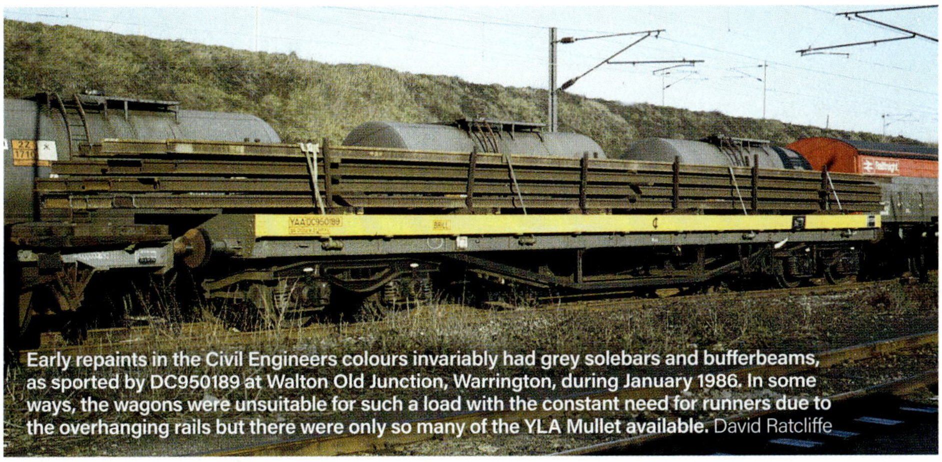

Early repaints in the Civil Engineers colours invariably had grey solebars and bufferbeams, as sported by DC950189 at Walton Old Junction, Warrington, during January 1986. In some ways, the wagons were unsuitable for such a load with the constant need for runners due to the overhanging rails but there were only so many of the YLA Mullet available. David Ratcliffe

This final batch of conversions was curtailed 300 wagons early as, like the opens, there was already an excess as traffic levels fell. Inevitably, late 1983 saw 250 or so wagons released to the Civil Engineers, most coming from the 950001-200 batch but also the more recently converted 950801-850 series. All were recoded YAA, given DC prefixes and took the fish name of Brill. As well as the mix of handbrake styles, there was also a contrast in liveries with freight brown still found on many of the earlier wagons and Railfreight red on the remainder.

Invariably, the Brill could be found carrying 60ft lengths of new rail or varying lengths of scrap rail. With a length of just 52ft, this meant that the rail loads would overhang the ends of the Brill, resulting in them having to operate with Bream runner wagons (see page 52). Repaints into yellow were underway by 1985 with initial wagons typically featuring grey solebars and bufferbeams, black only becoming common towards the end of the decade.

By March 1994, the number of Brill was down to 171, some having been converted into cable drum carriers while others had returned back to being BDA. This second trend was accelerated by EWS with a mass recoding back to the revenue earning fleet in the late 1990s, although affected wagons typically still ran in faded and battered yellow.

YLA Mullet/YQA Parr

In contrast to the Brill, the next type of bogie steel wagon was transferred en masse from the revenue fleet to the Civil Engineers in 1982. These bogie rail carriers, or Borails, were originally from batches built in 1959-61 and featured vacuum brakes. Once again, the need to retain part of the fleet into the 1980s and beyond saw 150 examples selected for refurbishment at Shildon Works between July 1981 and January 1982. The work included the fitting of air brakes and Y25C bogies while the sides and ends received steel strips to effectively create a one 'plank' high body. These sides acted as a mount for ratchet strap tensioners while the wooden planked floor was retained along with the bolsters. Repainted in Railfreight red, the modernised wagons were coded BRA and renumbered 967500-649.

By this time, the wagons had two main duties, the principal one being the movement of new 60ft rail lengths from steelworks, such as Workington, to BR depots, while they could also find employment carrying bridge beams and girders. As both duties were well within the remit of the Civil Engineers, the entire fleet was moved to departmental stock, becoming YLA Mullet. As a consequence, the BRA TOPS code became one of the shortest lived with some wagons having been refurbished for less than a year.

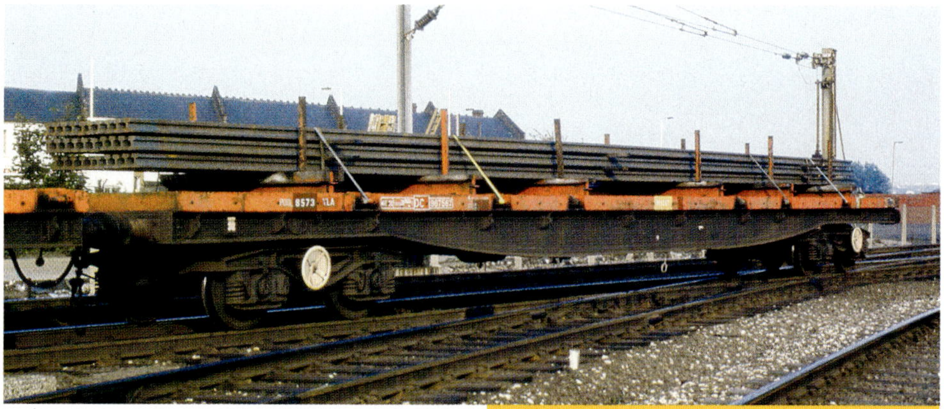

ABOVE: **Some 18 months or so after transferring to the Civil Engineers, DC967567 is seen at Mitre Bridge Junction, West London, in July 1984 with a load of new rail. Still carrying Railfreight red, the yellow-backed Mullet branding is positioned centrally on the side.** Simon Bendall Collection

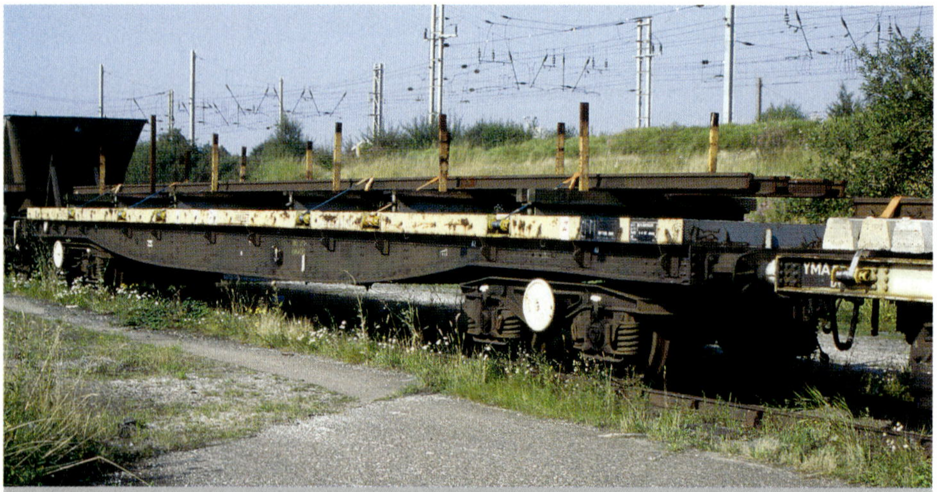

ABOVE: **The wagons became increasingly tatty as the years wore on and DC967510 is seen at Warrington Arpley on August 4, 1997, after a year in EWS ownership. Despite this, it is still in BR condition with the Mullet name on the yellow side and a Carlisle Currock depot sticker on the frame. This example has six ratchet tensioners, some had eight with an extra one at each end.** Trevor Mann

Many of the Mullet remained concentrated on moving new rails from the British Steel plant at Workington but they could also be seen carrying scrap rail for disposal at times. Livery wise, the normal pattern was followed with the Railfreight red initially retained and the requisite changes in branding applied, including the Mullet name in white on a yellow background.

Parr unveiled

Late 1985 saw an initial ten Mullet have their bolsters removed to be used on the Southern Region for carrying stacks of new concrete sleepers and, sometimes, 60ft track panels. To support the sleepers, heavy-duty timber baulks were laid longitudinally down each side of the wagon floor. As a result, DC96750 8/23/35/42/48/55/69/80/85 and DC967622 were renamed as Parr and coded YMA, taking the same TOPS code as used on air-braked Salmon. Interestingly, Parr is the name for young Salmon, showing that someone in the Civil Engineers department knew their fish!

These were also the first of the Borails to be repainted in grey and yellow, which saw the grey encompass the whole of the 'fish-belly' underframe with the black limited to just the bogies. Small lettering stating 'Load not to exceed 5 panels high' also appeared on the yellow sides. In later years, black would be more commonly used on the underframe as further wagons were repainted.

During mid-1990, another sizeable batch of YMA Parr was created to move concrete sleepers from the Costain manufacturing plant at Coltness, on the outskirts of Glasgow.

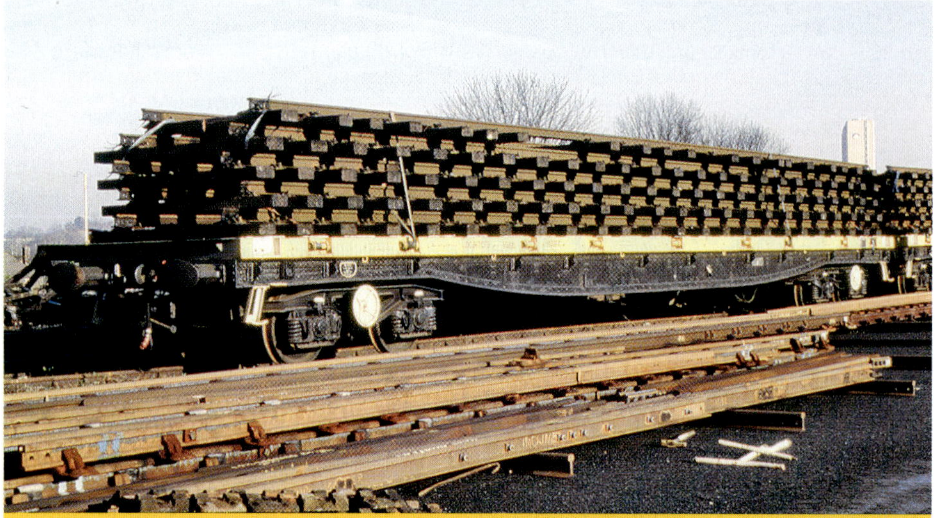

ABOVE: **Although the Parr are best known as sleeper carriers, they could carry 60ft track panels when required, as illustrated by DC967573 at Woking on January 8, 1990. Still coded YMA at this time, the load complies with the lettering to load no higher than five panels.** Roger Silsbury

Mulling over a Mullet by Mark Lambert

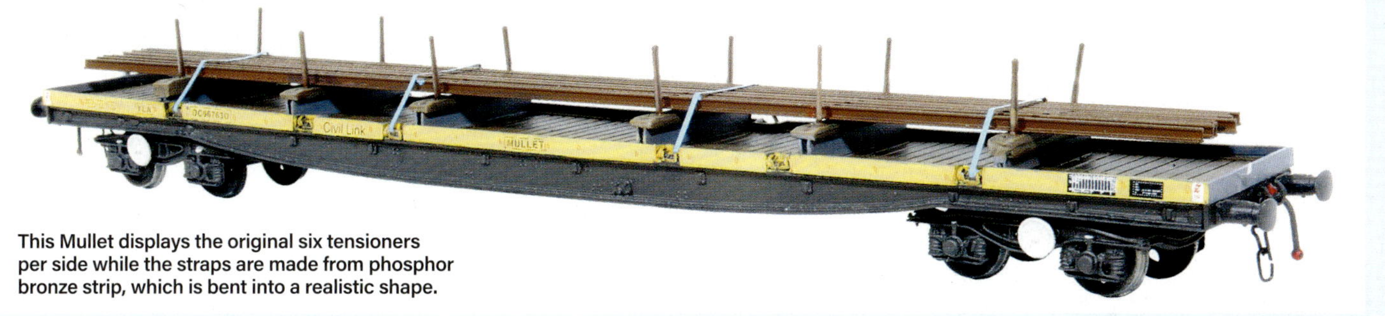

This Mullet displays the original six tensioners per side while the straps are made from phosphor bronze strip, which is bent into a realistic shape.

In the same way that the real wagons were refurbished, it is possible to replace the bogies on the 4mm scale Cambrian Borail EC/MB kit with Y25s from the same source. The newer one-piece mouldings with their nut and bolt fixings are a doddle to make and fit and allow this to be a far easier project than using the old three-piece bogie mouldings with the plastic pin.

Quite often with Cambrian bogie wagon kits, the floor comes in two parts. The nature of the Mullet conversion hides the join and the substantial underframe provides plenty of support, making this a solid wagon. The 'fish-belly' sides need to be filed to make sure they are square, which also correctly reduces the overall width slightly

The modernised wagons were furnished with low sides containing cut-outs for ratchet tensioners. Most wagons appear to have been given six cut-outs per side initially but at some point, those that stayed as Mullets often gained an extra two. I made the cut-outs before assembling the floor and underframe by taking a section out of the floor moulding for each one and fitting 10x125thou Evergreen strip to make the back and sides of the cut-out. These then need to be glued flush with the bottom of the floor before adding the rest of the new side pieces along the edge of the floor using the same plastic strip.

I added a second layer of plastic strip all along the sides once the first had cured, starting in the cut-outs again. This was fiddly but seemed to provide a more robust result.

The measurements for the cut-outs in both wagons were taken from drawings published in early editions of DEMU's Update magazine, while the ratchets themselves are S Kits castings.

Once the sides were dry, I laid longitudinal strips of 10 thou on the edges of the wagon floor in between the cutouts. On the real wagons, the planked floor was cut back and long timbers laid along the outer edge, so the strip represents this. On the first conversion, I used plastic cement to fix the strips but this caused them to sink into every plank moulding! With the second conversion, I filled the plank gaps first and then glued the strip on. Alternatively, you could use superglue to fix the longitudinal parts. The bolsters come with the kit and can be used without modification.

I used custom acrylic paint mixes for the yellow and a dark earth mix for the planks. For the underframe and bogies, I used the now discontinued Games Workshop colour 'Charadon Granite.' Army Painter produces a colour called 'Hardened Carapace' though, which is a good substitute. This gave me a faded and weathered wagon without the hassle of using weathering to fade the paint.

The load is 240mm lengths of C&L rail, superglued on and secured with phosphor bronze straps bent round the ratchets. On the wagon with two layers of rail, I added some 20x20 thou strip as stillage. The rail provides all the weight needed on this model. Transfers were from Appleby sheet 4T33 with overhead warning flashes from a Fox sheet, these being placed based on photos as no two Mullets were the same.

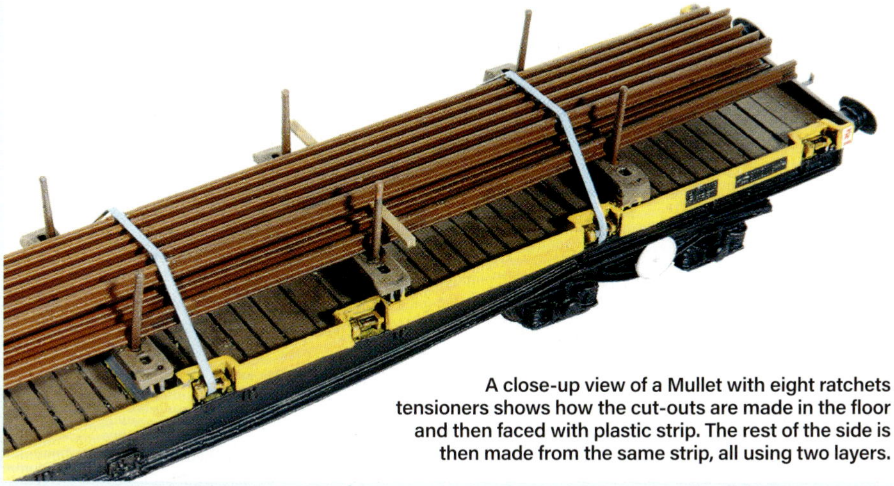

A close-up view of a Mullet with eight ratchets tensioners shows how the cut-outs are made in the floor and then faced with plastic strip. The rest of the side is then made from the same strip, all using two layers.

These were again stripped of their bolsters and fitted with baulks, their numbers being DC967500/02/03/34/41/52/56/58/60-62/71/81/94/99 and DC967601/09/11/15/16/18/23/39/42-47/49. However, by the end of the year, the potential for confusion with the TOPS code had clearly become apparent and all the Parr were re-coded as YQA. Further conversions would follow so that by March 1994, there were 80 Mullet and 69 Parr with one wagon withdrawn.

Both types remained in use throughout the existence of EWS, the company converting some of the Parr into Super Tench by adding low-height steel bodywork with mesh doors. The remaining Parr were withdrawn early in the 2010s but a much reduced fleet of Mullet and Super Tench still remain in use today with DB Cargo.

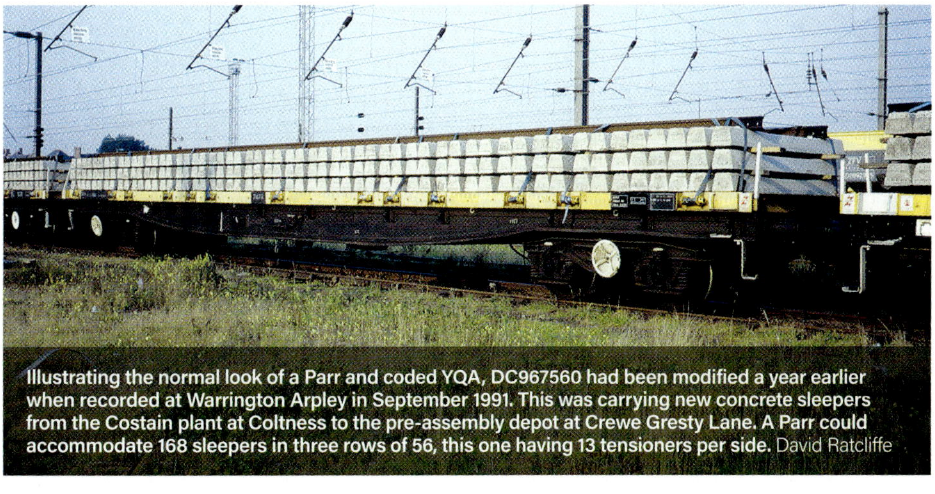

Illustrating the normal look of a Parr and coded YQA, DC967560 had been modified a year earlier when recorded at Warrington Arpley in September 1991. This was carrying new concrete sleepers from the Costain plant at Coltness to the pre-assembly depot at Crewe Gresty Lane. A Parr could accommodate 168 sleepers in three rows of 56, this one having 13 tensioners per side. David Ratcliffe

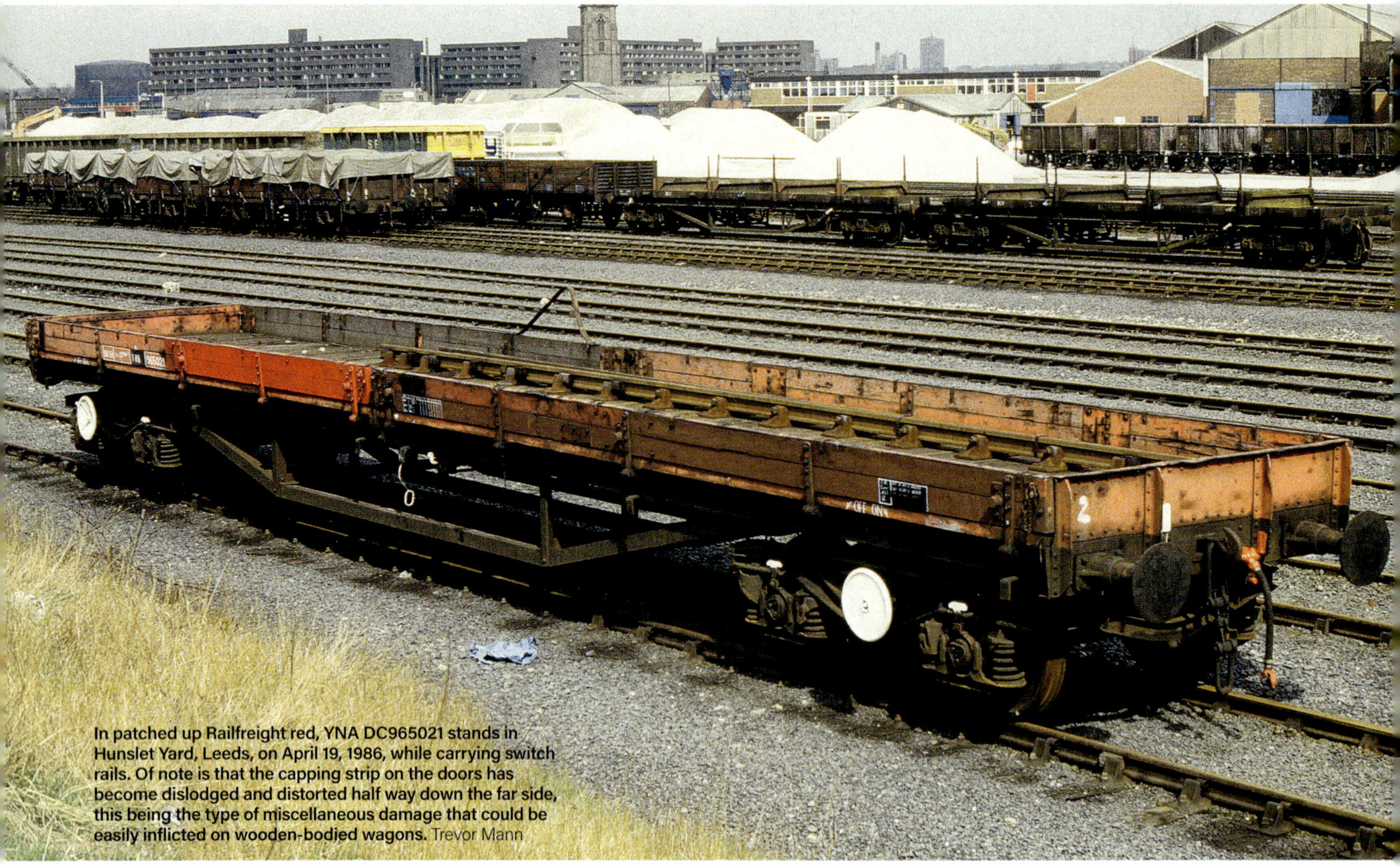

In patched up Railfreight red, YNA DC965021 stands in Hunslet Yard, Leeds, on April 19, 1986, while carrying switch rails. Of note is that the capping strip on the doors has become dislodged and distorted half way down the far side, this being the type of miscellaneous damage that could be easily inflicted on wooden-bodied wagons. Trevor Mann

YNA Boplate

The third type of bogie steel wagon to be transferred to Civil Engineers stock was some of the BPA Boplate fleet. These had begun life as unfitted or vacuum-braked bogie wagons for the movement of steel plate and other similar loads and featured a pair of two-plank doors on each side. During 1980/81, 80 wagons were selected for modernisation at Shildon, this bringing the fitting of air brakes and Y25C bogies along with a repaint in Railfreight red. A new TOPS code of BPA was applied while they were renumbered as 965000-079.

During 1984, 30 of these wagons were released to engineers' use, 965000-25/27-30 being recoded as YNA and given DC number prefixes. Surprisingly, no fish name was ever assigned to the type, making them one of the largest groups of Civil Engineers wagons to go un-christened. A handful of further transfers would occur later in the decade with some YNA gaining a coat of grey/yellow while others remained in red, the paintwork getting increasingly distressed as the doors were repaired over time.

Never the most conspicuous of types in engineers' use, they tended to carry specialist rail loads such as point vees and switch rails, which could just lie on the deck without restraint as their own weight and the low sides would retain them. After unremarkable careers, the YNA passed to EWS ownership in 1996 with some returning to their BPA codes; both versions continuing in use until the mid-late 2000s.

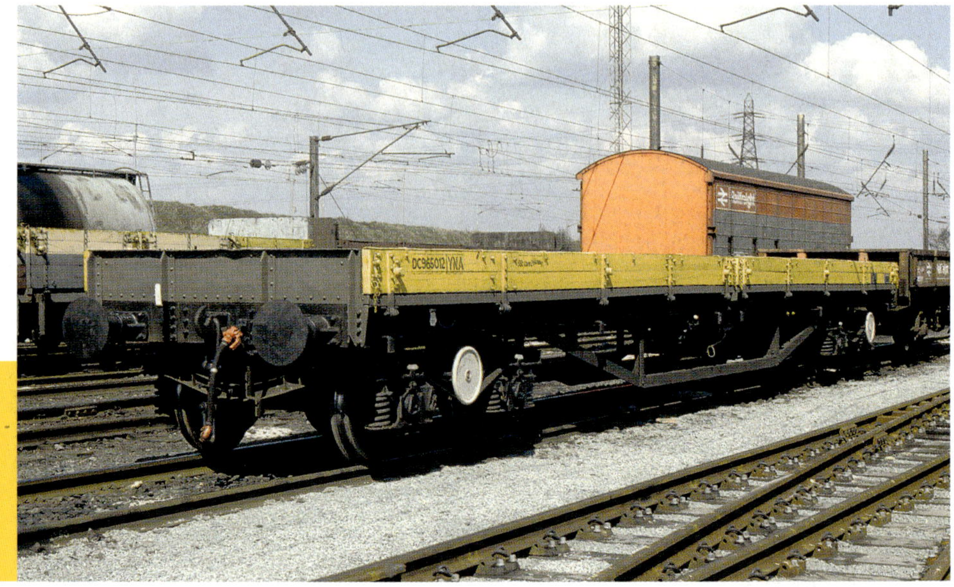

RIGHT: The YNAs looked particularly good in grey and yellow, the bright doors contrasting nicely with the rest of the grey bodywork, not that they stayed this way for long. A relatively freshly-painted DC965012 was residing at Walton Old Junction, Warrington, on April 15, 1989, in the company of a tatty ZAA Pike still in Railfreight red and a faded ZDA Bass behind. Trevor Mann

Building some Boplates by Mark Lambert

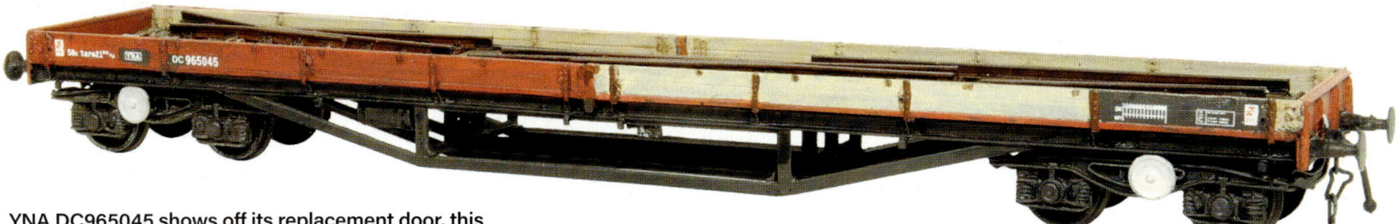

YNA DC965045 shows off its replacement door, this using a sand colour to represent unpainted wood.

These YNAs are another 4mm scale kit from the Cambrian range, being built straight from the packet and only replacing the buffers with castings from Lanarkshire Models and Supplies. As most of the parts come from the Bogie Bolster D kit, some care is needed to get the floor square and flat and ensure all the underframe trusses correctly line up.

After a good clean-up with a file of the flash on the parts, it is best to build the underframe to the upside down floor and let it dry before trying to fit the sides and ends to make sure everything is square and level. Once the floor is done though, this is an easy kit to put together, and the taller sides do give it a bit more rigidity than the bolster wagon kit.

I painted one of my YNAs in grey/yellow and the other in a variation of red with a replacement door. The photo I used for the latter actually had both doors on one side in unpainted wood, but I thought that might not look realistic on a model, so I only did one door as unpainted. This was completed with black patches for the lettering as per the real thing. The other door was painted in quite a dark red colour, certainly not Railfreight red which has a slight orange tint, as by the early 1990s, repaints of wagons would often use whatever was to hand.

I used Games Workshop acrylics straight from the pot for the red wagon, including a sand colour for the fresh timbers and a dark brown for all the metalwork, but for the 'Dutch' livery I mixed a custom yellow and grey to mimic a faded finish.

The load in one is scrap rail and sleepers, this using C&L offcuts, and laser-cut sleepers by Scale Model Scenery with a small sprinkling of ballast, all held down with canopy glue, which is a white glue that dries clear. The red YNA is carrying two point vees among its mixed load, these again coming from C&L. The transfers came from Appleby sheet 4T33 with the overhead warning flashes from a Fox pack. As usual, I put the transfers onto an area painted with gloss varnish and then gave the whole wagon a coat of gloss to seal the transfers, before spraying with matt varnish.

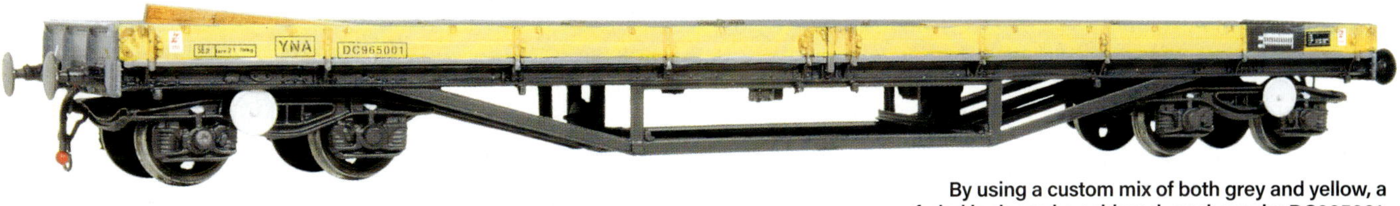

By using a custom mix of both grey and yellow, a faded look can be achieved, as shown by DC965001.

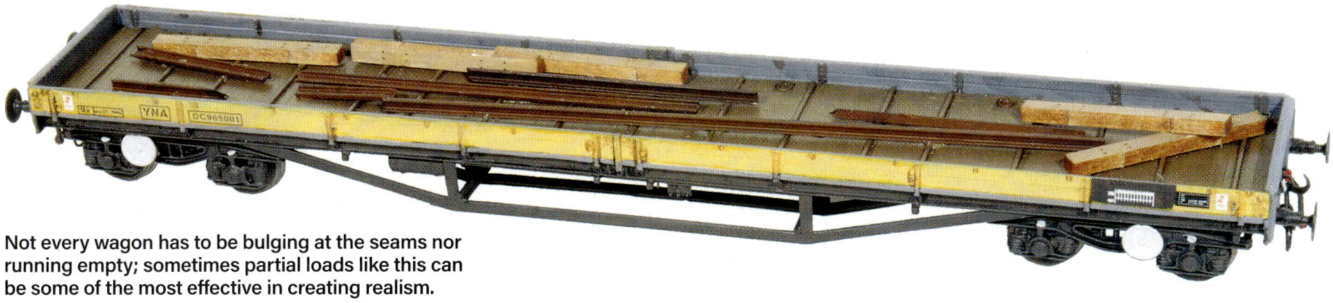

Not every wagon has to be bulging at the seams nor running empty; sometimes partial loads like this can be some of the most effective in creating realism.

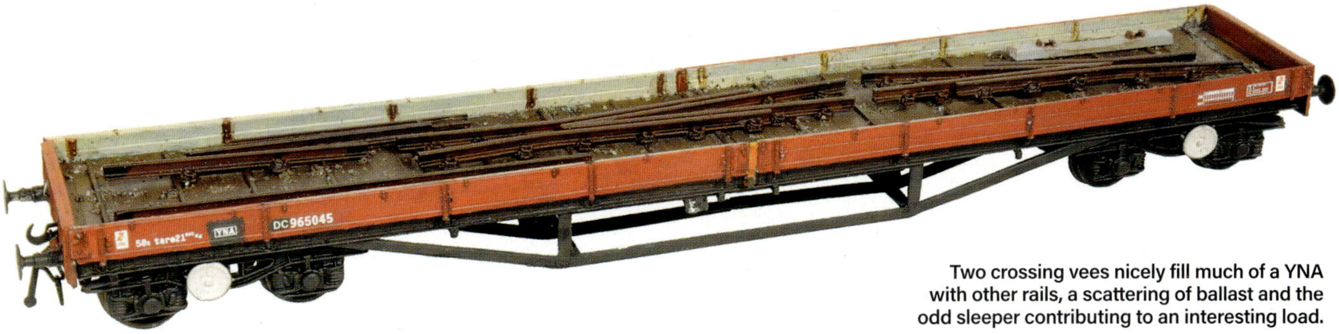

Two crossing vees nicely fill much of a YNA with other rails, a scattering of ballast and the odd sleeper contributing to an interesting load.

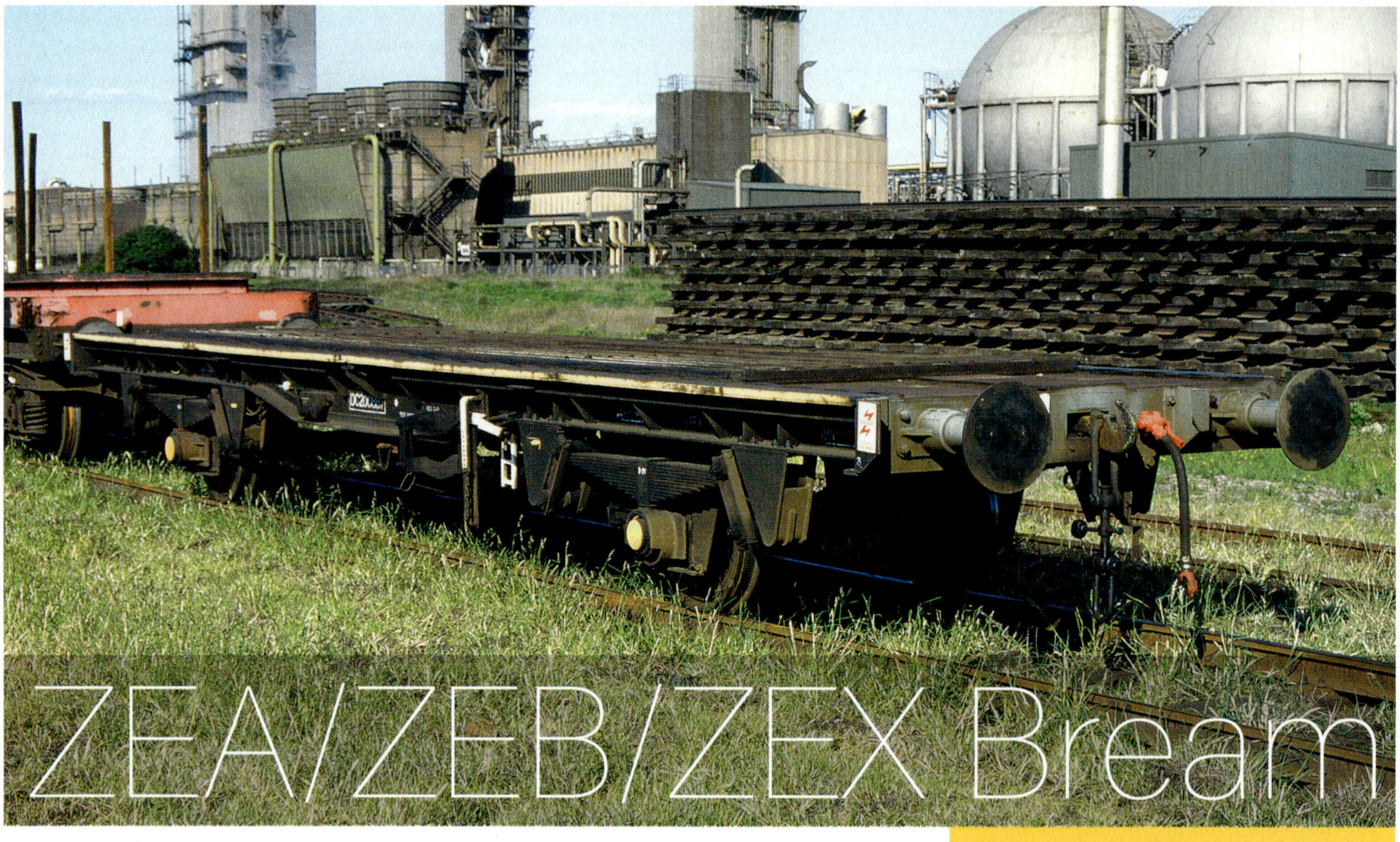

ZEA/ZEB/ZEX Bream

ABOVE: **The most numerous of the Bream were those converted from VDA vans by removing the body and adding scrap rail to the deck. DC200887 is seen at Tees Dock on May 27, 1996, at the dawn of its EWS ownership and yet to be recoded as RRA. Although finished in grey and yellow, this was largely limited to the edge of the floor and bufferbeam, respectively. Other examples had the solebars fully painted in yellow instead of black.** Trevor Mann

With the transfer of many air-braked Bogie Bolster D and all of the Boplates to the Civil Engineers, a new fleet of similarly equipped runner wagons was required to work with them. This also needed to be larger than before due to the under-length YAA Brill being regularly used to carry 60ft rails, a job that the likes of the more suitable Gane and older Salmon had previously performed before being replaced by these newcomers.

The fish name Bream was assigned to a number of different wagon types, but the key characteristic was that they had a flat deck. This allowed them to be positioned beneath overhanging loads without any problems with clearance and enabled coupling to take place normally at the outer end. The vast majority of Bream were two-axle types, but a handful of Bogie Bolster C were used in the 1980s, these having lost their bolsters and gained a through air-pipe. One of these was pictured in volume one of this series.

By mid-1984, three VCA and 18 VDA vans had already become RRA runners due to their bodies having suffered damage that was uneconomic to repair. These were all recalled to Derby Litchurch Lane that summer to be transferred to the Civil Engineers fleet, becoming ZEA. The main alteration was the addition of lengths of scrap rail to the deck to increase their tare weight, the previously bare chassis having been deemed too light. These initial Bream were ex VCA 200402/470/478 and ex VDA 200659/672/734/761/764/777/852/914/916/927/946 and 210210/225/231/251/273/295/333.

During early 1985, further redundant VDA vans were put through Doncaster Works to be stripped of their bodies and receive rails for additional weight, the arrangement of these differing slightly from the Derby batch. By the time the project was completed, 71 more Bream existed.

Other donors

A much simpler method of creating Bream was to transfer some of the SAA two-axle steel carrying flat wagons, a number of which were still looking for work after being found to be unsuitable for their planned role due to instability at speed. Just over 30 examples became ZEA with their numbers spread throughout the 400000-299 series. Any retaining their fold down end flaps had them removed for clearance reasons while most, but by no means all, also surrendered their hinged side stanchions.

The other wagons to be drafted in as

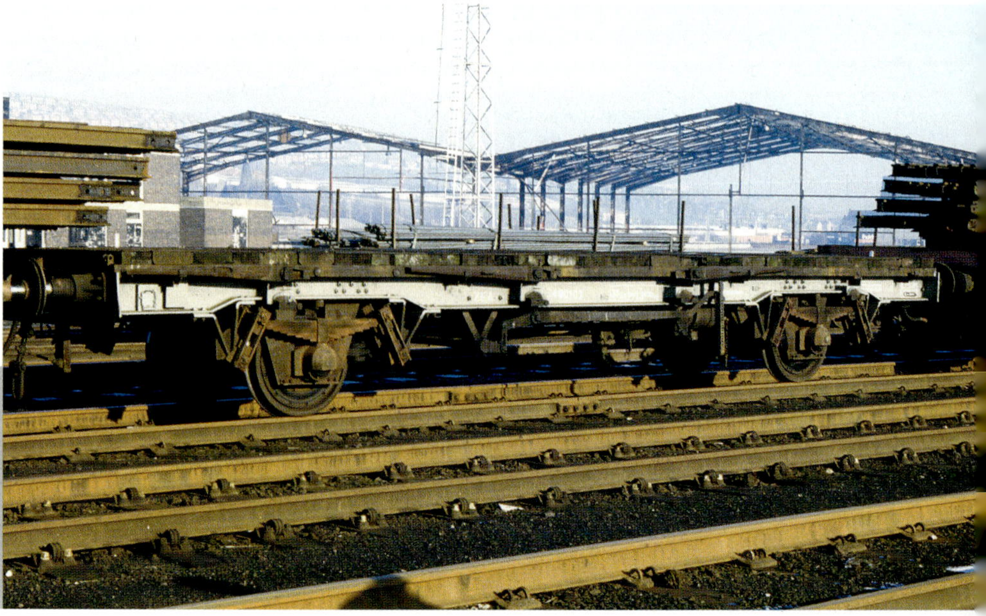

RIGHT: **DC400107 had seen little alteration from its days as one of the ill-fated SAA steel carriers when recorded at Sheffield Freight Terminal on January 26, 1986, as a ZEA Bream. While the end flaps have gone, it still retains its hinged stanchions in their lowered position along the sides. If ground staff were feeling mischievous, the runners could sometimes be seen operating with these raised.** Trevor Mann

I have a Bream

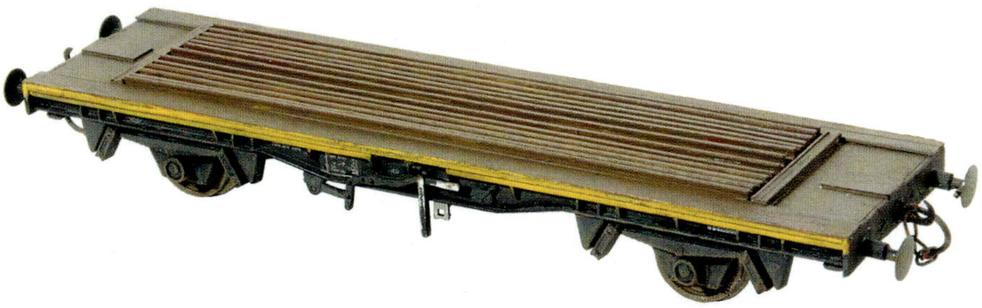

The Bachmann VDA offers a route to recreating the Bream conversions from the vans. With the body discarded, the pivoting axles have been fixed in position to improve the look of the wagon but could equally be replaced by etched W-irons and new whitemetal axleboxes to go even further. Meanwhile, the top of the chassis moulding has been cladded in plastic sheet around the edges to represent the metal plating that was added, including the raised sections over the couplings.

Lengths of Code 75 rail were cut to the necessary length and then progressively glued in place after test fitting. Typically, the pair of rails in the centre had wider gaps around them and this is reflected on the model. Final touches included adding Instanter couplings and surplus Heljan air pipes while the yellow and black were Humbrol with a rusty mix concocted for the deck. Appleby transfers completed.

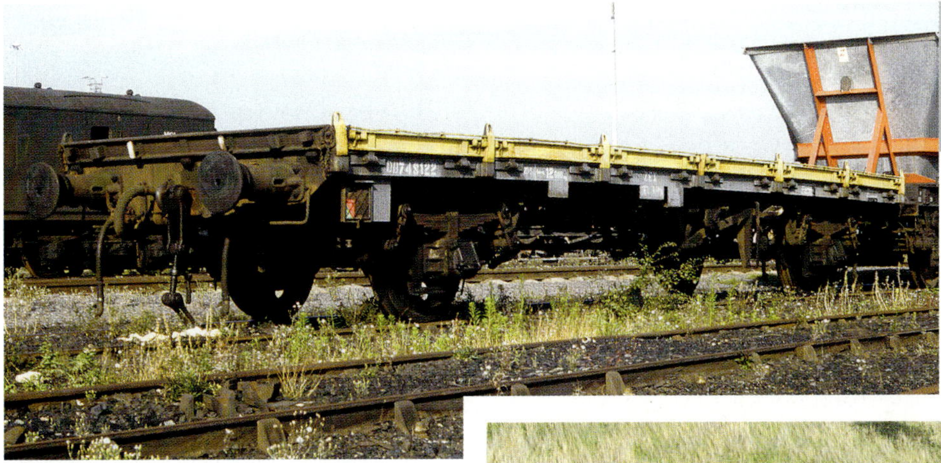

LEFT: **The Carfit C required no alterations at all for their Bream role beyond cosmetic concerns. Coded ZEX due to its dual brakes, DB748122 displays the full grey and yellow look at Toton Yard on September 20, 1986.** Trevor Mann

BELOW: **DB787422 was built as a pallet van for transferring Ford automotive components between the company's UK sites. By October 13, 1985, it had been reduced to a chassis at Tinsley Yard, becoming a ZEB, and was accompanying a YLA Mullet out of shot to the left. This image perfectly illustrates the role that the Bream played in allowing overhanging engineers' loads to move about the network.** Trevor Mann

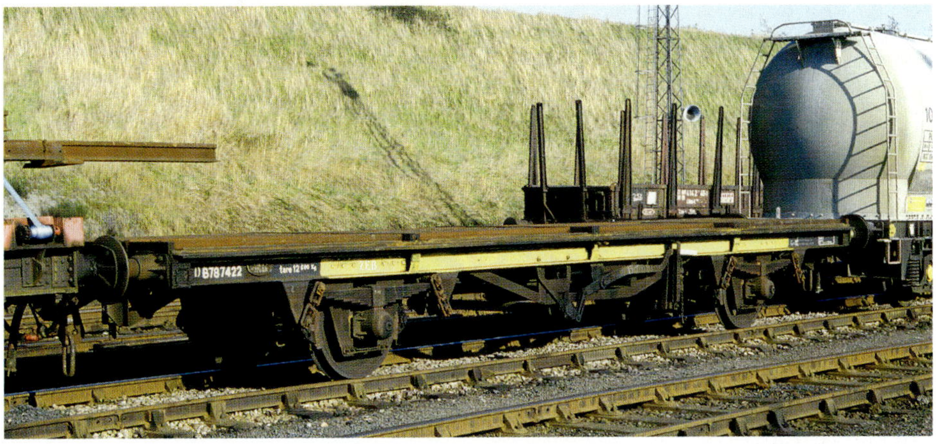

runners were more of a mixed bag. This included examples of the 40-strong Carfit C fleet, which had originally been built in 1958 to diagram 1/092 for train ferry traffic and numbered B748110-149. These dual-braked 20-ton flats required no alterations beyond a number prefix tweak and a new TOPS code of ZEX. Next were examples of the diagram 1/235 long-wheelbase pallet vans displaced from Ford traffic, specifically the VQB batch that was built in 1966 with air-brakes. These had lost their bodies in 1984 for use as runners on revenue traffic but many were surrendered to the engineers' fleet the following year, becoming ZEB.

Lastly, and the most obscure were five BR Plate wagon chassis that had previously lost their bodywork and gained air brakes and long-link suspension for carrying coal containers in Scotland. Coded FPB at the time, B934398, B935416/653/793 and B936129 became ZEB in late 1984.

The liveries on these five types were as diverse as their origins with a mix of grey, black, and yellow predominating in varying quantities. The two ZEA fleets in particular struggled to find a consistent look, some having just a thin strip of yellow while others received all-yellow solebars. Several examples of the ZEX Carfits made it through to EWS ownership along with a much smaller number of the two ZEB types but official withdrawal came around 2000. In contrast, both ZEA types were still very useful, and some remain in traffic today with DB Cargo, although recoded as RRA.

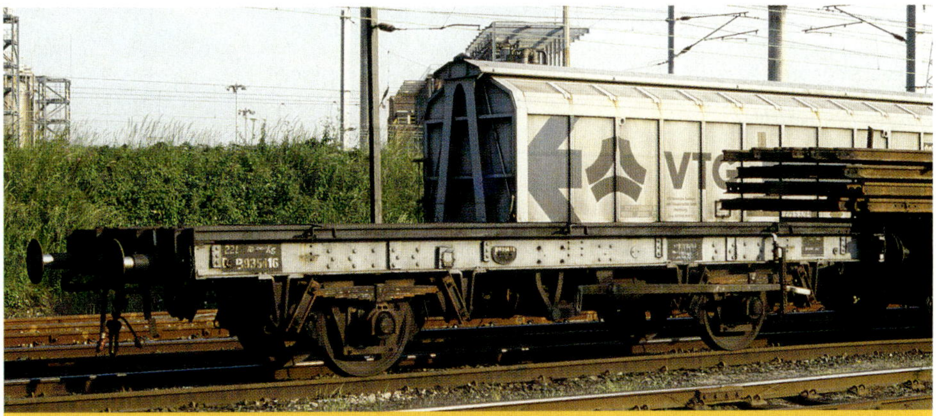

ABOVE: **The former Plate wagon chassis that was DB935416 shows off its modified suspension and air brakes at Walton Old Junction, Warrington, on June 18, 1989. This had been modernised for its previous role of carrying coal containers while the grey look was standard for these ZEB.** Trevor Mann

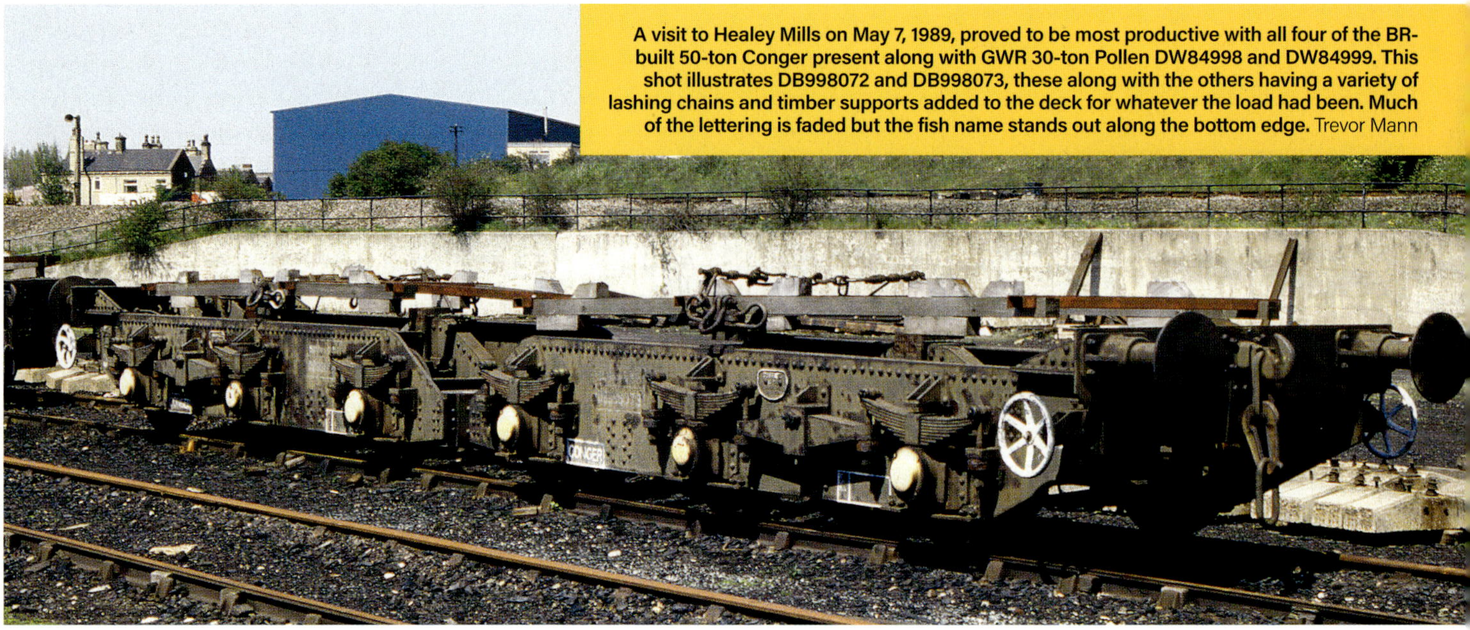

A visit to Healey Mills on May 7, 1989, proved to be most productive with all four of the BR-built 50-ton Conger present along with GWR 30-ton Pollen DW84998 and DW84999. This shot illustrates DB998072 and DB998073, these along with the others having a variety of lashing chains and timber supports added to the deck for whatever the load had been. Much of the lettering is faded but the fish name stands out along the bottom edge. Trevor Mann

YVO Conger/Pollen

These next vehicles are rather out of place in this section, being unfitted and not new transfers, but are included for completeness along with the involvement of air-braked stock at the end of their careers.

Pollen was the name given by the Great Western Railway to a series of vehicles developed from 1885 onwards to carry long heavy loads. As the design progressed, they essentially took the form of a pair or quartet of bogies that could be positioned at each end of a long load to enable it to move by rail, such as bridge girders of varying sizes.

In 1909 the Pollen E appeared, this being a set of four six-wheel bogies that were articulated together to form a wagon measuring 82ft 6in over headstocks. Initially assigned diagram A6, 84997 to 85000 were provided to carry gun barrels for naval battleships, a pair of special cradles being provided to hold the barrel on top

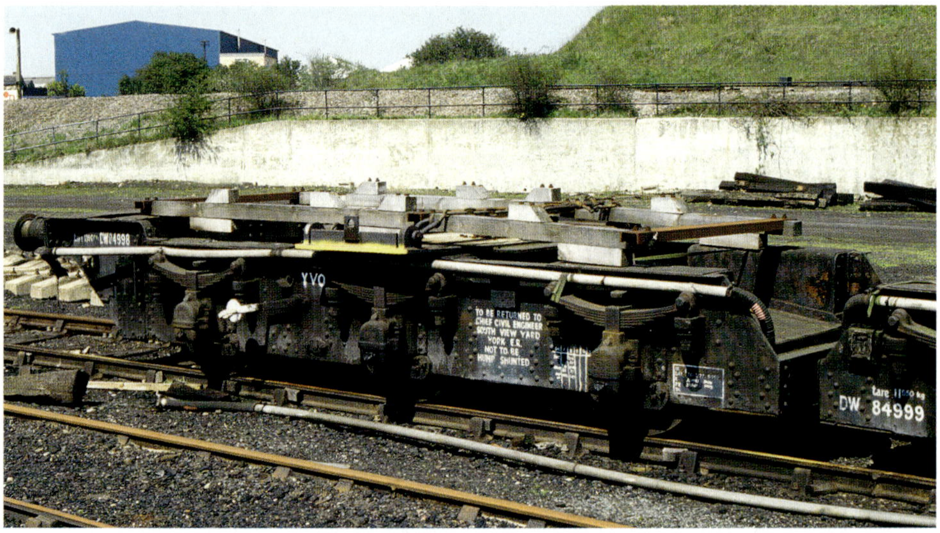

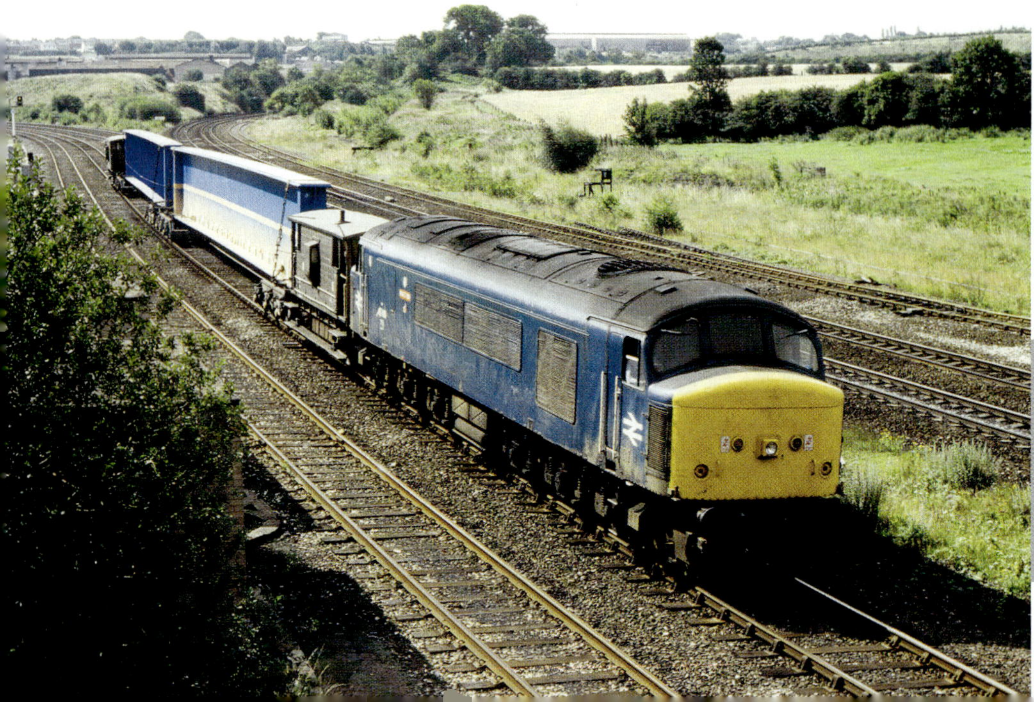

ABOVE: **In contrast, the lettering on Pollen DW84998 was much fresher, the instructions reading 'To be returned to Chief Civil Engineer South View Yard York ER. Not to be hump shunted.' Notably both it and DW84999 have been fitted with a through vacuum pipe, this being the grey pipe running down the side with flexible connections at each end. The work had clearly stopped for the weekend as another through pipe is lying on the ground alongside. The two types were easy to tell apart, even from a distance, as the Pollen had the Dean Churchward ratchet handbrake levers while the Conger had conventional handbrake wheels at the outer ends.** Trevor Mann

LEFT: **Both Conger sets are seen in action as 45149 *Phaeton* traverses Clay Cross Junction at a sedate pace during August 1987. The vehicles are carrying two substantial bridge beams with a brake van at each end. As these moves ran without a continuous train brake, they were heavily restricted in both speed and consequently the time of day when they could move.** Trevor Mann Collection

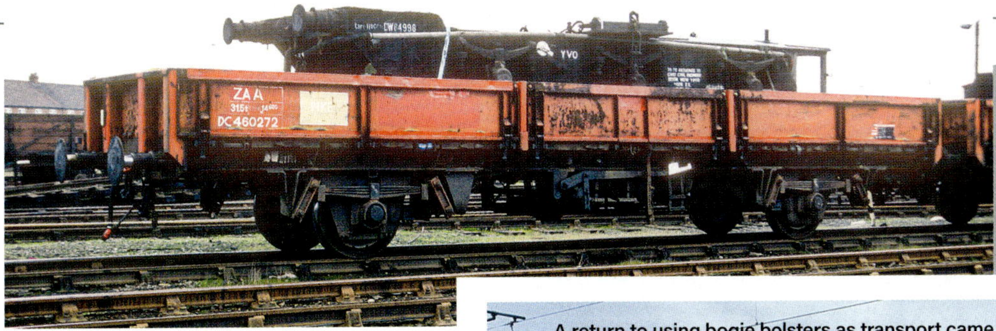

LEFT: **Illustrating the mid-1980s period when Pike were used to carry the bridge beam sets, DC460272 stands at York Leeman Road on February 20, 1988, with DW84998 loaded aboard while DW84999 is on another ZAA to the right.** Paul Bartlett

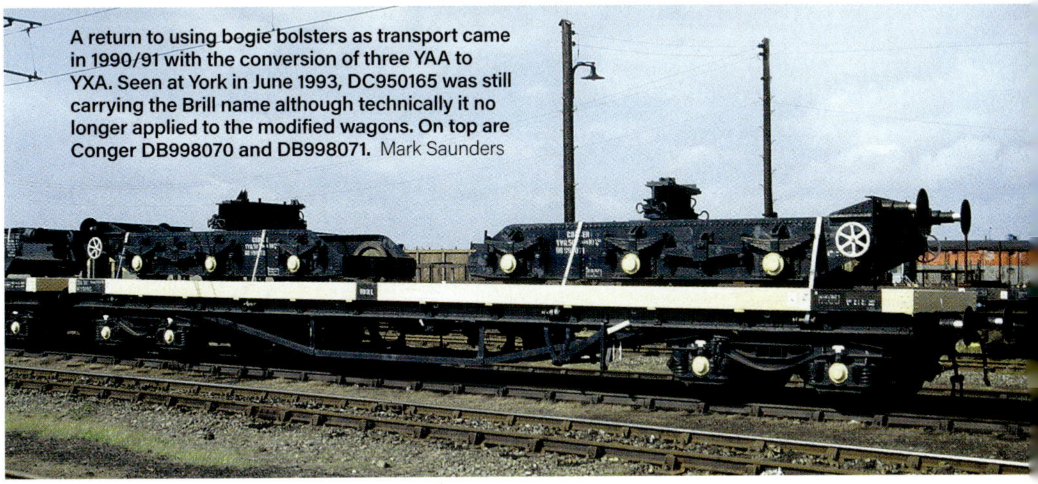

A return to using bogie bolsters as transport came in 1990/91 with the conversion of three YAA to YXA. Seen at York in June 1993, DC950165 was still carrying the Brill name although technically it no longer applied to the modified wagons. On top are Conger DB998070 and DB998071. Mark Saunders

of the wagons. The Pollen E could also be configured to carry industrial boilers weighing up to 120-tons.

Modifications were made to the set in 1930 with the pair of intermediate wagons, 84998/99, receiving removable buffers and drawgear. This allowed the four vehicles to be split and operate as two independent pairs when required, each capable of carrying 60-tons. Due to the modifications, new diagram numbers were issued with 84998/99 being diagram A9 and the original outer pair of 84997 and 85000 forming A10. The Pollen E were retained by BR, eventually passing to the Civil Engineers and becoming YVO DW84997-DW85000. Withdrawal came in 1996, 87 years after construction. All four are now part of the National Collection based at Didcot.

BR build

A number of girder-carrying sets were built by BR as part of its special wagons fleet, which were available for use by the Civil Engineers when required. However, a more heavy-duty quartet were constructed at Ashford Works late in 1970 to diagram 2/151, these being numbered DB998070-073 and coded YVO Conger. Operating as two pairs, each set was rated to carry up to 100-tons and again featured six wheels on each vehicle. The design was similar to the Pollen E but with modern enhancements such as roller bearings and hydraulic buffers.

As the railway was progressively modernised and speeds increased, the Pollen and Conger were an operational inconvenience with their lack of brakes and unconventional design. While this was unavoidable on the occasions they actually had to move bridge girders, it could be overcome when they were empty by loading them onto other wagons with Bogie Bolster C utilised initially. This method of transportation was updated to air-braked stock in the mid-1980s with both the Pollen and Conger being loaded into ZAA Pike when required, although this only allowed one YVO per wagon instead of two when bogie bolsters were employed.

A return to bolster wagon transportation came in 1990 when two YAA Brill, DC950153 and DC950165, were modified to carry the bridge bean sets to and from their York base. Both were recoded YXA to reflect the removal of their bolsters and other modifications made to their decks while a third example, DC950047, followed shortly after. Also provided at this time was former VCA van DC200511, which became a support vehicle to carry the specialist lifting tackle to get the bridge sets on and off the wagons. Notably, at some point, the Pollen name appears to have been dropped for the GWR examples with all referred to as Conger despite their different load capacities. The BR Conger also fell out of use in the mid-1990s but still passed to EWS ownership, being scrapped in the early 2000s after prolonged storage at York. ●

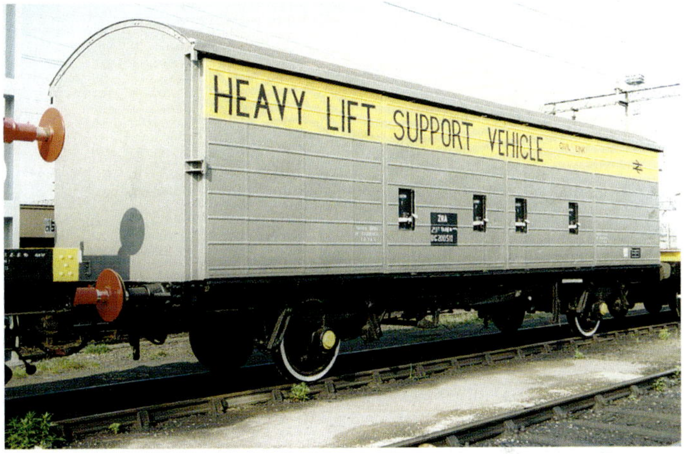

RIGHT: **Newly repainted ZRA DC200511 displays its 'Heavy Lift Support Vehicle' branding along with much smaller Civil Link lettering at the Bescot open day in June 1990, this carrying all the chains, tackle and other equipment required to lift the wagons from their transport. The bridge beam sets made several open day appearances around this time, the Civil Engineers department doubtless being keen to show off its new image.** Colin Wright/David Ratcliffe Collection

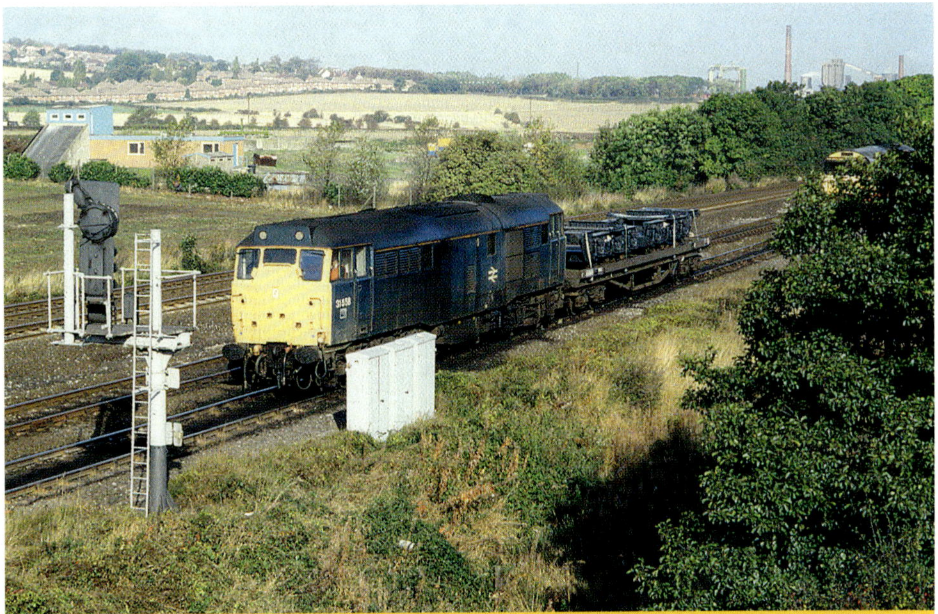

ABOVE: **Immingham's 31558 awaits the road at Tupton, south of Chesterfield, and the passing of the Class 58 that is emerging from behind the bushes in the summer of 1990. In tow is an air-braked Bogie Bolster D carrying two of the Pollen wagons on modified wooden blocks and strapped to the deck. This may well be one of the modified Brill prior to being recoded as YXA and receiving a repaint.** Simon Bendall Collection

Civil Engineers' oddballs

If there was one thing that the various BR engineering departments was good at, it was creating 'oddball' wagons that were designed for a specific role. These were usually completely unique or, occasionally, existed in twos or threes. Simon Bendall takes a look at some that fell under the remit of the Civil Engineers or its successors.

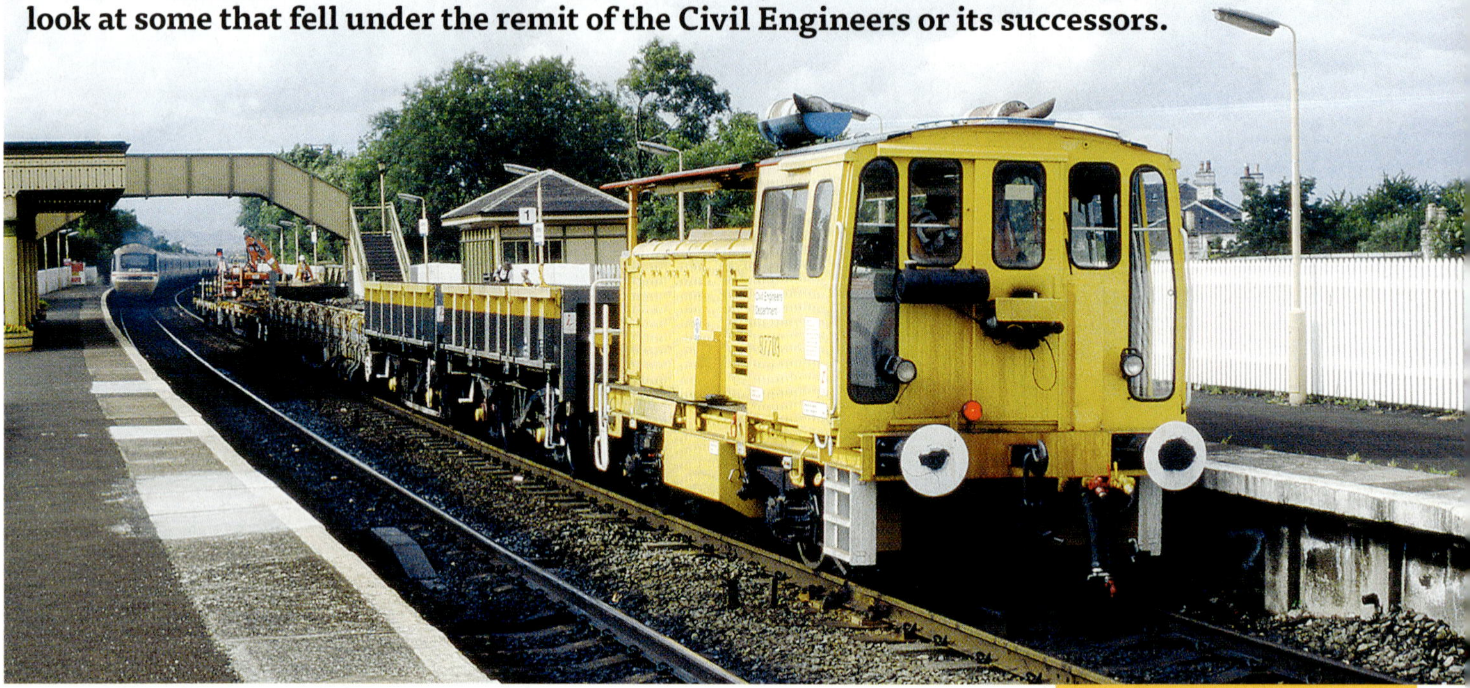

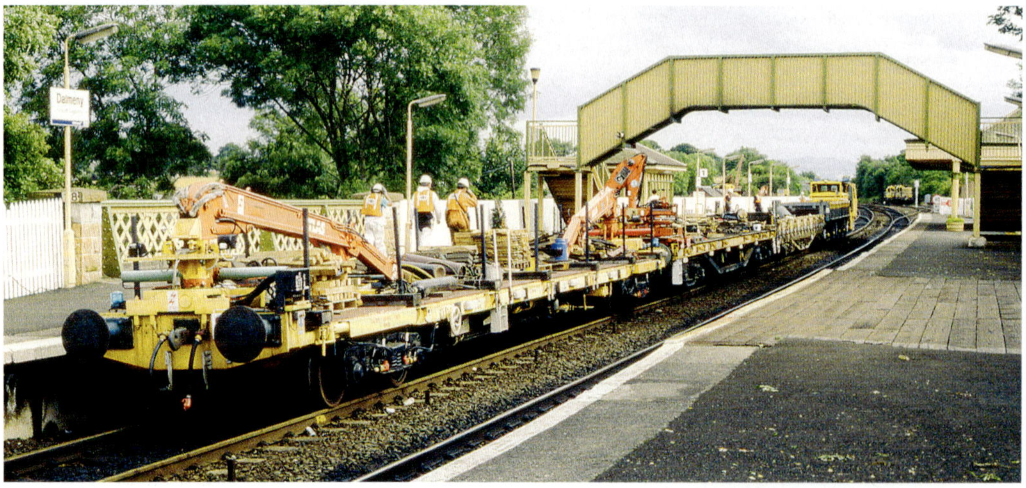

ABOVE & LEFT: **The rarely-pictured Forth Bridge maintenance train is recorded in action at Dalmeny on July 19, 1996, headed by 97603, although incorrectly numbered 97703. Three such 'locomotives' had been converted at Kilmarnock in 1986 from the power units of scrapped ballast cleaners for use as depot shunters. While they spent long periods out of use, 97603 eventually found a home based at Dalmeny while 97601/97701 was employed in a similar role at Dundee to power the Tay Bridge maintenance train. The second picture shows the train from the rear with the wagons being just as interesting as the traction. Nearest the camera is a converted ex-Freightliner flat DC611852, which has received drawgear at both ends and a sizeable Atlas hydraulic crane for use as a materials carrier. Next in line is Salmon DB996945 with a similar crane, the decks of both wagons being festooned with a wide range of materials and equipment, while making up the rest of the train is a YPA Tench and two ZBA Rudd. A second crane-fitted Salmon, DB996985, was also allocated to Dalmeny and the stowed crane of this can just be glimpsed behind the fence above the Tench. All three wagons were coded YXA and also numbered in the Civil Engineers Plant System (CEPS), the Salmon being 66300/01 while the former FGA was 66400.** Simon Bendall Collection

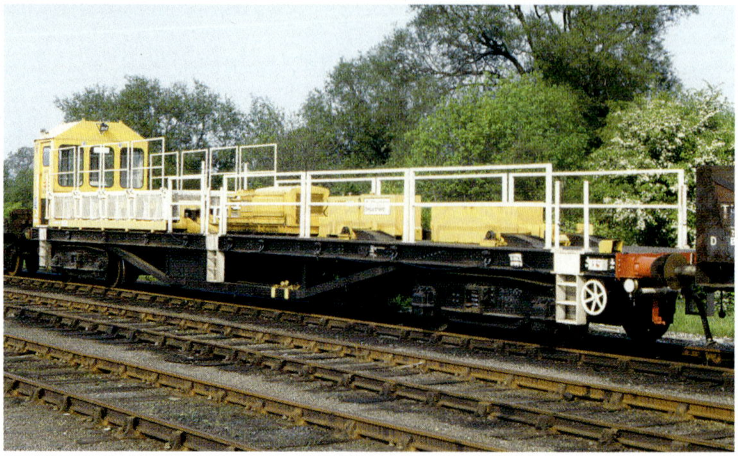

RIGHT: **Salmon DB996829 is seen at York Dringhouses yard on May 25, 1987, following conversion to a rail recovery winch unit, which has seen it also gain the CEPS number of 64007. Similar in concept to the Grampus and Tunny sets covered in part one of this series but the Eastern Region version, this was equipped with a diesel-powered winch to drag lengths of recovered rail onto its deck with rollers installed to help move them along. An operator's cabin was provided at the far end, this offering protection should the cable snap.** Trevor Mann

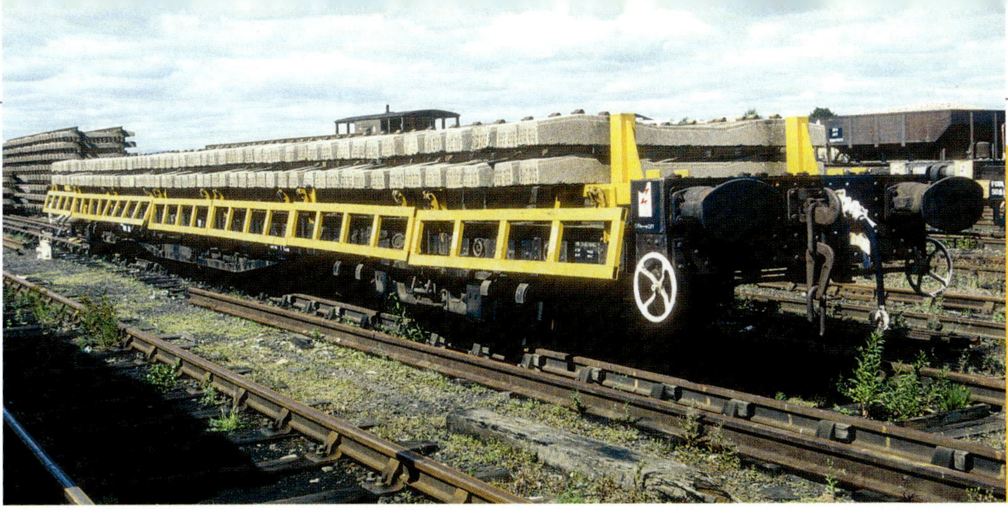

LEFT: **Sturgeon DB994176 is seen at Perth on August 1, 1989, after an experimental conversion into a concrete sleeper carrier. Its deck has been extensively modified with profiled bolsters to support the sleepers with new stanchions at the ends to prevent movement. Most obvious though are the new doors made of steel channel section to retain the load, which are seen here lowered. Coded YBQ, the wagon was unfitted but with a through air pipe. Seemingly over-complicated, especially the door hinges, it remained a one-off.** Paul Bartlett

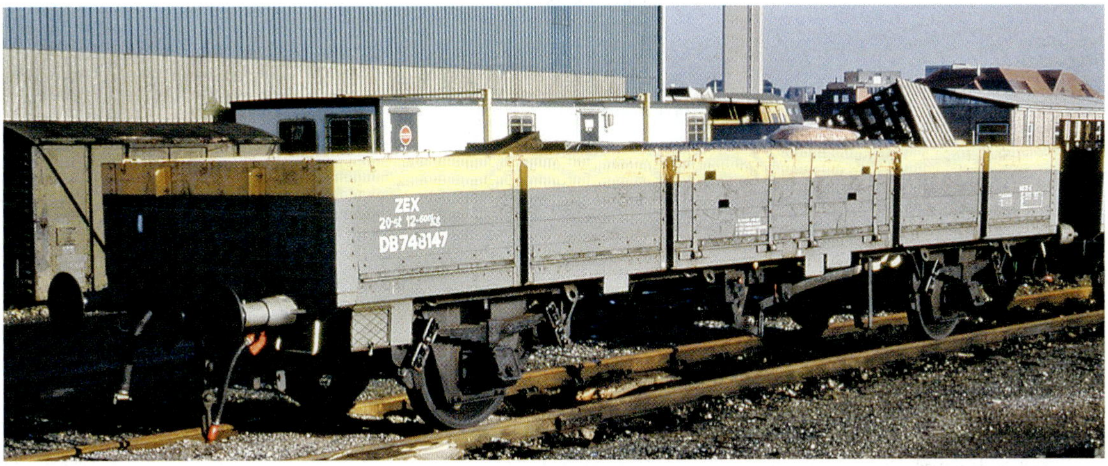

RIGHT: **Bearing some similarities to the Chub, two ferry-fitted Carfit C flat wagons were rebuilt at New Cross Gate in late 1982 with three-plank sides and ends. The sides incorporated a centrally-positioned and wide drop door and was seemingly an attempt to repurpose the useful dual-braked underframes. Never given a fish name, DB748147 is seen at Woking pre-assembly depot on January 8, 1990, carrying a TOPS code of ZEX and loaded with assorted rubbish. Its sister wagon, DB748126, is off to the right and was more appropriately lettered as a ZXX.** Roger Silsbury

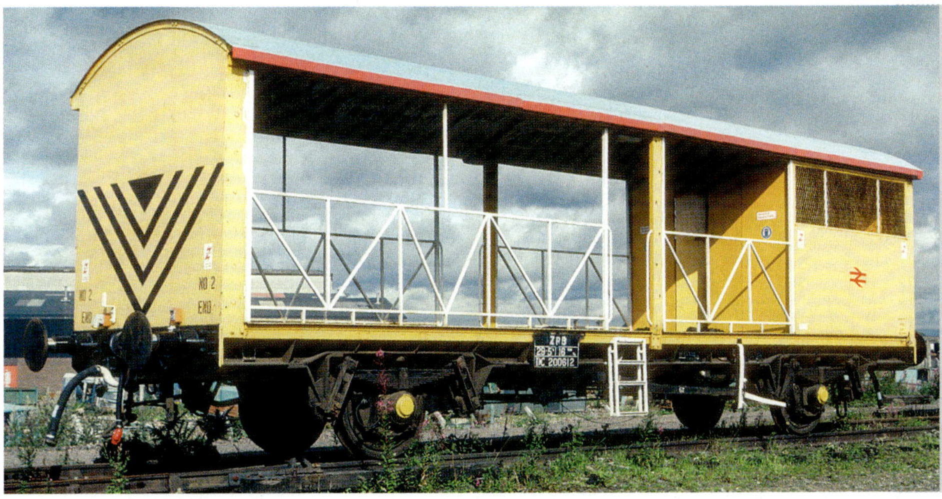

LEFT: **The summer of 1991 saw two air-braked vans converted into generator wagons at Polmadie for use with Sealion and Seacow ballast hoppers modified with electric lighting. These lost their sides with a compartment provided at one end to house the generator set and its fuel tank. Also fitted with a through vacuum-pipe, ex-VBA DC200612 and former VDA DC200875 were recoded as ZXB although, when the former was photographed at Mossend on August 13, 1991, it was incorrectly lettered ZRB. Neither appears to have seen much, if any, use in their intended role and were withdrawn by the mid-1990s.** Paul Bartlett

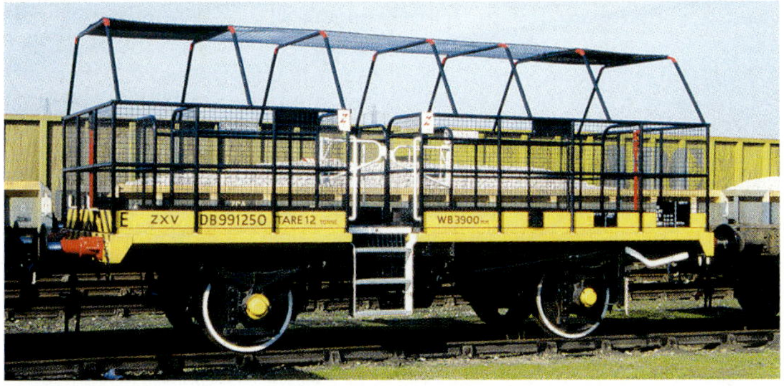

ABOVE: **Another conversion that proved of little value was that of ZCV Crab DB991250 into a ZXV propelling control vehicle. Completed at Ashford plant depot in the summer of 1994, this was intended as a riding vehicle for the shunter whilst controlling propelling movements by radio instead of walking alongside the moving train. Built for use within engineering possessions, the wagon was also equipped with a brake valve for use in an emergency. With most stock on the Southern being air-braked by this date, it was of limited use; a second conversion involving a more appropriate Rudd never coming to fruition. Seemingly deemed operationally inconvenient, it languished at Hoo Junction for several years, where it is seen on April 9, 1996.** Trevor Mann

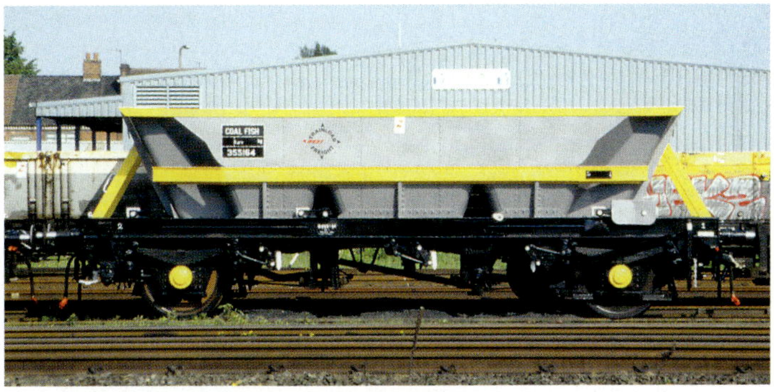

ABOVE: **Outshopped from Burton wagon works at the beginning of privatisation were three HAA hoppers converted into a new type of ballast wagon dubbed Coalfish. Funded by Trainload Freight West, later to become Transrail, the work involved cutting down the hopper body in a similar manner to the Tope. Seemingly deemed an immediate failure, 353163, 353220 and 355164 were never trialled nor given a new TOPS code. The last of the trio is seen at Burton WRD on May 28, 1994.** Phil Eames

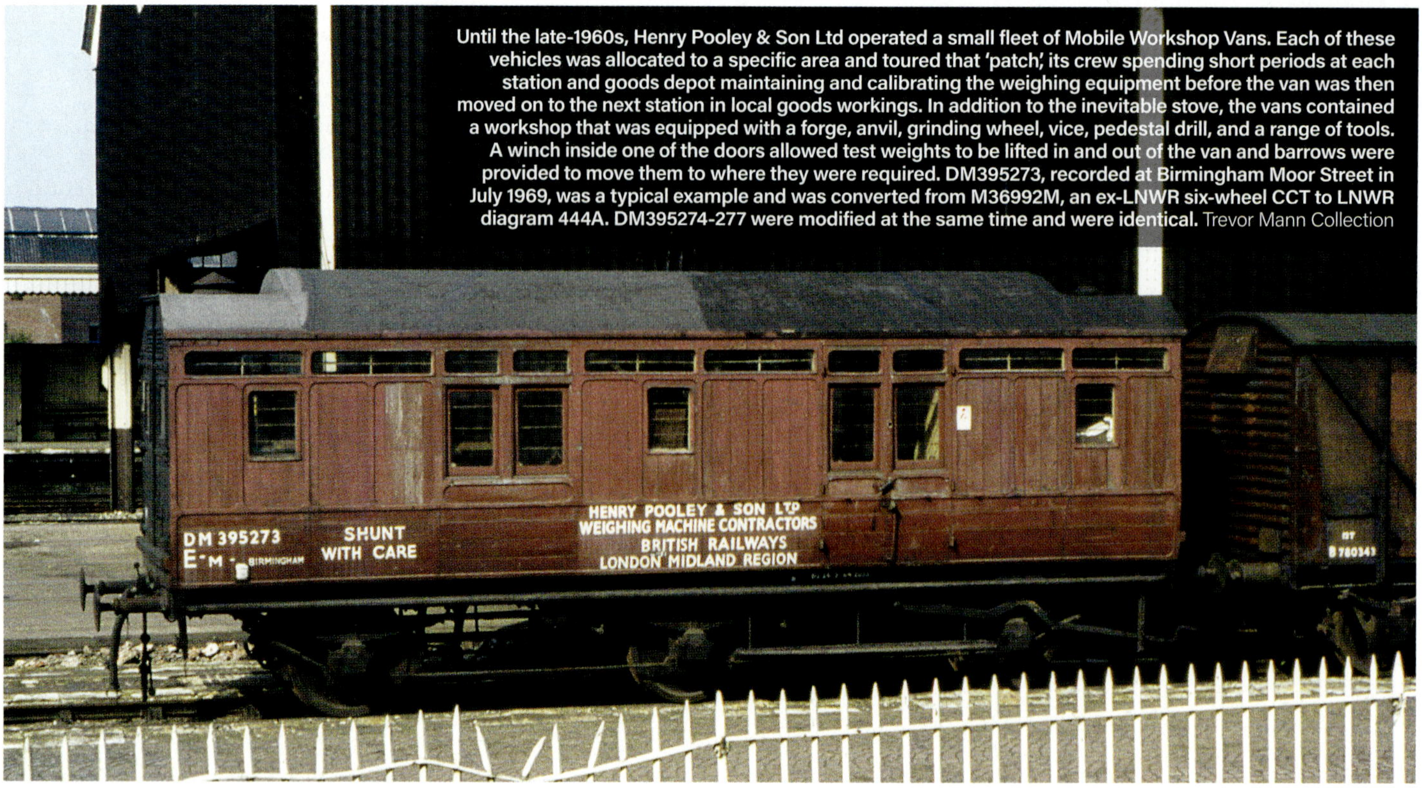

Until the late-1960s, Henry Pooley & Son Ltd operated a small fleet of Mobile Workshop Vans. Each of these vehicles was allocated to a specific area and toured that 'patch', its crew spending short periods at each station and goods depot maintaining and calibrating the weighing equipment before the van was then moved on to the next station in local goods workings. In addition to the inevitable stove, the vans contained a workshop that was equipped with a forge, anvil, grinding wheel, vice, pedestal drill, and a range of tools. A winch inside one of the doors allowed test weights to be lifted in and out of the van and barrows were provided to move them to where they were required. DM395273, recorded at Birmingham Moor Street in July 1969, was a typical example and was converted from M36992M, an ex-LNWR six-wheel CCT to LNWR diagram 444A. DM395274-277 were modified at the same time and were identical. Trevor Mann Collection

The Pooley fleet

A small part of the Civil Engineers remit, and unrelated to the fish types, was to provide a fleet of vehicles to Henry Pooley & Son Ltd, which was contracted to maintain all scales and weighbridges on the BR network. Trevor Mann provides an insight into this diverse group of vehicles, which included some historic gems.

With today's railways largely restricted to the operation of passenger trains and trainload freight, it is difficult to appreciate the importance of weighing equipment to day-to-day railway operations during the more traditional era. In those days, all parcels and sundries traffic along with the majority of wagonload freight movements were charged by weight, so even the smallest of wayside stations required scales for small packages and platform scales for larger, heavier items. Most had weighbridges, which were used to weigh road vehicles delivering consignments to be forwarded by rail, and larger goods depots were also equipped with rail weighbridges to assess the weight of traffic being consigned in bulk. Dock systems, many of which were railway-owned, were similarly equipped as, indeed, were many of the private sidings that served collieries, quarries, steelworks, large factories, and other railway customers.

Weights and measures legislation required that every one of these weighing machines, from the small scales used in station parcels offices through to the road and rail weighbridges was overhauled and calibrated annually, work that along with out-of-course repairs was entrusted to a specialist contractor - Henry Pooley & Son Ltd. Established in Liverpool during the late 18th century, Pooley's had long been associated with the railways, having made the very first

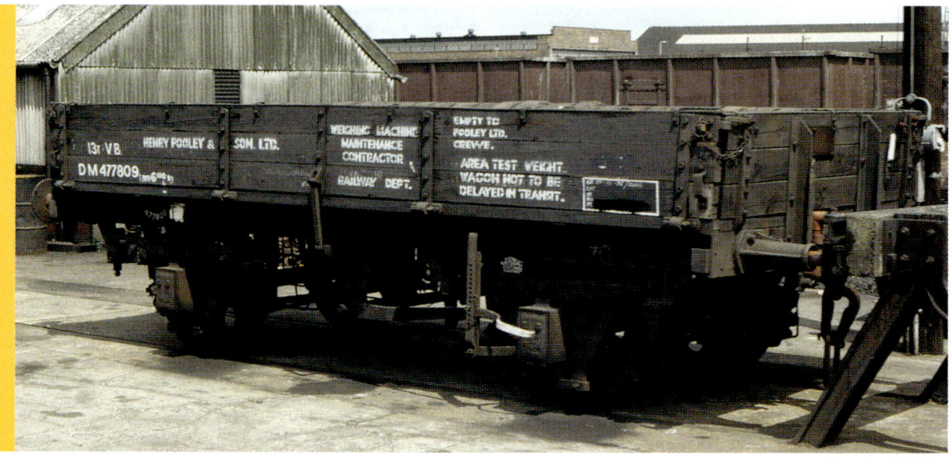

RIGHT: **On the London Midland Region, Pooley operated a number of ex-LMS 13-ton Medfits, which had been modified for use as test weight wagons in the early 1980s. DM477809 was typical, its rows of weights being just visible above the sides and ends when seen at Chester C&W Workshops on July 7, 1979. DM471131 carried an identical olive green livery and lettering but differed in having the shoe suspension and four-shoe vacuum brake of a wagon that had been built unfitted. In contrast, DM477532 and DM478397 retained the bauxite livery carried in revenue-earning traffic but had similar lettering; both also having auxiliary suspension and clasp brakes. Other regions converted different types for this role, the Western Region utilising 14-ton ballast wagons dating from the turn of the century for example.** Trevor Mann

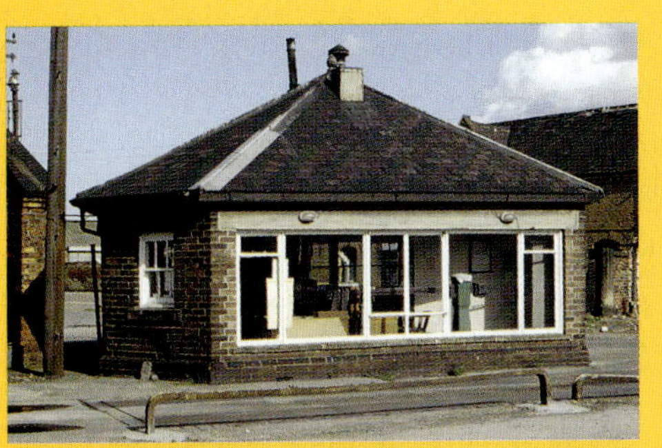

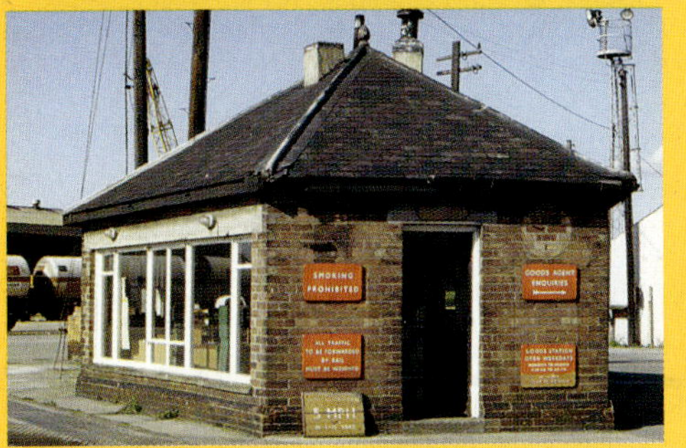

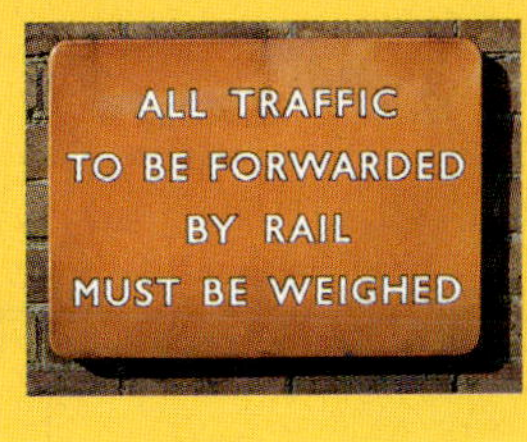

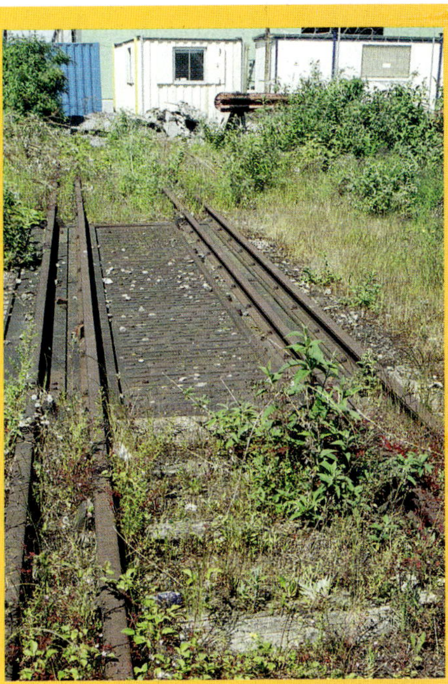

This weigh office at Middlesbrough Goods remained in day-to-day use into the 1980s and featured an array of North Eastern Region enamel signs, these being recorded on September 20, 1981. The road weighbridge was unusually long, enabling it to handle large lorries. The barrier, bent up from scrap rail, was designed to prevent damage to the delicate weighing equipment while the large window gave the clerk an excellent view of the vehicle being weighed. It also provides us with a glimpse of the weighing apparatus, notices, and other paraphernalia inside. In contrast, the rail weighbridge at Bridgwater was clearly out of use when seen in 2001. It had previously been used to weigh traffic being forwarded by rail from the goods depot and docks, similar installations being provided at busy locations across the network. One set of rails was used for weighing, the other pair bypassing the table; this allowed locomotives to shunt wagons over the weighbridge without damaging the mechanism. Trevor Mann/David Ratcliffe

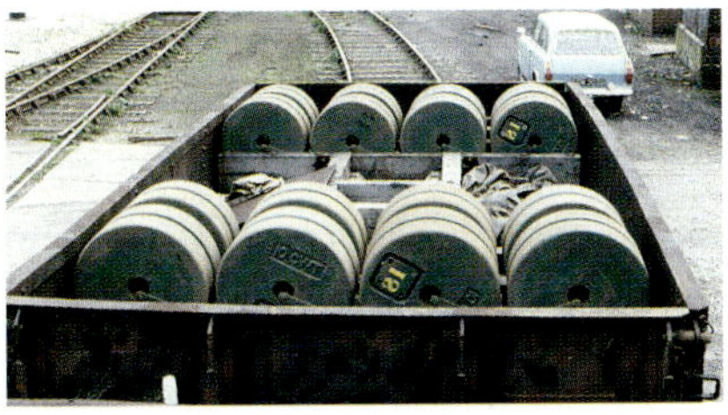

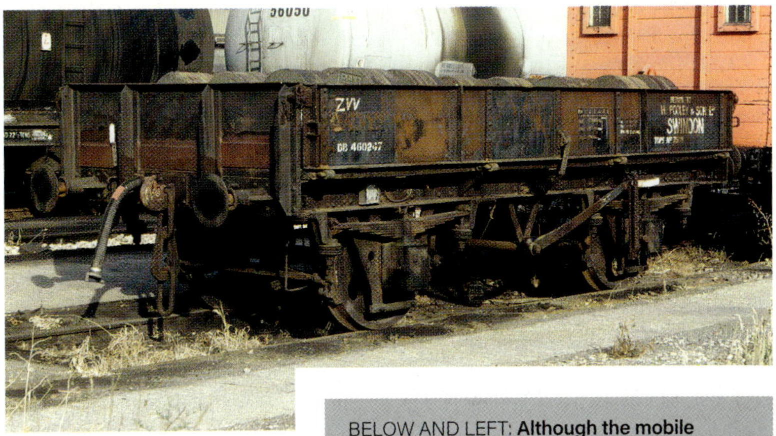

RIGHT: **During the 1980s and into the 1990s, BR standardised on test weight wagons adapted from 13-ton all-steel Medfits built to diagram 1/019, DB460247 being recorded in Cardiff Tidal Sidings in July 1983. Unlike the wooden-bodied wagons, these Medfits were rarely fully repainted with the heavily-rusted condition and the branding 'Return to H Pooley & Son Ltd, Swindon' being typical. On other regions, London Midland vehicles returned to Crewe and Southern wagons to Norwood Junction for example. The internal shot illustrates the racking that held the half-ton roller weights; these would be lifted out by a crane and rolled into position when a road weighbridge was being calibrated.** Trevor Mann

railway weighing machine that was installed at the Liverpool terminus of the Liverpool & Manchester Railway back in 1835. As the British railway network had grown, so had the company and in 1935, a century after that pioneering installation, Pooley's had been able to claim that 'nine-tenths of the railway traffic of Great Britain is today weighed over Pooley weighing machines.'

British Railways continued the practice of each of the 'big four' pre-nationalisation companies, and many of their pre-grouping predecessors, in providing Henry Pooley & Son with a small fleet of specialist vehicles to assist the company in fulfilling its maintenance contracts. A number, including some originating with the Great Eastern and the Great Western railways, were purpose built, but most, including all of the later vehicles, were conversions of redundant wagons and coaching stock. These were interesting vehicles, the sight of which enlivened many a railway journey into the mid-1990s!

BELOW AND LEFT: **Although the mobile workshop vans were dispensed with by the early-1970s, with any components requiring workshop attention presumably transported by road to a regional base, BR continued to provide staff and tool vans for use by the mechanics employed by Pooley. Two examples from what was a very diverse fleet of converted vehicles are illustrated. DW150169** (LEFT) **had been modified from W2660W, an ex-GWR 10-ton 'Bloater' passenger-rated fish van and was recorded at Cardiff Tidal in a distinctive red livery on July 20, 1983. In contrast, DB774443** (BELOW) **was a more modern conversion of a standard BR Vanfit and is seen at Edge Hill C&W, Liverpool on April 20, 1982.** Trevor Mann

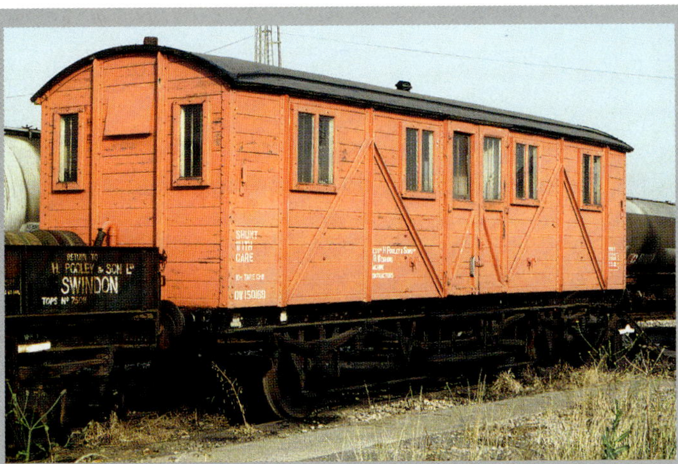

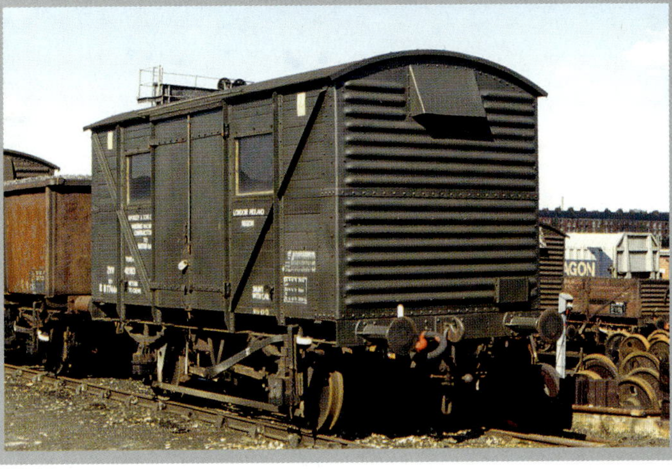

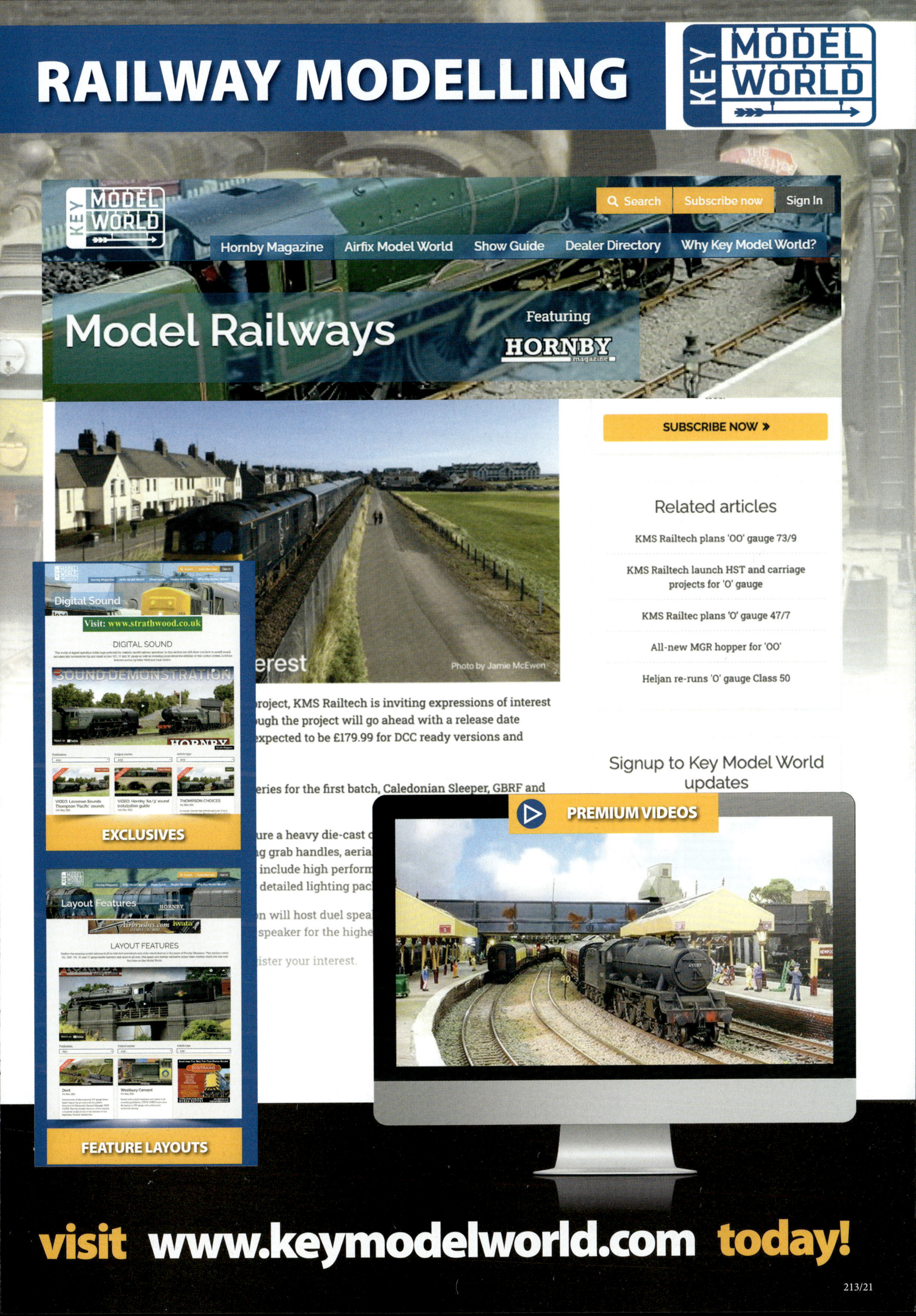
RAILWAY MODELLING
KEY MODEL WORLD
Search
Subscribe now
Sign In
Hornby Magazine
Airfix Model World
Show Guide
Dealer Directory
Why Key Model World?
Model Railways
Featuring
HORNBY magazine
SUBSCRIBE NOW »
Related articles
KMS Railtech plans 'OO' gauge 73/9
KMS Railtech launch HST and carriage projects for 'O' gauge
KMS Railtec plans 'O' gauge 47/7
All-new MGR hopper for 'OO'
Heljan re-runs 'O' gauge Class 50
Photo by Jamie McEwen
erest
roject, KMS Railtech is inviting expressions of interest
ugh the project will go ahead with a release date
xpected to be £179.99 for DCC ready versions and
eries for the first batch, Caledonian Sleeper, GBRF and
ure a heavy die-cast c
g grab handles, aeria
include high perform
detailed lighting pac
n will host duel speal
speaker for the highe
ister your interest.
Signup to Key Model World updates
Digital Sound
Visit: www.strathwood.co.uk
DIGITAL SOUND
SOUND DEMONSTRATION
EXCLUSIVES
Layout Features
LAYOUT FEATURES
FEATURE LAYOUTS
PREMIUM VIDEOS
visit www.keymodelworld.com today!
213/21

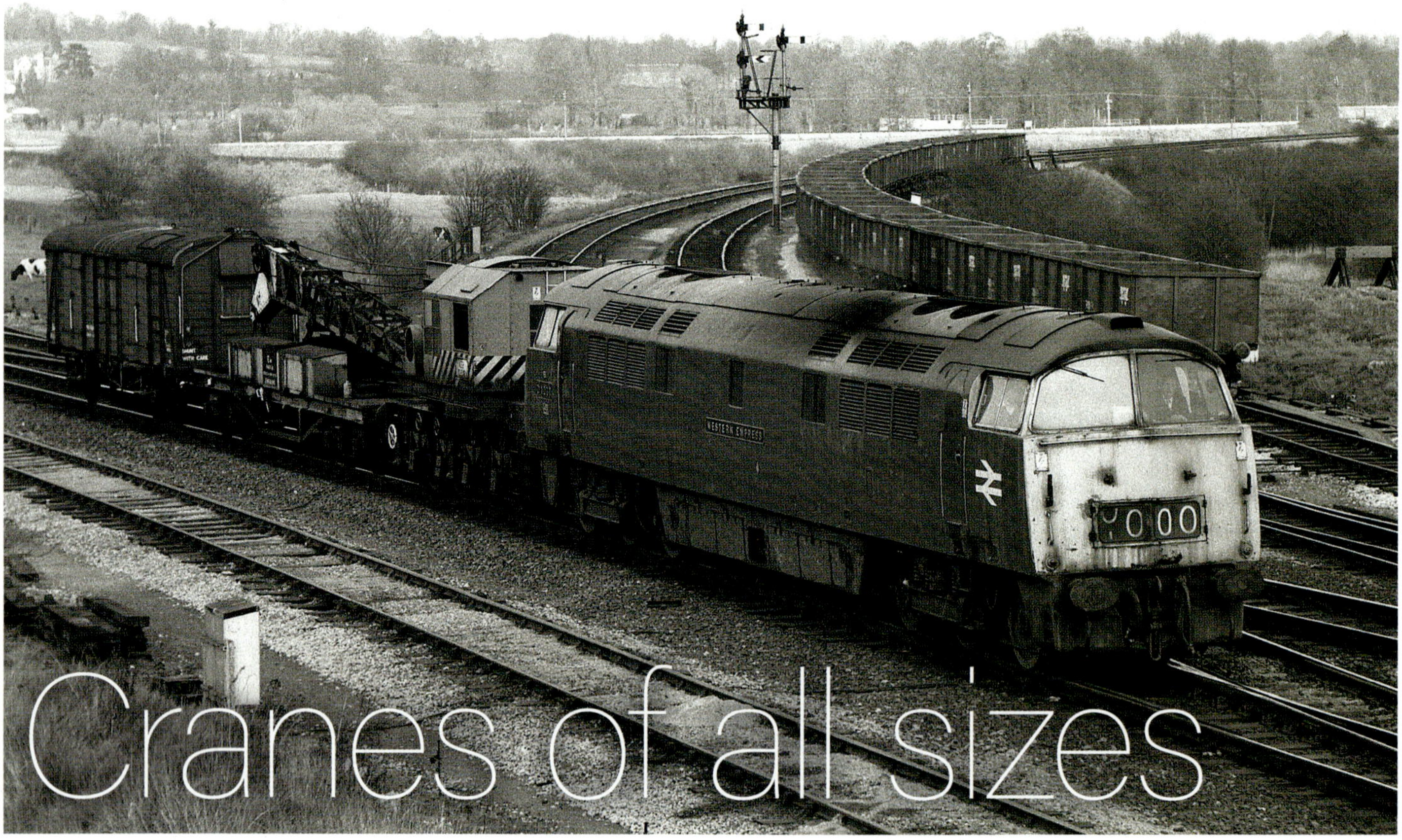

Cranes of all sizes

The Civil Engineers had a sizeable array of cranes available during the British Rail era, these progressing from steam powered to diesel types with three different forms of transmission. Simon Bendall gives an overview of the subject and illustrates a selection.

Mention cranes in a railway context and the subject that most likely will come to mind is that of breakdown cranes, these being the heavy lifting types that lived on locomotive depots until they were called into action to deal with incidents and accidents. While they did see use on civil engineering duties, such as lifting bridge girders, they belonged to the Mechanical and Electrical Engineers and were not provided for run of the mill maintenance and renewal work.

Instead, the Civil Engineers had an extensive collection of smaller cranes that could handle most of the tasks required. This was a truly eclectic fleet with a range of builders, power sources, sizes, and capacities, all with their own foibles and spread out across different regions. The subject is a complex one and can only be covered in passing but for an in-depth study, I would recommend *Railway Cranes Volume 3* by Peter Tatlow (Crecy Publishing 2018), where the subject of engineers' cranes is covered across all of 222 pages and that does not even include the track relayers! The previous two volumes in the series cover the development of the aforementioned breakdown cranes in even more detail.

While the railways initially relied on steam power for all but its lightest cranes, diesel types began to appear as early as 1938 under the LMS. These initial types used a mechanical transmission to operate the crane but as this did not necessarily allow for fine control, some manufacturers moved into electric transmission as well. Neither were ideal systems which lead to the development of hydraulic transmission, the first such cranes being delivered unsurprisingly to the Western

ABOVE: **With only a month to go until withdrawal, D1037 *Western Empress* had been reduced to an engineers' trip on April 3, 1976, as it arrives at Westbury. In tow is one of the diesel hydraulic cranes built by Booth Rodley in 1958/59 for the Western Region, this being the first application of hydraulic transmission to a BR order. Finished in grey at this time, this type was numbered DB347-56, later DRA81547-56, and lasted into the early 1990s.** Simon Bendall Collection

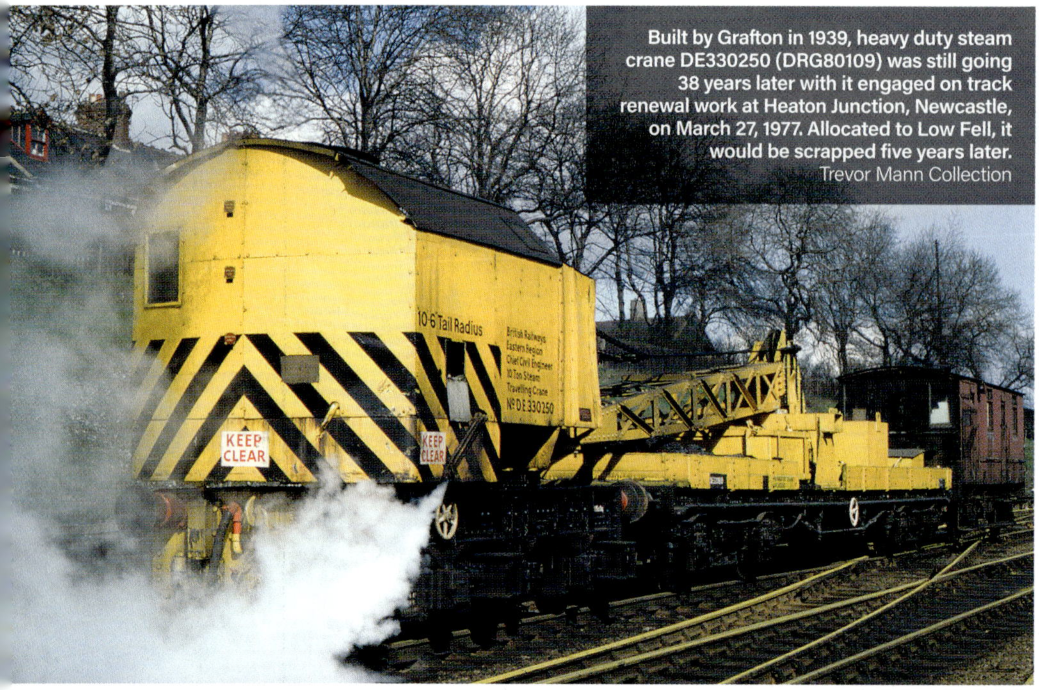

Built by Grafton in 1939, heavy duty steam crane DE330250 (DRG80109) was still going 38 years later with it engaged on track renewal work at Heaton Junction, Newcastle, on March 27, 1977. Allocated to Low Fell, it would be scrapped five years later. Trevor Mann Collection

Region in the late 1950s.

The subsequent two decades therefore saw BR operating both steam and three different types of diesel crane simultaneously. The numbering of these was also chaotic with the regions initially applying their own internal identities before a form of central numbering using the DB965xxx series was introduced from 1957, this taking a decade to be fully adopted. Even then, some older cranes that had existed before its creation, particularly on the Western, were never renumbered.

Modernisation

While steam locos may have finished in 1968, no such edict applied to steam cranes, and it was not until 1986 that the final remaining Civil Engineers pair was stood down. These were the exception though as most had been withdrawn earlier in the decade following the commencement of a modernisation programme towards the end of the 1970s that saw new diesel hydraulic cranes purchased from both Plasser & Theurer and Cowans Sheldon.

In 1974 a new numbering series was introduced, known as the Civil Engineers Plant System (CEPS), which was similar to TOPS. This grouped together different categories of track machine by type and sub-type. For cranes, Civil Engineers machines were re-numbered into the 80xxx series for steam and 81xxx for diesel while those belonging mostly to the M&EE went into the 95xxx series for steam and 96xxx for diesel. They were also rated by lifting capacity with a light duty crane being up to eight tonnes and a heavy duty anything above this.

Like the wagon fleets, all were prefixed with DR with a letter added in front of this to denote the owning department if it was not the Civil Engineers, such as 'A' for M&EE. Uniquely, the cranes also gained another letter after the DR to identify the manufacturer, such as 'P' for Plasser. The table gives a breakdown of the Civil Engineers categories.

As the 1980s progressed, widespread withdrawals of the diesel mechanical examples took place followed by the diesel electric types, there usually being a few stragglers confined to internal use at yards and pre-assembly depots. By 1995, it was only the Plasser and Cowans telescopic jib designs that really survived, these passing to the new infrastructure maintenance companies to receive all manner of new brandings and liveries. However, they too progressively succumbed as road/railers took over and only a handful of Plasser examples remain in main line use today.

Civil Engineers cranes CEPS numbering details

Number range	Power	Type	Builders
80000-80005	Steam	Light	Grafton, Marshall Fleming, Smith, Taylor Hubbard
80100-80173	Steam	Heavy	Booth, Clark Chapman, Grafton, Taylor Hubbard
81000-81053	Diesel Mechanical	Light	Grafton, Jones, Smith, Taylor Hubbard
81100-81141	Diesel Mechanical	Heavy	Smith, Taylor Hubbard
81200-81264	Diesel Electric	Light	Coles, Smith, Taylor Hubbard
81300-81373	Diesel Electric	Heavy	Coles, Cowans Sheldon, Smith, Taylor Hubbard
81401-81403	Diesel Hydraulic	Light	Jones
81501-81556	Diesel Hydraulic	Heavy	Booth, Cowans Sheldon, Plasser & Theurer, Smith

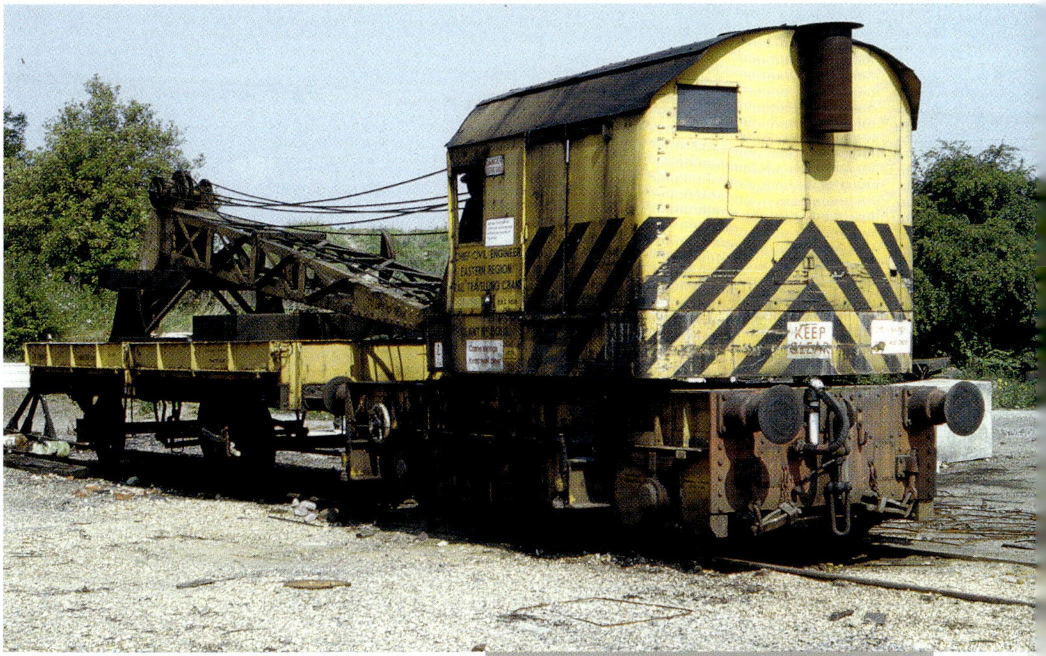

ABOVE: **Another Grafton product but this time from 1954, DRG80118 was carrying its CEPS number at Hitchin permanent way depot on August 26, 1980. An Eastern crane throughout its life, the chimney for the boiler is in its inverted travel position. It was cut on Tyneside four years later.** Trevor Mann

Taylor Hubbard was one of the principal builders of BR's engineering cranes, contributing numerous different types over the years. This one is from the light duty diesel mechanical category and dates from 1939, it displays both its initial DM1403 identity along with the new number of DRT81003. Seen at Chester carriage and wagon sidings on March 1, 1980, it was less than three years from disposal, while the jib runner is an ex GWR bolster. Trevor Mann

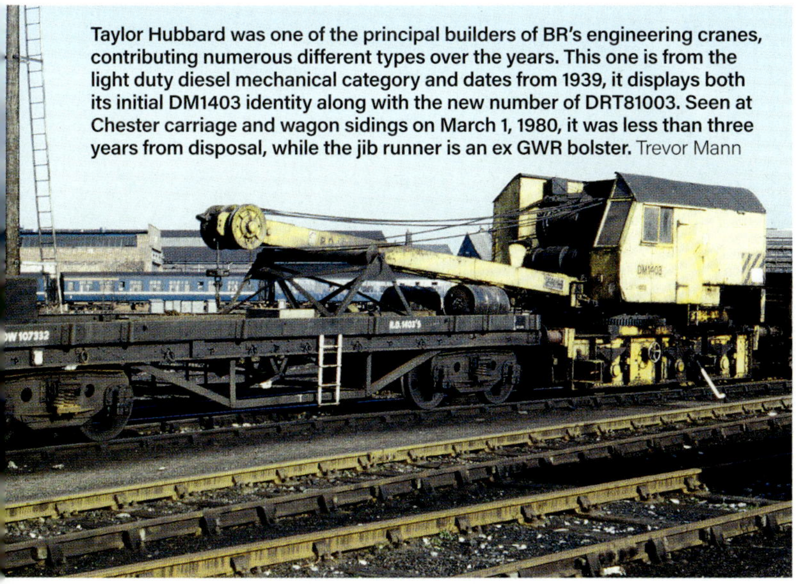

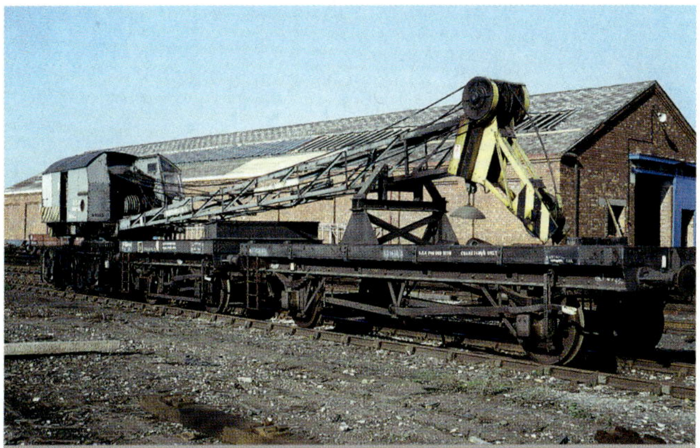

ABOVE: **Recorded at Northampton engineers' yard on October 21, 1979, DRT81033 (DM1433) was built by Taylor Hubbard in 1958 and allocated to Watford for much of its life. Both runners are repurposed ex revenue stock with the nearest, TDM311891, being an ex LMS double bolster, while TDB917090 was built by BR as a single bolster wagon.** Simon Bendall Collection

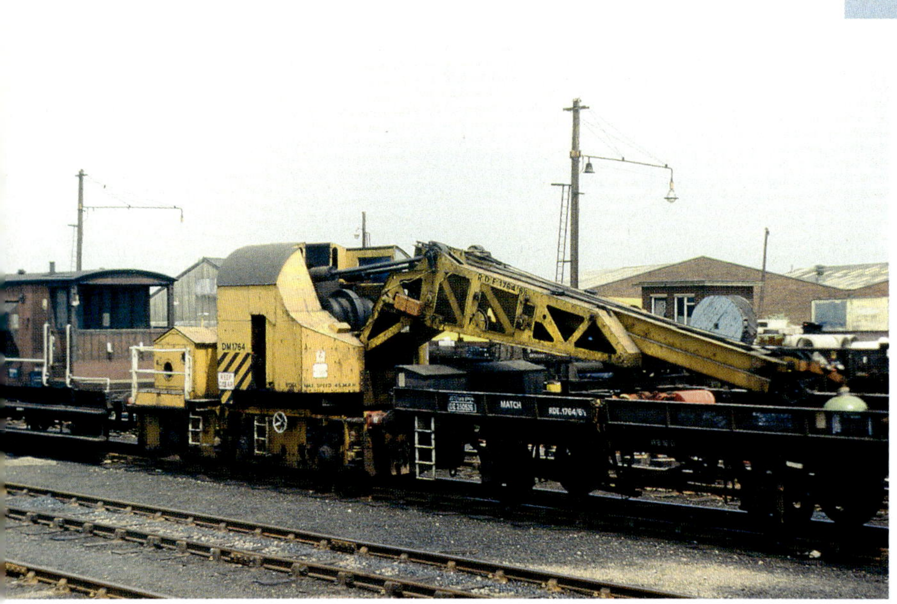

ABOVE: **Another Taylor Hubbard product but this time a light duty diesel electric type, DM1764 (later DRT81264) was a unique crane. Built in 1960, it was the first experiment into using a telescopic jib as BR looked to develop a new group of cranes that could work under overhead electrification. Although innovative, it was limited to lifting just 6½ tons. Seen at Watford Junction on July 7, 1979, it had Plate wagon DE250526 as a runner and would be scrapped in 1988.** Simon Bendall Collection

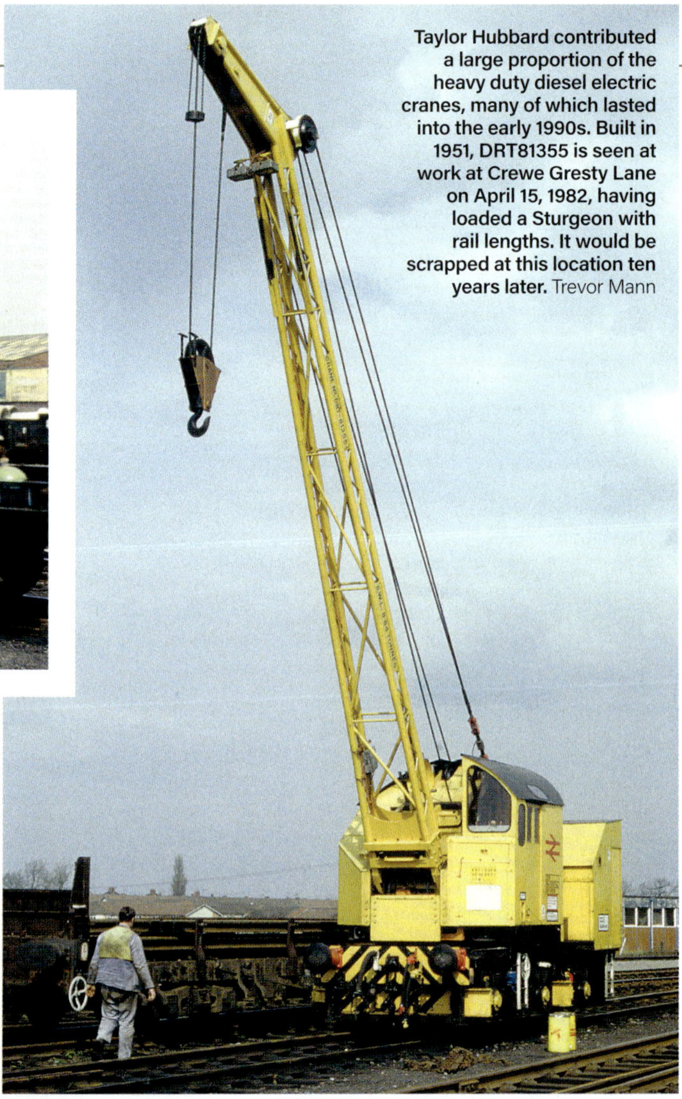

Taylor Hubbard contributed a large proportion of the heavy duty diesel electric cranes, many of which lasted into the early 1990s. Built in 1951, DRT81355 is seen at work at Crewe Gresty Lane on April 15, 1982, having loaded a Sturgeon with rail lengths. It would be scrapped at this location ten years later. Trevor Mann

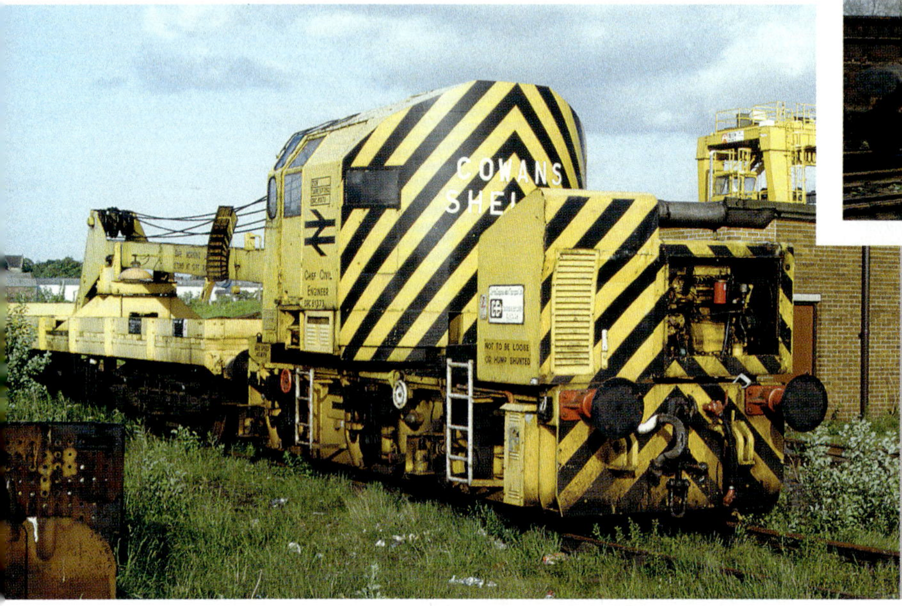

LEFT: **Cowans Sheldon was not overly involved in providing rigid jib cranes to the Civil Engineers, but it did contribute a few heavy duty diesel electric examples. Built in 1972, DRC81373 was recorded at Castleton pre-assembly depot on June 16, 1983. It would be transferred to the M&EE fleet five years later, being renumbered as ADRC96418 and based at Romford. Scrapping followed in 1996.** Trevor Mann

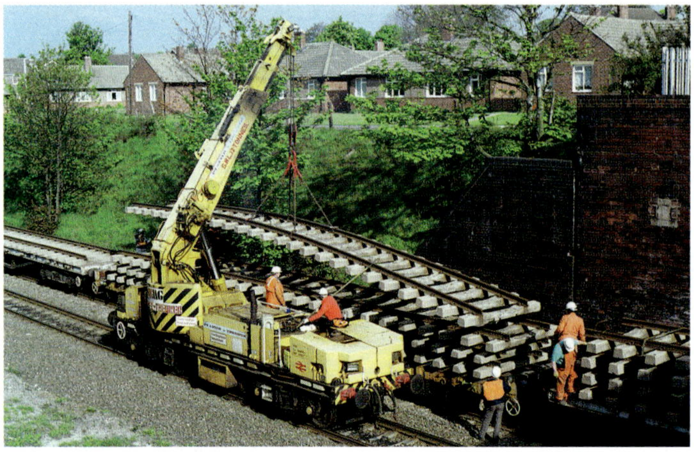

ABOVE: **The most recognisable of all the Civil Engineers cranes is the telescopic jib Plasser & Theurer GPC-72 design, DRP81503-32 being delivered between 1977 and 1981. With some still seeing use with Balfour Beatty, they could handle most jobs, including lifting tack panels as DRP81527 displays at Horbury in May 1991. The sagging of the 60ft track section also illustrates why track relayers were preferred for such jobs.** David Ratcliffe

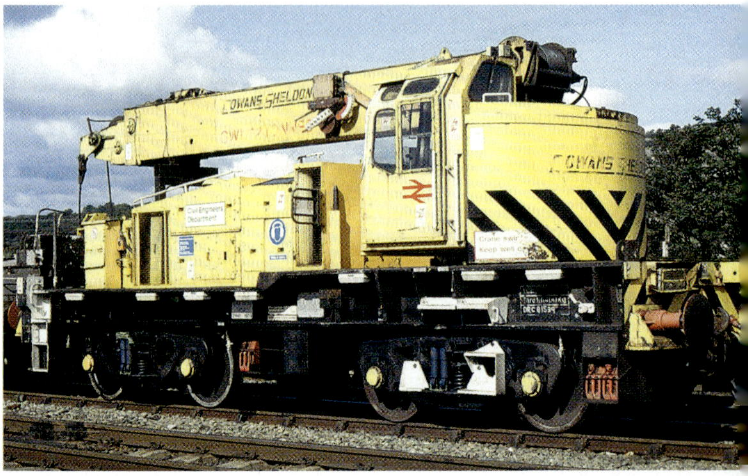

ABOVE: **The Cowans Sheldon version of the telescopic jib crane is illustrated by DRC81539 at Carnforth Bottom End Sidings in March 1989. There were 14 examples delivered in 1978/79 as DRC81533-46, these seeing particular use in the north of England and Scotland whereas the Plasser type was more common in the southern half of the country.** David Ratcliffe

Relayers evolve

The development of the track relaying machines, or twin jib cranes, followed a similar evolution to the cranes, with early machines being diesel powered to control the jibs but not being self-propelled. The first batch capable of moving themselves arrived in the mid-1960s with the 1978-1980 period again bringing a replacement programme that was shared once more between Plasser and Cowans. These were the last twin-jib track relayers to be built, their subsequent journey into privatisation mirroring that of the same companies' cranes.

Civil Engineers track relayers CEPS numbering details			
Number range	**Propulsion**	**Type**	**Builders**
78000-78011	Non-powered	Light	BR
78100-78122	Non-powered	Heavy	BR, Cowans Sheldon, Taylor Hubbard
78200-78238	Self-propelled	Heavy	Cowans Sheldon, Smith, Plasser & Theurer, Taylor Hubbard

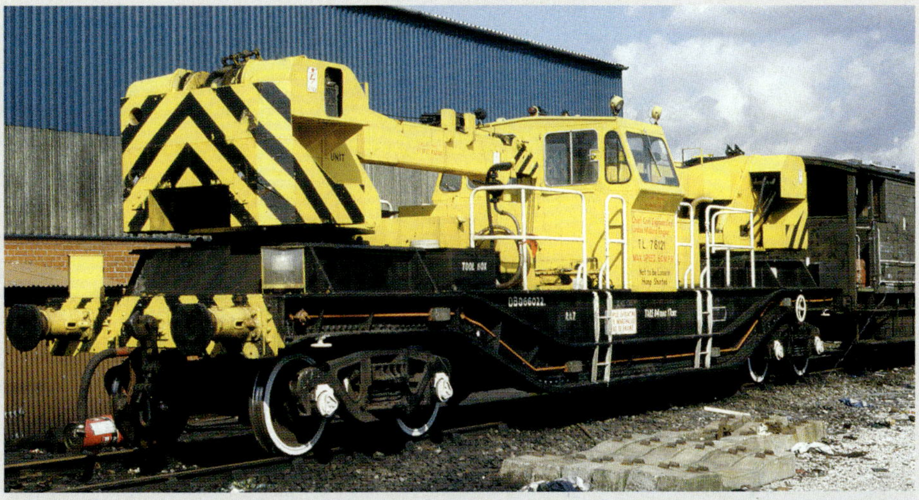

RIGHT: **Many of the early heavy duty track relayers were built using a Warwell wagon as the frame, as demonstrated by DRB78121 (DB966022) at Guide Bridge on March 29, 1988. Built by BR in 1975, it would be scrapped in June 1992.** Trevor Mann

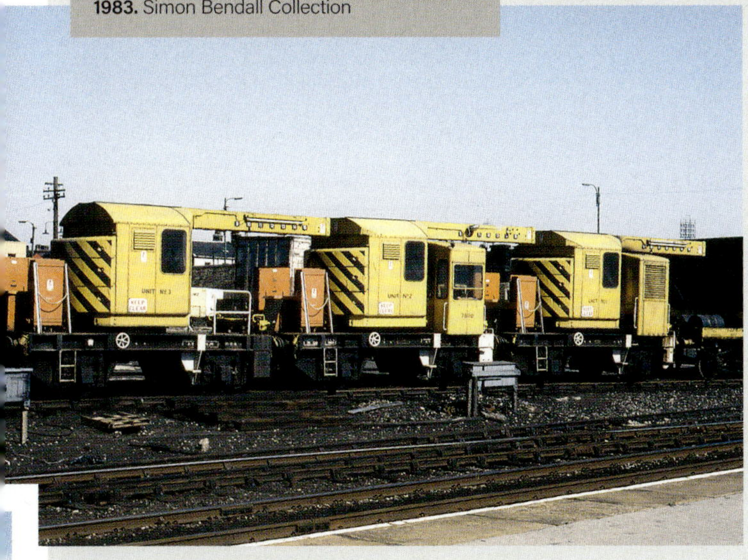

BELOW: **The contribution of Cowans Sheldon to the early track relayers was certainly a unique take on the matter, it providing a pair of these three jib units. DRC78110 is seen at Bolton during August 1978 with the central part featuring the operator's cabin with the diesel power unit at the right hand end. Built in 1960, both it and DRC78111 would be scrapped in early 1983.** Simon Bendall Collection

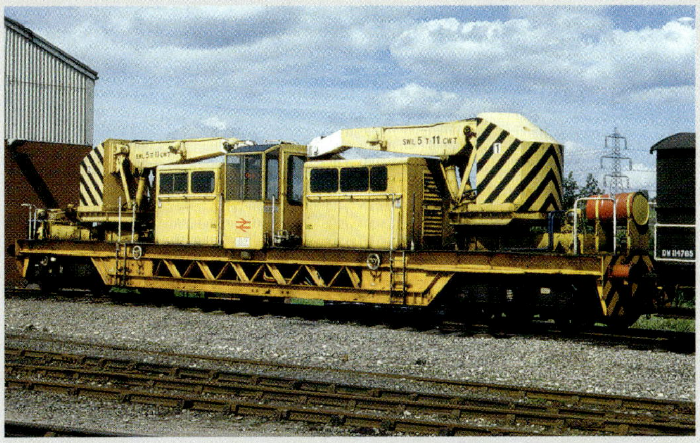

ABOVE: **The Smiths-built track relayers undoubtedly had a presence with their sturdy underframes and sizeable counterweights on the back of the cranes. These were also the first of the self-propelled track relayers, DRS78203 dating from 1965. Seen at Beighton on June 23, 1985, it was scrapped in 1999 after passing to Balfour Beatty ownership.** Trevor Mann

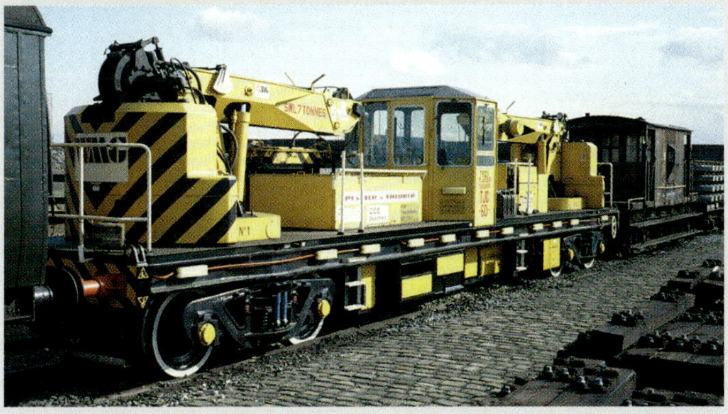

ABOVE: **Built in 1977, DRP78211 was the first of the Plasser & Theurer TJC-60 relayers with 13 more following by 1980. It is seen at St Helens Shaw Street during April 1984 and still exists today in the ownership of Track Engineering Ltd, where it is available for hire. Several others remain in main line use.** David Ratcliffe

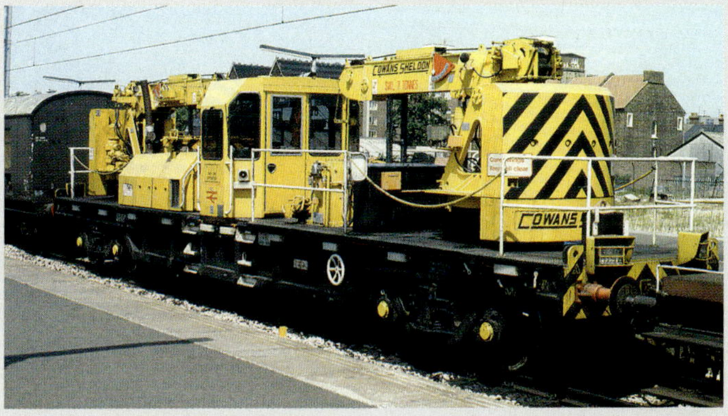

ABOVE: **Cowans Sheldon also provided 14 track relayers to BR in 1980 with DRC78236 recorded at Bedford in July 1983. Very similar in design to the Plasser version but with more bulk, it was scrapped in 2007 after seeing use with Centrac, GTRM and Carillion. Two sister machines remain in use with Colas Rail.** Simon Bendall Collection

BR conversion for a Booth crane by Steve Farmer

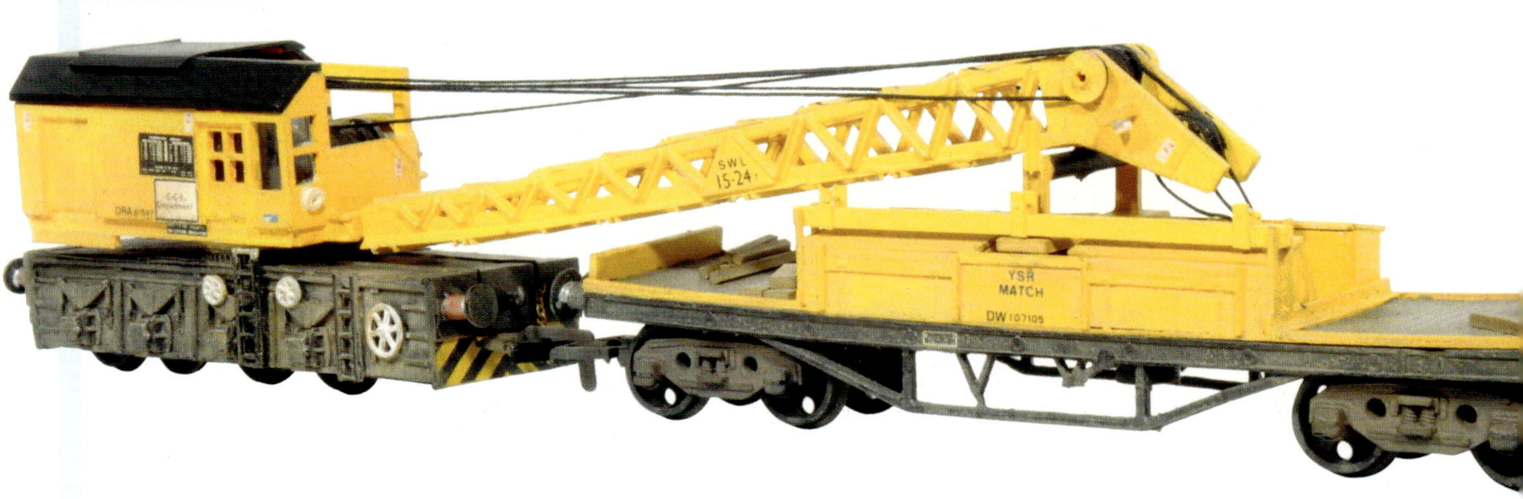

The basis for this crane was the Airfix plastic kit, as now produced by Dapol. This portrays an industrial version of a diesel hydraulic crane built by Booth Rodley, it has two bogies. BR ordered a similar version of the same crane but with a rigid underframe, ten examples being delivered to the Western Region in the late 1950s and which lasted in service into the mid-1990s.

The kit therefore needs to be modified in the same manner and, although this particular model was built some 20 years ago, the process is still the same today, give or take the odd product. Starting with the chassis of the crane, the only option is to scratchbuild new sides. These were formed from 40thou styrene sheet with holes cut in the appropriate positions to fit brass bearings for the wheelsets. Once glued to the remainder of the chassis, whitemetal springs and axleboxes can be glued in position; these castings were sourced from a long forgotten supplier but the likes of Rumney Models, Wizard Models and MJT all offer such items today.

Romford wheels are used but with the flanges filed off the inner four wheels to allow the crane to negotiate tight curves. Next, the tension lock couplings were fitted on plastic mounting blocks and then the lower part of the bufferbeams fabricated from plastic strip and glued in place under the couplings. With this completed, I had a mobile crane base that could be trialled on the layout to see if it ran alright.

Bodywork

The body and jib were mostly built as per the kit but with the roof initially omitted. The engine grille on the side was opened up and an etched brass grille put in place behind while the jib had a representation of the lights made up from plastic strip. Both parts were then primed and sprayed with Humbrol yellow (No.24), after which both were given a coat of Railmatch gloss varnish. Transfers were a mix of Fox for the data panel lettering with the remainder being from alphabet sets, all of which were then coated with Railmatch matt varnish. The cab was also glazed at this time using clear glazing sheet.

The body and jib were then assembled, being cautious as the jib was not fastened solidly. Some vertical movement of the jib would be required for good running when resting on the runner wagon. The crane was then rigged using fishing line with reference to pictures to see where it all went and using the hook supplied with the kit. With this completed, the roof of the cab unit was glued into position and painted black with a coat of Railmatch matt varnish to finish it off.

Going back to the chassis, further items were added including access steps before the whole unit was sprayed black. The lower bufferbeams received their wasp stripes while the assorted handwheels were painted white and glued in position. The body and jib were

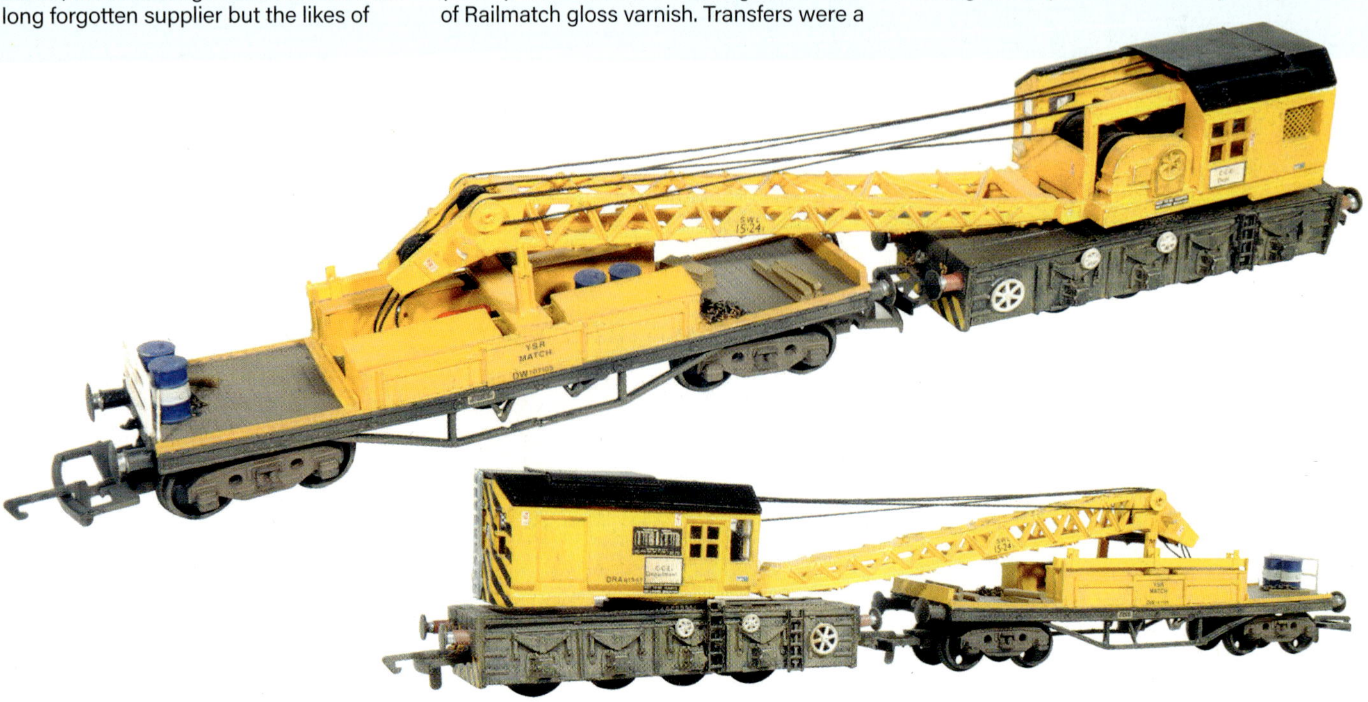

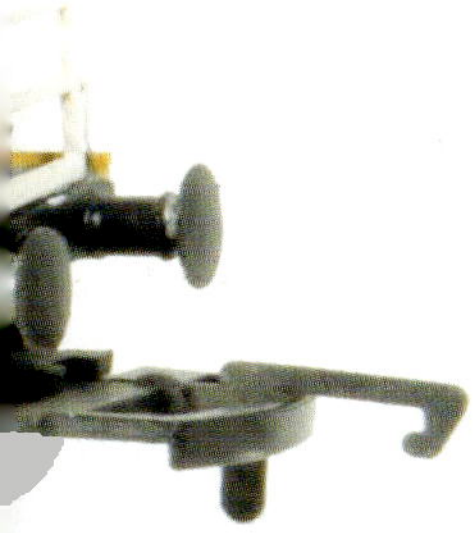

LEFT: **The Airfix/ Dapol kit is the easiest way to produce a Civil Engineers crane in 4mm scale but still requires a fair bit of work to depict a BR version. Built over two decades ago, this example sees use on Tonbridge West Yard.**

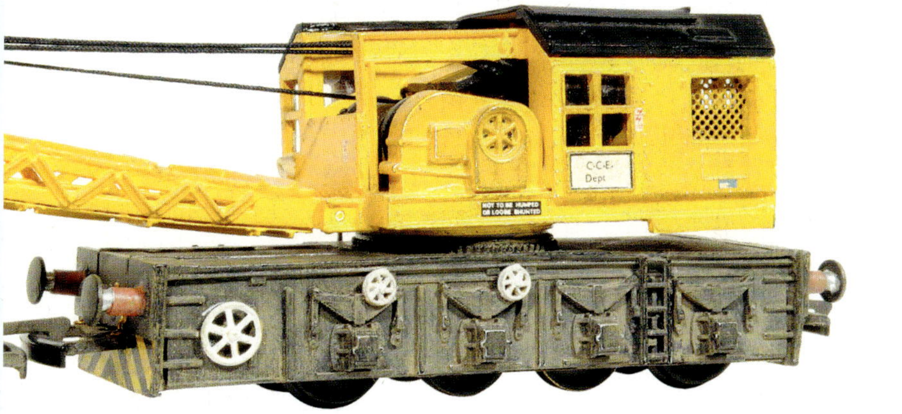

A close-up of the crane showing the scratchbuilt sides to the chassis and lower bufferbeams, these being grafted to the remainder of the plastic kit. The crane body pushes into place on the chassis.

then mated with the chassis, ensuring that the body could rotate freely in its housing to again ensure good running.

Runner wagon

Attention then turned to the runner wagon as nothing is supplied with the kit. I opted to use the old Mainline Macaw bogie bolster wagon as the basis, this having a good likeness to the real runners. This received a new floor made from embossed planked plasticard while the storage lockers and jib support were all fabricated from plasticard and strip. The lifting spreader beam is also made from strip, and this sits in a holder on top of the lockers

The runner was primed, and the floor painted in Humbrol natural wood (No.110) with the rest of the bodywork finished in yellow. Transfers and varnish were added as per the crane while Romford wheels were fitted to the existing bogies. The end handrails were created from plastic strip with drums and chains added along with plastic strip painted to resemble packing timbers. With the crane complete, more testing was required to see how it would work on a layout. This showed that the jib would derail the runner on curves as it pushed against the support cradle. This was solved by adding an upright piece of brass wire through the jib support roller on the runner while the jib received a small plasticard strip with a hole in to suit the upright brass wire. With the wire passed through this hole, this acts as a pivot point and keeps the jib central on the cradle.

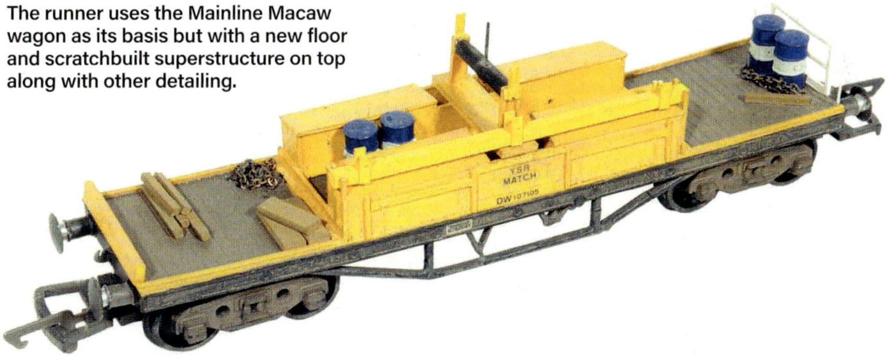

The runner uses the Mainline Macaw wagon as its basis but with a new floor and scratchbuilt superstructure on top along with other detailing.

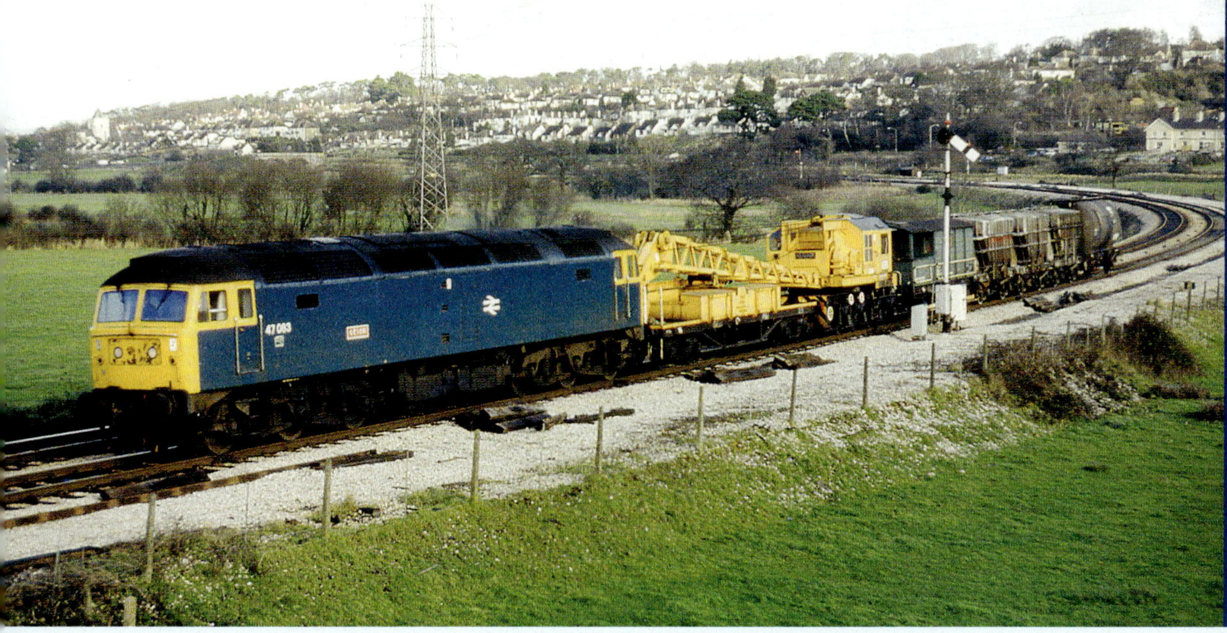

LEFT: **Sporting a replacement painted name, 47803 *Orion* rounds the curve at Aller Junction as it heads west with a mixed consist on January 7, 1983. With a Booth Rodley crane heading the formation along with its staff van, also included are three Presflo cement wagons and a Shell-BP tanker.** Simon Bendall Collection

Building a baby Cowans by Paul Wade

The Mechanical and Electrical Engineers had two 30t diesel mechanical cranes available, these both being based at Horsham Yard in West Sussex for use by the Southern-based Power Supply Section. As the name suggests, the PSS was responsible for maintaining and renewing the third rail 750V DC system with these cranes being used for heavy lift duties, such as transformer installation.

Both were built by Cowans Sheldon in 1961 and strongly resembled the larger 76t breakdown cranes in appearance. Numbered ADRC96100 and ADRC96101, the latter was chosen to be modelled, this depicting its ex-works condition after overhaul at Ashford Crane Repair Depot in 1993. The real crane was scrapped in 2008, three years after leaving Horsham for a few years at the Dean Forest Railway, while ADRC96100 also still exists but in derelict condition at West Coast's Carnforth depot

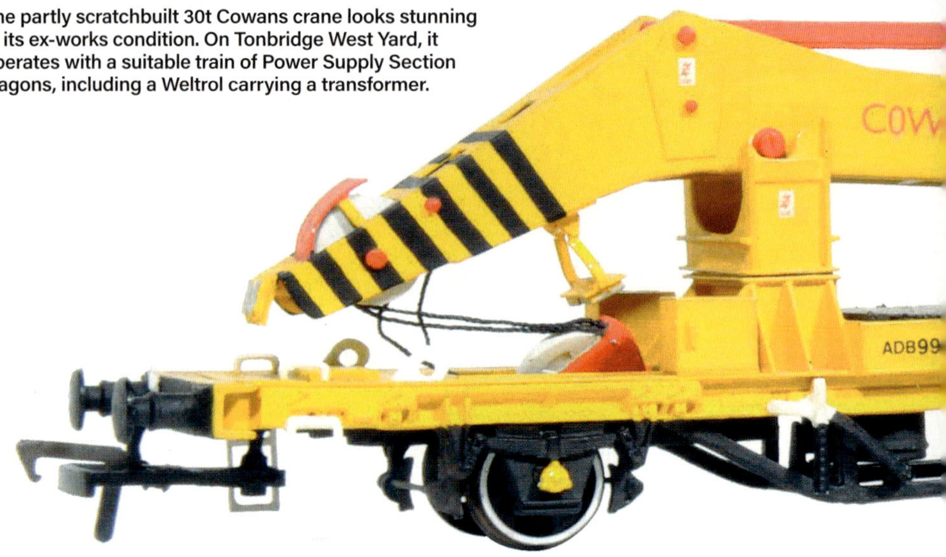

The partly scratchbuilt 30t Cowans crane looks stunning in its ex-works condition. On Tonbridge West Yard, it operates with a suitable train of Power Supply Section wagons, including a Weltrol carrying a transformer.

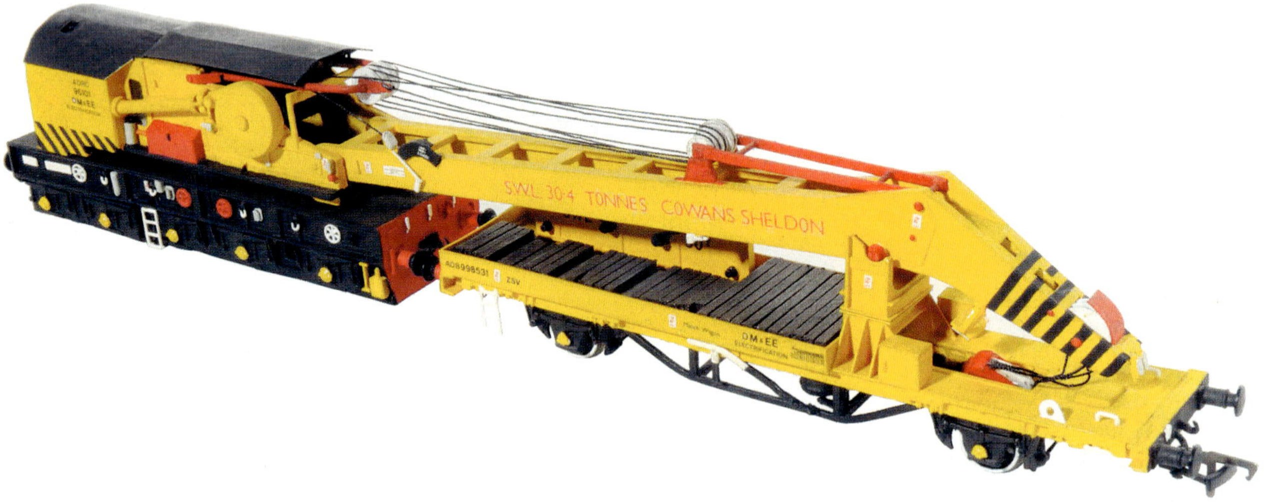

The venerable Hornby 76t breakdown crane was the starting point for this model. As this was produced considerably under scale length to suit trainset curves, the cab/engine section and jib length are actually close to the size of the 30t cranes. I did not have any measurements or plans of the crane, so studied my photos to estimate sizes and positions which was all I could do. The book *Railway Breakdown Cranes Volume 2* by Peter Tatlow (Crecy Publishing 2013) was not out when I made my model. This contains a plan but the scale on it is incorrect, although it provides all of the measurements you would need.

Conversion work

The first task was to modify the Hornby chassis to reflect the five-axle look of the 30t cranes, these having a fixed three-axle section and then a two-axle bogie at the rear. All of the chassis beneath the solebars was removed with the main frame then lengthened using plasticard to give the extra length required to accommodate the bogie.

The replacement fixed section of the side frames was made from plasticard with the springs and roller bearing axleboxes being as close a match as I could find in my parts collection. The rest was built up using various sizes of plastic strip and rod. The bogie was of similar construction, being pivoted to the bottom of the chassis. New bufferbeams, which are of different depths front and back, were made from 20 thou plastic sheet, to which were added whitemetal buffers and lamp irons made from plastic strip A scale Smiths screw coupling was fitted to the jib end to couple to the runner wagon and a small tension lock on the other end. The

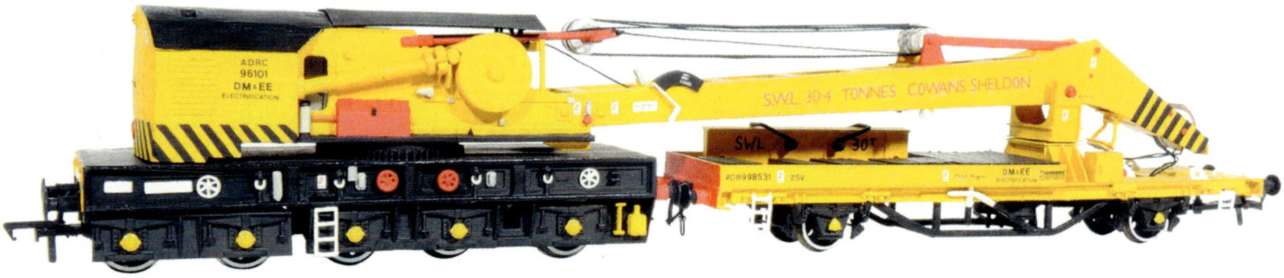

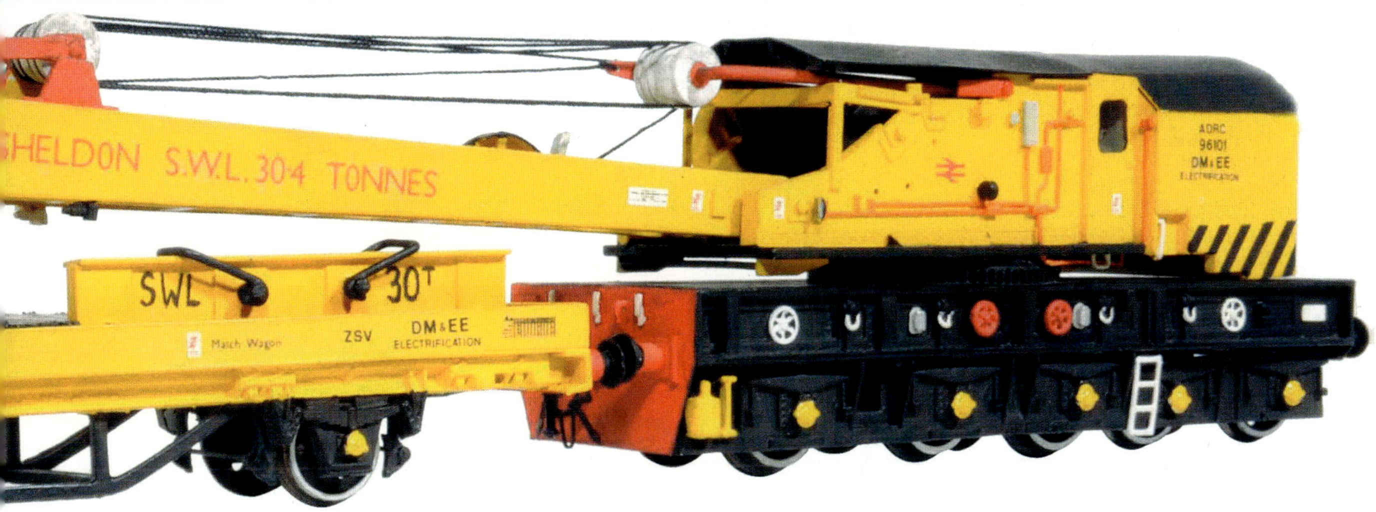

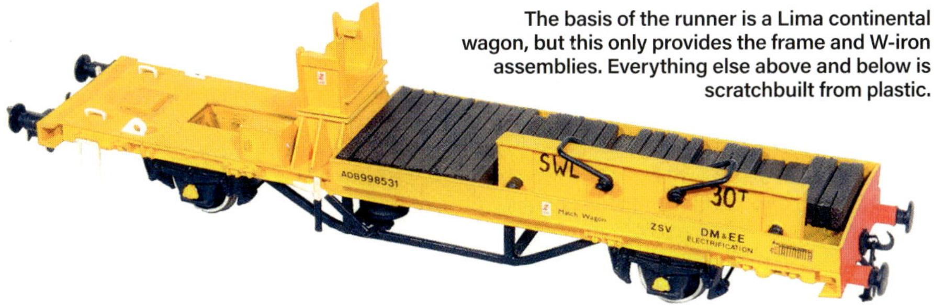

The basis of the runner is a Lima continental wagon, but this only provides the frame and W-iron assemblies. Everything else above and below is scratchbuilt from plastic.

solebars also received brake handwheels, lights, and other small details.

The cab/engine section was also altered, plastic sheet being employed to make the larger cab with new sides, doors, windows, and grilles. On the operator's side, conduit runs, junction boxes and lights were made from plastic and put in place while the other side received the driveshaft and wheel. The jib rope wheels were made from washers and mounted on a thick wire frame fixed to the centre of the cab with a frame made from plastic strip to support it. The roof over the operating area, which rose with the jib, was shaped from plasticard, and just clips in place on the model.

The cab turning wheel was a circular piece of plastic I found which was close to the required diameter, this being fixed on top of the chassis. The wheel teeth on the outside were added with short lengths of plastic strip. The front of the jib was reshaped from plasticard, and I used different sizes of washers to make the rope wheels on the jib and the front of the cab. The rope wheels were added on a frame mounted on top of the jib. Other details were added including the indicator for the jib angle and floodlights with black cotton used for the jib rope.

New runner

The runner wagon supplied with the Hornby model was unsuitable for re-use, being under length for one. Instead, I employed a long-wheelbase European container wagon made by Lima as the basis of the new runner. This had all the un-necessary parts stripped off the deck and underframe before a new plastic floor was fitted along with plastic 'U' section bufferbeams. The low sides to the packing area were added while the jib support was fashioned from plasticard sections; the top half of this is separate and pivoted so it turns as the crane goes around curves.

The front section of the runner has a plain floor with a central well cut-out to accommodate the hook when travelling, these again all being made from plastic sheet as were the stowage boxes alongside. Other touches included etched brass ladder sections glued to the solebars, whitemetal buffers and vacuum pipes. The underframe trussing was fabricated from plastic strip with a vacuum cylinder, brake shoes and handbrake levers made from strip also added.

On the runner deck, handrails and shaped lifting eyes were put in place along with a substantial amount of wooden packing, this once again being formed from plastic sections glued together and painted in a dark wood shade. Finally, the lifting beam was plastic sections with the shackles made from thick wire.

Painting was done with Humbrol yellow and a host of other colours for various details with transfers mostly being alphabet and number sheets of different sizes and colours. Handwritten lettering on the lifting beam was the final touch for what was a very satisfying project to produce a unique model.

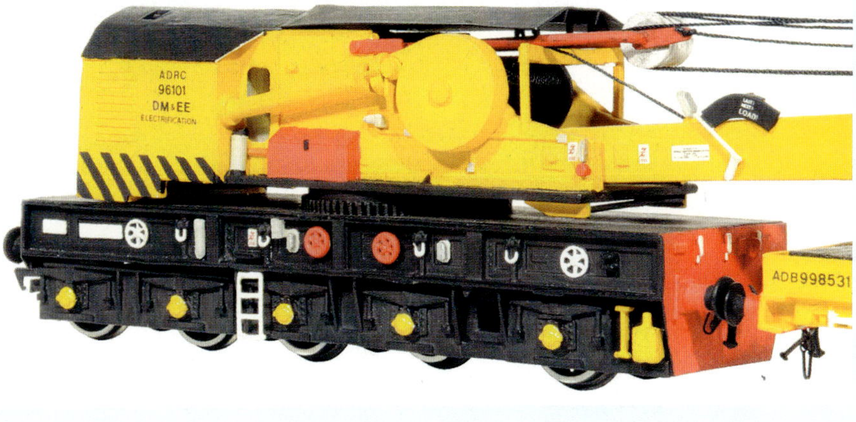

RIGHT: **The main section of the crane incorporates parts of the Hornby model such as the main frame but a lot of it is made from scratch. This includes the substantial side frames, which feature a three-axle rigid section and two-axle bogie at the rear as per the real crane.**

Tayloring a Hubbard by Paul Wade

I photographed several of these Taylor Hubbard heavy duty diesel-electric cranes in Kent, which made them an ideal type to model for Tonbridge West Yard with Ashford-based DRT81341 as the chosen example. The basis of the OO gauge model was the Airfix/Dapol Booth Rodley crane kit along with one of Hornby's generic Southern Railway coaches of the 1980s, this surrendering its chassis for the runner. Scale drawings of the crane were found on a BR Civil Engineering information sheet, this giving one side elevation along with an end and top view, while I also measured one of the runners that had survived into preservation. These, along with my photographs gave me enough to make the model. The book *Railway Cranes Volume 3* by Peter Tatlow contains a plan but, if using it, check the scale is correct as some are not.

The Dapol kit chassis was modified to the required length with thick 80thou plasticard bufferbeams cut to shape and glued to the ends. Although not immediately obvious, these cranes were a bogie design with the substantial side frames being scratchbuilt, including the spring, jack, and step detail, while whitemetal castings were employed for the axleboxes. Behind the side frames, Cambrian bogie frames were employed as a 'cheat' to ensure smooth running with the cosmetic ones glued in front.

The cab employed the floor from the kit with scratchbuilt sides and ends from plasticard, these having the door and window cut-outs added along with the engine grille and handrails. The roof was made from a Parkside wagon roof cut to shape with plastic strip added for the joints and a window formed over the driver's cab. A chair and controls were made from plasticard and fitted in the cab.

The Taylor Hubbard crane uses parts of the Airfix/Dapol kit as its basis, but the body and jib are largely scratchbuilt. The considerable length of the runner compared to the crane was noticeable on this type.

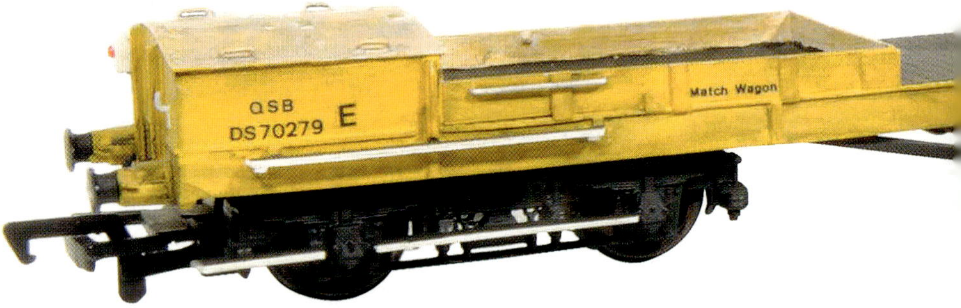

Making the jib

The hinge for the jib along with the beams for the ropes were made and fitted on wire bars to allow them to move in the centre section of the cab. Wheels for the beam ropes were from the Dapol kit. The jib was made from 40thou plasticard sides and ends with the diagonal strengthening bars at top and bottom being fashioned from plastic strip. The hook end of the jib was modified from the kit one and grafted onto the scratchbuilt section while the rope wheels at the hook end also came from the kit. Other details included spotlights made from plastic strip along with lifting data panels made from 10thou plasticard rectangles and glued to the cab end of the jib.

The match wagon consisted of the coach chassis with an embossed plastic wood-

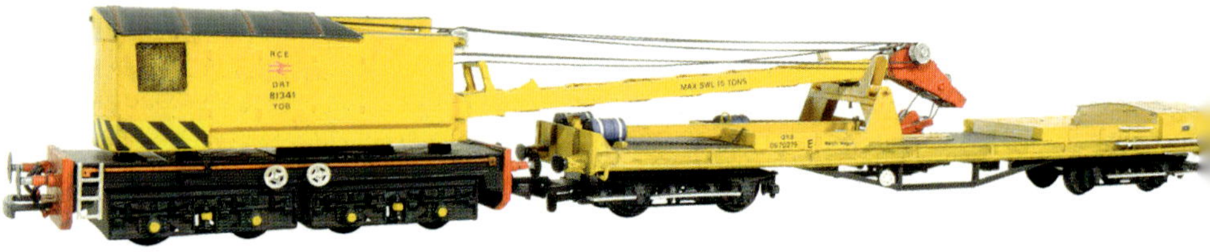

This design of Taylor Hubbard crane was not the company's best looking with its slab-sided crane body. The underframe is again largely scratchbuilt with the fact that it was a bogie design being well disguised by the chunky sideframes.

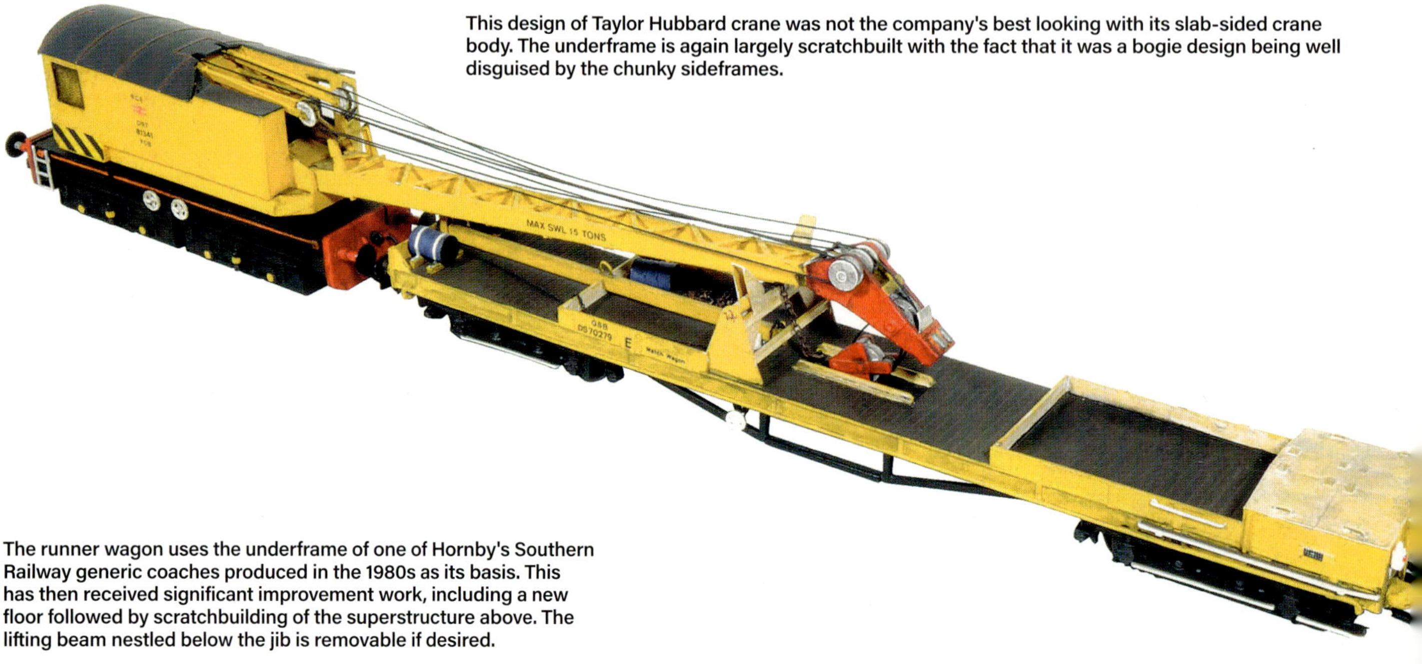

The runner wagon uses the underframe of one of Hornby's Southern Railway generic coaches produced in the 1980s as its basis. This has then received significant improvement work, including a new floor followed by scratchbuilding of the superstructure above. The lifting beam nestled below the jib is removable if desired.

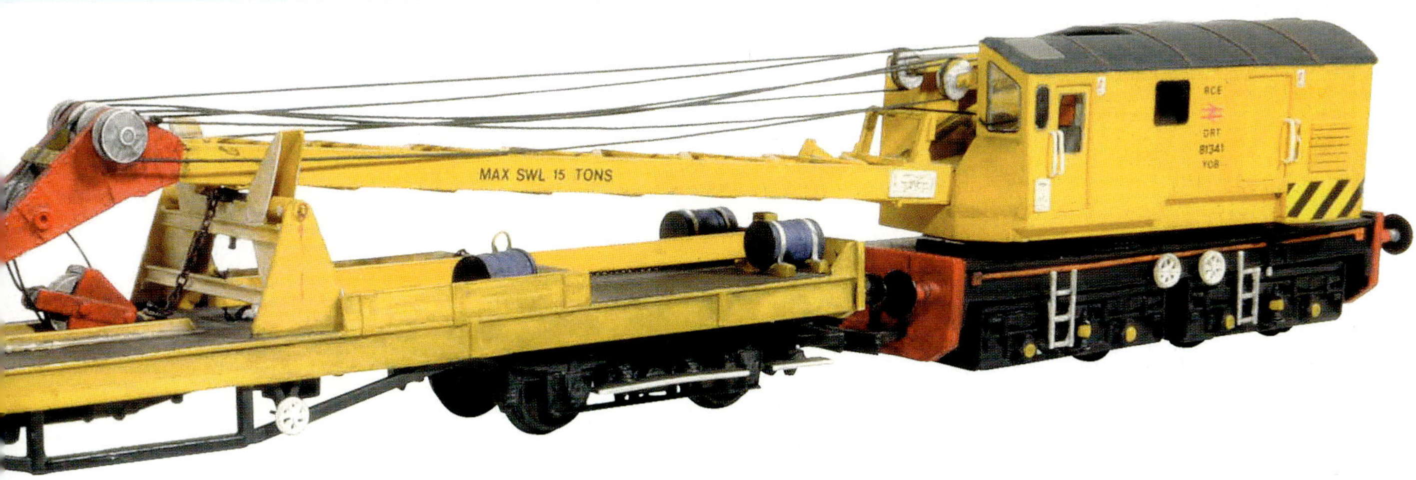

The runners were built on the underframes of former EMU vehicles, which accounts for their excessive length. In this case, DS70279 used the frame of 6-Pan Trailer First Corridor S12270S.

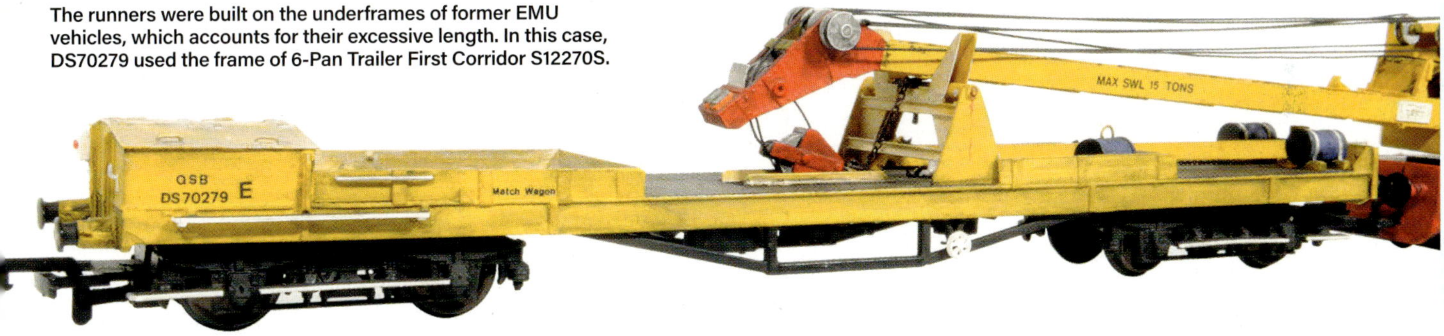

effect floor with the toolbox, low-sided stowage sections and jib platform made from plasticard. A hole was cut in the floor for the hook well with the sides added from plastic strip. The spreader bar was 40thou plasticard with oil drums mounted on cradles formed from plasticard. Buffers were a whitemetal heavyweight EMU type with the bogies being Bachmann's Southern design with the stepboards added.

To keep the jib in position while going round curves, I fitted a 0.9mm diameter brass pivot on the top of the jib rest. On the underside of the jib and in line with the pivot, I added a piece of plasticard with a hole to locate the jib on the pivot. The hole was larger than the 0.9mm pivot to allow the jib some sideways and back and forth movement. This method has worked well to keep the jib in a central position with no trouble.

Finishing

Painting was with Humbrol paints, with yellow for the cab and jib along with the runner wagon body, solebars and lifting beam. Otherwise, it was black for the underframe and bogies, wood brown for the floor of the runner, medium grey for the crane roof and the other colours as per the pictures. The transfers were mostly from alphabet and number sheets of different sizes with the BR arrows coming from a Network SouthEast EMU sheet. The black hatching on the back and sides of the cab was from Fox Transfers.

Cotton was used for the rigging ropes attached to the hook and run round the wheels on the end of the jib and those on the top of the cab. My photos were very handy for this process. Lastly, I fixed a 30mm length of fine chain to the hook which goes onto the match wagon rest pivot.

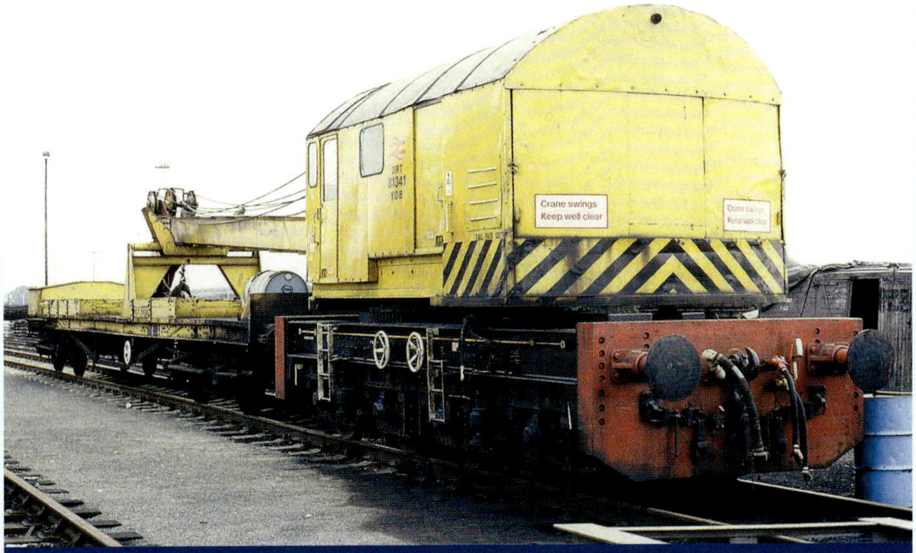

ABOVE: **Illustrating the actual crane modelled here, DRT81341 was awaiting its next job at Ashford on August 24, 1980, along with runner DS70279. Both survive today at the Keighley and Worth Valley Railway.** Simon Bendall Collection

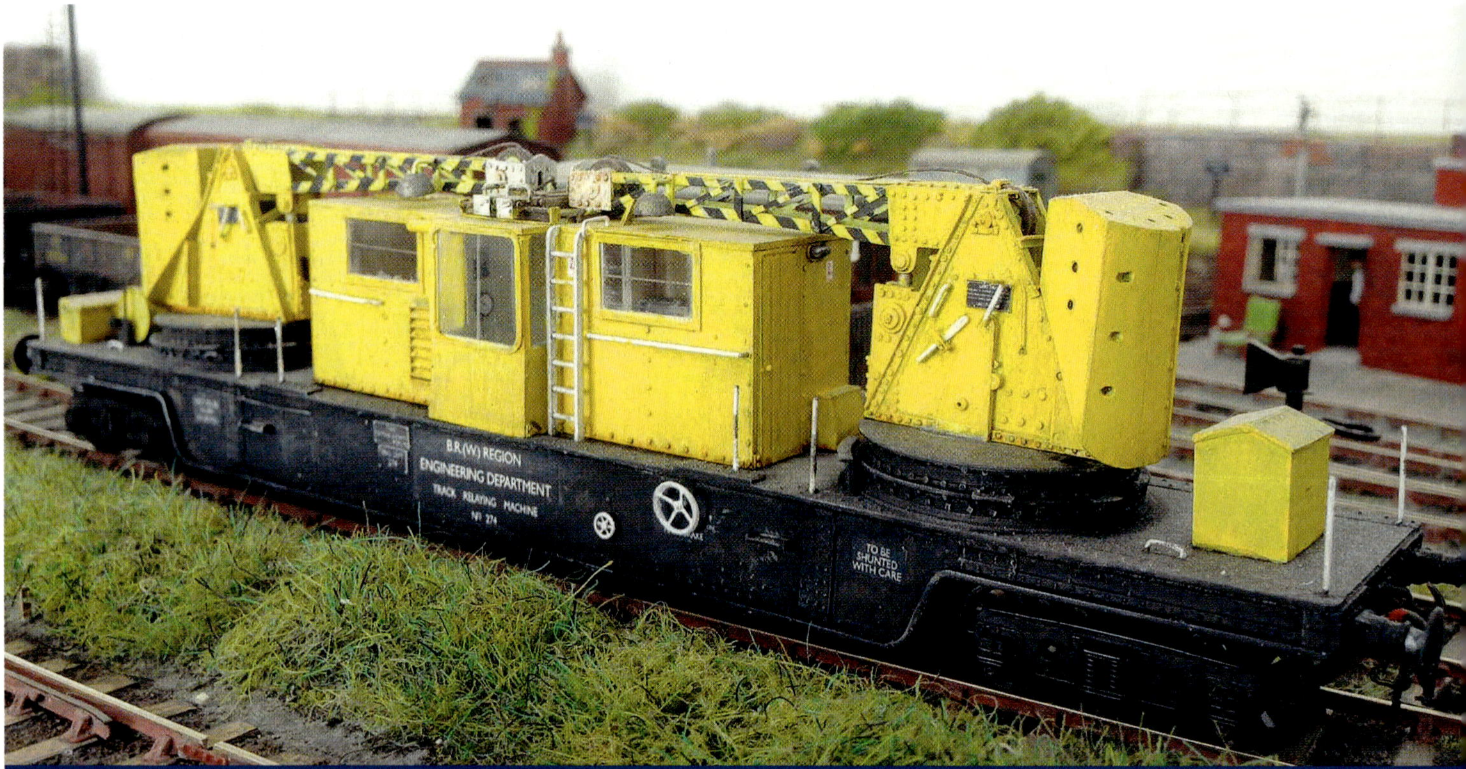

Scratchbuilding a Track Relayer by Hywel Thomas

ABOVE: **Western Region track relayer TRM274 stands ready for action on Morfa Bank Sidings. Although such vehicles are often called twin jib cranes, the correct terminology is track relaying machine or unit and, as the term suggests, they were designed to lift and position track panels using both jibs together.**

This style of Track Relaying Machine, or TRM as the Western Region referred to them, was designed at Swindon Works in the early 1950s. At that time, the Western was already operating the early 1948-built track relayer DW215, which was based on two old hand crane chassis and built for tracklaying in the Severn Tunnel. The Southern was the proud owner of its first tracklaying machine dating from 1947 and a few early North Eastern Region units were also in operation.

The first of the five to this design emerged from Swindon in 1952 and in appearance looked like an early GWR-design Crocodile well wagon with similar, possibly reclaimed, spoked-wheel bogies fitted and heavy-duty riveted frames. The central control cabin housed the operator and the diesel generator that powered the two winches. These were simple counter-weighted affairs positioned at each end on a turntable with the two jibs pointing inwards for travel.

When built, they were actually fitted with Churchward ratchet handbrake levers, adding some credence to suggestions that they did in fact use at least parts from redundant Crocodiles, but these were replaced with handbrake wheels soon after 1956 and certainly by 1961. Each machine featured a number of small detail differences from the others as their 30-year careers progressed.

Allocations

Of the five, the first was an Eastern Region machine with three for the Western following in 1953 along with one example for the Scottish Region. The Eastern numbered its as 78/002, it also carrying DB966480, later to become DRB78104, while the Scottish machine was numbered TRM 1/10; this also carried DB965311 and then DRB78100. The three Western Region examples were TRM274 (later DRB78114), TRM275 (later DRB78115) and TRM276 (later DRB78116) and none of these were allocated numbers in BR's DB96xxxx series.

The Eastern example featured yellow cabins, grey cranes, and a black underframe from new, while the Scottish machine may have been in black livery, but no colour views have surfaced. The Western, in typical non-conformist style, initially painted its trio in all-over black with a BR 'cycling lion' emblem on the cabin sides but at some time in the 1950s, applied a rather fetching crimson and cream scheme. All later gained yellow upper parts with a black underframe.

In use the units, certainly on the Western, were nominally allocated to the pre-assembly depots such as Radyr but in reality, seem to have just travelled to wherever they were needed. They could often be found tucked away in sidings awaiting weekend or overnight possessions, sometimes in the company of one of the Western's fleet of Ruston & Hornsby PWM shunters, later to become Class 97/6.

The relayers all lasted until the early 1980s; 78/002 was scrapped at Stockton in July 1982 while TRM 1/10 was cut up at Mossend in March 1982 along with TRU276, which had moved north to Scotland in 1979. Of the other two, TRM274 was scrapped at Hereford in February 1983 while TRM275 was the only example to succumb at its birthplace in Swindon during March 1982.

Seeking to build something a little different in 4mm scale for my layout Morfa Bank Sidings, one of these TRMs appealed greatly. The following photos detail how I went about scratchbuilding one of the Western examples.

1 **The basis for the model was a pair of venerable Mainline Weltrols, which are still produced by Bachmann today. With no plans or diagrams to work from, the overall length was calculated from the relationship between the crane jibs and the standard 60ft track panels they were designed to lift. The first wagon was cut down the centre and a lengthening piece removed from the well of the second example.**

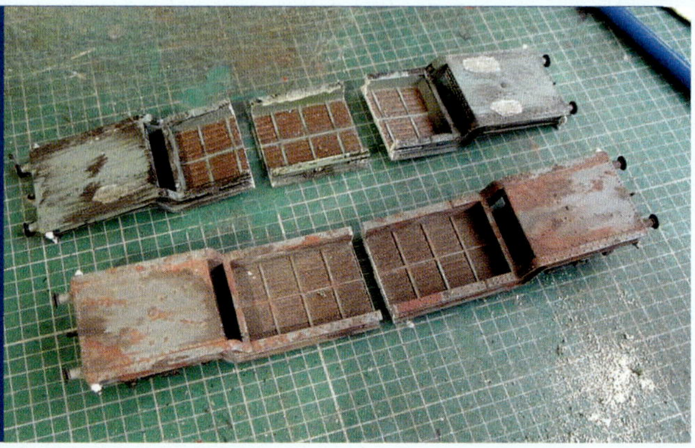

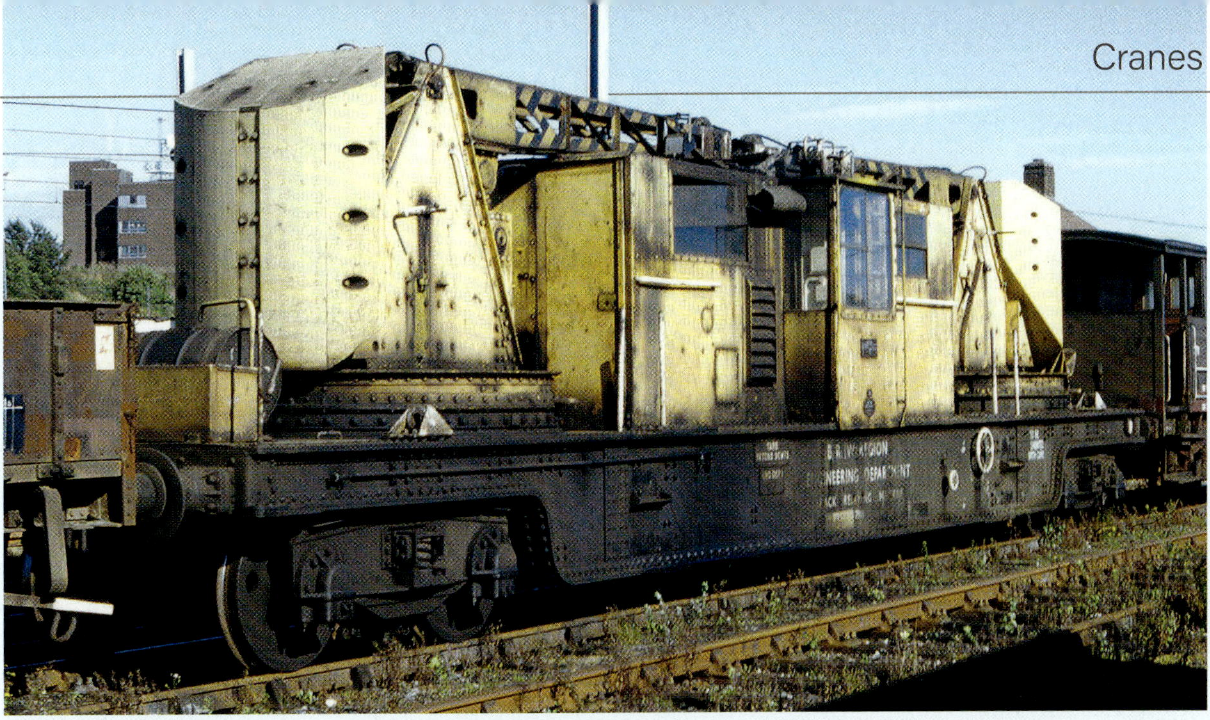

LEFT: **Originally allocated to the Western Region, DRB78116 was moved to the Scottish Region in January 1979. Some 18 months later, the former DW276 was found back across the border at Carlisle Upperby on August 14, 1981. It would be scrapped in the spring of the following year on site at Mossend Yard after a working life of just under 30 years.** Trevor Mann

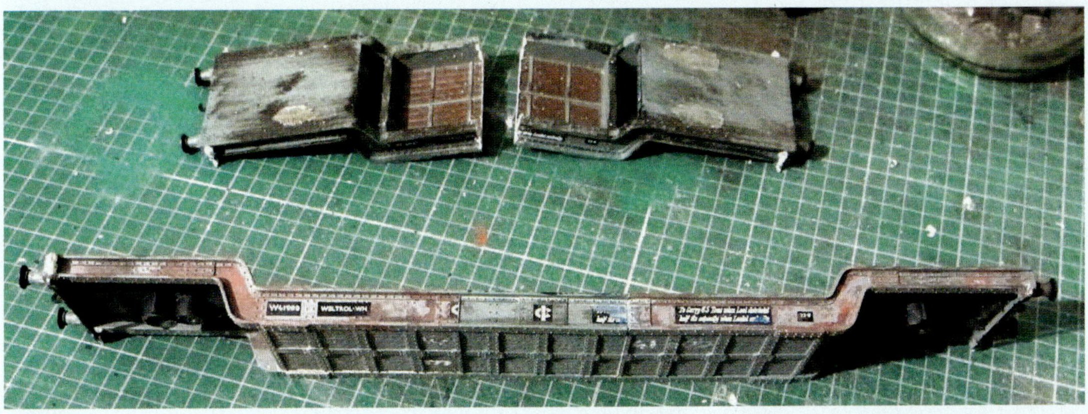

2 **Here we can see the extra piece spliced into the original body using copious quantities of solvent. The original bogies were re-used. Even after all these years, the quality of the Mainline moulding still stands up well against current day ready-to-run offerings.**

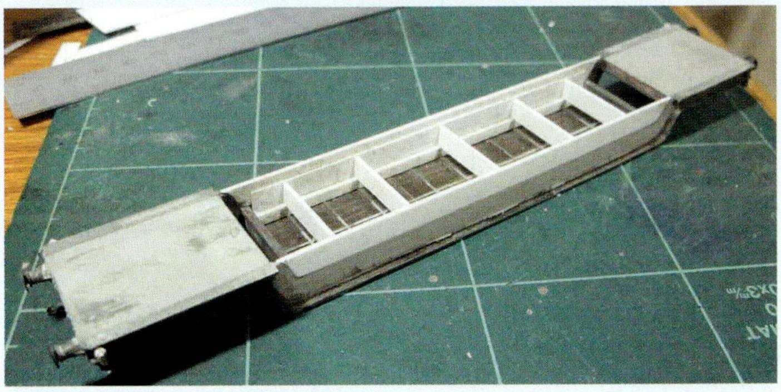

3 **Sadly, the nicely moulded rivets on the sides had to go and new sheet plastic extensions were fitted. Extra bracing was also fitted to the inside of the well to provide some strength once the upper works were fitted. The end platforms were also filed flat at this stage ready for the new deck.**

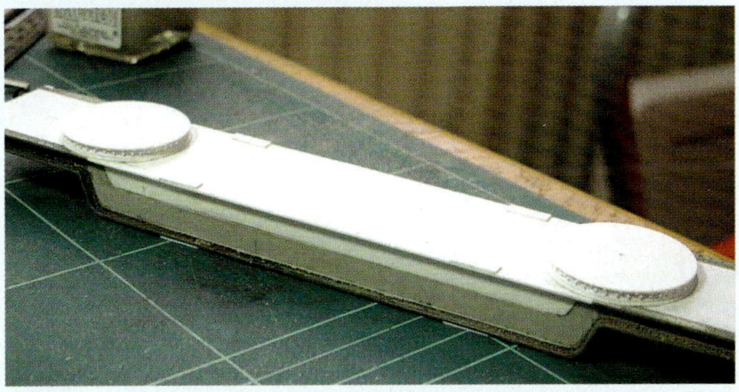

4 **The new deck has now been fitted along with the edging to match up with the original wagon ends. The two turntables have also been fitted, complete with the substantial bolt heads around the circumference.**

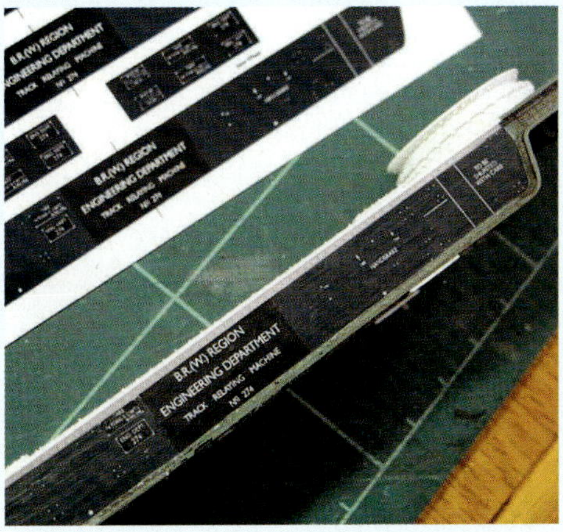

5 **In something of an experiment, the lettering, and the location of the rivets on the side panel were printed out from a computer. Some time was spent adjusting the fonts to the correct style and getting everything lined up correctly. In the end, sticking the rivets to the card base proved too messy and unpredictable, so the lettering panels were cut out for re-use and then inlaid into new thin plastic side overlays.**

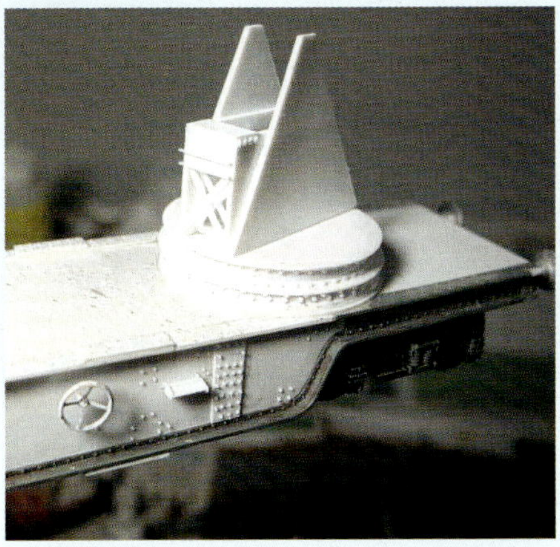

6 **The new plastic overlay panels have now been fitted along with a lot of plastic cube rivets, steps, and a test fit for the handbrake wheel. A start has been made on the cranes too. The unusual triangular side pieces and bracing are also starting to appear as the build progresses along with the top section of the circular turntable. Despite initially being made to revolve, this was later fixed in place.**

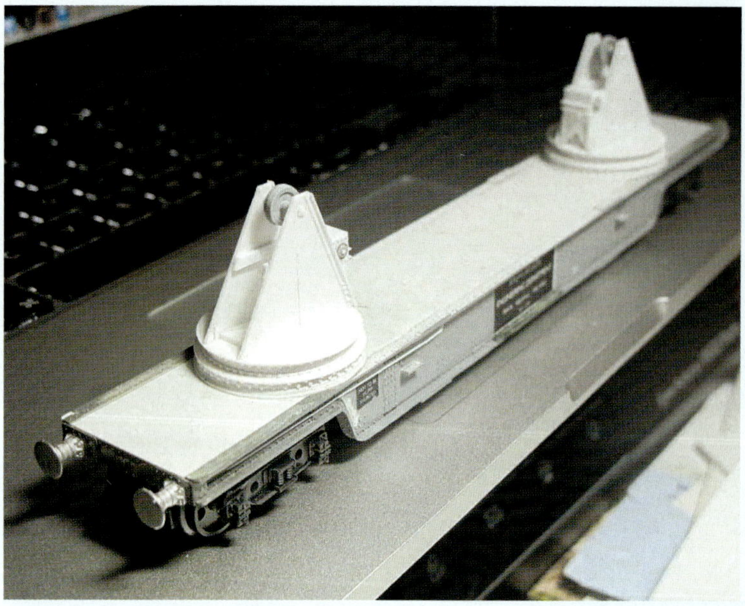

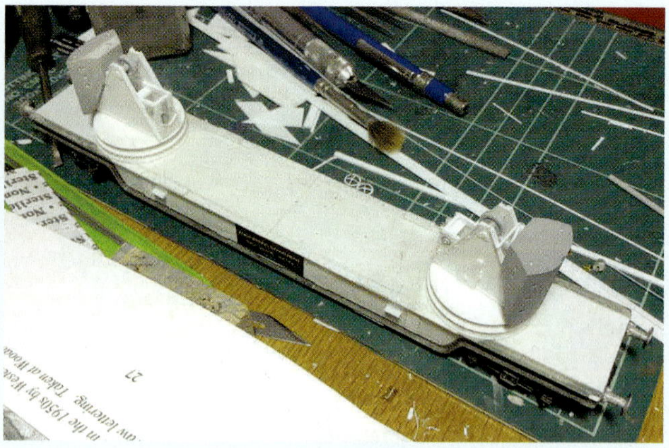

8 The substantial balance weights have been temporarily positioned. These were a particularly complicated shape, and several false starts were required before they began to look the part. Further rivet detail is starting to appear on one of the cranes. The state on the workbench shows just how many widths of Evergreen strip were used on this model!

7 With a bit more detail on the cranes and some pulley wheels fitted (sourced, I think, from an old Airfix kit), the character of the relayer is starting to appear. The now flush lettering panels were masked off and a light coat of grey primer applied to check for any issues. The new rivets show up well, as they did prominently on the real machine. Heavy duty cast buffers have also been fitted.

9 A cruel close-up of one of the cranes with the riveting finished and the various wire details appearing. Once the crane was finished, I did not tackle any further riveted scratchbuilds for a while!

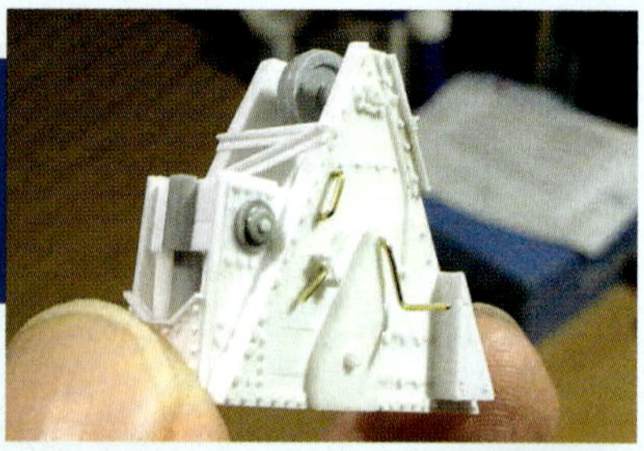

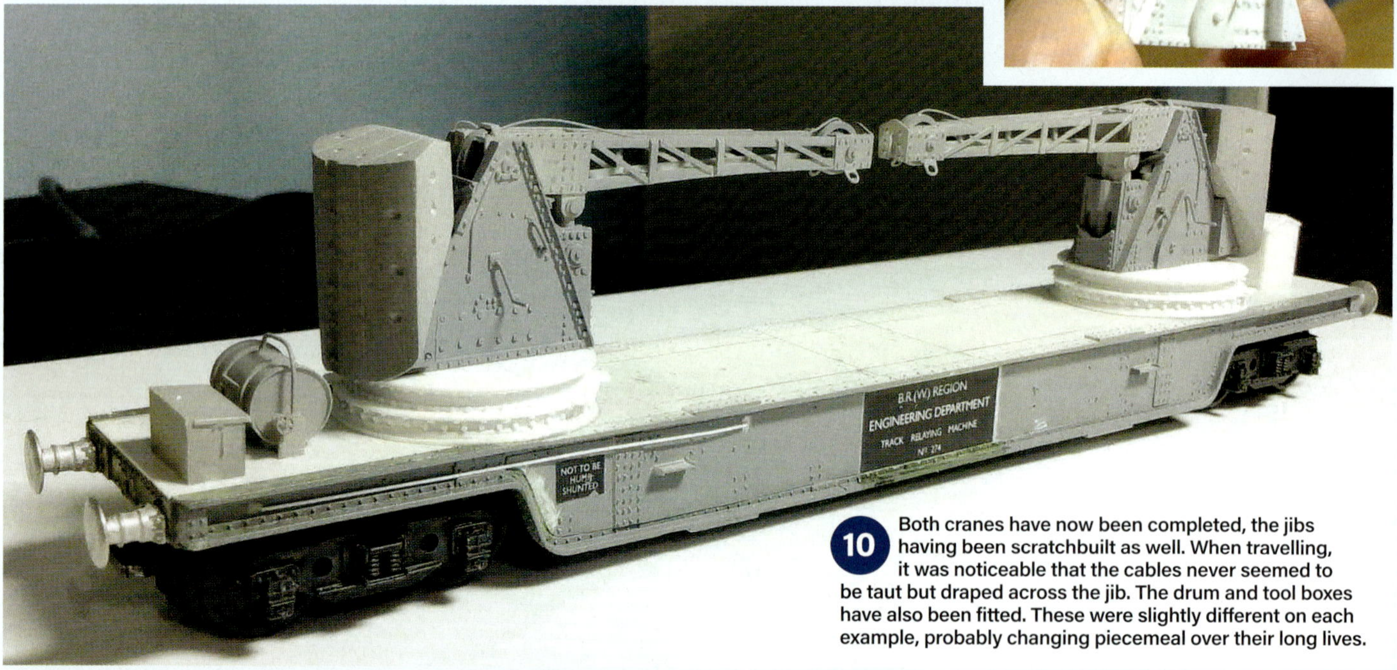

10 Both cranes have now been completed, the jibs having been scratchbuilt as well. When travelling, it was noticeable that the cables never seemed to be taut but draped across the jib. The drum and tool boxes have also been fitted. These were slightly different on each example, probably changing piecemeal over their long lives.

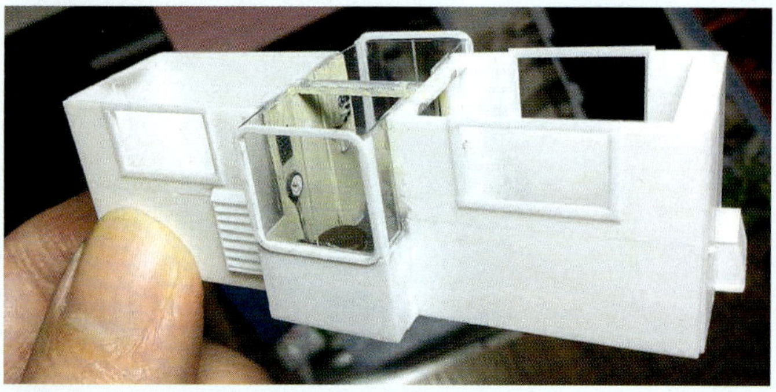

11 With the chassis and cranes completed, it was time to move onto the cabin. Despite seeming to be a simple shape, it turned out to be quite complicated with those large windows, which, of course, meant that the interior needed to be modelled too. This then had to be made and painted before the rest of the cabin.

12 The cab interior is nearly completed, and part painted with a pair of hi-viz vests hung up at the far end. In 1972, it seems those vests spent more time hanging in cabs than actually being worn! This is very different to today and the head-to-toe orange army.

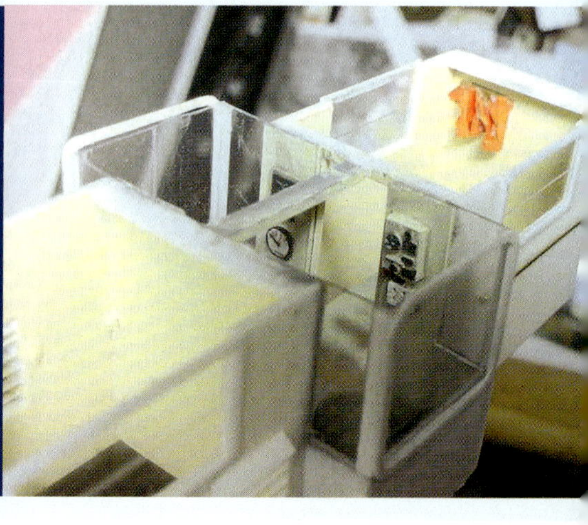

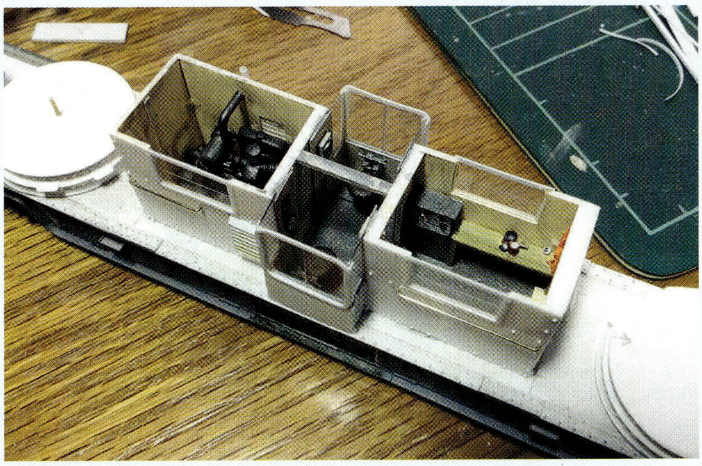

13 The interior of all three sections of the cabin are now complete. The generator sits at one end with the bench and electrical cabinet at the other. The operator's cab had been fitted with the simple mechanical controls and the small stool that served as a seat. Handrails also now added.

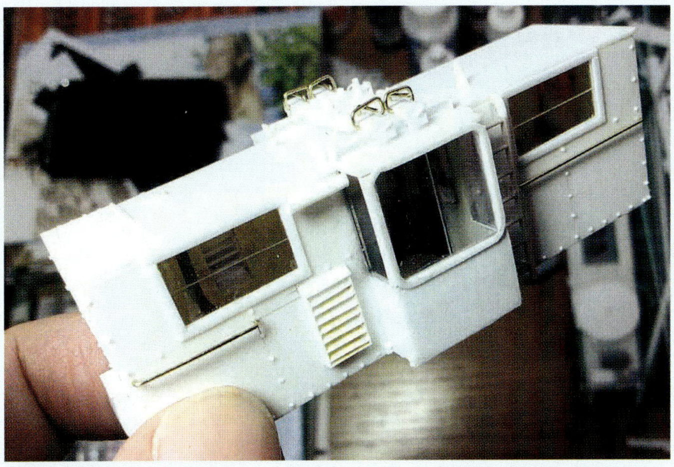

14 The flat roof has been fitted, complete with the lifting brackets attached to their travel cradle above the operator's cab. Some more rivets have been added and the roof access ladder. The whole vehicle is now ready for painting.

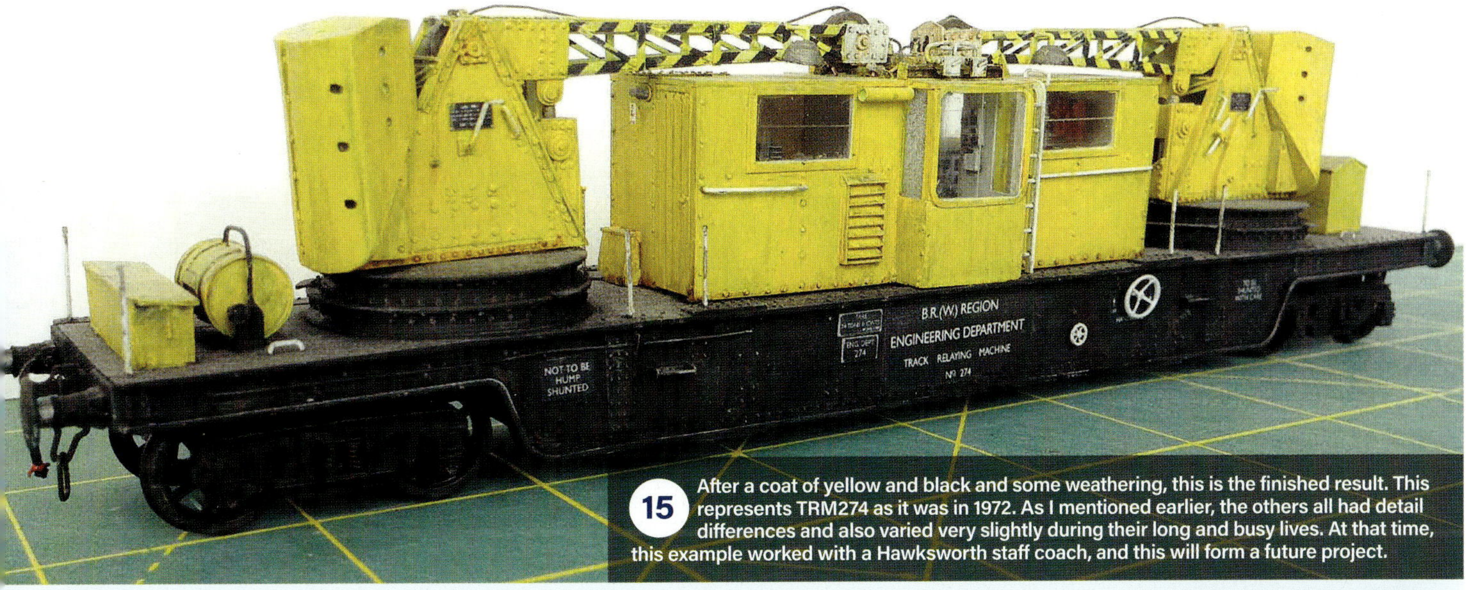

15 After a coat of yellow and black and some weathering, this is the finished result. This represents TRM274 as it was in 1972. As I mentioned earlier, the others all had detail differences and also varied very slightly during their long and busy lives. At that time, this example worked with a Hawksworth staff coach, and this will form a future project.

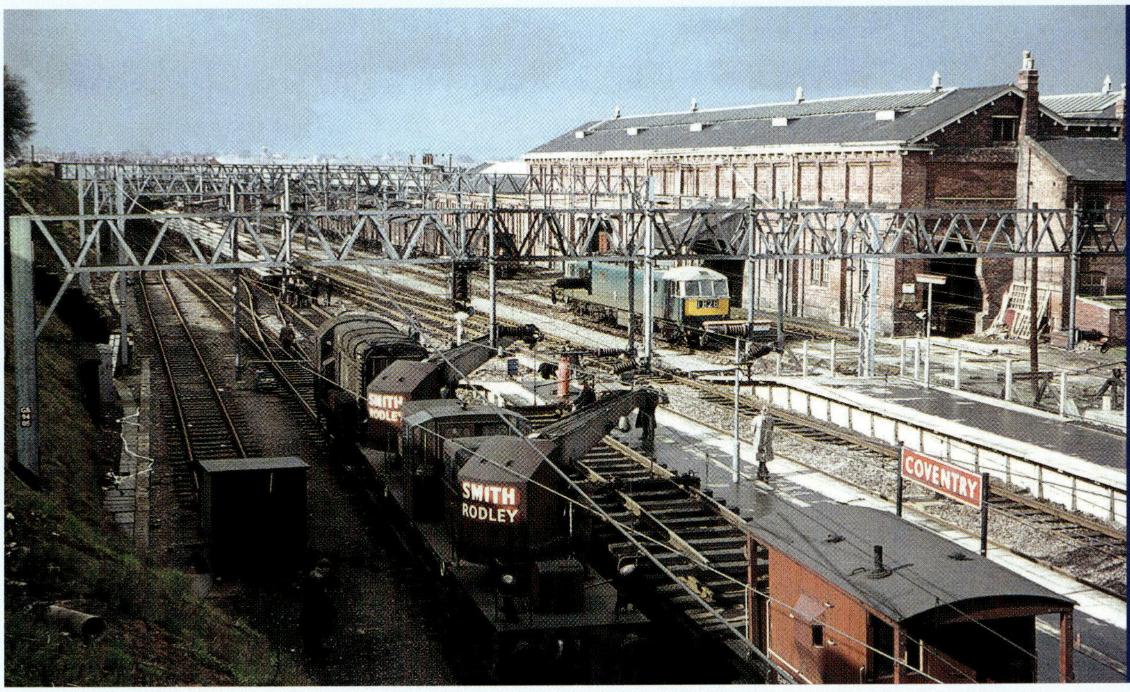

LEFT: **Although a different make of track relayer, being built by Smith Rodley rather than in-house by BR, the operating principal was the same. The two jibs would work together to lift 60ft track panels off flat wagons, such as Salmon and Sturgeon, positioned alongside and then move them to where they needed to be laid. Early examples were unpowered and had to be hauled to and fro, as shown here with a Class 08 attached, but later builds were self-powered. The relayers could also recover redundant track panels in the same manner. This is the scene at Coventry on an unrecorded date in 1967.** Trevor Mann Collection

Plasser perfection by Mark Lambert

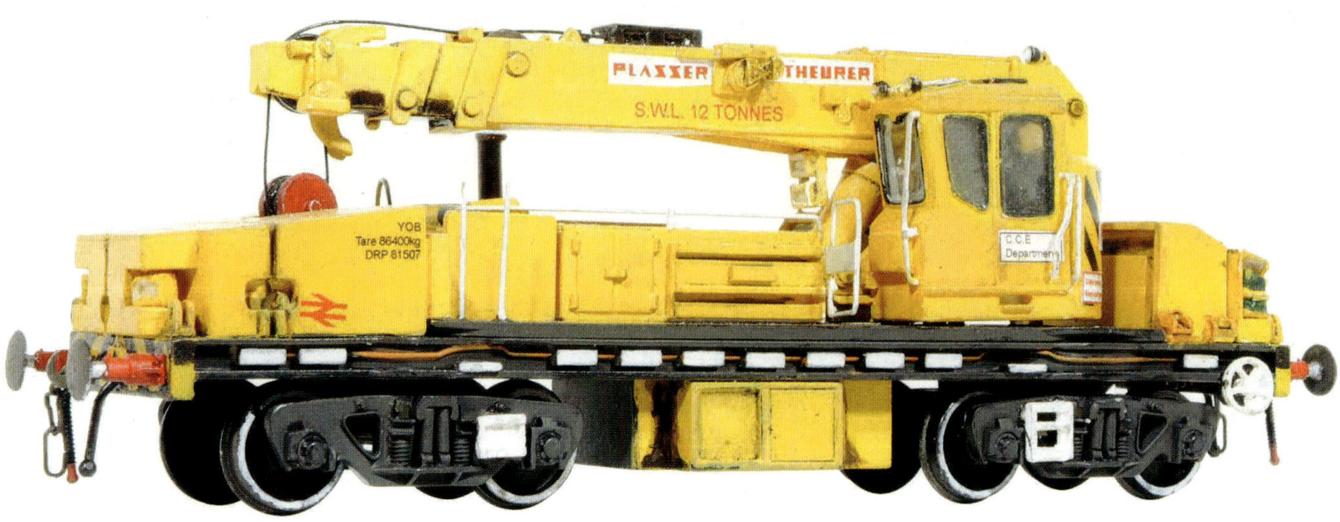

This is a 4mm scale resin kit by Make Your Mark Models that assembles into a very good representation of the Plasser & Theurer GPC-72 15-tonne Civil Engineers' crane. Also produced in hand-built ready-to-run form by the company, both options are sadly now out of stock and have been for some time.

The resin parts are all perfectly cast and fit in such a way that they lock most of the bodywork together. There are a fair number of handrails to add from wire, which is not supplied, but the exact style and placement of these varies with the age of the prototypes and the operator so it is best to work from period photos to get the correct layout. I also added the guard rails over the window in the top of the cab. Glazing is supplied but this is quite thick acrylic sheet that fits into the casting cut-outs; I replaced most of it with thinner sheet but in hindsight, the supplied parts would have been fine.

Buffers are not supplied as these again varied widely over time. I used Lanarkshire Models and Supplies 18in head Oleos, but some cranes had 22in heads, which is typically a DMU buffer and also available from the company. The GPC-72 is a diesel-hydraulic crane that can move itself at a low speed in possessions and yards via a torque converter on one bogie. However, I shied away from trying to replicate the large drive unit on the jib-end bogie as it would most likely foul the wheelsets in OO gauge.

I opted to undercoat all the parts before assembly to make sure the paint got into all the corners and crevices. However, I then had to sand all the locating pins down as the tolerances are so fine that the pins no longer fitted the holes! If the kit reappears and I do a second one, I will assemble the jib and body parts before undercoating to avoid this problem.

Hoses and cables

I fitted the main hydraulic lines on the jib by very carefully drilling 0.5mm holes in locations determined from photos and fitted thin layout wire, with the outer sleeve cut back a little, into the holes with superglue. For the crane hook rigging, I used copper wire sold for model cars glued into 0.7mm holes at strategic locations. The cable run is not quite correct as modelled, having examined some further photos sent to me. The pulley block on the side is not connected directly to the hook, the cable goes into the jib (and possibly doubles back towards the cab) and re-emerges nearer the end to go over the hook pulley and back up to an anchor point. The cable that runs alongside the jib is a power supply to the spotlights on the end of the jib and is paid out from a drum near the hydraulic distributor.

The smaller spotlights again vary from crane to crane, so I added some that were supplied with the kit and supplemented them with a few jewelled headlights I had in the spares box from about 25 years ago. The crane jib is permanently fixed in place, but I painted it before final assembly to ensure I could get at all the parts with a paintbrush. The paint shade is a custom mix of Games Workshop 'Averland Sunset', 'Yriel Yellow' and 'White Scar' to give a mix of faded yellow shades across the components. The baseplate and silencer were painted with Railmatch bauxite and the frame and bogies with 'Charadon Granite'. Other details were variously picked out in orange and white as required.

I then used brown and grey acrylic and enamel washes to add shading and grease to the underside of the crane jib and across the underframe as these cranes do seem to leak fluid and grease quite readily. All the main transfers come from a sheet sold by the manufacturer but there are more small notices on the real thing than are supplied, so some warning placards were sourced from spares (mostly military models).

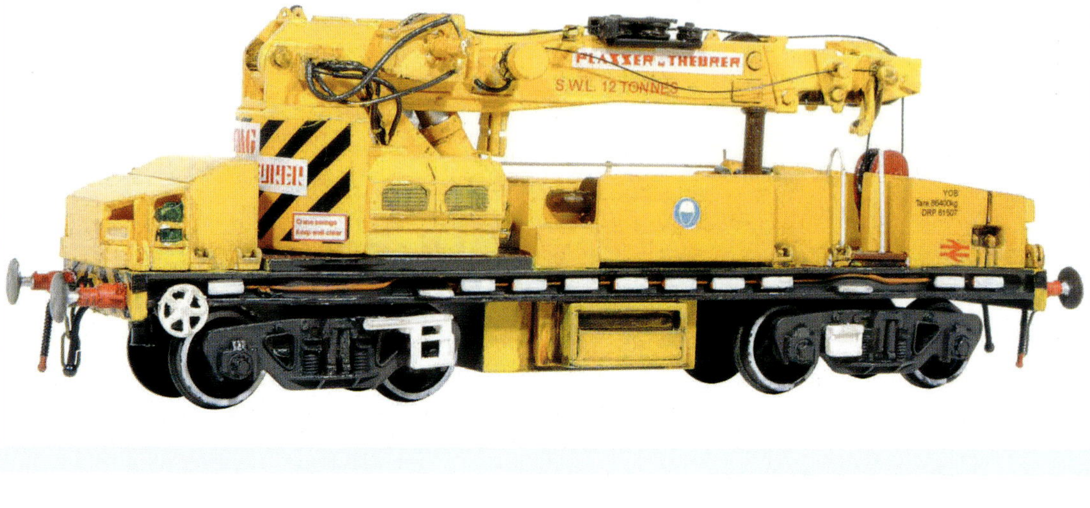

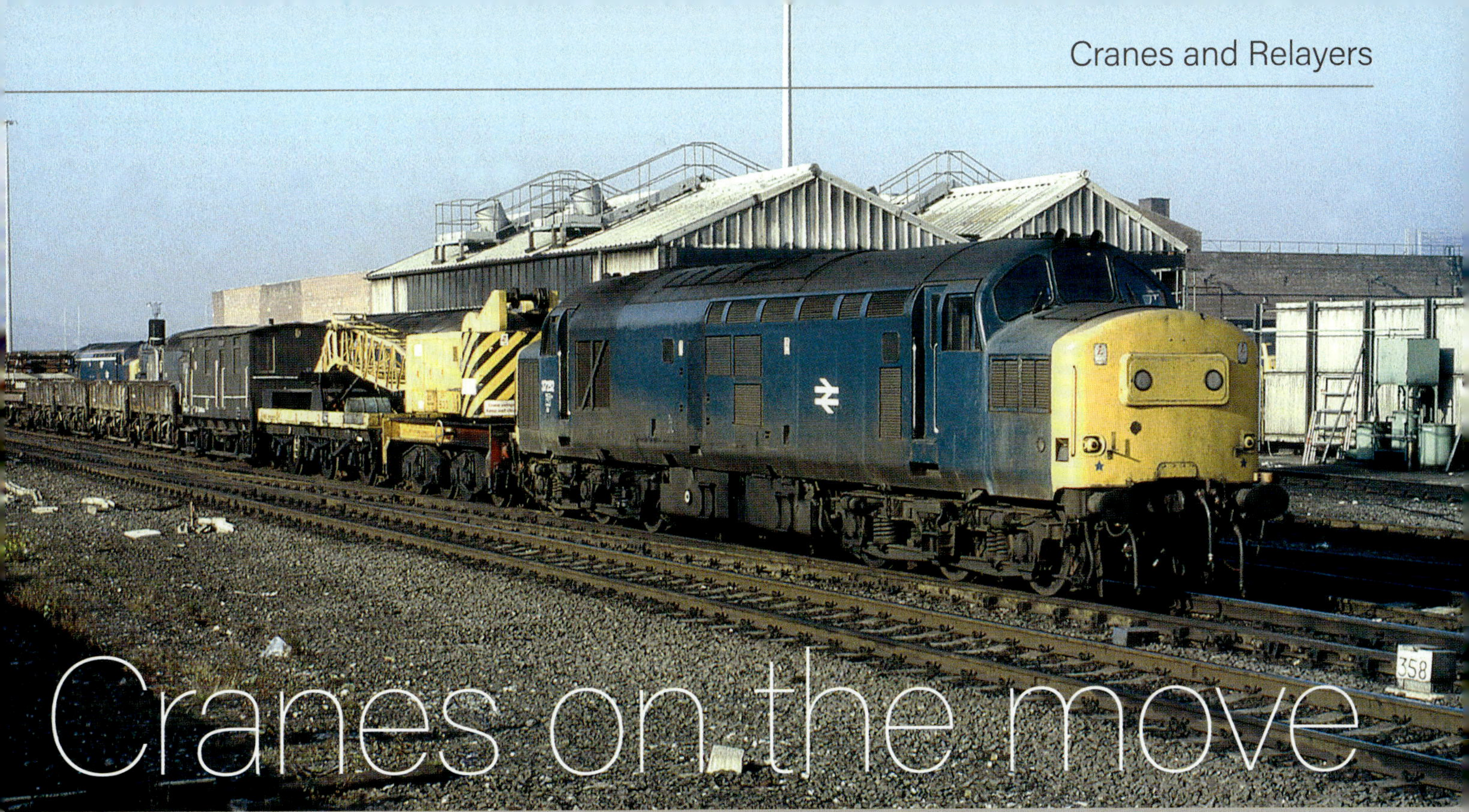

Cranes on the move

During the BR period, cranes were seldom seen moving alone, usually being accompanied by a brake van at the very least or with a staff van and support wagon. They could also be formed in permanent way trains, be they long or short, on the way to worksites. Simon Bendall showcases a selection of images with different types of cranes on view.

ABOVE: Two cranes for the price of one as 37252 drifts past Gateshead TMD during October 1985 with a works train. In the background, the depot's Cowans breakdown crane is raised to its limit, but it is the crane behind the Class 37 that is arguably more interesting. This is one of four 10-ton diesel electric cranes built by Coles that ran on two substantial plate-frame bogies. Numbered DRF81312-15, they were normally found in the northeast in BR ownership. The accompanying staff van is also comparatively unusual, being one of the 26 ballast brake vans ordered by the LNER just prior to nationalisation, while the crane's runner is a three-axle design.

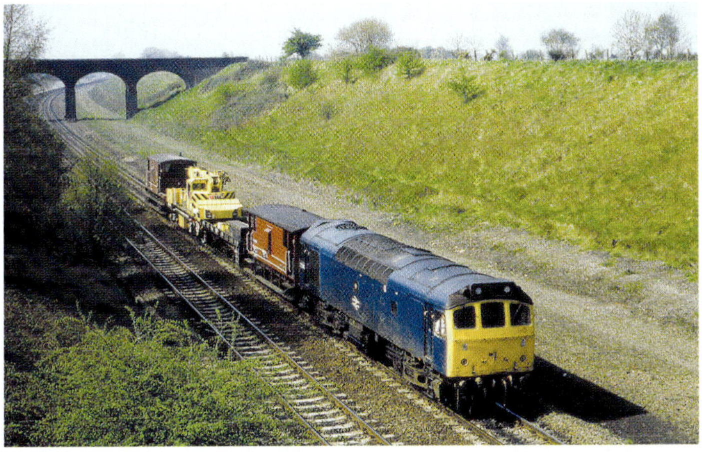

ABOVE: Spring is coming as 25296 ambles along at Saltney Junction, near Chester, on April 27, 1984, with a Plasser GPC-72 telescopic jib crane, its support wagons, and a BR brake van. During the1980s, it was common for these cranes to have an open wagon and staff van assigned to accompany then, although the precise nature of what was used varied across the regions. The London Midland often used a Plate wagon to carry drums of fluids, lifting tackle in a tool box and other assorted material while the mess van was invariably an LMS design brake.

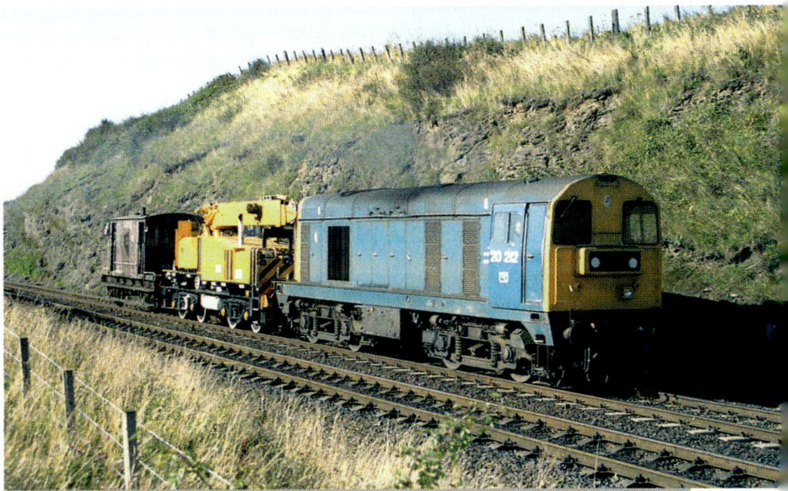

ABOVE: A lightweight load for 20212 on September 10, 1986, as it passes Seafield, near Leith, with a crane transfer. In tow is one of the Cowans Sheldon 12-tonne diesel hydraulic cranes, which as a telescopic jib design were a direct rival to the Plasser version. These were something of a bulky machine, especially from this side, when compared to the sleeker look of the Austrian product.

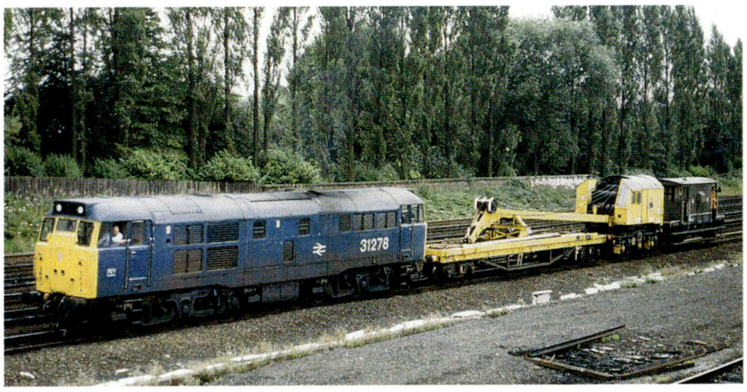

LEFT: Displaying the Thornaby trademark of large numbers, 31278 passes York Holgate on August 23, 1988, with one of the lighter weight Taylor Hubbard designs in tow, these coming in several different versions. As was often the case for BR cranes, the runner was a repurposed wagon rather than a new build, in this case a Bogie Bolster C.

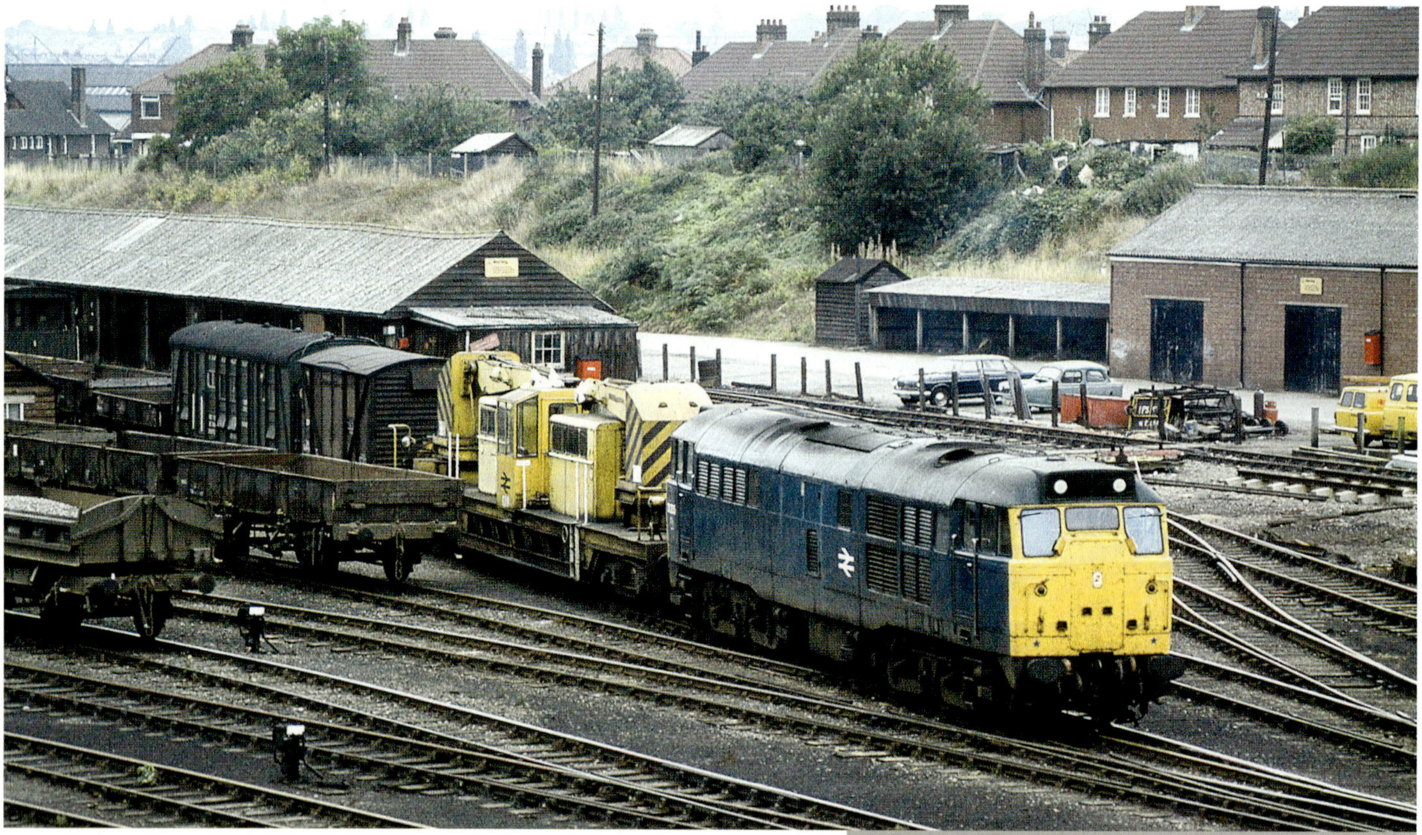

ABOVE: **During September 1981, 31245 awaits departure from Ipswich engineers' yard with one of the imposing Thomas Smith track relayers in tow, this being a self-propelled example. Accompanying it is a 12-ton van along with a Southern Railway-design Parcels and Miscellaneous Van (PMV) which has been converted into a staff van.**

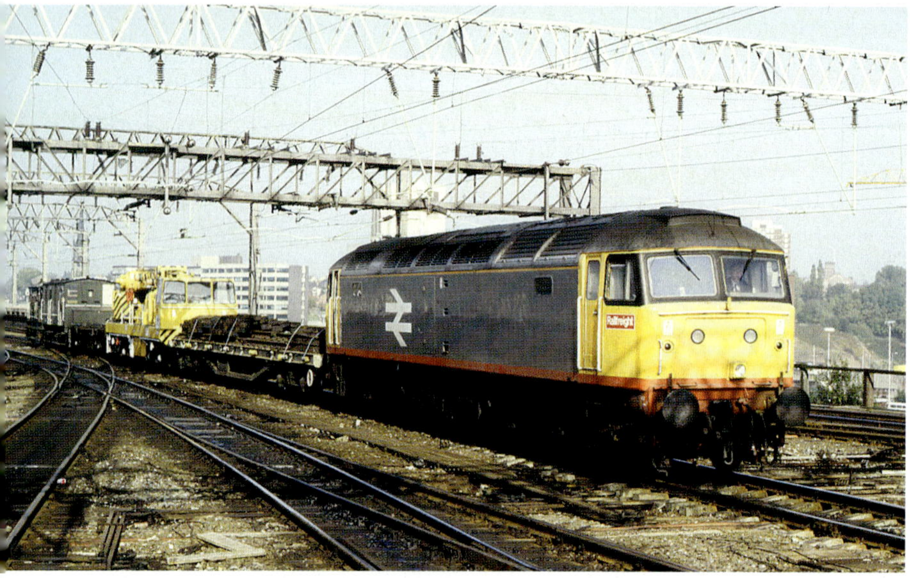

LEFT: **Railfreight Red Stripe-liveried 47339 is seen approaching Stockport on October 15, 1988, with one of the distinctly unusual Thomas Smith 18-ton diesel hydraulic cranes in tow. Built in 1970, DRS81502 was another variant on the telescopic jib design but had a full width operator's cabin at the opposite end to the jib. Only two were built and they were not a success, being found to be unstable both in use and transit. On this occasion, the working also featured a Salmon with recovered track, another of the LNER ballast brakes as a mess van and a BR standard brake van. The runner behind the crane is also a rarity, this being DB710253, one of two experimental Conflat D prototypes now transferred to departmental use as a ZSV.**

RIGHT: **A Plasser & Theurer TJC-60 track relayer is the machine of interest as 37038 passes Aller Junction on April 10, 1992. The train also includes a former Mk1 Carflat carrying a lifting beam, a Salmon with packing timber strapped to its deck and an ex-Southern PMV staff van. Bringing up the rear are three ZBA Rudd, these all being the Grampus conversions, two having the replacement ends only while the one on the back is a full re-body.** All Simon Bendall Collection

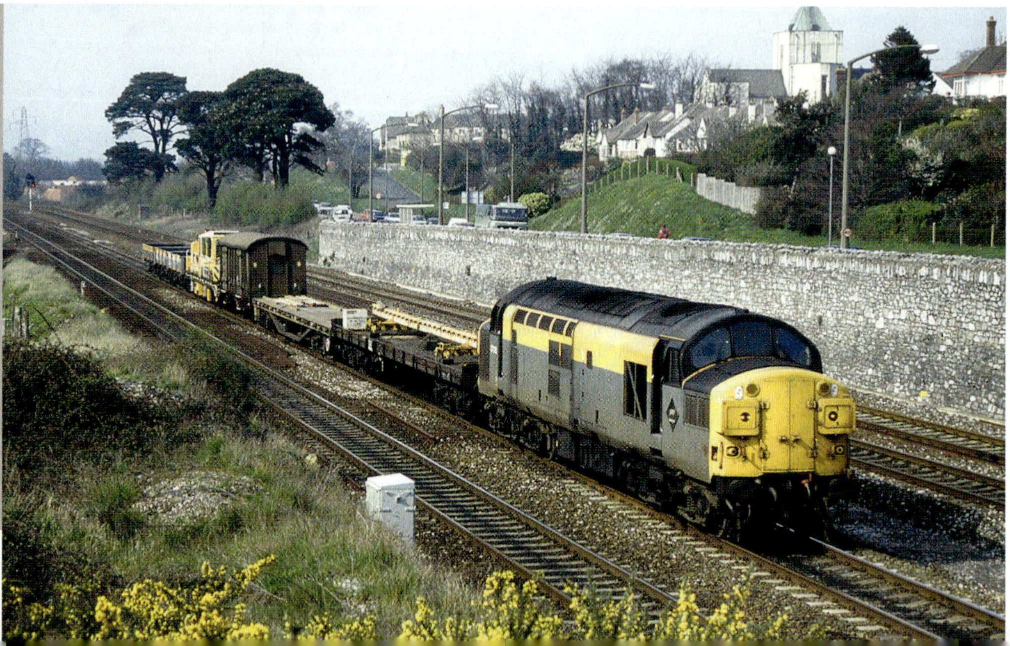

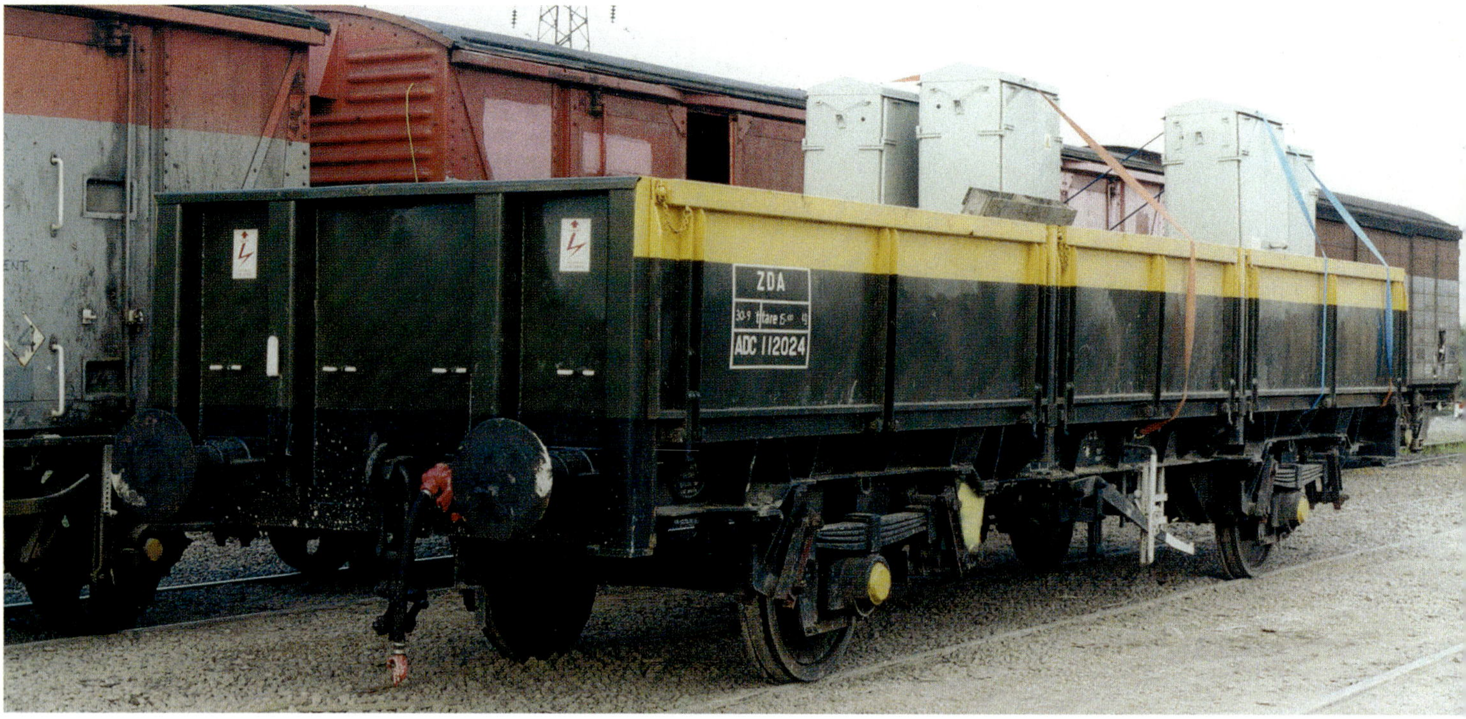

Rail Stores services

Falling under the remit of the Mechanical and Electrical Engineers was a diverse range of wagons used to transfer rolling stock parts across the country. Like other engineering departments, this fleet was progressively updated during the 1980s to use air-braked stock and David Ratcliffe recounts the types involved.

By the early 1980s, British Rail's plan to gradually switch all freight traffic into air-braked wagons was gathering pace, which meant that the engineers' rolling stock needed updating. While the approach that the Civil Engineers took to this process has already been detailed in the preceding pages, it was not the only department affected. In a similar manner, the Mechanical & Electrical Engineers (M&EE) began to receive quantities of redundant air-braked and long-wheelbase wagons from 1982, albeit in much smaller quantities than the voracious needs of the Civil Engineers.

ABOVE: **Repainting its wagons was never a priority for the M&EE but ZDA ADC112024 did receive an unusual yellow and olive green livery. When spotted at Ripple Lane in May 1994, it was on loan to the Signal and Telecomms department and loaded with relay cabinets.** Colin Wright/David Ratcliffe Collection

In total, the M&EE department took on 36 open wagons, comprising 10 OBAs and 26 OCAs, along with 40 vans, initially mostly VCA, and 40 SPA plate wagons. These were used to replace an even more varied collection of vacuum-braked and unfitted vehicles that were in use conveying a wide range of miscellaneous loads under the rail stores banner. Typical loads included locomotive and carriage brake blocks, diesel and electric locomotive and unit parts, steel castings, wheelsets and wagon springs, test weights, new buffers, electric batteries, wagon sheets, bags of locomotive sand and

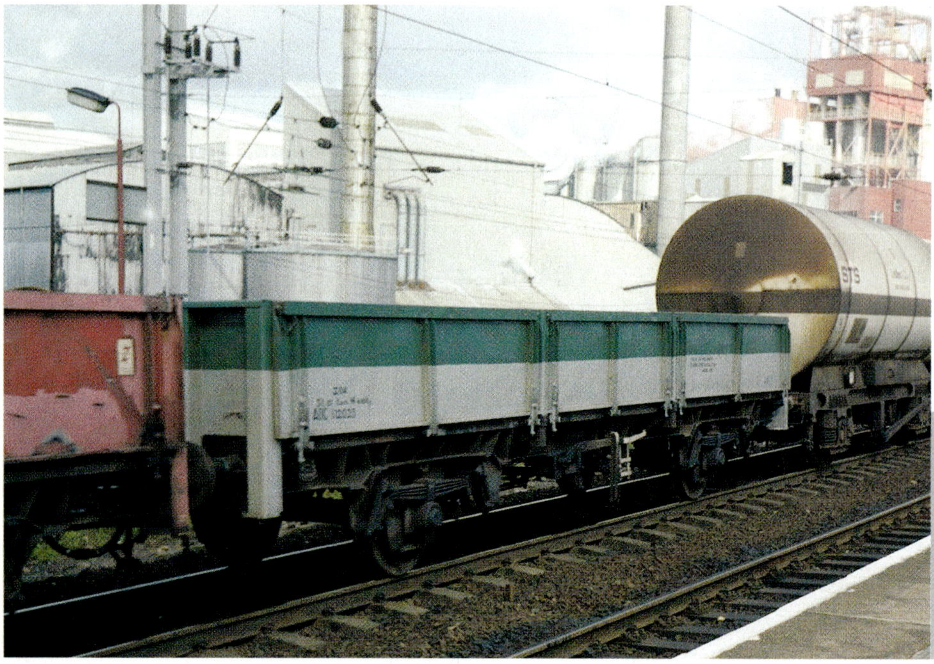

LEFT: **During 1985, two former OCAs allocated to carry stores traffic between Swindon Works and Plymouth Laira, ADC112022 and ADC112023, were painted in green and grey but without any Rail Stores lettering. Seen some way from its designated circuit, the second of these ZDAs passes through Warrington Bank Quay in September 1986 while working from Crewe Works to Longsight TMD.** David Ratcliffe

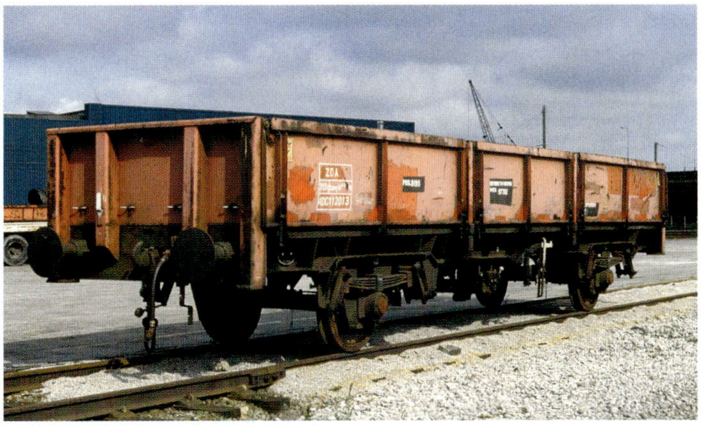

ABOVE: **More commonly, the M&EE's former OCAs retained their original Railfreight red livery, such as ZDA ADC112013 recorded at Warrington Dallam in June 1987. Lettered 'Pool 8195' and 'Return to Burton MGR', this was one of three former OCAs allocated to the merry-go-round wagon repair depot at Burton upon Trent for the carriage of refuse and stores.** Trevor Mann

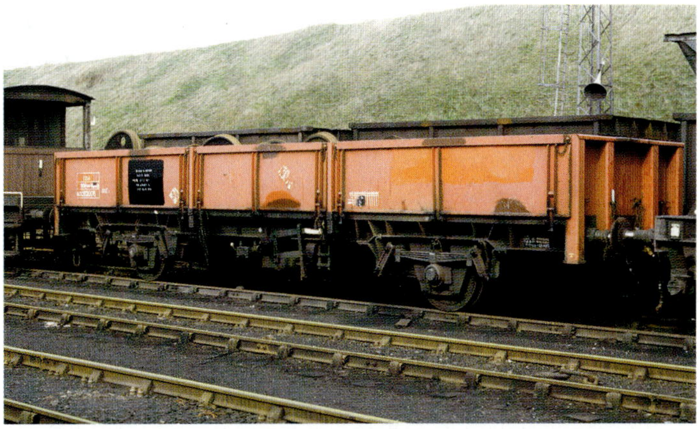

ABOVE: **Recorded at Tinsley Yard on March 11, 1984, ADC 112005 was loaded with scrap wheelsets destined for one of the Sheffield scrapyards. The lettering reads 'To work to and from Eastern Region M&EE depots only. For authority to load Tel 032 3776', this being all in capitals on the wagon.** Trevor Mann

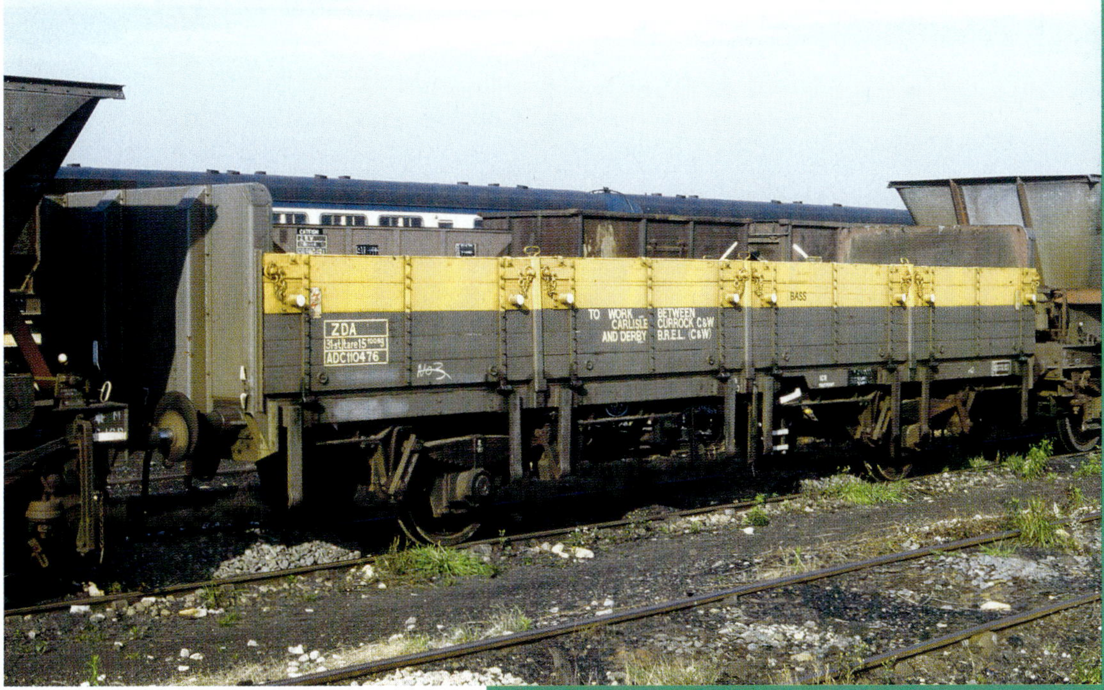

LEFT: **Despite carrying grey/yellow and the Bass name, ZDA ADC110476 was a M&EE wagon when seen in Toton Yard on September 20, 1986. This was one of just ten OBAs transferred to the department for stores use and was lettered 'To work between Carlisle Currock C&W and Derby BREL (C&W)' in white capitals. C&W in this instance stood for carriage and wagon, be it sidings, depot or works.** Trevor Mann

BELOW: **During 1983, over 30 VCA vans that were no longer required for tinplate traffic were reassigned to the M&EE as the type's wide central door aperture suited the engineers. Still in its original Railfreight maroon scheme but now recoded ZRA, newly transferred ADC200390 was at Cardiff Tidal on June 17, 1983.** Simon Bendall Collection

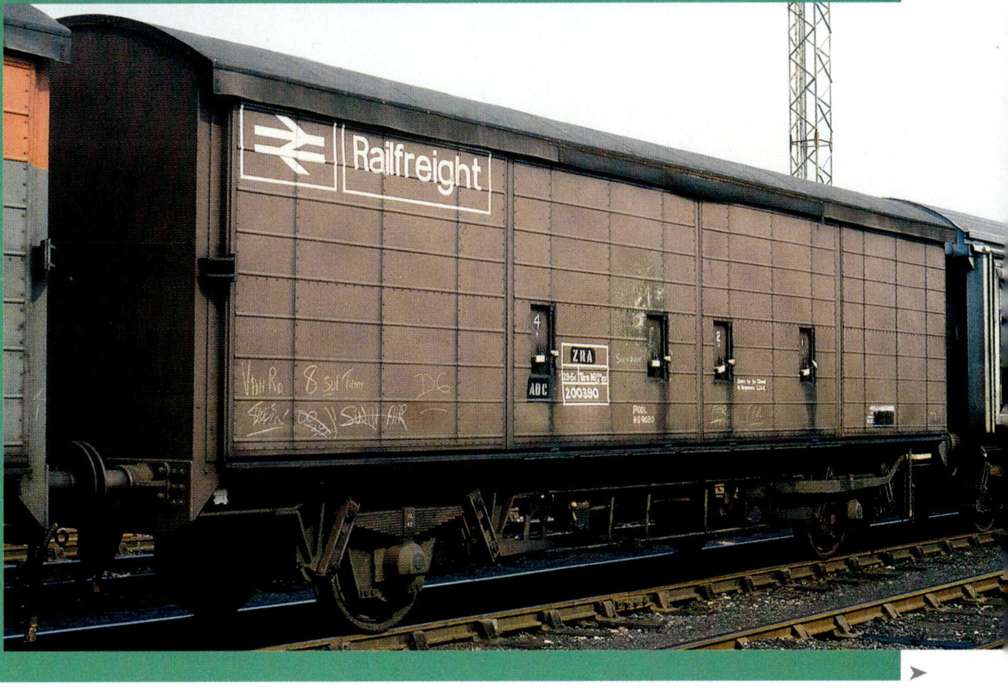

even drums of lubricating oil.

In addition, the early 1980s also saw the M&EE receive a dozen 13-ton Highfit opens and 20 Palvans and Vanfits, all of which had been experimentally fitted with air brakes and long-link suspension back in 1970. Eight of the Highfits, now recoded ZGB, joined most of the ZAA (ex-SPA) wagons in brake block traffic from the BREL workshops at Horwich while the other Highfits, together with all of the Palvans and Vanfits, were assigned to the Rolling Stock Engineer Southern Region (RSE-SR) for stores traffic.

Twelve of the dual-braked, 21-ton, eight-plank Ferry High wagons were also allocated to the M&EE, most of which were rebuilt either as electrification cable drum carriers or overhead line maintenance wagons. However, a couple remained in original condition for carrying general stores traffic around the Southern Region.

In a similar vein, the 20-strong 22-ton Ferry Tube fleet also went to the RSE-SR, six of which retained their UIC numbers in order to continue being used on cross-Channel traffic, these moving wagon spare parts, such as buffers, brake pipes and wheelsets,

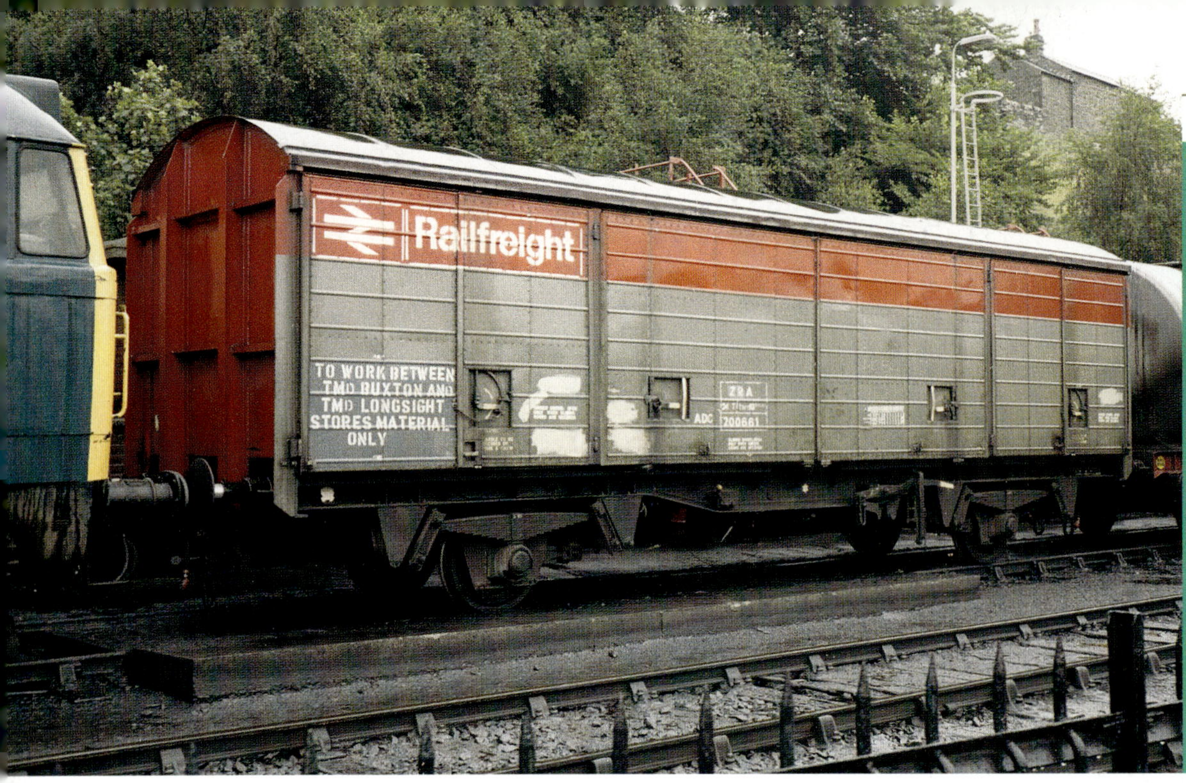

LEFT: **While most of the air-braked vans in the M&EE fleet were in a nationwide pool, a handful were assigned to a specific circuit working. Once a VDA, ZRA ADC200661 was lettered 'To work between TMD Buxton and TMD Longsight. Stores material only' when found at Buxton in July 1985.** David Ratcliffe

BELOW: **Still in olive green livery, ZRB Palvan ADB781864 was en route from Cardiff Cathays to Carlisle Currock when recorded at Walton Old Junction, Warrington, in August 1987. The most obvious sign of the upgrading of these vintage vans was the new suspension linkages and rearranged brake equipment.** Trevor Mann

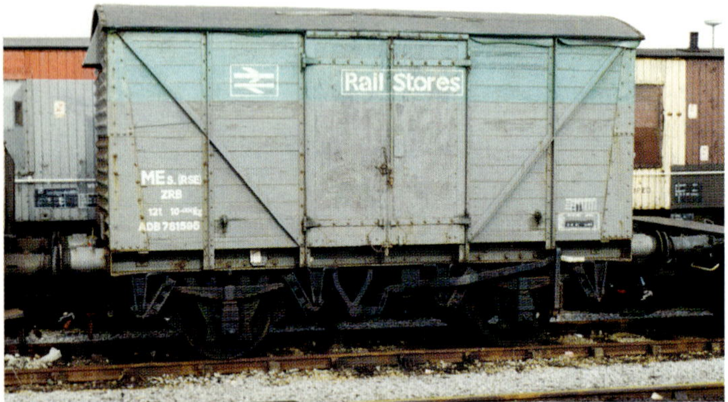

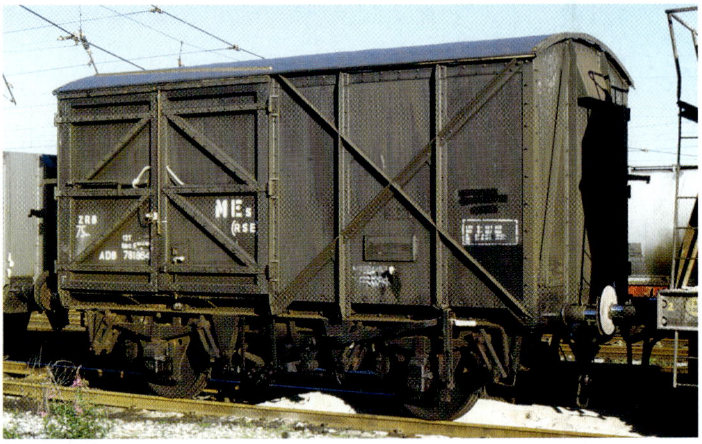

ABOVE: **At least eight of the air-braked Vanfits in the M&EE fleet were eventually painted in the Rail Stores green and grey livery, the first being ADB781007 in early 1985. By 1989 though, only five remained in regular main line use. ZRB ADB781595 is pictured at Dover in October 1988.** Colin Wright/David Ratcliffe Collection

between Dover and Dunkerque. These six Ferry Tubes also regularly ventured outside of the southeast of England. For example, a pool enquiry on February 14, 1994, showed that while two were at Dover and one at Dunkerque, the other three were to be found at Three Bridges M&EE Sidings, BREL Doncaster Works and Marcroft Engineering in Stoke.

Unlike the Civil Engineers department, which chose to paint many of its wagons in the grey and yellow livery, the majority of the M&EE fleet retained their former revenue colours or were repainted in olive green. In addition, the M&EE did not make use of the aquatic codenames, even if the same type of wagon was utilised by both departments. However, a few of its air-braked wagons did receive a new green and grey livery, usually but not always embellished with Rail Stores lettering, although this scheme was always a rarity.

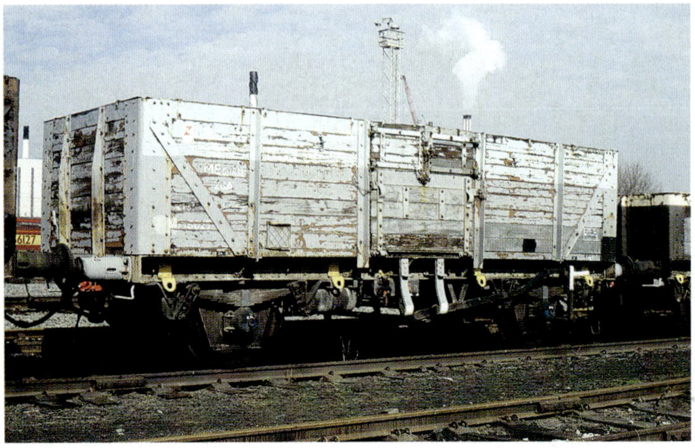

ABOVE: **At least two 21-ton Ferry Highs were repainted in the Rail Stores livery, ADB715013 and ADB715027 also being recoded as ZGA following removal of their vacuum brake equipment. The latter was at Warrington Arpley in April 2000, having gained an erroneous 'M' prefix to its number.** David Ratcliffe

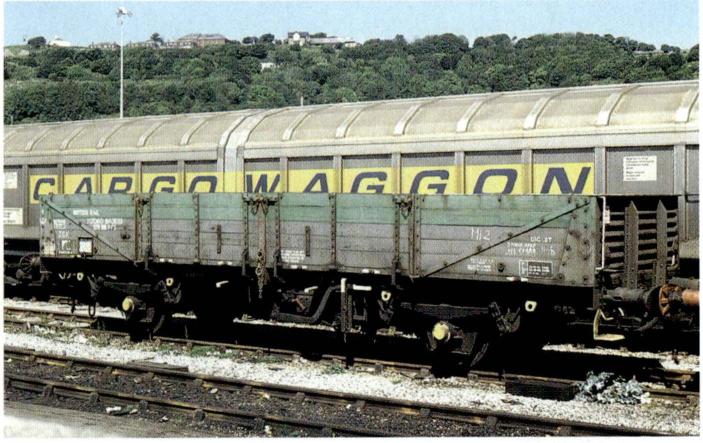

ABOVE: **Until the final sailing of the cross-channel train ferry in December 1995, a handful of Ferry Tubes were used to carry spare wagon parts to and from the continent. Dual-braked ZDX 21 70 6094 053-3 had been repainted in Rail Stores livery when spotted at Dover in May 1989.** Trevor Mann

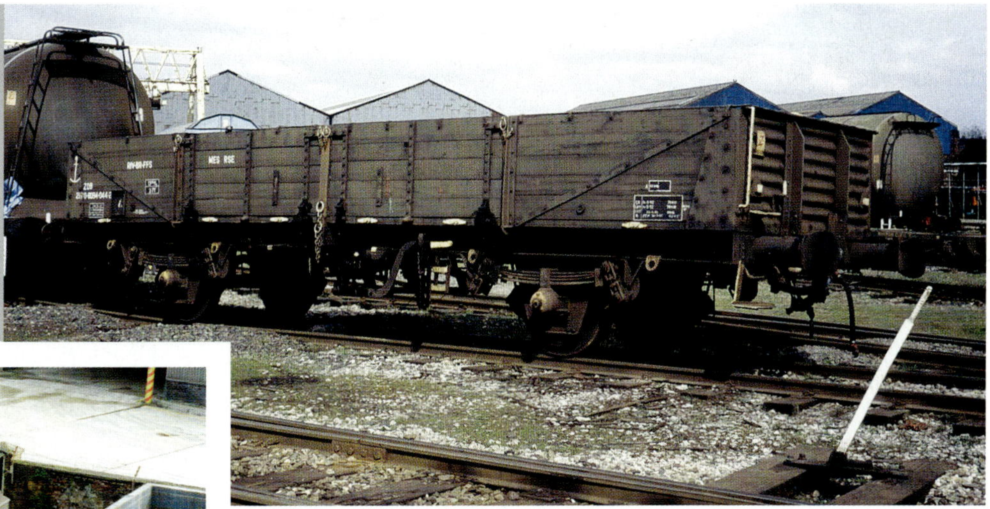

RIGHT: **In contrast, sister Ferry Tube 21 70 6094 044-2 had been reduced to air brakes only but with a through vacuum pipe when recorded at Marcroft's wagon works in Stoke on April 8, 1995. As a consequence, it was now coded ZDB and still retained olive green.** David Ratcliffe

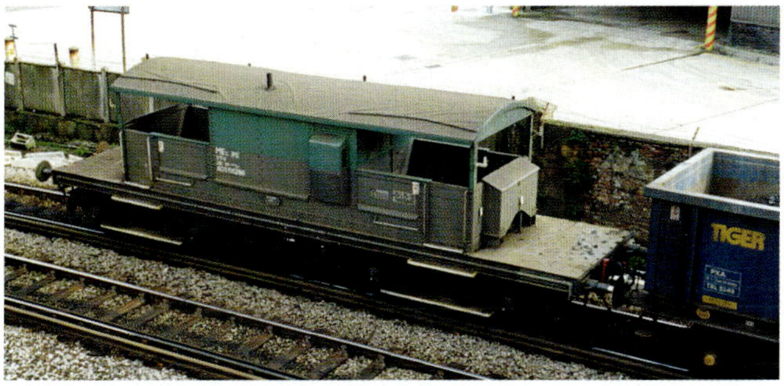

LEFT: **Another wagon to sport the green and grey colours was Queen Mary bogie brake van ADS56286, which when recorded at Dover in October 1988 had been allocated to the M&EE's Power Supply Section at Horsham. Incorrectly coded YTV, it was dual-braked and is seen bringing up the rear of a Shakespeare Cliff to Sevington Channel Tunnel construction spoil train.** Colin Wright/David Ratcliffe Collection

Brake blocks from Horwich

Horwich Works, six miles northwest of Bolton, was opened by the Lancashire & Yorkshire Railway in 1887; locomotive building ending there during the 1960s. By the early 1980s, the works was scheduled for closure but, while most rail activity at the 150 acre site came to an end in 1983, the recently installed automatic iron furnace continued in operation to produce railway brake blocks.

Pool 4825 contained 40 ZAA (ex-SPA) air-braked plate wagons, which were allocated to the M&EE to carry these new brake blocks to works, depots and carriage sidings across the network. A pool enquiry on February 22, 1986, found 14 wagons were at Horwich awaiting loading while the rest could be found either at, or were en route to, some 24 other destinations.

These comprised Glasgow Shields, Haymarket, Corkerhill, Carlisle Currock, Crewe Electric, Chester C&W, Liverpool Edge Hill Downhill CS, Newton Heath, Oxley, Duddeston C&W, Bescot, Toton, Derby Litchurch Lane, Willesden, Leeds Neville Hill, Gateshead, Thornaby, Norwich Crown Point, Ilford, Stratford, Old Oak Common, Bristol St Philip's Marsh, Swansea Landore, and Ramsgate EMU depot.

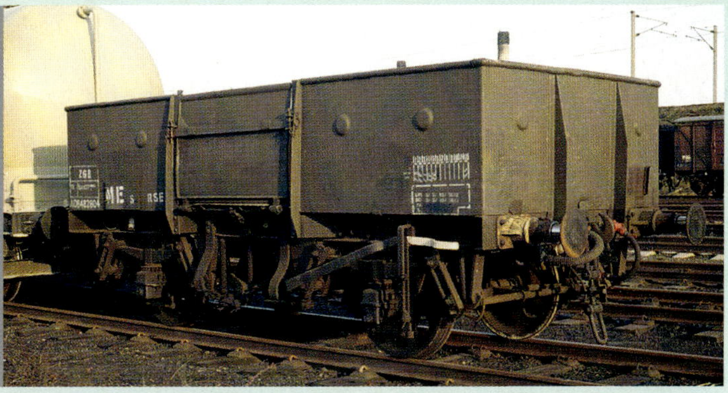

RIGHT: **Air-braked ZGB Highfit ADB482804 was carrying new brake blocks for Carlisle Currock when recorded at Warrington in March 1986, despite being lettered as part of the Southern Region allocation.** David Ratcliffe

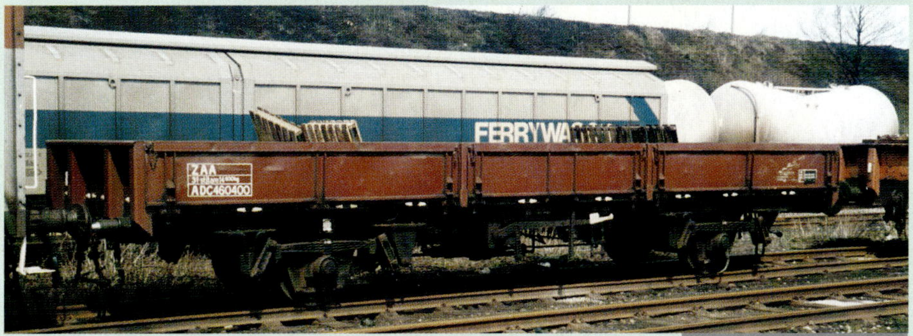

ABOVE: **Carrying freight brown, ZAA ADC460400 had been recently repainted when spotted at Warrington in April 1986 loaded with brake blocks for Inverness TMD. At least ADC460345 was similarly painted in late 1984.** David Ratcliffe

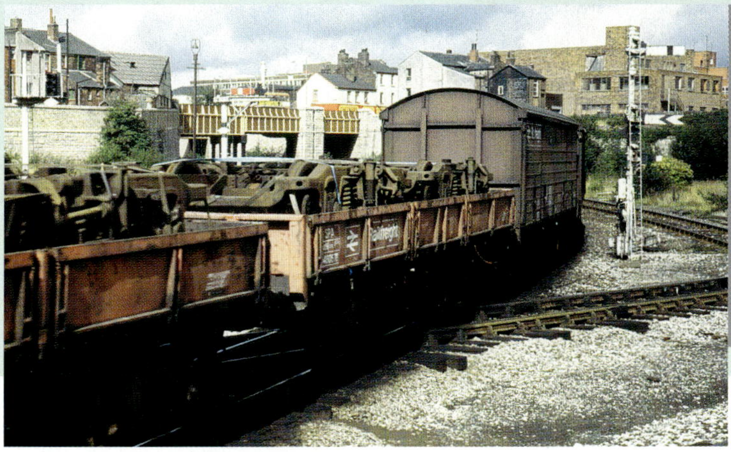

LEFT: **Prior to their official transfer from the revenue fleet, several SPA wagons were already to be found working from Horwich Works and, in addition to carrying new brake blocks and springs, they were also used to convey parts such as carriage bogies. Seen at Bolton during August 1983, 460938 was loaded with Commonwealth bogies recovered from coaches recently scrapped at Horwich and was destined for Derby Litchurch Lane.** David Ratcliffe

Ferry Tubes and Highfits by Mark Lambert

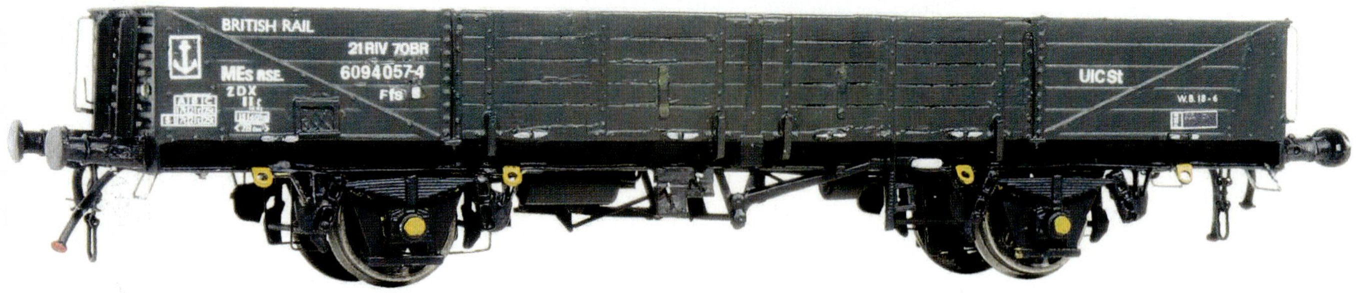

On the face of it, a Ferry Tube wagon in 4mm scale seems an easy conversion, combining a Parkside Tube kit, a Parkside Pipe kit, and some homemade resin spring/axlebox castings. However, inevitably, it turned out to be not so simple!

The bodywork was fairly straightforward, this seeing the middle of the Tube sides removed and replaced with 'cut and shut' Pipe sides as the new wider doors. Dimensioned drawings can be found in *An Illustrated History of BR Wagons Volume 1* (OPC 1985). The floor moulding of the Tube was then modified by cutting squares out of some of the plank edges for the recessed lashing rings that these wagons had when new, although it seems in later years some floors were repaired with plywood sheet that covered them over. The rings themselves were made from fuse wire wrapped around a drill bit and cut into loops.

I used Wizard Models strapping along with plastic strip to add the thicker strapping either side of the central drop doors and some spare etch to represent the strips that hit the door bangers. There are a number of continental fittings, such as handrails, steps, tie downs and lamp brackets, that need to be added from plastic and brass. The brass is mostly scrap etch and the plastic is various widths of 10 thou strip.

Tricky brakes

The best way to tackle the complex dual-braked underframe is to strip the Tube underframe back to its most basic state and rebuild from the ground up. The resin springs and axleboxes are based on the Hornby ferry van with the hangers made from 10x30 thou plastic strip, while the buffers are S Kits oval-headed continental pattern. The brake equipment largely came out of the spares box, namely some from the Tube kit and more from the Parkside VEA underframe kit. Where needed, some pieces were scratchbuilt based on photos and the curved part of one handbrake lever was bent up from some scrap etch to match the drawing.

The changeover levers are just plastic blocks with a piece of thin wire glued to the outer face; the top end being flattened first in a pair of smooth-faced pliers to represent the knob. The vacuum pipes are Lanarkshire castings, and the air pipes are Replica Railways mouldings, which are a little over-scale but robust. The distinctive continental pattern label holders are made from tiny pieces of netting, as sold for chain link fencing, with a plastic strip surround, although S Kits does an etch for these.

I undercoated the wagon to key all the different materials before giving the body a top coat of Railmatch olive green and the underframe Games Workshop 'Chaos Black.' All of the transfers are from a Railtec sheet for the VIX ferry vans, with some of the letters and numbers substituted with individual items from the company's packs for three and four inch lettering.

Air-braked Highfit

The Parkside kit for the LNER-designed but BR built Highfits can be modified to represent those fitted with air brakes and new suspension and later deployed on Rail Stores services. The conversion again requires the VEA underframe kit as this provides the springs, air cylinder and distributor.

Although the Highfit comes with the correct pattern of LNER brakegear, the 'V' hangers have to be moved inboard to reflect the changes associated with the air-brake conversion, which was achieved using photos for reference. The brake linkages are a hugely compressed version of the arrangement applied to early air-braked long-wheelbase wagons and were built entirely from plastic strip (10x30 thou) and rod (20 thou). The handbrake levers are cut down from plain levers intended for a longer wheelbase wagon.

The only body modification is to reduce the size of the moulded chalk panel on the sides

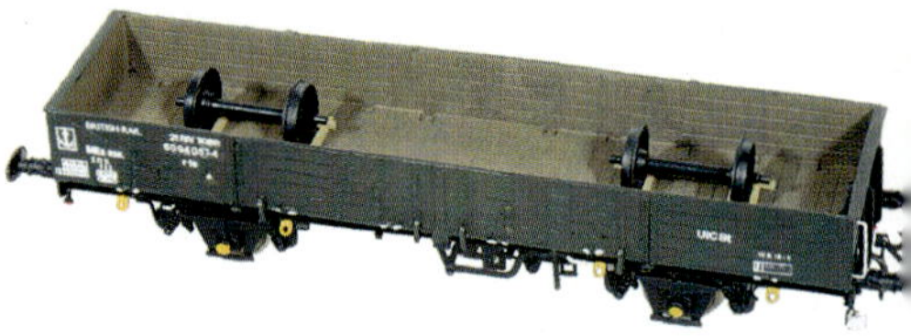

as the LNER one is much larger than the BR version. I did this using a curved blade to gradually remove material before finishing with a file, all done before the body was assembled. The lost bolt detail on this panel was replaced using slivers of plastic rod. The Lanarkshire Oleo buffers this time were 1ft 8½in long with a 13in head with brake pipes the same as the Tube.

The underframe received Games Workshop 'Charadon Granite' and the body was painted with LifeColor faded olive drab which is a good match for the early 1990s condition. The repainted patches are a mix of Games Workshop 'Chaos Black' and 'Castellan Green' to give a slightly faded olive shade, while a brown wash replicated the dirt around the surfaces The transfers are from Fox sheets for individual wagon TOPS panels, except for the MEs branding which is Railtec. The extended TOPS panel was made by splicing two transfers together.

Both wagons received a load of two wheelsets, these receiving new axles to give a better representation of the real thing and with squared-off ends. Plastic strip was used to make transport cradles for them, which were painted to represent new wood and glued to the wagon floor.

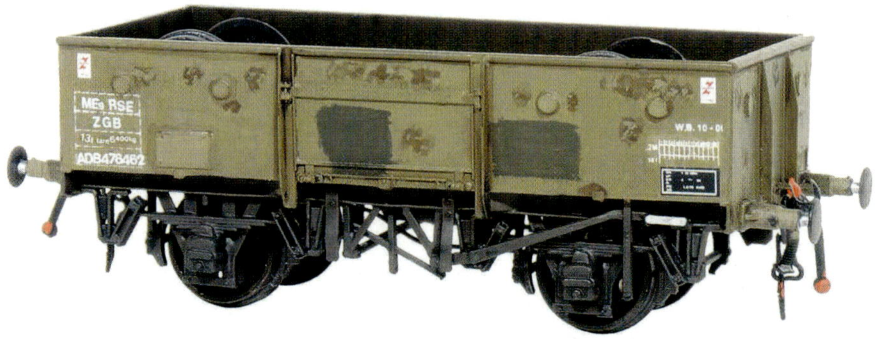

Rail Stores wagons by Mark Lambert

To build an accurate Ferry High in 4mm scale requires something between kit-bashing and scratchbuilding. Beginning with the chassis, you need the underframe from the Airfix/Dapol Class B tanker kit, preferably an Airfix one as the mouldings are somewhat sharper. The Ferry High had a wheelbase of 14ft 10in with the tanker's being 15ft, which was deemed close enough, so it was left unmodified.

The outer ends of the donor do need reducing though to match the required frame length, this being based on the drawing in *An Illustrated History of BR Wagons Volume 1* (OPC 1985). Also on the chassis, the holes for all the various fittings need to be filled with 40thou rod and all the spring, axlebox and brake gear details filed off, leaving the detail of the changeover lever. New springs and axleboxes come from the Parkside VEA underframe kit. As the VEA underframe has a solid suspension mounting on one corner, you actually require two underframe kits to get four of the regular open design of mountings but as they are cheap enough, this is not much of an issue,

The eight-plank body can be assembled in two ways using parts from various Cambrian kits. The central section with the door always comes from a Southern Railway eight-plank wagon kit (reference no. C96) but the remainder of the sides and the ends can be cut from a second kit of the same type, albeit with the diagonal strapping needing removing on the inner sections. Alternatively, an eight-plank acid tank wagon kit (C75) can be used, which needs the lower two large planks filled and re-scribed. The ends on this second wagon are additionally more like those on the Ferry High and the sides do not need filing down, so this is the route I opted to take.

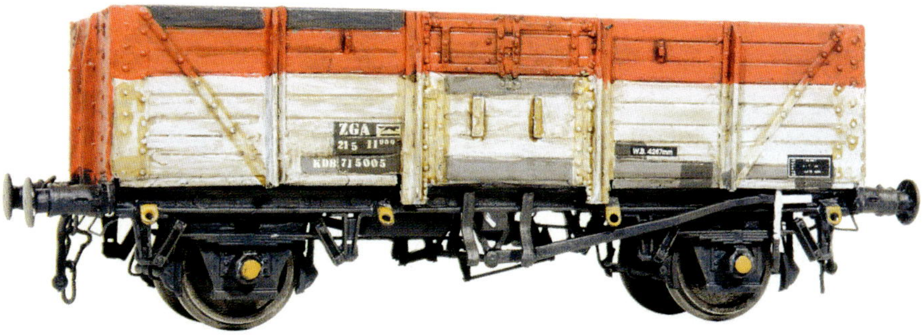

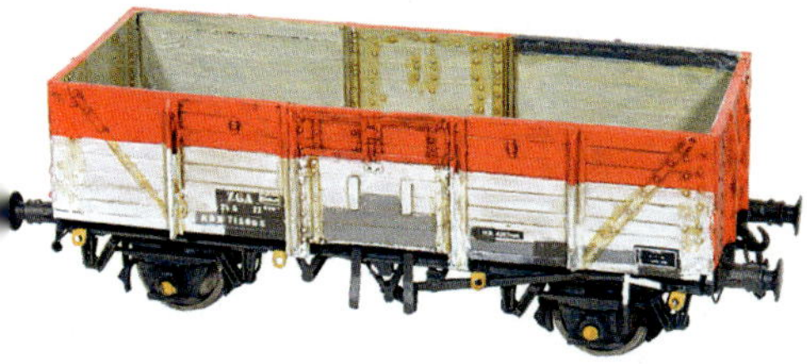

Strapped in

Even then the diagonal strapping is not quite right; it is possible to file off the Cambrian detail and replace it with strapping made from 10x40 thou strip with Archer's rivet transfers completing the look. Some vertical strapping made in the same way is needed for the bodysides in any case. The buffers are Lanarkshire Models and Supplies continental pattern round-headed (B31) and the underframe parts are a combination of etched 'V' hangers from Wizard and Southern Pride along with parts from the spares box and 0.33mm wire for the commode handles under the buffers and safety loops. The ferry tie-down eyelets also came from Wizard Models.

The drawing in the book shows the original vacuum-braked and air-piped arrangement; in later years the vehicles were dual-braked and later still some were reduced to air brakes only. I had to check photos to see which parts of the brake gear were still in use for the selected wagon and period. The brakes come from the VEA underframe but need tweaking to clear the slightly larger wheels as, being a ferry wagon, the wheels are one metre not 3ft 1in. This means that the Hornby 12.6mm wheels sold as spares are a perfect fit.

The particular wagon I built had lost the continental pattern label holders at some point, so I did not need to worry about those. Painting the wagon was by far the easiest part of the build, using Games Workshop shades to produce the very faded Railfreight red/grey patch-painted livery with much of the lettering and numbers coming from Fox Transfers.

ZRA Stores vans

This pair of former VDA vans were both in use with the M&EE's Southern Rolling Stock Engineer in the early 1990s. ADC200185 appears to have been repainted in late1990 or early 1991 in freight brown with just the door instructions and TOPS panel initially remaining in the way of lettering. A short time later, it gained small 'MEs RSE' lettering on each side. This is a repainted Bachmann model; I found it is easier to repaint an EWS liveried wagon than remove the tampo printing from a bauxite one. The RSE lettering and door instructions were made up from Railtec transfers with the Fox range providing the number panel, this needing extending in width by splicing two boxes together to match the real thing.

The moulded axleboxes are not right for a VDA as Bachmann uses a generic moulding that is more suited to the open wagons, so I removed them. Replacements came from the Chivers/Five79 range, these being the hooded design that come as spares in the company's MDV mineral wagon kit.

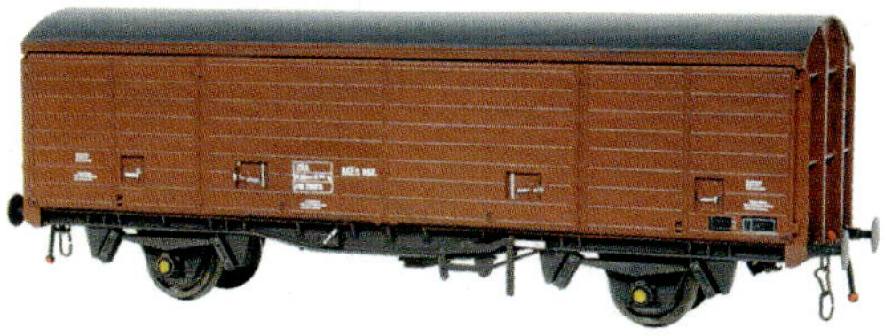

For the red/grey ZRA numbered ADC210271, I started with a factory weathered Railfreight model and repainted the roof with a mid-grey acrylic. In addition to the new axleboxes, I also replaced the handbrake levers with the longer etched type available from Stenson Models and added external hinges to the cupboard doors. These are made from plastic strip and only feature on a particular batch of the vans.

The renumbering is prototypically crude using Railtec letters and numbers while, likewise, the painted out VDA code and other lettering used different shades of paint, Games Workshop 'Codex Grey' and 'Charadon Granite', to achieve the right look. The whole underframe was brush painted with the granite shade as the factory weathered colour was very light. Replica Railways air pipes and Smith's couplings then completed the job.

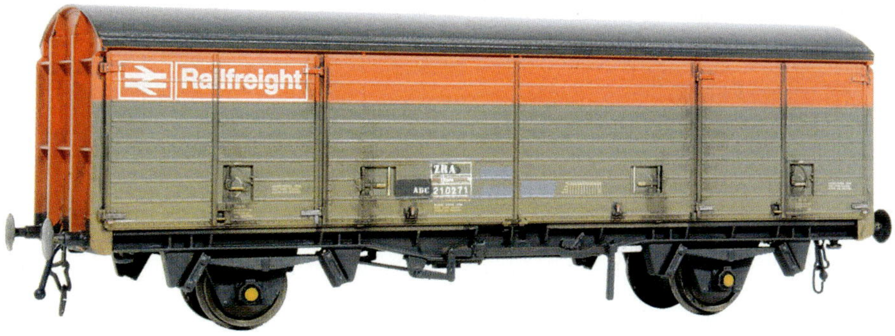

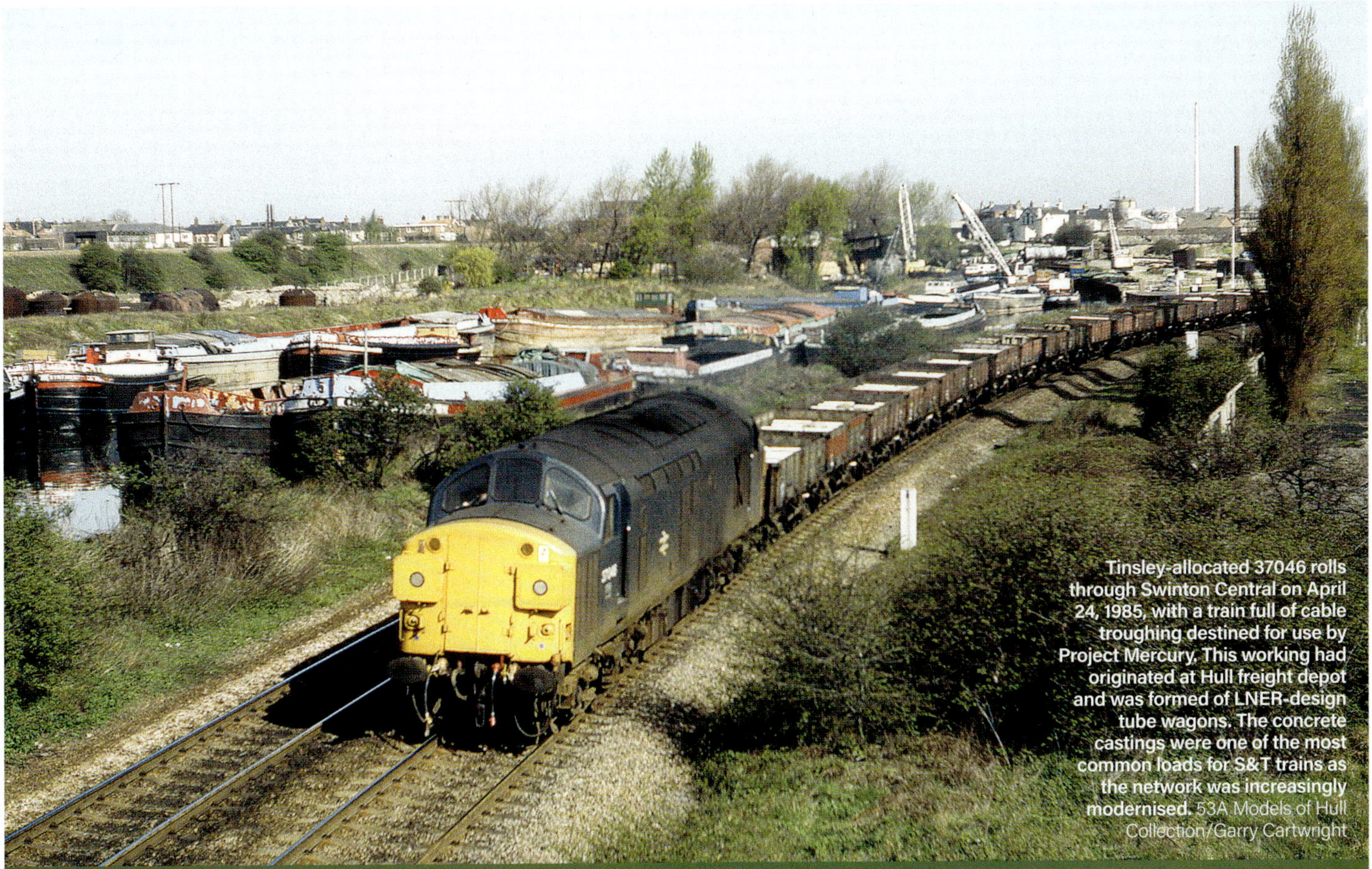

Tinsley-allocated 37046 rolls through Swinton Central on April 24, 1985, with a train full of cable troughing destined for use by Project Mercury. This working had originated at Hull freight depot and was formed of LNER-design tube wagons. The concrete castings were one of the most common loads for S&T trains as the network was increasingly modernised. 53A Models of Hull Collection/Garry Cartwright

Maintaining the signals

While the Civil Engineers department was in charge of many aspects of maintaining and renewing the rail network, the complex task of providing signalling was left to the specialists of the Signal & Telegraph Engineers. This department also had its own sizeable wagon fleet that initially encompassed many 'traditional' designs which David Ratcliffe details.

The Signal and Telegraph Engineers (S&TE) operated a diverse fleet of vehicles in support of its activities and, while this was overall smaller in size than the Civil Engineers, it included many specialist conversions for specific roles. Originally, in the 1950s, the department received a small number of new build wagons that were given aquatic names of their own, such as the Prawn and Winkle. Such wagons were typically copies of standard revenue-earning designs, in this case 30-ton Bogie Bolster C and 22-ton Plate, respectively.

However, their meagre numbers meant that they were supplemented by many ex-revenue vehicles, such as Boplates and Tubes. The S&TE's two-axle wagons were commonly used to carry cable troughing, signal box steps and relay cabinets, while its bogie vehicles conveyed longer items like level crossing barriers and gates, signal posts and ladders.

Also assigned to the S&TE were over three dozen special wagons including Flatrols, Protrols and Lowmacs, while its fleet also included a number of vans, which were used to carry miscellaneous loads including rolls of signal wire, lever frame equipment and point motors. Various vehicles were also converted to carry cable drums in cradles, these including Bogie Bolster C, two-axle Conflats and even a few ex-Mk.1 coach underframes. Many of these unfitted and vacuum-braked designs lasted into the early 1980s and some of the latter into the 1990s until replaced. ●

RIGHT: **One of the S&T's most famous installations was Reading Signal Works, the former GWR signalling workshops being located alongside Reading General station but at a lower level. Between 1957 and 1981, shunting was undertaken by BR-owned Ruston & Hornsby 88DS No.20 (later to become 97020) but, following withdrawal, it was replaced by 06003. Renumbered as 97804, the former Scottish shunter pottered around the fascinating site until its closure in 1984 and is seen surrounded by all the expected paraphernalia in early 1983.** Simon Bendall Collection

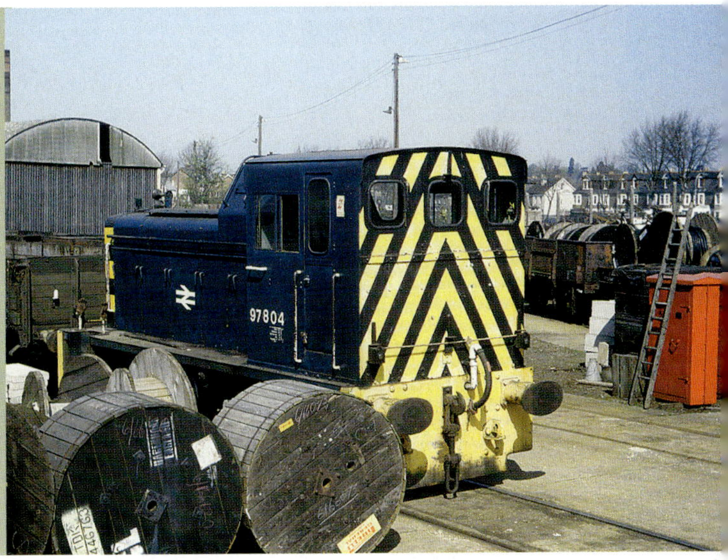

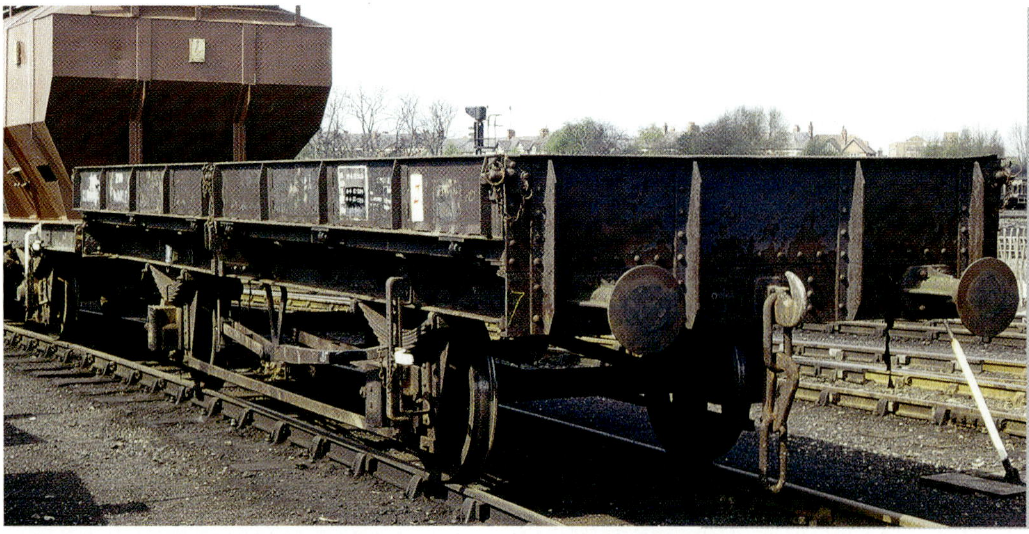

LEFT: **Shildon Works built 43 22-ton Plate wagons to diagram 1/431 for the S&TE in three batches between 1951 and 1956, these being numbered DB997500-542 and coded Winkle. They were initially allocated to the London Midland and Scottish regions but later travelled further afield. Carrying the TOPS code of ZVO, KDB997514 was at Chester wagon repair depot on April 17, 1982.** Trevor Mann

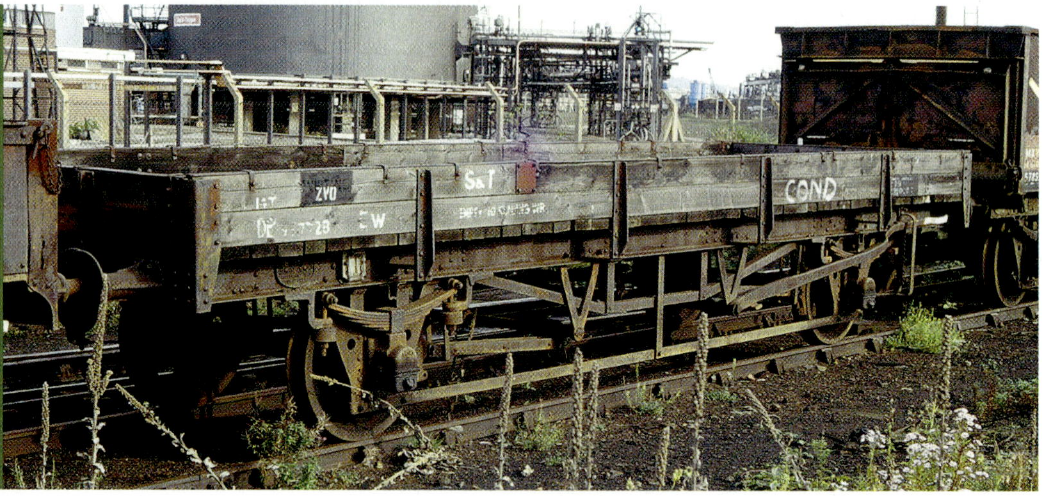

RIGHT: **The two-plank 14-ton Whiting were a GWR design for S&T use that was perpetuated by British Railways to diagram 1/622. Built in three groups between 1952 and 1957, construction of the 50 wagons was split between Swindon and Wolverton with the numbers being DB997700-46 and DB995250-52, this trio being the last built. Normally found on the Western Region, ZVO DB997728 had migrated to Broughton Lane, Sheffield, by October 1983 to await scrapping. The faded lettering includes the Ew allocation and 'Empty to Reading WR' lettering.** Trevor Mann

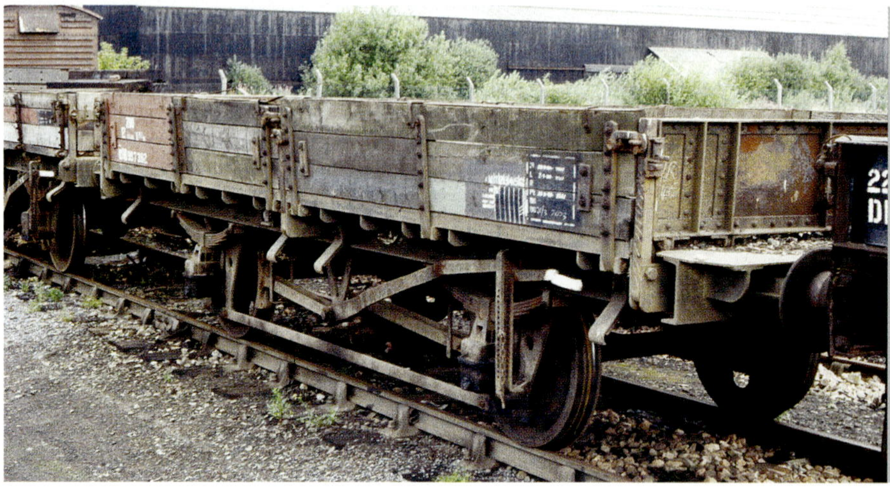

LEFT: **During 1955, Wolverton built six 12-ton open wagons to diagram 1/619 for the S&TE which had wooden dropsides and fixed steel ends. No codename was allocated to DB997300-05 but all were assigned to the Scottish Region where they were used as miscellaneous material and spoil carriers. ZDO KDB997302 is seen at Rutherglen permanent way depot on August 18, 1981.** Trevor Mann

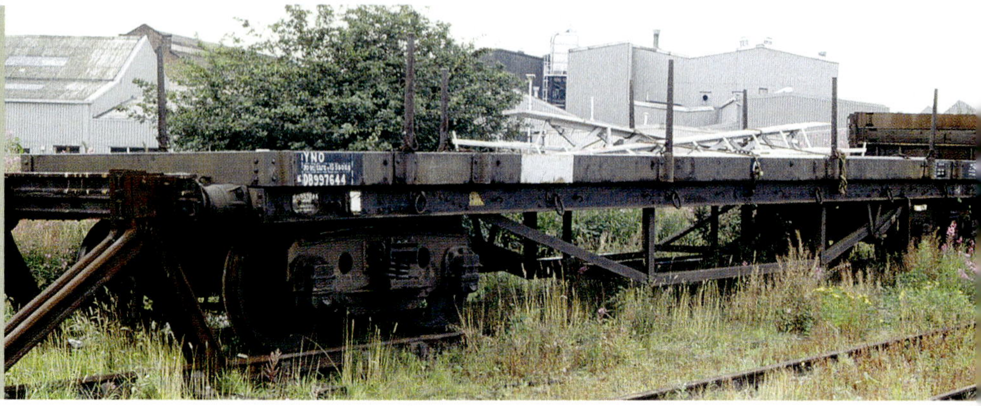

RIGHT: **Another copy of a revenue-earning design were the 69 Bogie Bolster C wagons built specially for the S&TE fleet between 1952 and 1954 as part of diagram 1/471. Coded Prawn, they took the numbers DB997600-47 and DB997649-69, allocations from new being to the London Midland, Eastern and Western regions. YNO KDB997644 was loaded with a set of crossing barriers when seen at Bamber Bridge permanent way depot on August 14, 1981. One final design built for the S&TE in 1954 were two diagram 1/490 Boplates, these being coded Whelk and numbered DB997400/01. Sent new to Scotland, photographs are exceptionally rare despite the duo lasting until 1981!** Trevor Mann

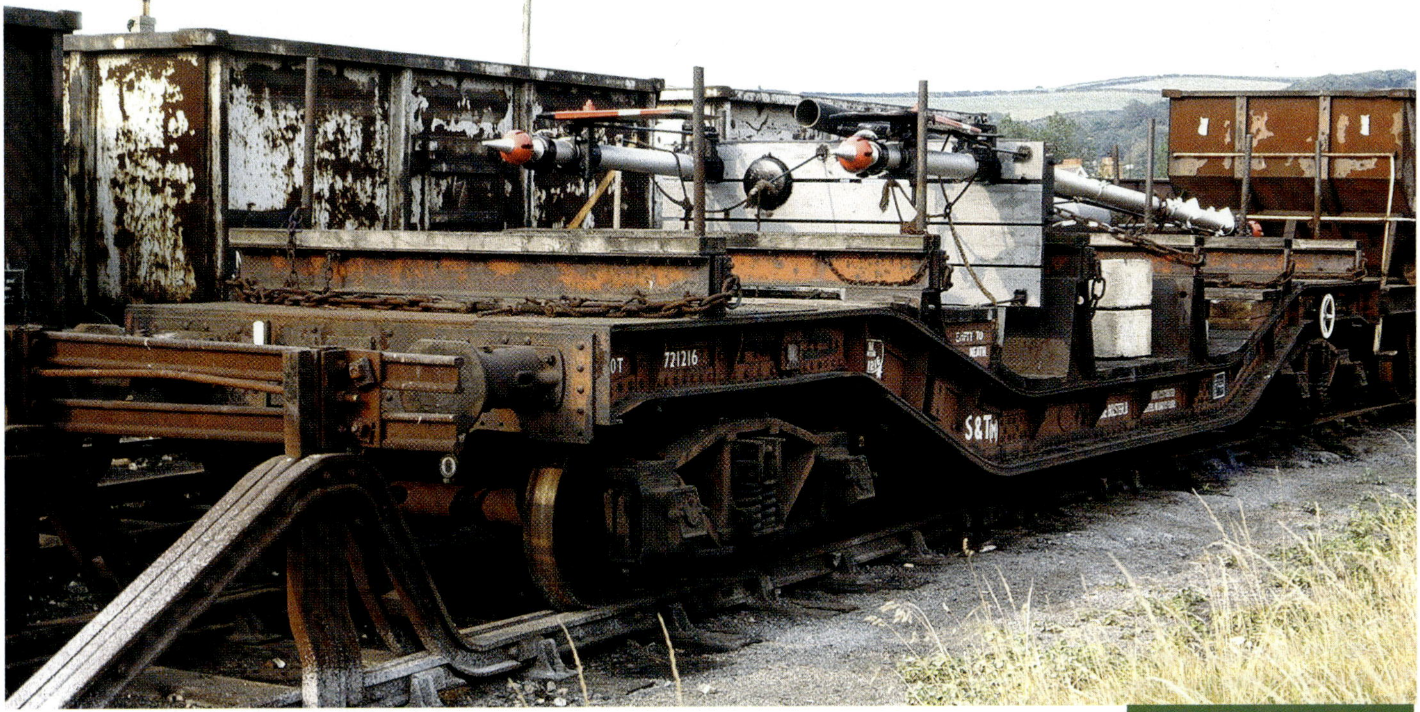

ABOVE: **Former Warwell KDM721216 had been rebuilt as a Bogie Bolster B in 1949. Later assigned to the S&TE, it was recorded at Burry Port in August 1981 while carrying a new double bracket semaphore signal, complete with arms in place. The wagon is lettered 'Empty to Neath'.** Trevor Mann

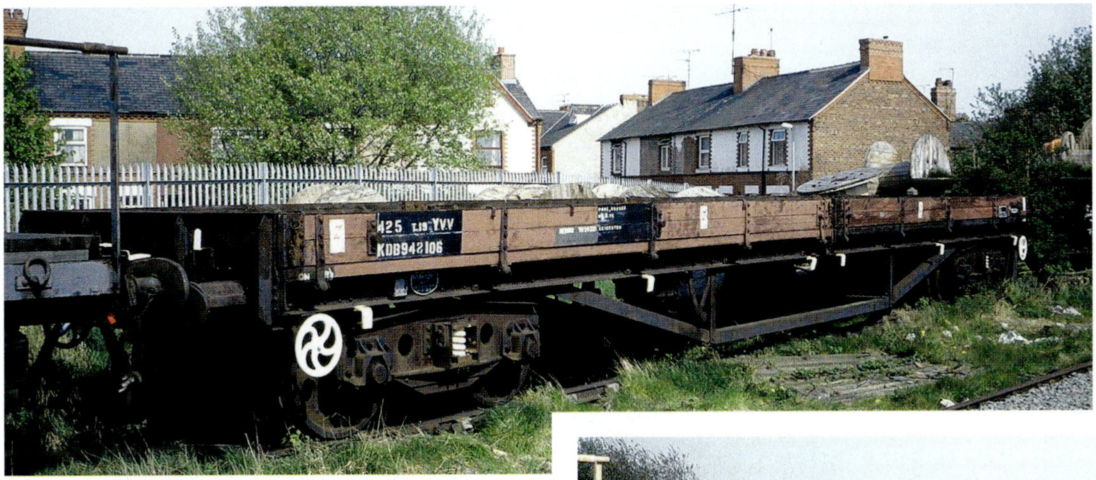

ABOVE: **The S&TE also used a number of ex-revenue Boplates to convey lengthy items. Vacuum-braked YVV KDB948106 is seen in the S&T sidings at Chester on May 2, 1994, and is lettered 'Return to 59221 Leicester', the number being the TOPS location code.** David Ratcliffe

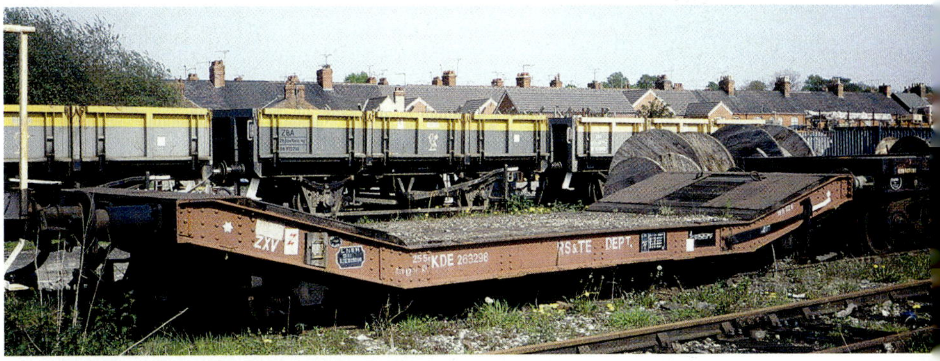

RIGHT: **The S&TE retained a number of Lowmacs to carry bulky items. One of these, ZXV KDE263298, is pictured at Chester S&T sidings on May 2, 1994, this being a 25-ton rated Lowmac EP.** David Ratcliffe

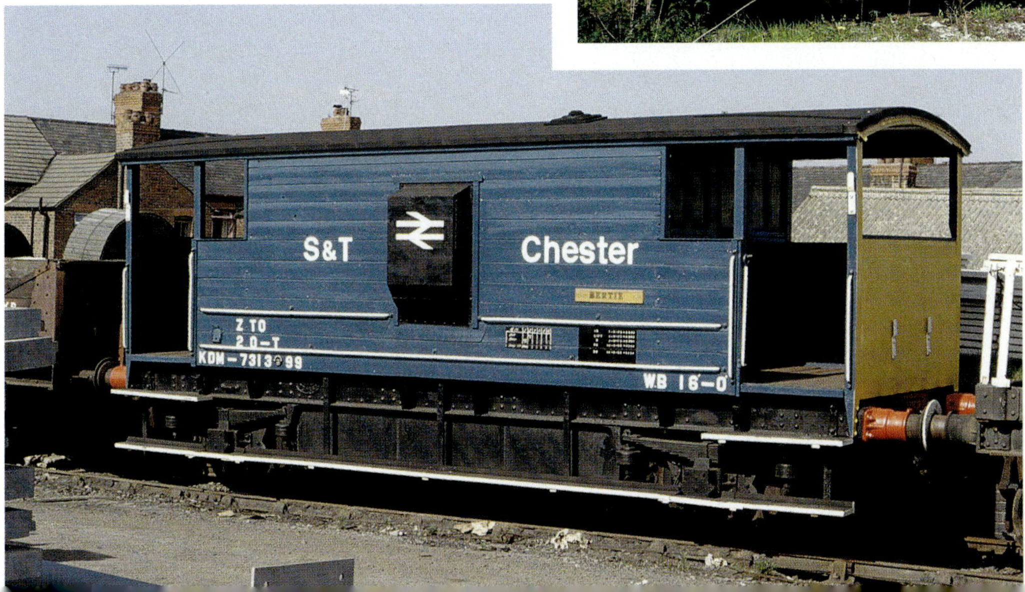

LEFT: **Built by British Railways in 1949 to diagram 2068, KDM731399 had never looked like this before as it sports a locally-applied mix of blue, yellow, red, and black at Chester on April 20, 1981. Also carrying a *Bertie* nameplate, the LMS brake van, coded ZTO, was assigned to local S&T workings.** Trevor Mann

RIGHT: **Among the more specialist vehicles allocated to the S&TE at Chester was 50-ton Borail KDM720905. Now coded YVO, this had been built in 1937 and was originally a revenue-earning version of the LMS-design Salmon. Seen at Chester station on April 20, 1981, it had been fitted with a Pelloby crane and was used in the installation of new equipment. Accompanying it was KDW105742, an equally vintage GWR Mogo van.** Trevor Mann

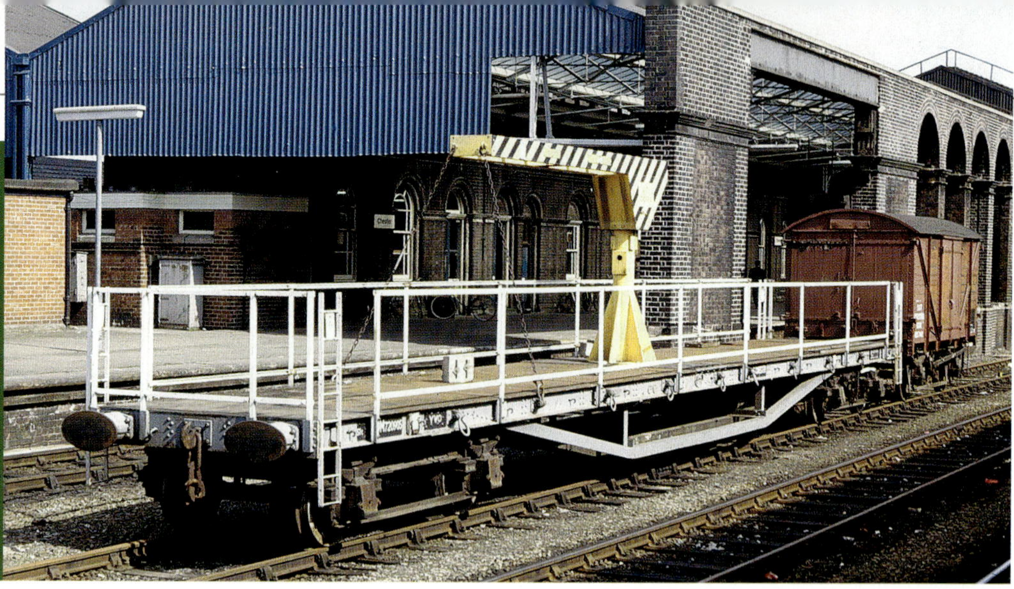

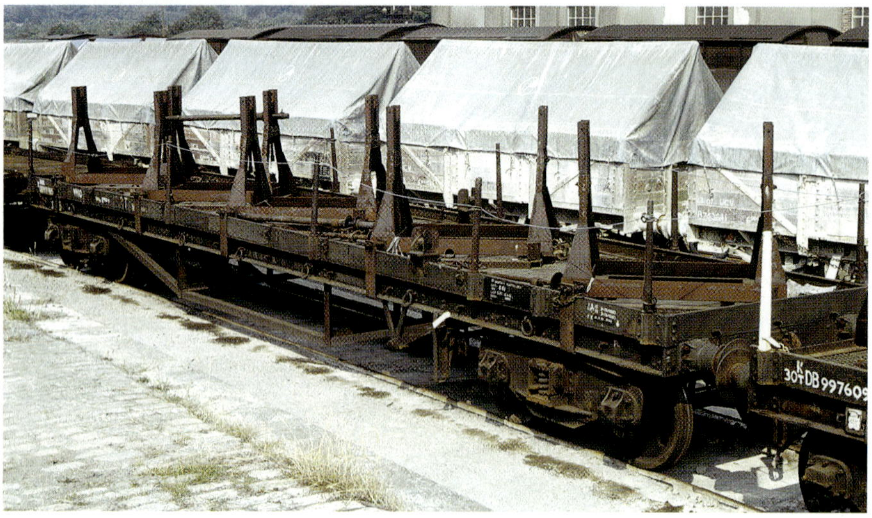

LEFT: **Several of the Prawn were fitted with cable drum cradles over time, including YNO KDB997655 seen at St. Blazey on August 29, 1981, it being lettered 'S&T (W) Reading'.** Trevor Mann

BELOW: **Several ex-revenue Bogie Bolster C wagons were also converted into cable drum carriers and by the mid-1980s, many had been fitted with a mesh canopy to provide protection for staff when working beneath overhead catenary. Air-piped and lettered 'S&T BRB' on its olive green livery, YNW KDB922520 was recorded at Ardwick West in April 1986. BRB stood for British Rail Board and indicated a vehicle used nationally rather than regionally.** David Ratcliffe

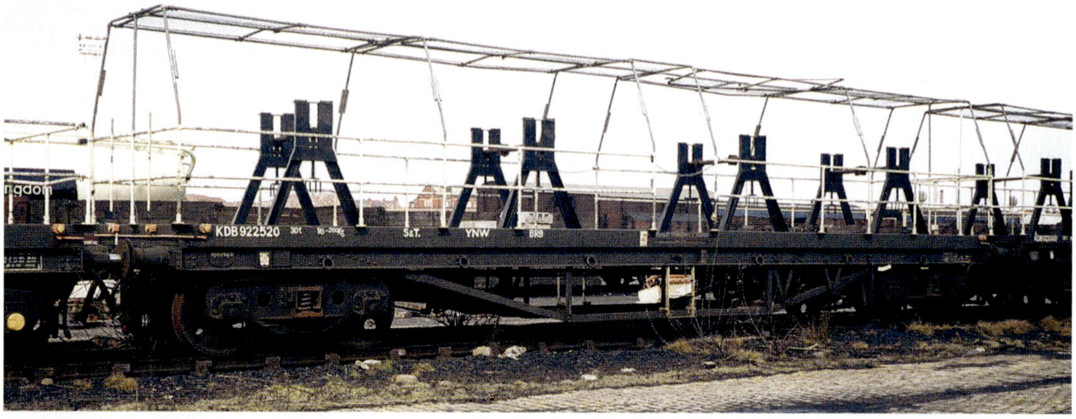

BELOW: **In addition to the bogie bolsters, 18 Mk.1 coach underframes were converted into cable drum carriers for the S&TE. Recoded QVV, the former coaches were all based on the London Midland Region at Crewe, Leicester or Warrington Central. KDB975106 (originally SK 24745) is seen at Liverpool Spekeland Road in September 1994.** David Ratcliffe

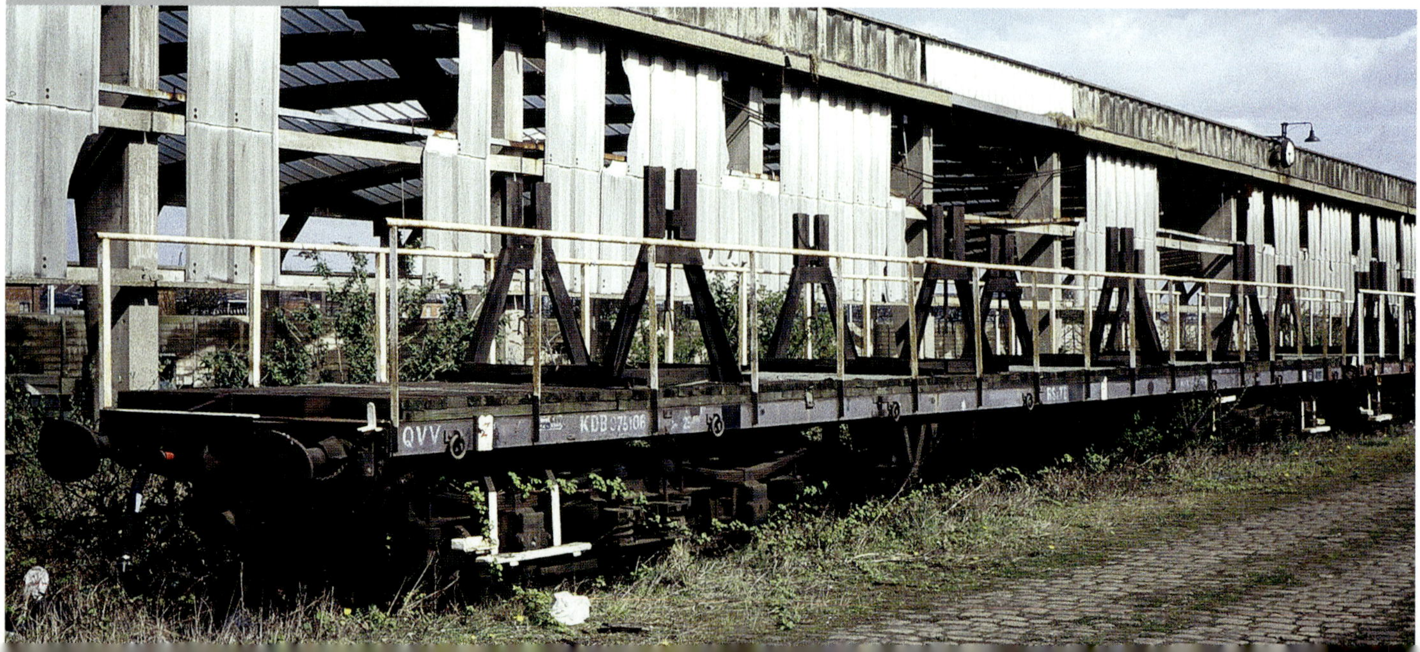

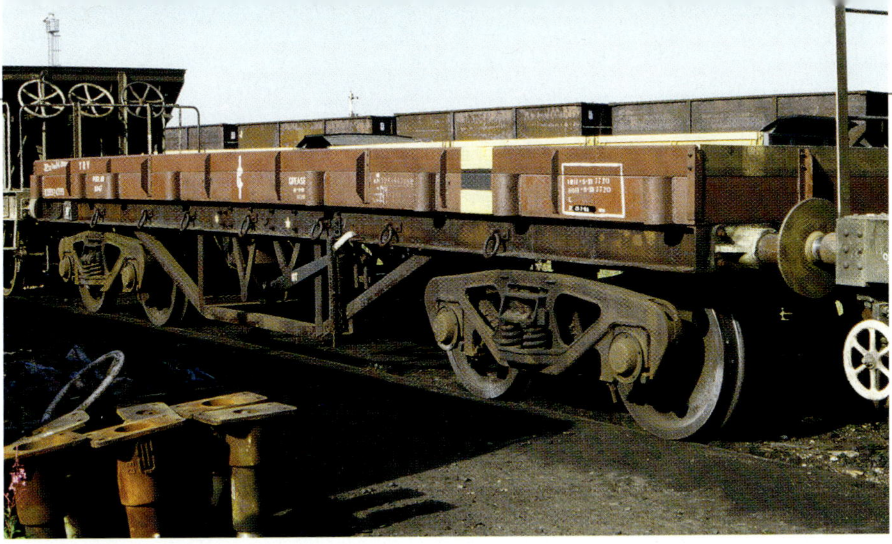

LEFT: **KRV KDB924399 was one of a small number of Bogie Bolster E wagons that were modified in 1981 at Dunfermline Townhill to carry concrete troughing and is seen at Ayr Falkland Yard on July 23, 1984. Initially, all were allocated to the S&T depot at Irvine but by the late 1980s some had been transferred to Chester. The yellow and black striped logo was that of the S&TE in Scotland.** Trevor Mann

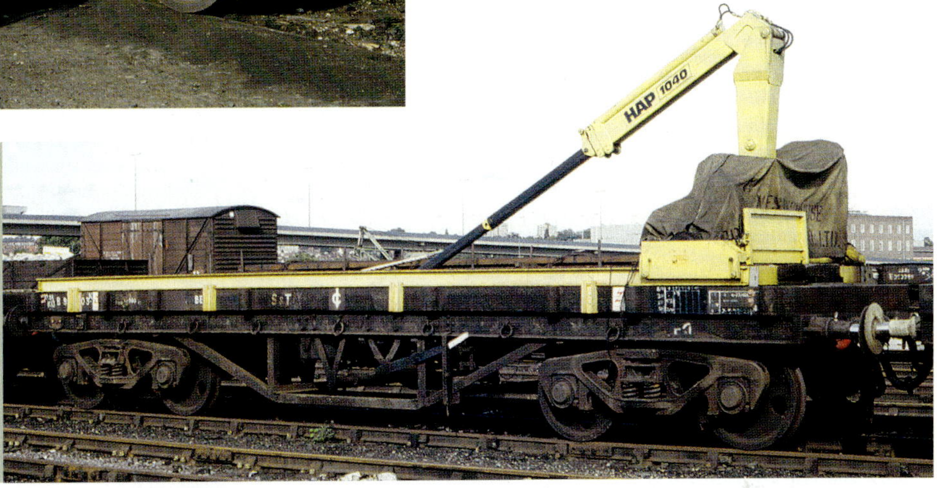

RIGHT: **Another modified Bogie Bolster E, KDB924203 had been fitted with a HAP hydraulic jib for use by the S&TE to unload concrete troughing and presumably also pick up used and damaged troughs. Seen at Brent Yard, Cricklewood, on October 13, 1979, it was still in use in the early 1990s albeit repainted. The lettering is somewhat confused as, although correctly prefixed KDB, the wagon was still carrying its BEV TOPS code from its revenue earning days.** Trevor Mann

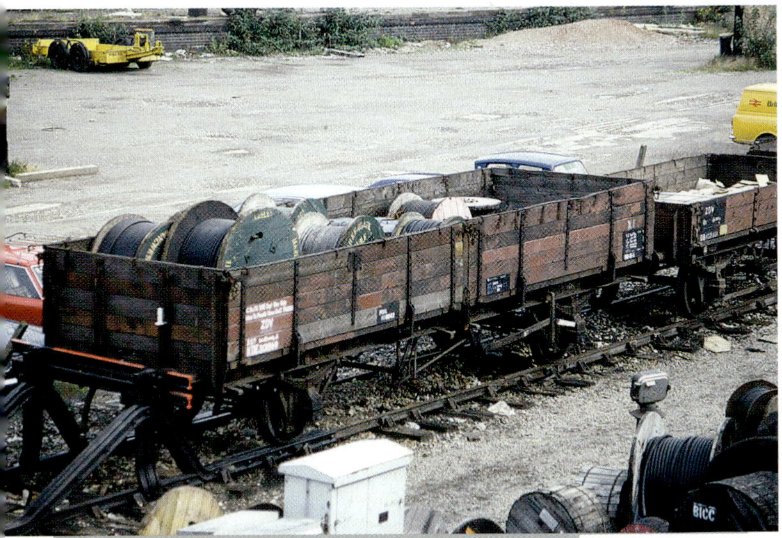

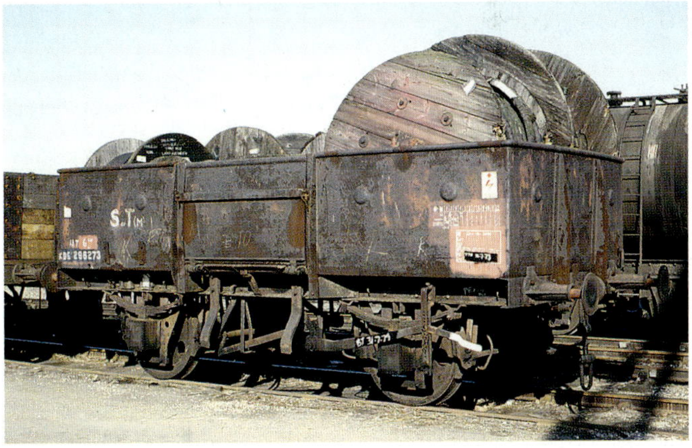

ABOVE: **Much use was also made of the vacuum-braked 13-ton Highfits, be they wooden or steel bodied and BR or pre-nationalisation builds. Carrying a diverse load of cable drums, KDE296273 soaks up the sun at Cambridge on August 28, 1979.** Simon Bendall Collection

ABOVE: **The LNER-designed tube wagons were much liked by the S&TE due to their length and pair of drop doors which, although heavy, gave unrestricted access for loading. In contrast, the LMS design, which had been preferred by BR, was not favoured as they only had a small central door. Much used for carrying cable troughing, they could also move cable drums as shown by KDE301569 at Newport S&T sidings on July 13, 1980. The Medfit alongside, which is Civil Engineers allocated, is loaded with an assortment of cardboard boxes, including a particularly large one and squashed empties.** Simon Bendall Collection

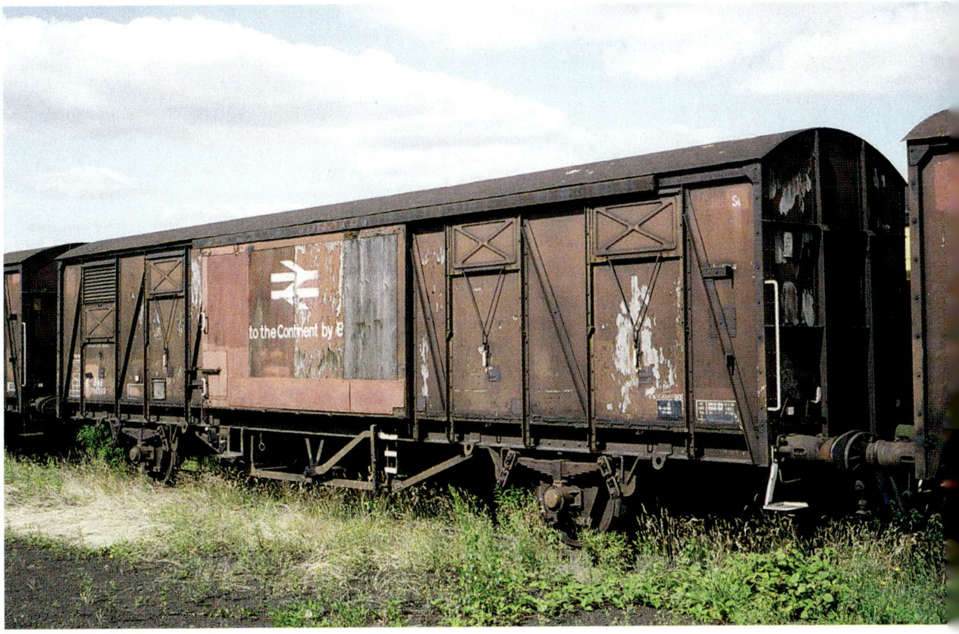

RIGHT: **During the 1980s, many of the BR 20-ton ferry vans that were now no longer required for cross-channel traffic were moved to the departmental fleet to replace some of the shorter wheelbase 12-ton vans then still in use. In some respects, the vans were ideal for the engineers with the wide door making miscellaneous equipment easy to load while their dual brakes provided operational flexibility. Some would remain in service long enough to sport the colourful liveries adopted by the Civil Engineers and the S&TE. However, ZRX KDB786910, which had recently been used as a stores van by the S&TE, still retained some of its original 'Through to the Continent by British Rail' lettering when photographed at Goole in July 1992 after withdrawal.** David Ratcliffe

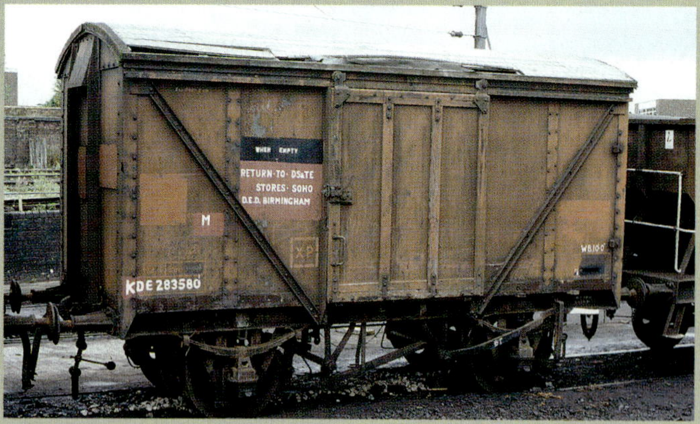

ABOVE: The S&TE employed numerous 12-ton vans into the 1980s for moving stores, including pre-nationalisation desig ns. LNER-built KDE283580 is seen at Duddeston wagon repair depot on August 19, 1981, while undergoing roof repairs, it being part of the local Soho allocation.

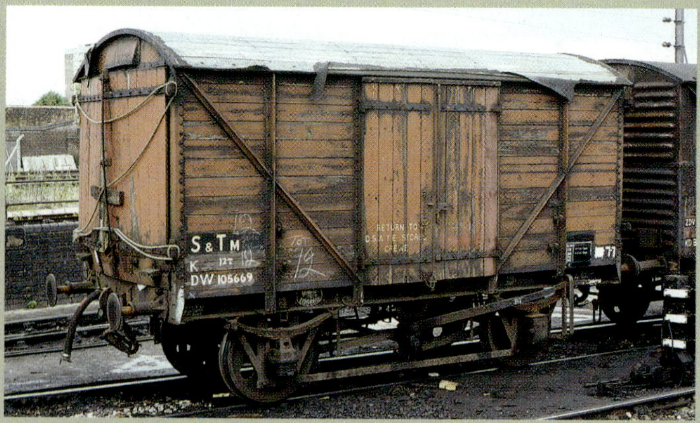

ABOVE: Also at Duddeston on the same day was KDW105669, this being a particularly distressed GWR Mogo with its end door restrained by rope and also in need of a new roof canvas. Built to carry motor cars, several found a role in S&T use, this one being lettered to return to Crewe.

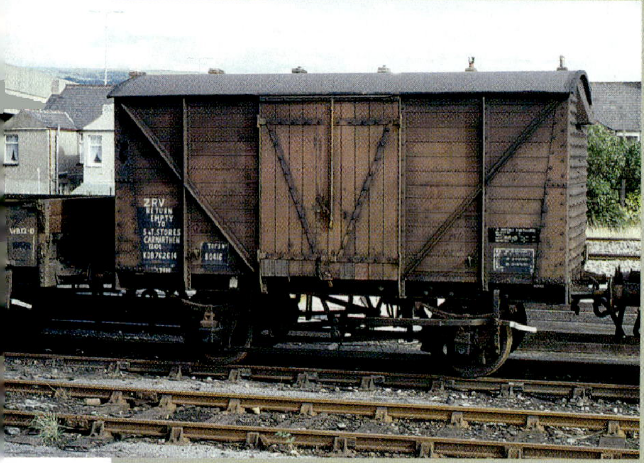

LEFT: Naturally, much use was made of BR's standard 12-ton vans built to diagram 1/208, as typified by KDB762614 at Neath on September 16, 1981. Coded ZRV, this was neatly lettered 'Return empty to S&T stores Carmarthen' and 'TOPS No. 80416' for the location code.

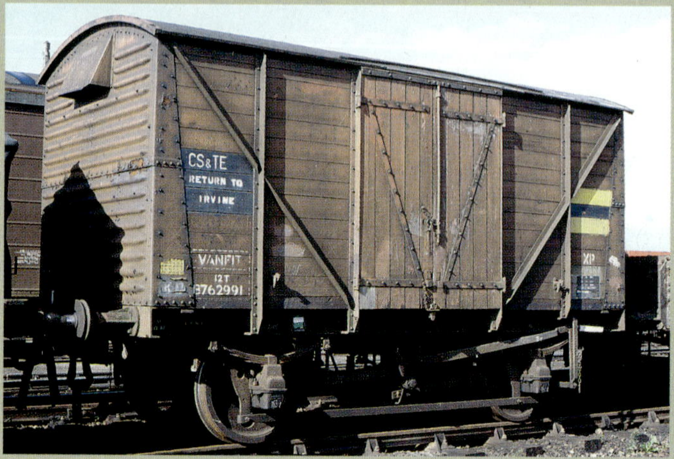

ABOVE: Another 1/208 van, KDB762991 was recorded at Motherwell on September 28, 1981, this displaying the yellow and black stripes of the Scottish S&TE. It is also lettered for return to Irvine but carries no TOPS code, it still having its Vanfit lettering despite the other branding changes.

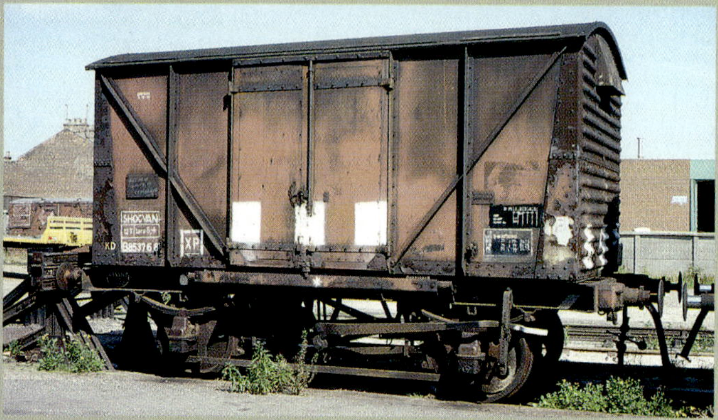

ABOVE: In contrast, you would be hard pressed to tell that shock van KDB853768 was even in S&T use if it were not for the 'KD' prefix added in front of the wagon number. Built to diagram 1/218, all the other markings were as per revenue use when seen at King's Lynn on August 28, 1979.

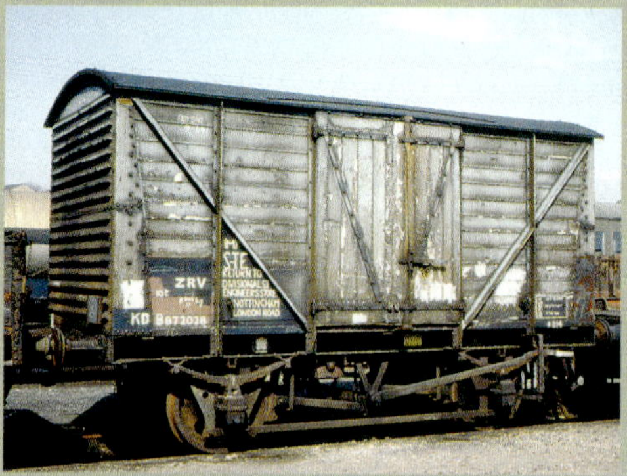

LEFT: From the rarer end of the scale is this 10-ton insulated meat van, KDB872028 being from diagram 1/251. Still in its original white livery, the ZRV was lettered 'Return to Divisional ST Engineers Store. Nottingham London Road,' where it was to be found on April 21, 1979. All Simon Bendall Collection

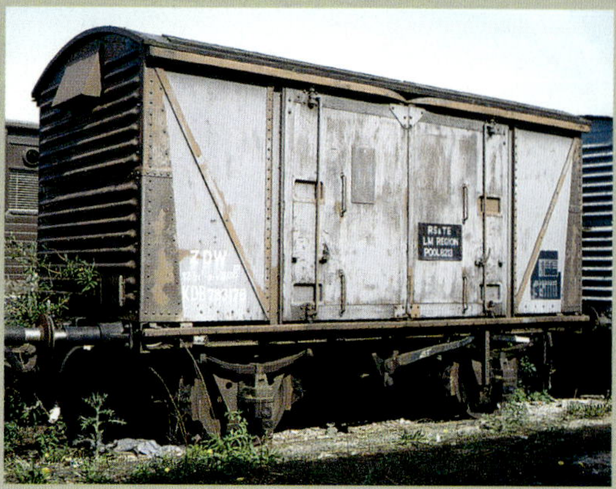

RIGHT: With little in the way of paint remaining, Vanwide KDB783176 was spotted at Chester S&T sidings in May 1994, this having received a through air pipe to make it a ZDW. It is also lettered 'RS&TE LM Region Pool 8213' on a separate plate, 'R' standing for regional. David Ratcliffe

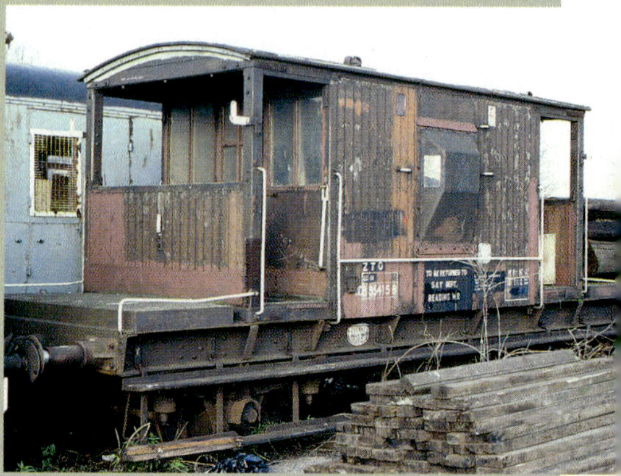

RIGHT: Naturally, the S&TE had numerous brake vans on its books of the commonest designs. Built to diagram 1/506, a tired KDB954158 was to be found at 'home' at Reading on April 15, 1982, it being lettered 'To be returned to S&T Dept. Reading WR' under the ducket. Simon Bendall Collection

S&T wagons for Morfa Bank by Hywel Thomas

The small S&T fleet that operates on Morfa Bank Sidings makes occasional visits to the yard, usually stabling ahead of weekend or overnight engineering work in the local area. In reality, the nearest S&T depot to the layout's imaginary location in Port Talbot was the one at Neath, a few miles to the west, so most of the small fleet are based on wagons from there.

Bogie Bolster B (ex Warwell)

The centrepiece of the S&T stock is Bogie Bolster B DM721216, as pictured on page 89. Having seen this former Warwell on a trip to Swansea in the late 1970s loaded with either a new or refurbished fully finished signal gantry, it was an obvious choice for the layout. The model is a Hattons example with only minor modifications. The main alteration was to the bogies, which needed a considerable amount of work to widen them in order to take EM gauge wheelsets. A full repaint in Gulf Red followed and then some complicated work cutting up various transfers to replicate the lettering.

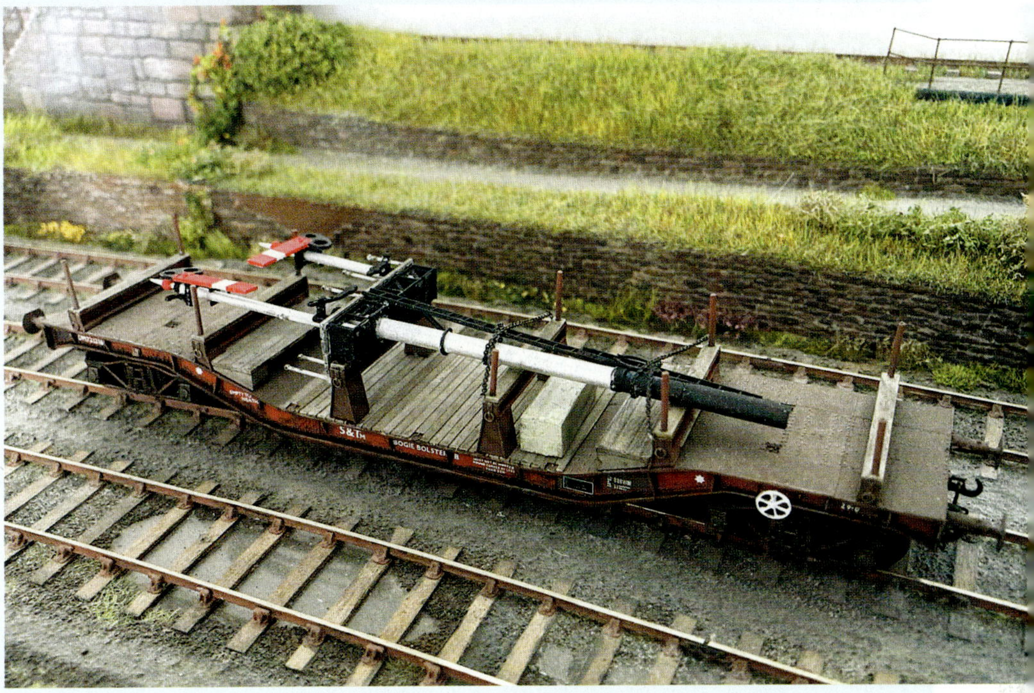

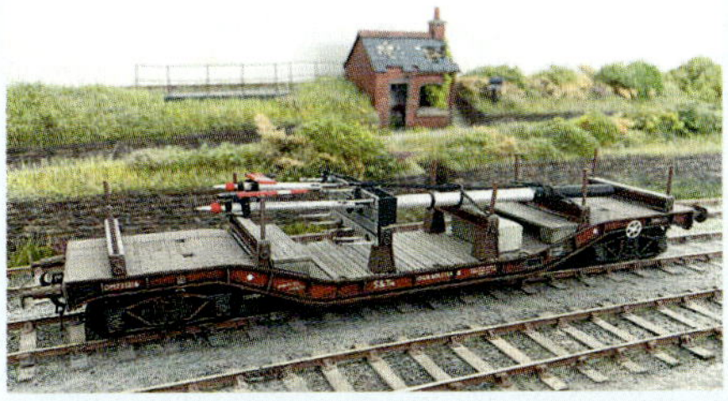

Moving onto the signal gantry, the wagon will also appear on the layout with other loads, so it needed to be removable. From photographs and a sketch of the initial sighting, the Ratio GWR gantry kit seemed the best way forward. It was built as per the instructions except for the extension of the main tube, which on the real thing slotted into the concrete foundation block; the latter is also modelled sitting in the well underneath the post.

The other alterations to the kit saw one of the signal arms dropped parallel to the post to keep it within gauge, as per the real thing, and the ladders strapped to the main post. The chains fitted to secure the load were fine 34-links to the inch examples and were kept rigid by coating them in superglue before positioning them, which also allowed the entire load to be removed as planned.

Plate wagon

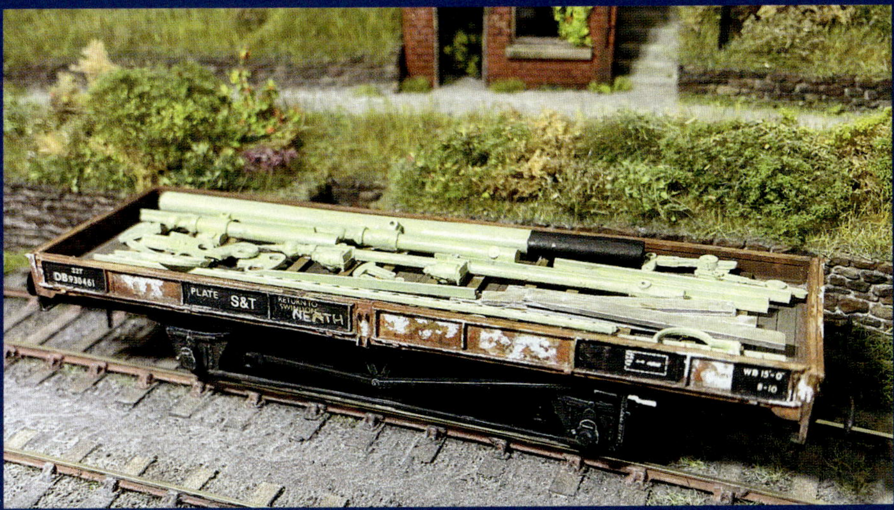

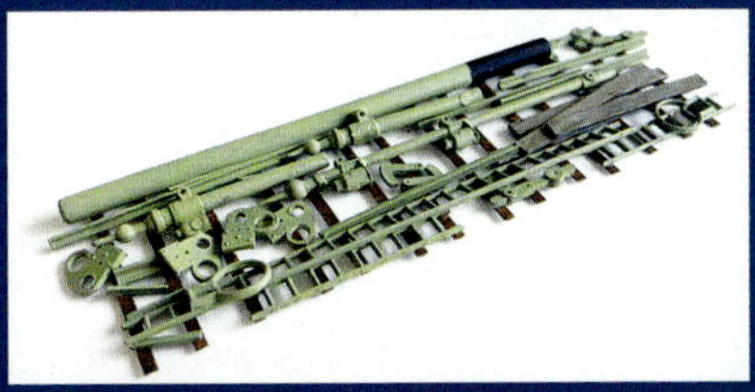

The next wagon in the fleet is a Parkside plate wagon built exactly as per the instructions. It was lettered up as an ex-revenue example that had been transferred to the S&T department. Although branded for Swindon, it has been crudely reallocated (or pinched) for Neath! The load represents a fairly common sight working out of the signal works at Reading, essentially a signal kit and based on a load I saw travelling west through Cardiff around 1980. These parts were painted in a green chromate primer (with the base of the post painted in black protective bituminous paint) and assembled and painted on site. The wagon contained everything except the signal arms, the connections into the signal rodding and the foundation block (unless it was replacing an in-situ example).

Once again, a Ratio kit provided most of the parts along with some Plastruct and Evergreen strip, all given a good coat of chromate green. In order to make the load removable, 10-thou strip was cut to fit the top of all the battens on the original kit floor but not glued to them. The various signal parts were then carefully attached with solvent to these strips (out of the wagon), some pieces overlapping others to create, effectively, a spider's web of parts that was rigid enough to hold together.

S&T wagons for Morfa Bank

Shock open

Shock open wagons were particularly common in the Western Region S&T fleet with most allocated to Reading and were regularly seen carrying both new and reclaimed parts plus scrap when needed. This example is a Bachmann RTR wagon repainted and re-lettered. As usual, removable loads were a must for this wagon and this open so far has two. The first represents a full load of cable drums on their way to a major project or into store at Neath ready for use. The drums came from various sources and were wrapped with copper wire. Aberdare Cables was one of the local providers of electrical cable and the outer wraps were created on the computer. The dunnage sack is used to wedge the drums and prevent movement.

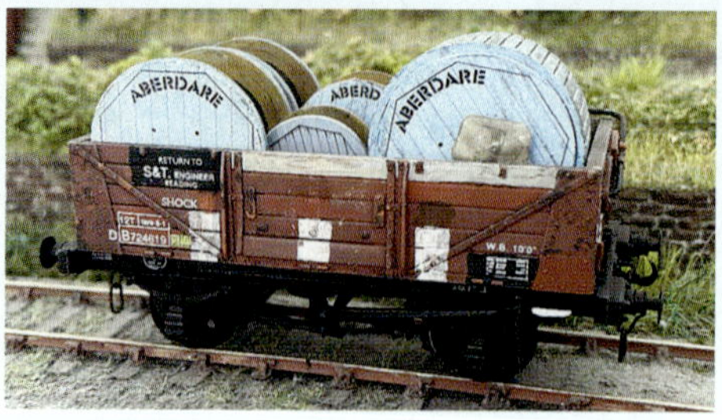

The other load represents the opposite end of a project with the collection of scrap cable. A lot of soft copper wire was wound around various cylindrical objects. To save on making any more of these bundles than necessary, I looked for something to represent the cable lower in the wagon. Rubberised horsehair seemed to have potential and so a piece was cut to fit and carefully trimmed before receiving a liberal coat of primer. The primed copper wire was then stuck on top using superglue. This was then sprayed with a top coat of satin black acrylic car paint from a spray can.

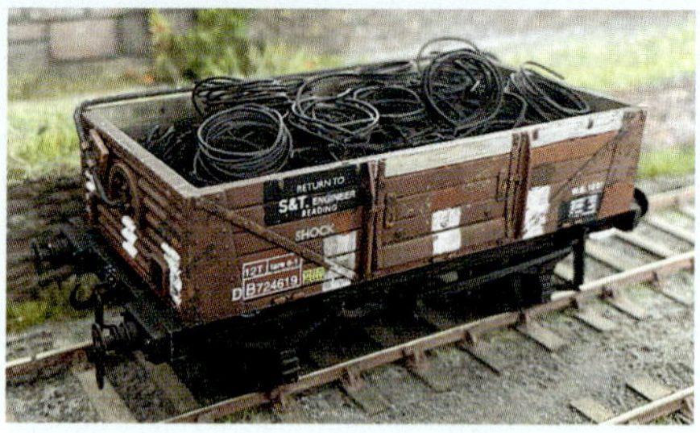

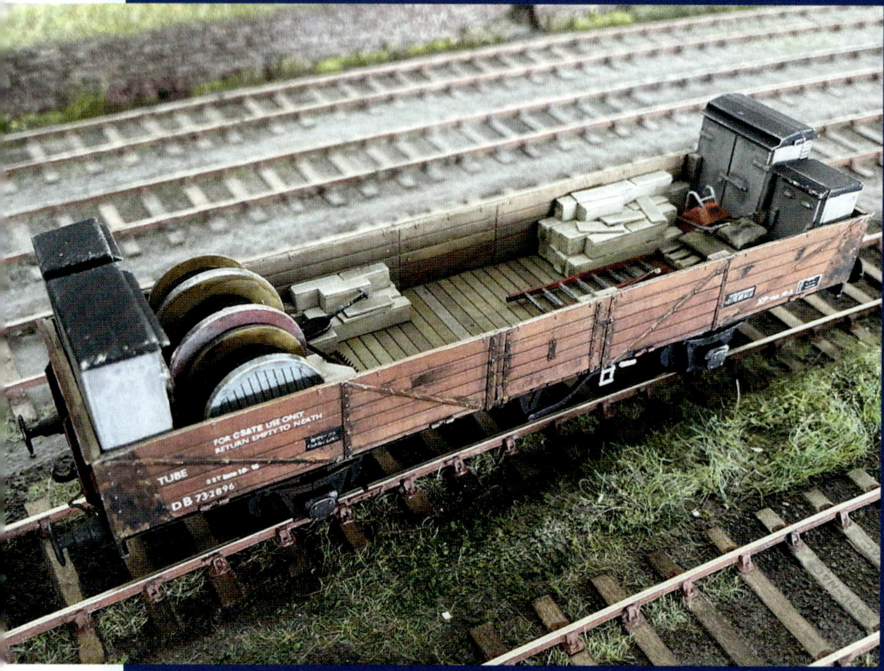

Tube wagon

Another Parkside kit, this one for the BR standard tube wagon, is also part of the fleet and represents an example photographed at Barry and lettered up for the S&T depot at Neath, which was recreated using transfers from various sources. Wearing pretty much the standard livery for vacuum-braked wagons, only the D prefix and the additional S&T instructions mark it out from the revenue fleet. Another removable load is carried by this wagon and features lineside equipment cabinets en route to a worksite along with everything the engineers would need.

The four cabinets (from the excellent Wills sets) are carried at each end and kept apart from each other using dunnage bags and wooden blocks. At one end, three small cable drums are wedged by wooden chocks and kept clear of the cabinets by the use of an old pallet. At the other end in front of the cabinets is a pallet carrying some sand and cement bags, while alongside is a stack of cable troughing, with a few more at the other end of the wagon to equal up the weight. There is also some spare wood packing, various tools, a wheelbarrow, and ladder.

GWR open

This wagon, an early Ratio kit for a former GWR Open C, represents another tube wagon that had been transferred from the revenue fleet to the S&T engineers. Built as per the instructions many years ago, it has now been repurposed as part of the Neath fleet after some refurbishment work. This wagon carries a load of salvaged point and signal rodding for reuse or scrap. As the wagon already carried some packing and old rope that had been stuck in when it was first built, the removable load had to be fitted around this. The base of the load used Evergreen strip fitted to clear the existing packing and prevent the new load from moving in the wagon. On to this, modified

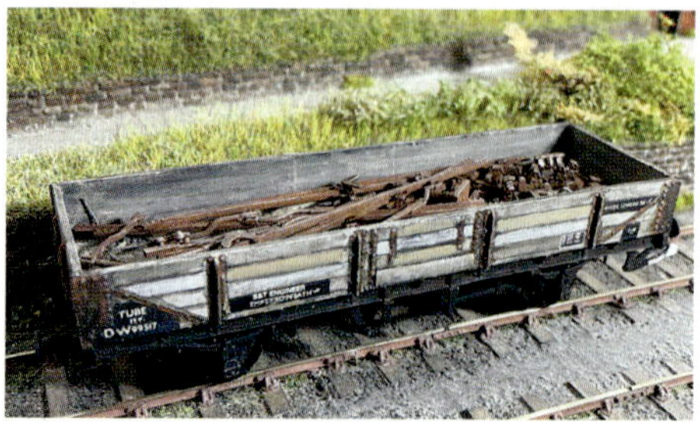

parts from the Wills point rodding kit were added in similar fashion to the plate wagon, creating a spider's web of bits for strength. The rodding has been separated from the rollers as these were loaded separately and assembled on site. All of the various parts were added to the base strips using solvent and then sprayed with primer followed by a mix of acrylic and pigment. Finally, after a coat of matt varnish, some of the parts were given an oily finish to represent the greased moving parts.

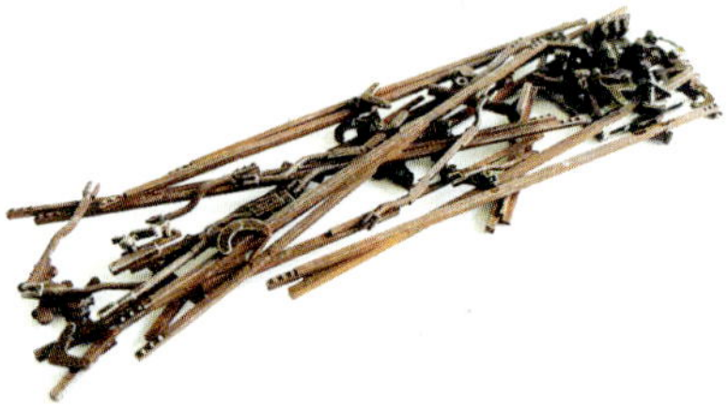

Satlink rebranding

The end of the 1980s brought a significant new look for the Signal and Telegraph Engineers with an amended name, new logo, and striking livery, all of which transformed the image of the department's rolling stock into the 1990s as Simon Bendall explains.

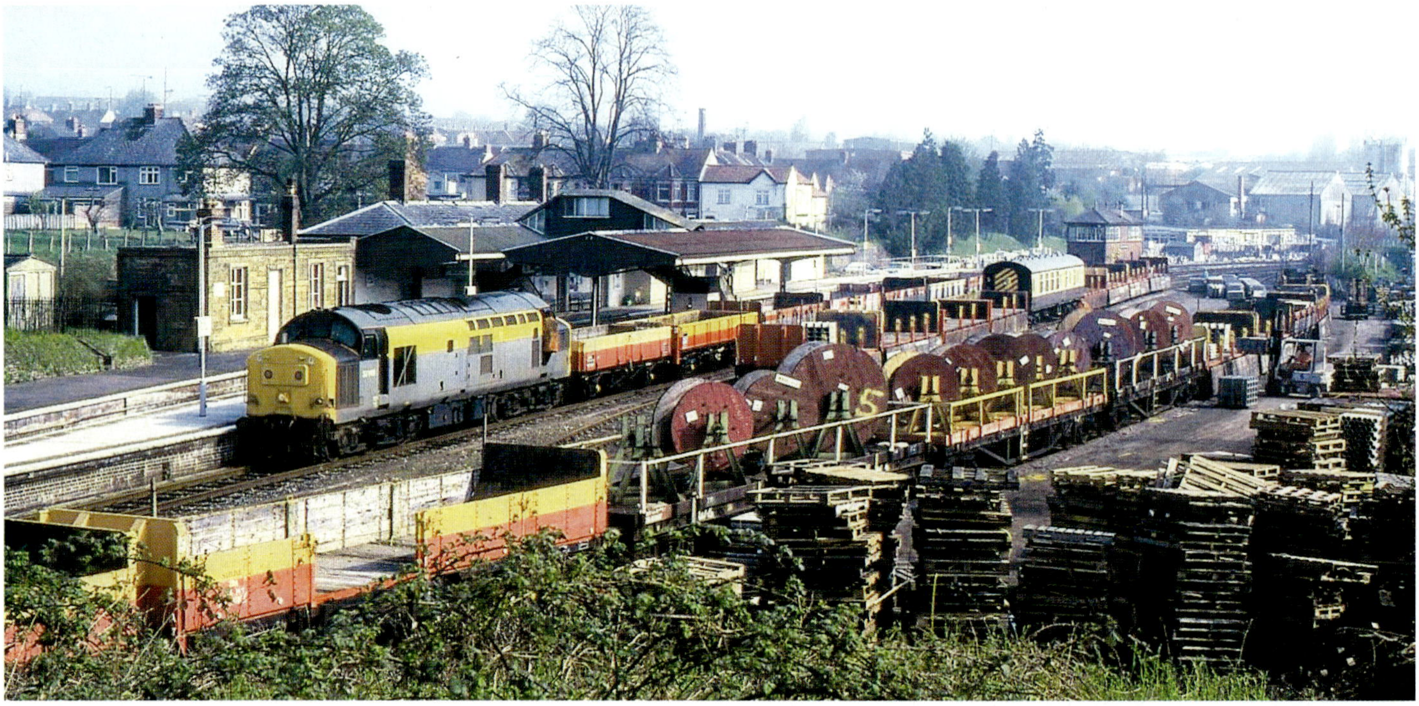

ABOVE: The normally sleepy yard at Yeovil Pen Mill was transformed into a hive of activity in January 1993 as a signalling renewal project commenced over the 'Mule', the former Southern Railway route to Exeter. This involved the overnight installation of new concrete troughing and signalling cables amongst other work. On January 19 that year, 37146 had just arrived with the 7Z46 09.30 working from Westbury, conveying empty open wagons. Leading the formation is an air-piped ZDW tube wagon, which is followed by a ZDA (ex OCA) newly repainted in Satlink colours and then five more ZDA. The latter would be on loan from the Civil Engineers and encompass three ex OBA in Railfreight red/grey, an ex OCA in grey/yellow and an ex OAA also in Railfreight. The sidings are also full of ex OBA and OCA, mostly in Satlink colours, with their doors lowered in preparation for loading with concrete troughing, which is underway on the right hand siding using a forklift. Also prominent are three cable drum carriers converted from Bogie Bolster C while the ex Mk.1 BSK staff and dormitory coach is DB975220, which was again on loan from the Civil Engineers and had received chocolate and cream colours at Exmouth Junction just three months earlier. Steve McMullin

With the late 1980s and early 1990s bringing a host of re-signalling projects across the network, the need to modernise the S&T fleet was clear. This period saw a major investment in the wagon fleet, surplus air-braked stock being drafted in to work alongside the best of the vacuum-braked designs and specialist conversions, many of which were fitted with a through air pipe to give brake compatibility, while much of the elderly stock was condemned.

The introduction of air-braked wagons also meant that vehicles could be moved via the Civil Engineers' network of Civil Link services when required, allowing materials to be transported across the country quickly. The modernisation brought the introduction of a striking new red and yellow livery and the brand name of Satlink, both of which were in evidence during 1989 and became ever more prevalent in the early 1990s. The department itself was also re-named with 'Telegraph' replaced by 'Telecomm' to project a more modern image and a new red and blue stylised S&T logo introduced.

Satlink Western

The S&T wagon fleet assigned to the Western Region was amongst the department's largest and busiest, thanks in no small part to the high profile early 1990s re-signalling project on the West London approach into Paddington along with the accompanying installation of Automatic Train Protection on part of the Great Western Main line. Several hundred wagons were given the new red and yellow image, many emblazoned with Satlink Western branding. The other regions were far less keen on adopting such a legend though, although Satlink LM or variants thereof was quite common on the Midland routes.

Among the Satlink Western fleet, a small proportion of the wagons, particularly the ex VDA and ferry vans, were used solely to transport stores that were too bulky to go by the preferred method of road, these including signal posts and gantry components, relay cabinets and point motors. Meanwhile, some open wagons worked out of the Taunton Concrete Works with cable troughing sections and other concrete fabrications.

The rest of the Satlink Western fleet was deployed on re-signalling projects and all the associated work that this entailed. Typical S&T duties at worksites would include delivering and installing both concrete troughing and relay cabinets, cable laying in the troughing, cement pouring for signal bases and the installation of signals. For the cable laying, a fleet of modified bogie bolsters carrying cable drums was provided while crane-fitted Lowmacs or similar would lift the relay cabinets into position. A dedicated concrete mixing train was available, this consisting of a modified Weltrol carrying the mixer, a water tanker, and flat wagons, such as Plates, for carrying supplies.

With the coming of privatisation, the S&T wagon fleet was divided up first amongst the passenger sectors in 1992 and then between the shadow freight companies two years later before passing to EWS ownership. While the air-braked open wagons would return to revenue use, most of the specialist vehicles would soon be withdrawn.

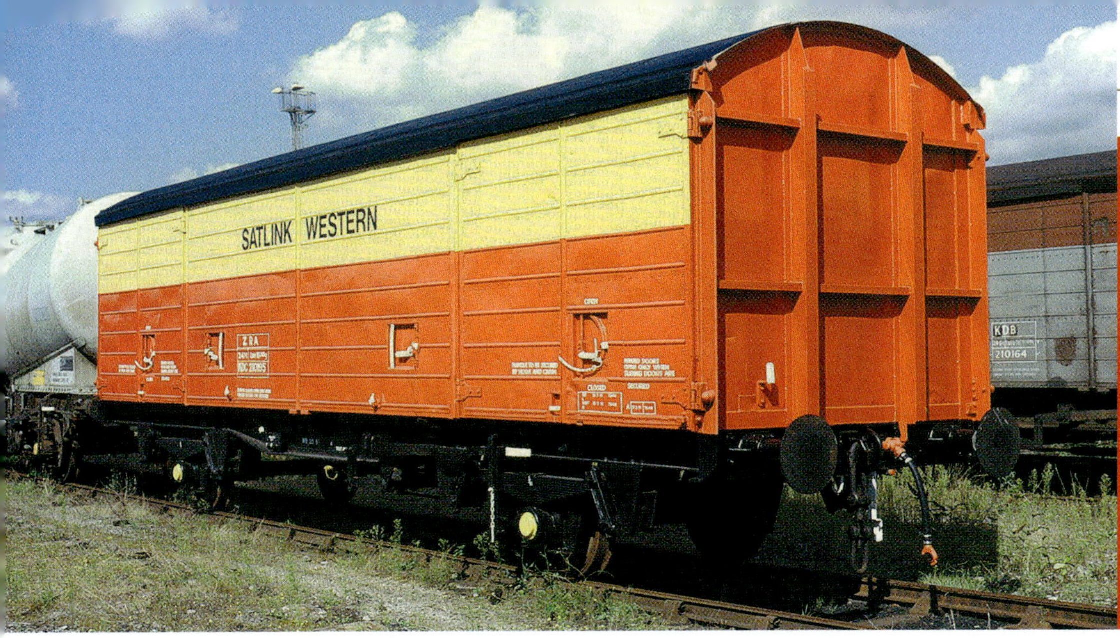

LEFT: **The 'poster boys' for Satlink Western were the VDA vans that looked particularly striking when freshly painted in red and yellow and recoded as ZRA. These were used to carry all manner of bulky stores and equipment to S&T depots but faced competition from more economic road movements. KDC210195 displays the 'full fat' version of the livery with all the lettering correctly applied when recorded at Radyr in August 1991. Conversely, once the paint started to fade, which it did rapidly, the vans looked terrible in pink!** David Ratcliffe

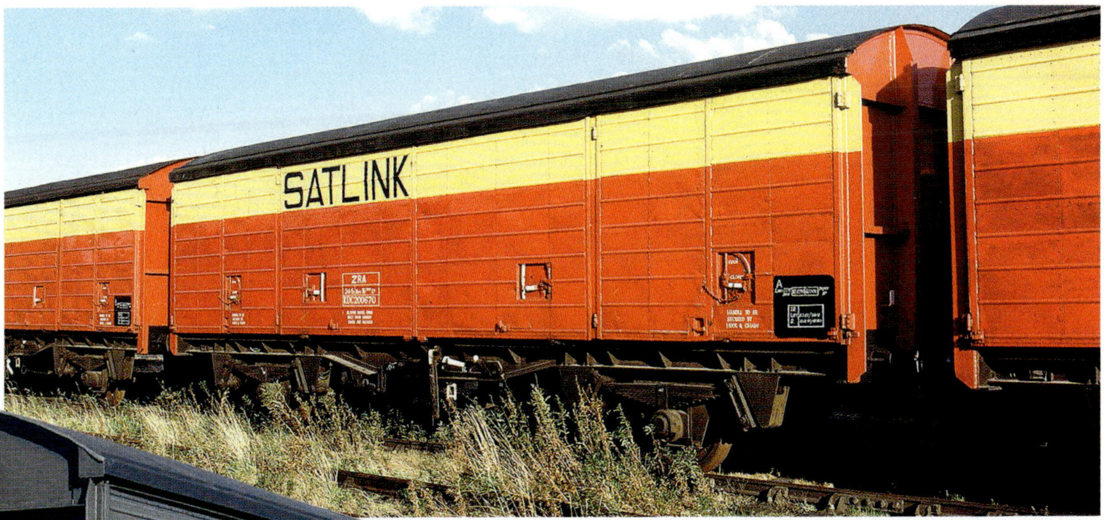

RIGHT: **In contrast to its fellow ZRA, KDC200670 displays much reduced lettering at Goole in October 1991, especially in terms of door locking instructions. The Satlink legend also has a rather amateurish look to it but illustrates the sort of variation that can be modelled on otherwise similar wagons.** David Ratcliffe

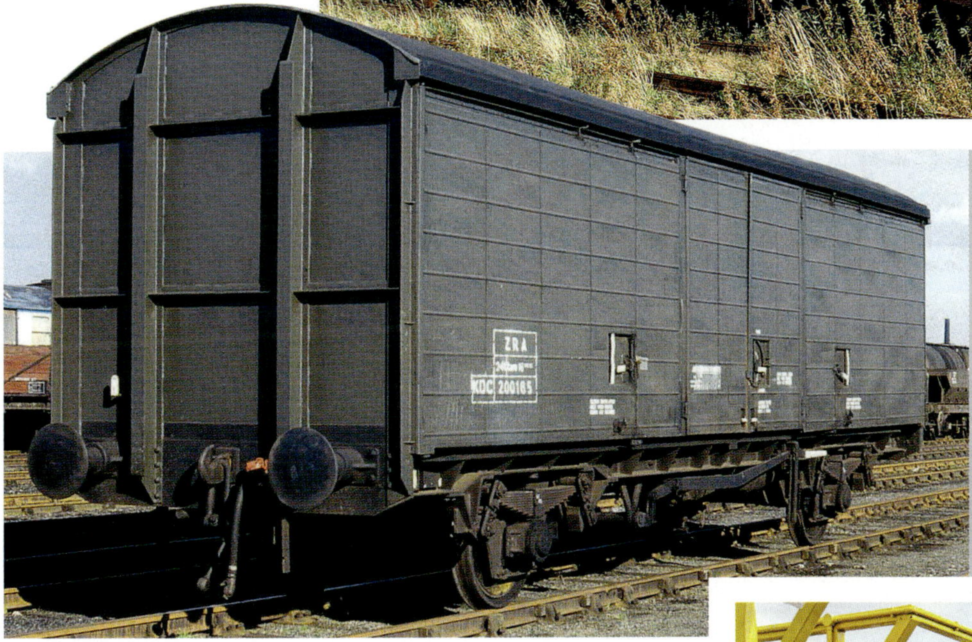

LEFT: **The engineers' fleet would eventually become home to most of the one-off and prototype air-braked wagons including the two VAB that had been experimentally rebuilt during the 1970s to test different door configurations. Recoded VDB, 200165 received a pair of centrally-positioned cupboard doors flanked by larger sliding doors but this design proved unsuccessful. When photographed at York Leeman Road on August 20, 1985, it had lost its vacuum pipe to become a ZRA, gained a KDC number prefix and was with the S&TE working a diagram from York to the signalling depots at Crewe Gresty Road, Wimbledon Stores and Reading, before returning back to York. It would be withdrawn in early 1994.** Trevor Mann

S&T
Signal & Telecom

RIGHT: **Newly converted at Cardiff Cathays, cable drum carrier KDC950046 stands in Radyr Yard following release on April 26, 1992. At this point, it was coded YXA, but this would later be altered to YVA while it also still had to receive the cradles for carrying the cable drums. Denoting the new ownership structure that was introduced for engineers' stock that year, it is lettered 'NSE S&T'.** Hywel Thomas

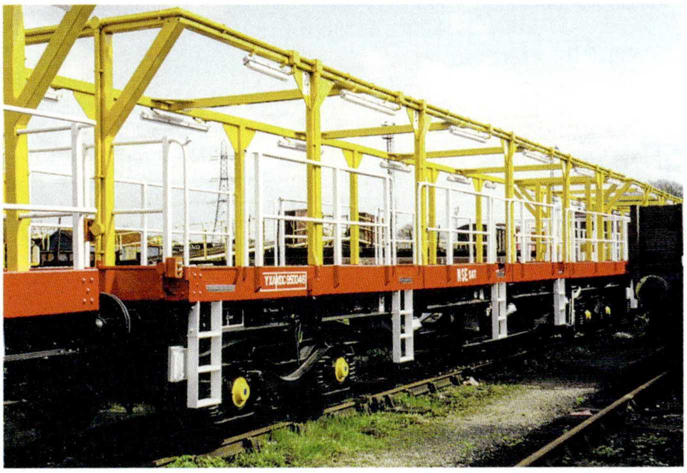

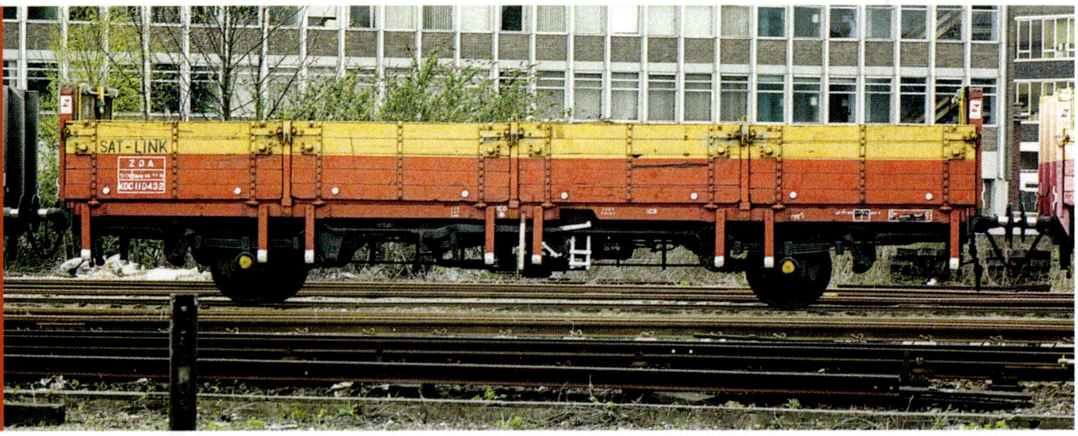

RIGHT: **The Satlink-liveried ZDAs (ex-OBA) were particularly common on former Southern Region metals for a time due to the various re-signalling projects then underway. However, by April 9, 1995, KDC110432 belonged to Mainline Freight but was physically unaltered by the ownership change. Seen at Redhill, it carries a rarer version of the livery with the curb rail and door bangers painted in red when these were normally black. Notably the paint has faded far less than the other ZDA to the right.** Ian Cuthbertson

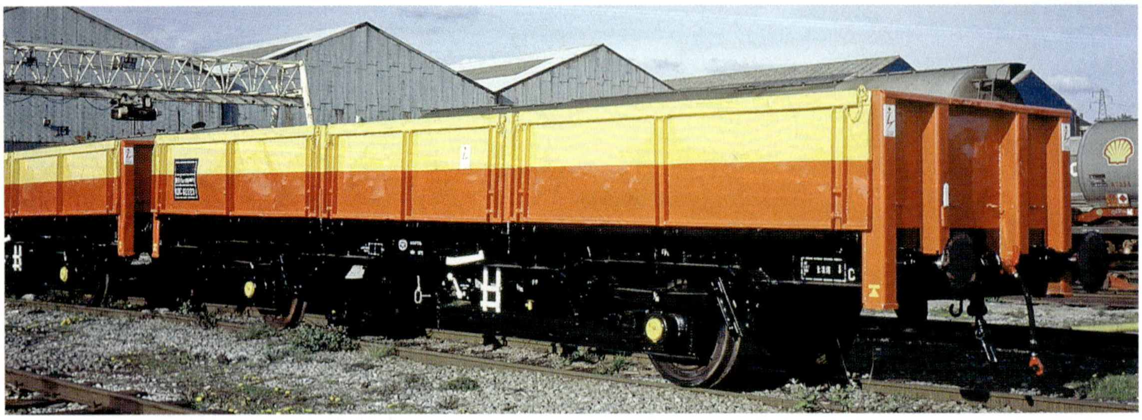

LEFT: **Fresh from the Marcroft Engineering paint shop, former OCA KDC112223 stands outside the Stoke wagon works in May 1992 while awaiting the application of its ZDA TOPS code. Like the other open wagons used by the S&TE, these could carry a wide range of loads.** David Ratcliffe

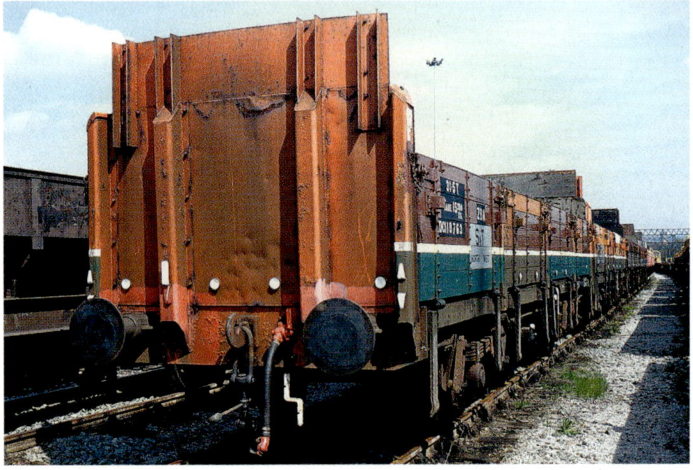

ABOVE: **Not all of the air-braked wagons transferred to S&T use were repainted, particularly if they were taken on towards the end of the British Rail era. Previously modified for Plasmor block traffic, ZDA KDC110763 had retained that company's orange and green livery when seen at Guide Bridge in April 1994, just receiving 'S&T North West' lettering instead.** David Ratcliffe

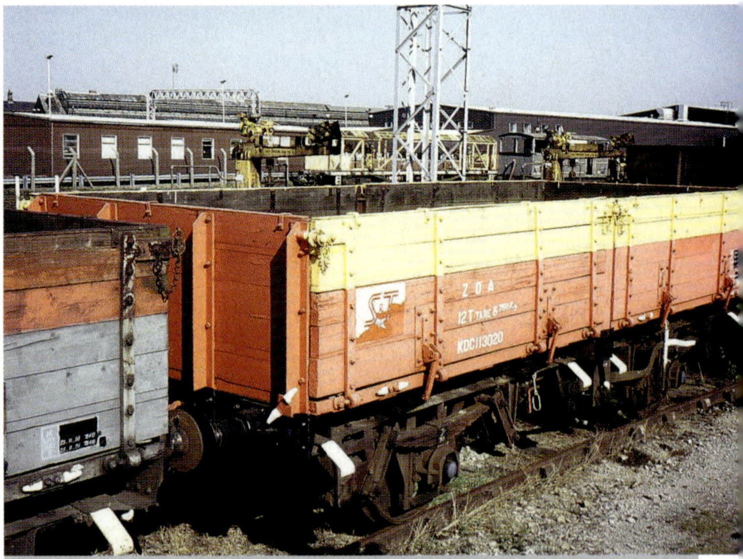

ABOVE: **The 50-strong fleet of air-braked ODA open wagons, 113000-049, were comparatively late transfers to departmental stock. The first tranche was not released to become ZDAs until the middle of 1991 following the closure of the Speedlink wagonload network and the scaling back of Ministry of Defence traffic to which the ODAs had been largely dedicated. The remainder had followed by the summer of 1993, being split between Regional Railways and InterCity infrastructure pools. With its paint already heavily faded, KDC113020 was at Chester wagon repair depot on April 12, 1995. This wagon also displays a partly removed S&T logo, the application of which to the entire Satlink wagon fleet was not particularly common.** David Ratcliffe

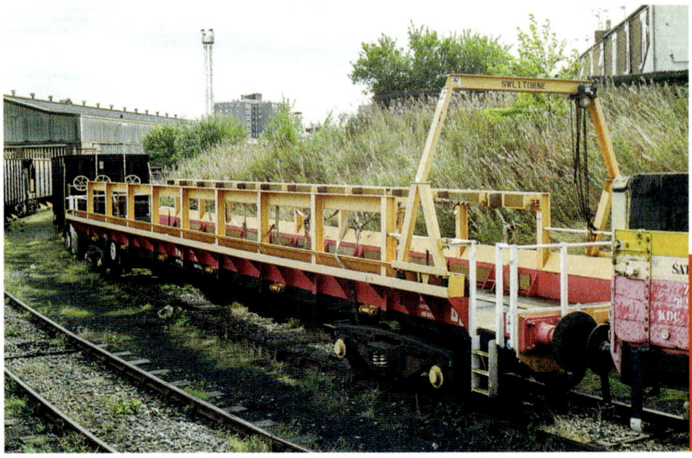

LEFT: **Once used for Far North Line container traffic on the back of passenger trains, single Freightliner flat KDC601999 found an altogether different purpose in the mid-1990s. Converted at Ashford in the spring of 1993, it was an experimental YSB relay cabinet carrier, which would be lined up along its length and then unloaded using the hoist at one end. Seemingly unsuccessful, it was captured at Chester wagon repair depot in September 1995.** David Ratcliffe

YVA Cable Drum Carriers in N by Carl White

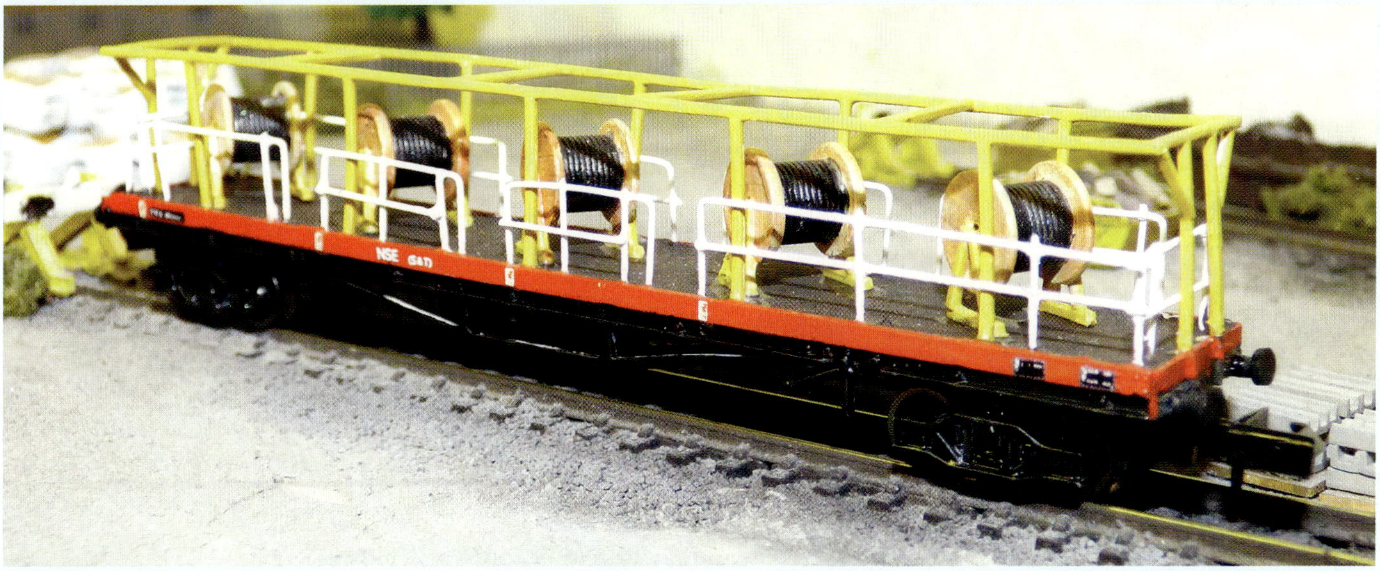

The base model for this wagon is a N Gauge Society BDA bogie bolster kit, which was built as per the instructions but with the omission of the bolsters. During my research into the cable drum carriers, I found a line drawing of the wagon on the Barrowmore Model Railway Group website, which I used in combination with photographs for the measurements of the handrails and framework.

The frame was constructed using plastic strip cut to size and glued together with Plastic-Weld. As I knew that I would require more than one of these wagons, during the construction of the first frame I made a cardboard jig and marked on all the sizes and positions of the frame components. With the model being in N gauge, some compromises were required with the frame, such as omitting the triangular strengthening plates at the top of the vertical supports. The frame was also constructed as a completely separate item so it could be painted with Phoenix Precision engineers' yellow before attaching it to the rest of the wagon.

Turning to the handrails, I marked and drilled all of the holes required into the floor of the wagon before constructing a further jig showing where the holes go to again aid with the construction of further wagons in due course. Lengths of 0.4mm brass rod were cut and bent to size and then glued in place using superglue. The wagon was next given a coat of white primer from an aerosol can. Once this had fully dried, the floor was painted using a brown Humbrol with the sides painted with Signal red and the underframe finished in black.

The cable drums are a 3D-printed item that I purchased from Shapeways.com while the cradles for them were a simple construction using the same plastic strip I had used for the framework. These were built and painted separately from the wagon and glued in place after painting was complete, with the transfers being a mixture of Fox and Railtec.

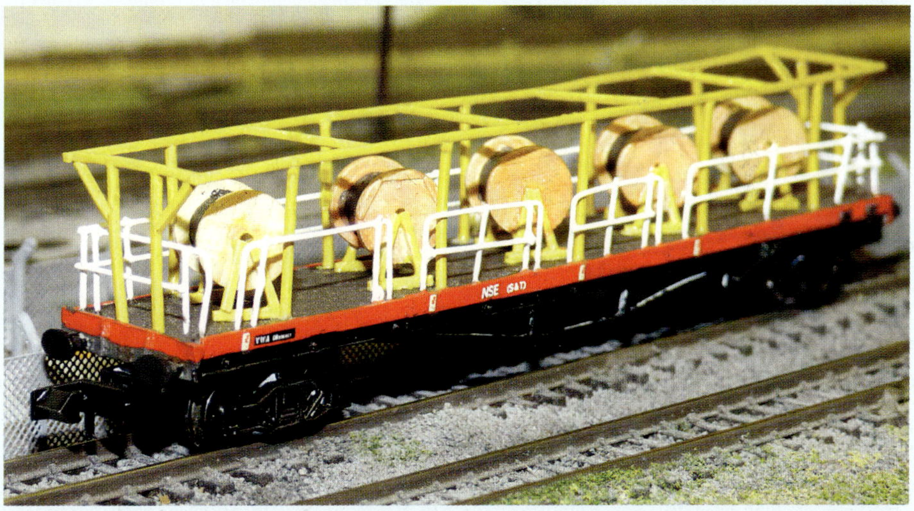

Southern YVA

The YVA cable drum carriers first appeared in the summer of 1992 with 22 examples eventually emerging from Cardiff Cathays for use by Network SouthEast. Maintained at Three Bridges and Ipswich, four sets of four wagons were created with six maintenance spares, all being finished in Satlink red and yellow. Each could carry five drums with the cradles being fitted at an angle to make it easier to unspool the cable. Numbers were KDC95 0034/37/46/48/56/64/82/9 3/98, KDC950113/38/79/83, KDC950221, KDC950330/ 57/69, KDC950400/44, and KDC950807/48/49, the final three being from the batch of BDAs that had bogie-mounted handbrake wheels with the rest having handbrake levers on the underframe.

To provide power for the on-board lighting, five generator vans were converted from VDAs at the same time with four in use and one spare. These were again painted in Satlink colours with their identities being KDC200800/879 and KDC210164/209/280. Remarkably, 11 of the YVAs survive today in DB ownership and see occasional use, although after spending several years in store, shabby does not really describe their condition! Also still with them is ZXA KDC200879, this working with EWS-liveried ZXA 200493 to power the lights. As the cable laying train is now longer, a van is marshalled at each end to supply half the set.

Simon Bendall

Satlink general material carriers by Paul Wade

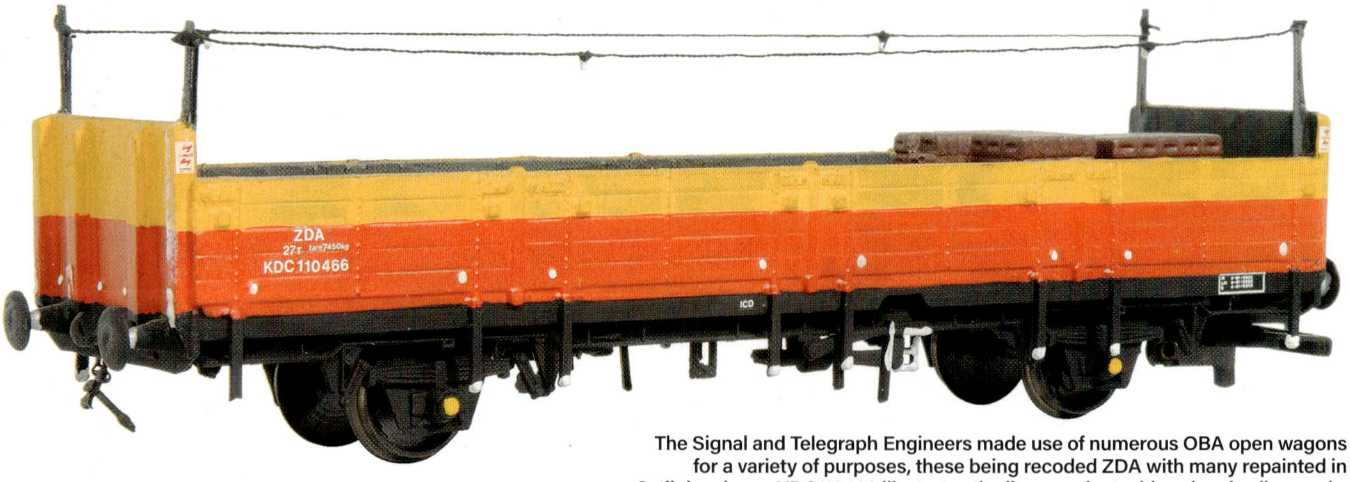

The Signal and Telegraph Engineers made use of numerous OBA open wagons for a variety of purposes, these being recoded ZDA with many repainted in Satlink colours. KDC110466 illustrates the livery variant with red and yellow ends.

Satlink wagons feature on my OO gauge layout Tonbridge West Yard due to the extensive re-signalling project that was taking place in its early 1990s time period, this being the Ashford Integrated Electronic Control Centre scheme. There were project depots at Ashford, located between the Wheel Shop and the Crane Repair Depot in the former Ashford Works site, and at the country end of Tonbridge station where the old motive power depot had been sited. At both these locations, wagons were loaded with various materials to replace the existing signalling. Tonbridge West Yard was used for marshalling rakes and storing wagons when not required.

For the mainstay of these works, air-braked OBA wooden-bodied open wagons were overhauled and outshopped in the bright Satlink red/yellow livery. However, due to the volume of renewal work being undertaken, older vacuum-braked Tube and Pipe wagons were utilised as well, often in the same livery. The OBAs were recoded ZDA and appeared to be overhauled at several locations judging by the livery and marking variations that occurred. Two main styles predominated, both having the top two planks finished in yellow while the ends either featured a red/yellow split to match the sides or were completely red .

The first livery variant had white lettering directly on the red planks while the second style had the lettering applied on black background panels. Other differences included the style and positioning of the Satlink legend and the presence or not of overhead warning flashes on the corners of the ends. One other livery variation had the red extending lower down the body and onto the door bangers.

A couple of the Plasmor conversions with extended ends were included in the

Table 1: **ZDA (ex-OBA) end painting style**
Red/yellow ends: KDC110005/12/16/28/32/51/52, KDC110157/58/67/78/80, KDC110207/36/64, KDC110309/23/48/63/67/71, KDC110404/16/66/83.
All red ends: KDC110545/79, KDC110612/36/89.
All red ends with red curb rail/door bangers: KDC110008/20/91, KDC110432.

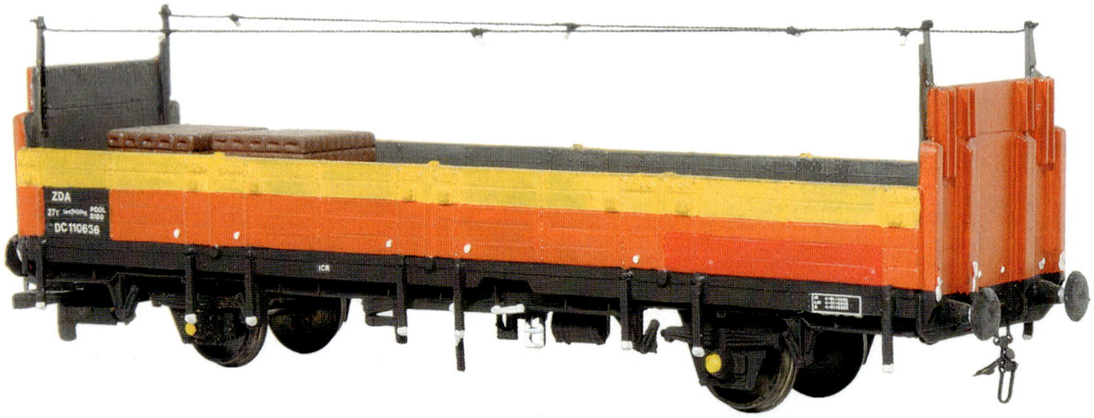

A number of the OBAs fitted with extended ends for use on Plasmor block traffic made it into the S&T fleet once made redundant. A few received a red and yellow repaint, this one being DC110636, the 'K' of the prefix being absent. It also has all red ends and the numbering details on black panels.

Table 2: **Personnel carrier brake vans**

Type	TOPS	Number	Livery
SR Pillbox	ZTR	DS55532	Olive green
SR Pillbox	ZTR	KDS55560	Satlink red/yellow
SR Pillbox	ZTR	KDS55997	Satlink red/yellow
SR Pillbox	ZTR	DS56119	CE grey/yellow (faded)
SR Pillbox	ZTR	KDS56153	Satlink red/yellow
SR Pillbox	ZTP	KDS56400	Satlink red/yellow
SR Pillbox	ZTR	DS56454	CE light grey/yellow
BR Standard	ZTR	KDB954672	CE grey/yellow (faded)
BR Standard	ZTR	KDB954429	Satlink red/yellow

Table 3: Sample ZDA train formations

ZDA x4	ZTR (SR) x2	ZDA x4		
ZDA x3	ZTR (SR)	ZDA x3		
ZDA x3	ZTR (SR)	ZDA x5		
ZDA x6	ZTR (SR)	ZDA x4		
ZDA x5	ZTR (BR)	ZDA x8		
ZDA x6	ZTR (BR)	ZDA x3		
ZDA x5	ZTR (BR)	ZDA x4		
ZDA x3	ZTR (SR)	ZDA x3	Atlas crane Warwell	ZDA x3
ZDA x3	ZTR (SR)	ZDA x3	HAP crane	ZDA x3
ZDA x3	Atlas crane Warwell		ZDA x3	

RIGHT & BELOW: **Some of the ZDA wagons received rudimentary lighting, KDC110180 being modelled with a representation of the festoon lash-up. This uses plastic strip for the poles and small scraps for the lights themselves while cotton thread represents the cabling.**

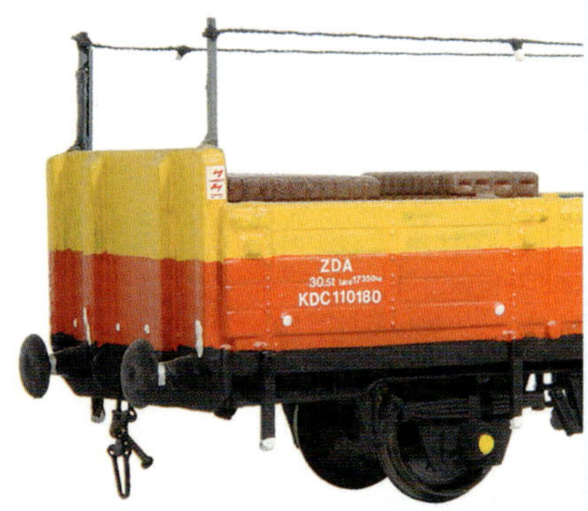

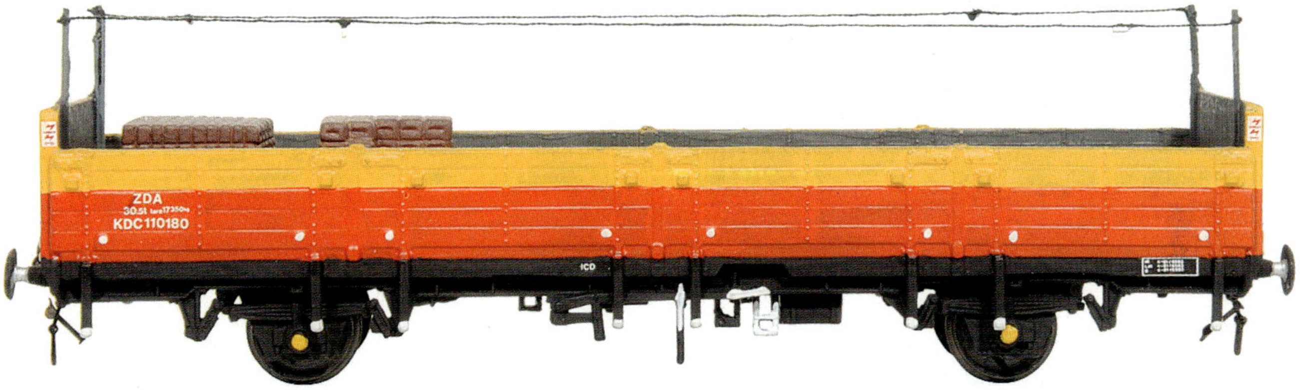

programme, these being KDC110545 and KDC110636. Table 1 gives the details of the end painting style on wagons that I photographed, showing that the red/yellow split was the most common.

Lighting up

Some of the wagons were soon fitted with a crude lighting system in the form of wooden posts nailed to the inner ends with 110-volt festoon lighting strung between them and taped to the posts. The cables were not split between wagons, just left long enough for going round curves. There must have been some inline plugs and sockets, but these are not clear in photographs.

A typical train formation would have a brake van towards the centre where a portable generator would be sited, this being connected to the strings of festoon lighting. The brake vans were also used as personnel carriers with a dedicated pool including several overhauled and repainted examples. Table 2 details the brake vans that were used in these trains around Kent, none of which were employed in their traditional role.

Some ZDAs did receive a more permanent lighting installation, this consisting of metal conduit posts on the inside of the ends with 110-volt sockets feeding flood lamps and with end-mounted jumper cables between the wagons. This was a superior system, but the earlier crude design was the more common arrangement. The permanent system soon fell out of use with the upright conduits and lights being removed while some wagons never received lighting additions of any kind. In later years, the festoon light fittings were also removed as the wagons became general user.

Loads and formations

Typical loads included pallets of concrete troughing sections with separate lids (both coming in various sizes), ducting, concrete sections used at the base of lineside cabinets, bricks, posts, relay and telecoms cabinets, and sacks of stone and sand. After the re-signalling project was completed, the wagons were used for recovering scrap materials made redundant by the scheme, especially cable, which was usually cut into short lengths to make loading easier.

Not all of the ZDAs were fitted with lighting, some just receiving the posts on the insides of the ends, as illustrated by KDC110579. The red on most Satlink stock faded badly over time to give a pink look, although these particular wagons are modelled in largely ex-works, early 1990s condition.

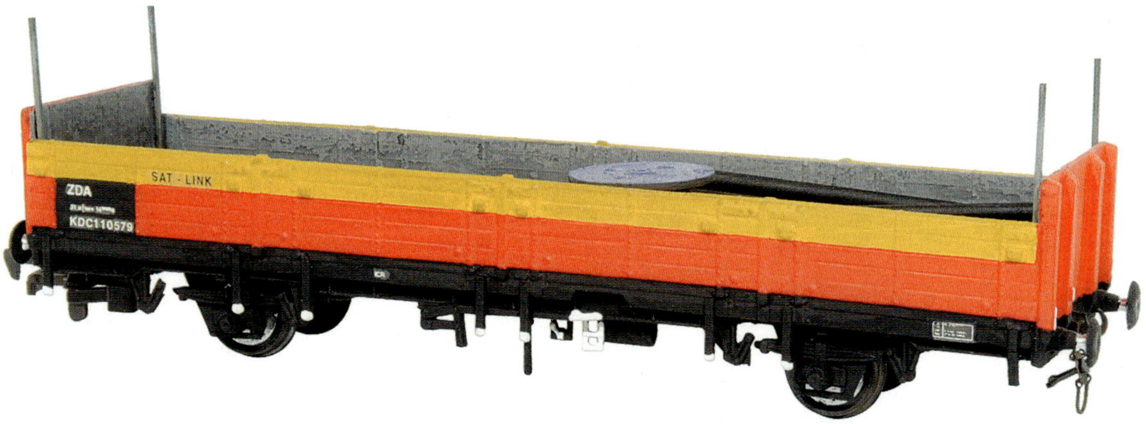

Satlink general material carriers

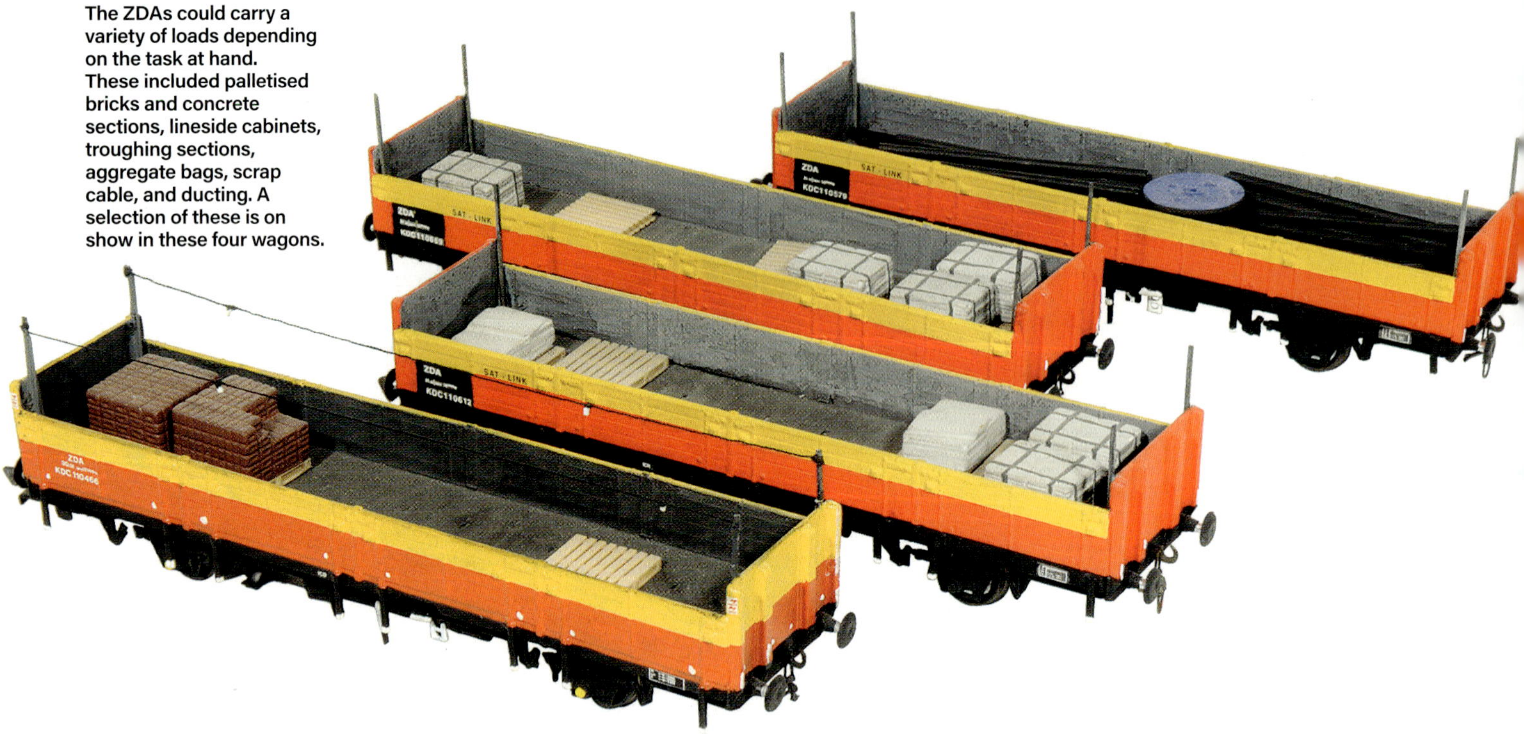

The ZDAs could carry a variety of loads depending on the task at hand. These included palletised bricks and concrete sections, lineside cabinets, troughing sections, aggregate bags, scrap cable, and ducting. A selection of these is on show in these four wagons.

Table 4: **Air-braked cable-laying sets**

Base	YVA cable layers	ZXA generator	ZTR brake	ZDA opens
Tonbridge	KDC950034/037/807/849	KDC210164	KDS55560	KDC110148/301/425
Three Bridges	KDC950056/098/369/444	KDC210209	KDS56153	KDC110051/128/588
Ashford	KDC950064/093/113/138	KDC200800	None	None
Ipswich	KDC950046/179/183/848	KDC210280	None	None

Some typical ZDA train formations are shown in Table 3. Due to the inclusion of the ZTR personnel carrier brake vans, which were only air and vacuum piped, they had to be marshalled within the formations with a minimum of three fully braked wagons on either side if the train was to be reversed on its journey. They therefore often stayed in rakes for long periods, especially once rigged up with the festoon lighting. Some of these trains were of a nice short length while, as the table shows, other specialist crane wagons sometimes joined the formations.

Once their work in Kent was completed, the wagons moved on to other Network SouthEast signalling projects as well as becoming more general user with civils workings in later years. The wagons featuring red and yellow ends seemed to fade faster than the red-ended versions, the red soon going pink while the yellow also faded badly too.

From 1993, some ZDAs joined the air-braked cable laying wagon sets formed from converted BDA bogie bolster wagons. The Tonbridge and Three Bridges sets were formed with four cable wagons designated YVA, one ZXA generator van (ex VDA), one Southern Pillbox ZTR personnel carrier brake van and three ZDA opens. Prior to these sets being formed, older former Plate and bogie bolster cable layers were used. See Table 4 for full details of the air-braked cable laying sets.

Modelling the ZDAs

I have used Cambrian kits for all of the ZDAs built so far. These go together very well and have much thinner sides and ends than the Bachmann model, not that this was available when I built mine! These were assembled as per the instructions, which involves mounting the sides and ends onto the floor before adding the solebars underneath followed by all the underframe equipment. The buffers can be replaced with cast or sprung versions if desired as can the plastic brake disc inserts with etched versions. On one example, I added the optional taller Plasmor ends.

With brass bearings added, the W-iron units can be folded up and glued. I used plastic X-Acto clamps to hold them to shape with the wheels inserted. The springs on the W-irons were of the correct type for the wagons I modelled so the alternative design provided in the kit was not required. I used the swivelling wheel units with the centring spring as this works for me. For added weight, I fitted several strips of self-adhesive window lead under the floor. The wagons were undercoated with white car primer before employing Humbrol No.24 yellow for the top planks followed by Phoenix Precision Railfreight red for the remainder of the sides and ends. Medium grey was used for the interior with black for the underframes.

The seven wagons I built were divided up with two having red/yellow ends, four with red ends and black panels for the numbering data, and one with red ends, curb rails and door bangers. Some of the wagons were fitted with screw couplings at both ends or with a screw coupling at one end and a tension lock at the other. This allows scale couplings to be used on most of the set but with the ability to couple easily to locomotives and brake vans.

As they were done many years ago, transfers were a mixture of Fox and Woodhead with the Satlink brandings made up from lettering sets. When finished, the wagons were matt varnished and the interiors lightly weathered. For loads, I added brick stacks and concrete sections on pallets, empty pallets and, in one wagon, piles of ducting lengths with a cable drum.

On three wagons, I added the festoon lighting using plastic posts (although brass would give added strength), cotton thread glued between the posts, and little bits of

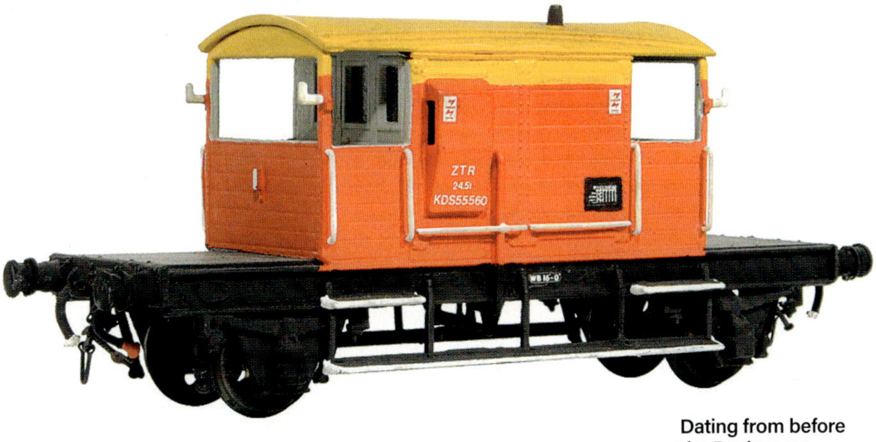

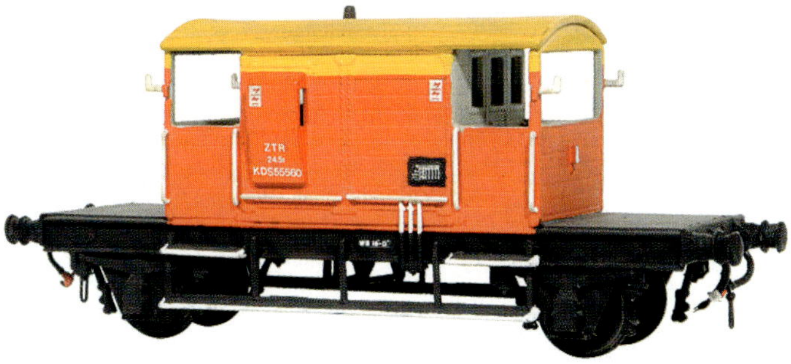

Dating from before the Bachmann version, the Cambrian kit of the Southern Railway Pillbox brake van builds up into a nice model. Used as personnel and generator carriers, they were marshalled in the middle of trains as they lacked train brakes. They were however air and vacuum piped as evidenced by the bufferbeam fittings and the different pipework styles on the sides.

styrene strip glued to the cotton to represent the lamps, which were then picked out in white. On another three wagons, I just added the posts without lighting. The final touch was to glue Replica Railways tail lamps on the outer end wagons of the rake.

ZTR personnel carrier

This model again used the cleverly designed Cambrian kit for the Southern Pillbox brake van. This can be built with left or right hand duckets along with even or mixed planking styles. My model of KDS55560 has left hand duckets and was built by first adding the solebars and bufferbeams to the floor with the body then built up on top. The underframe equipment and stepboards were fitted to the chassis as were screw link couplings to the bufferbeams along with cast vacuum and air pipes. The stepboard design differs depending on whether the brake van has left or right hand duckets.

Lamp irons and handrails were fitted around the verandas while roof rain strips were made from styrene strip. The style of the latter varied from van to van due to repairs over time. The stove chimney was added by drilling a 1.5mm hole as the instructions indicated while the roof remained unfixed until the model was painted and glazed. The vacuum pipe into the van body on one side was a length of 0.9mm brass wire while, on the other side, three 0.5mm lengths of brass wire represented the air pipe connections.

The wagon was primed, painted, and varnished in the same manner as the ZDA opens. The inner bodywork on the verandas was painted mid grey with the lamp irons, handrails, vacuum and air pipes, and stepboard edges picked out in white. Transfers were again from Woodhead with small black patches painted as a background where the maintenance data panels were sited. Once glazed, I glued a large metal nut inside the body to give weight to the wagon before the roof was fixed in place.

I have also modelled two other Pillbox brake vans, grey/yellow DS56454 and olive green DS55532, which I sometimes use in the ZDA rake. There is also a BR brake van, KDB954672, available for use in the set, which employed the earlier Hornby model as its basis.

ZXA generator van

The generator wagon for the cable laying train was a converted VDA van. The only external changes were the addition of steps on the solebars to access the interior, light fittings and switches on the solebars, an exhaust on the roof and jumper cables and boxes on the ends to connect to the YVA cable wagons. The 240-volt generator was hidden inside the body with no external ventilation grille provided.

I used a Hornby VDA as the basis for the model as the superior Bachmann model had not been produced at the time. The steps, lamps, switches, and jumper boxes were all made out of different sizes of styrene strip, with the exhaust pipe on the roof fashioned from 0.9mm wire.

The un-prototypical vent on the roof was filed off and the roof ribs rebuilt from plastic strip. Painting and finishing were as previously with transfers again mostly coming from the old Woodhead Fine Print range while the NSE lettering was from a rub-on sheet.

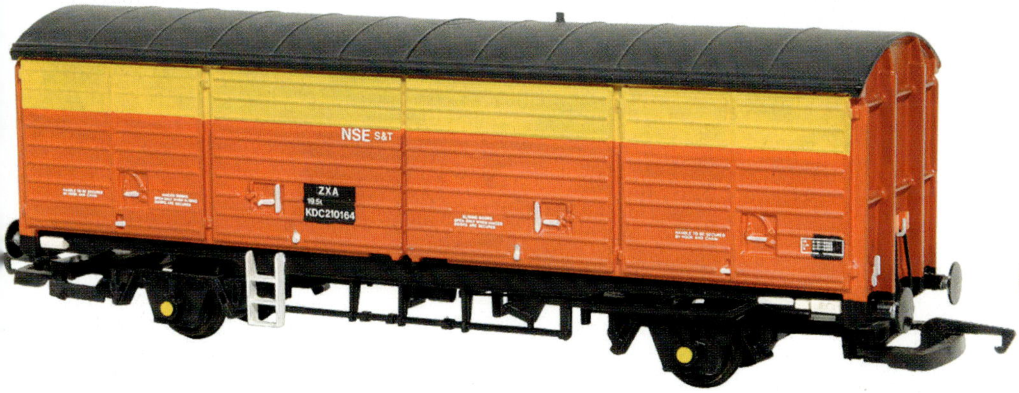

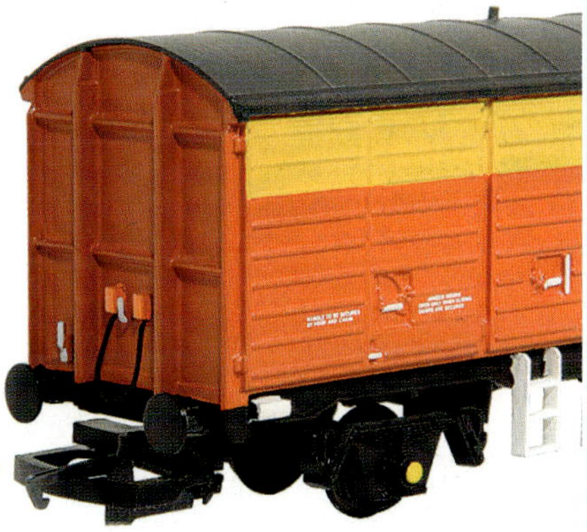

If you were modelling a Satlink ZXA generator van today, the obvious starting point would be the Bachmann VDA van. However, when this model was built, the elderly Hornby version was all that was available. Modifications include the roof exhaust, solebar steps and lighting, and the jumper cable connections on the ends.

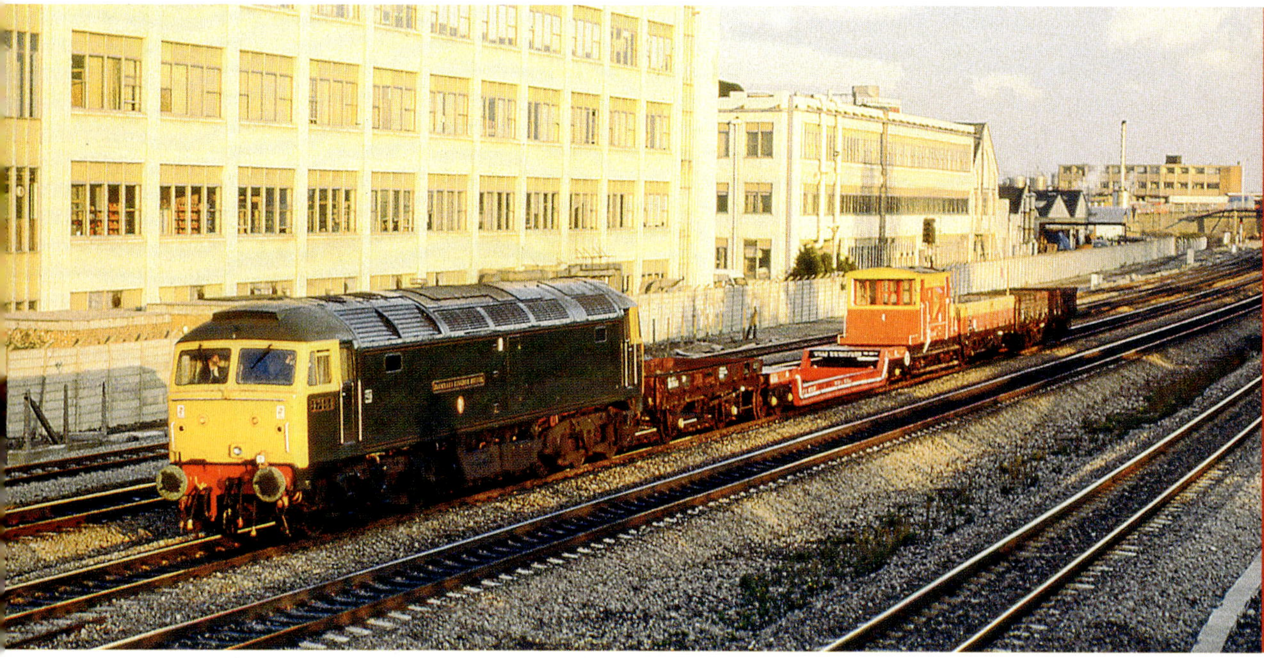

LEFT: **47484 *Isambard Kingdom Brunel* dodges the lengthening shadows as it heads into the evening sun at Hayes & Harlington, West London, on an unrecorded date in mid-1990. The westbound S&T working shows the transformational effect that the Satlink livery had on the wagon fleet with the well wagon, personnel carrier (ex brake van) and Tube all standing out in their newly-applied colours. In contrast, the Plate wagon at the front of the formation along with another Tube and a Pipe at the rear are dismally drab.** Simon Bendall Collection

Satlink expansion

The red and yellow Satlink colours were not just for air-braked stock, the livery expanding rapidly to vacuum-braked wagons following its introduction in 1989. The same was true of the various specialist vehicles that were retained into the 1990s as Simon Bendall details.

BOTH BELOW: **Built to BR diagram 1/446, these two Tube wagons are both to the LNER design with two drop doors giving full access for loading. Commonly used to carry palletised concrete troughing, they are showing different region allegiances with KDB730329 lettered Satlink LM at Chester during April 1990 while KDB730243 at Radyr in August 1991 was carrying Satlink WR. The latter wagon had also received a through air pipe, making it a ZDW, while the other was still just a ZDV.** David Ratcliffe

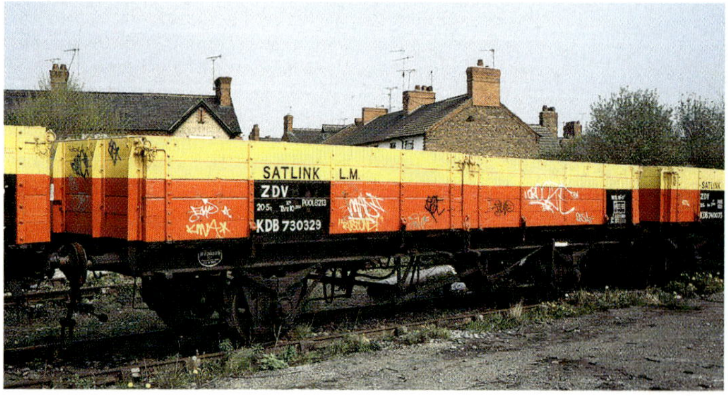

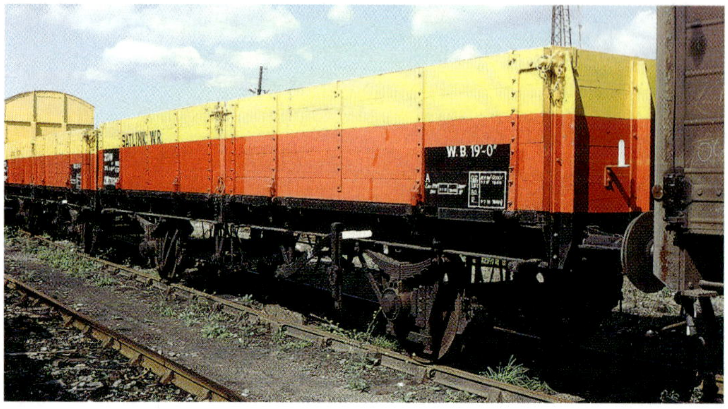

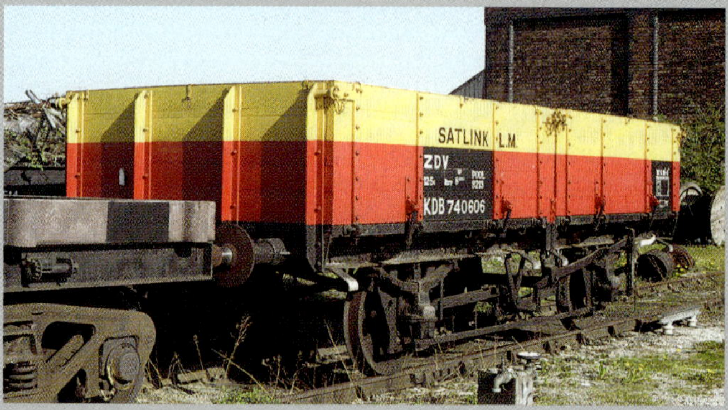

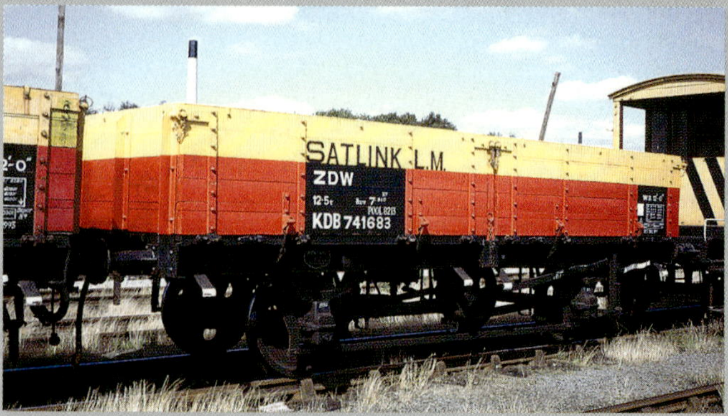

BOTH ABOVE: **It was a similar situation in terms of brake characteristics for these two 12-ton Pipe wagons with KDB740606 at Chester S&T Sidings in April 1995 having remained un-piped as a ZDV. In contrast, another of the Satlink LM pool, KDB741683 had been air-piped some three years earlier and become a ZDW when photographed at Ellesmere Port in July 1992.** David Ratcliffe

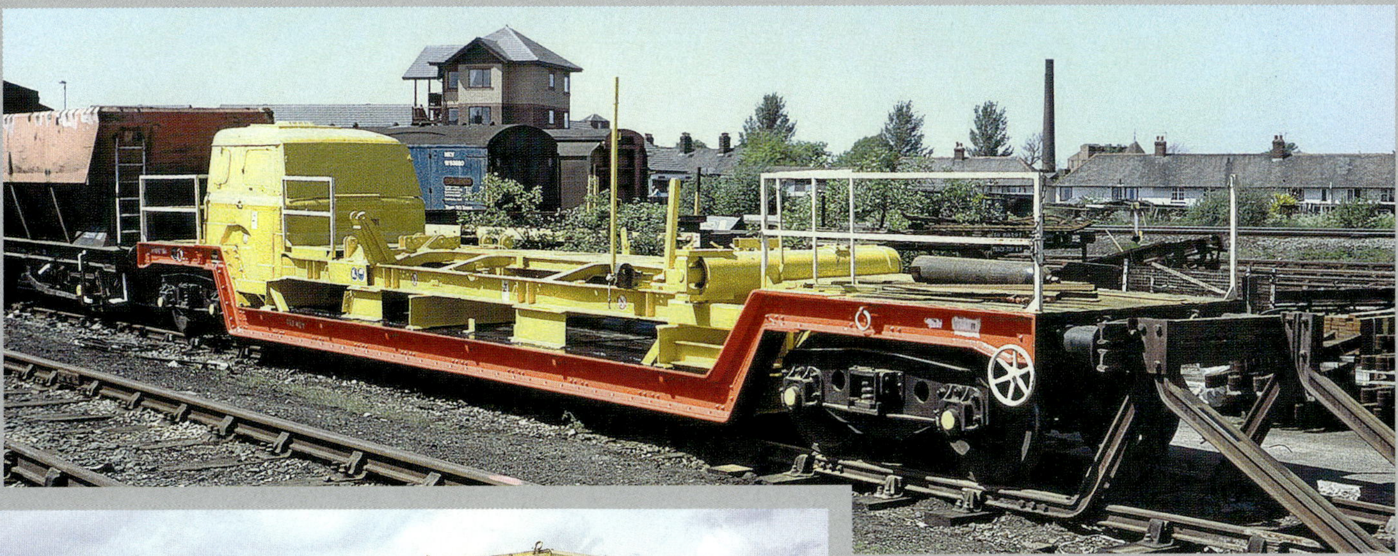

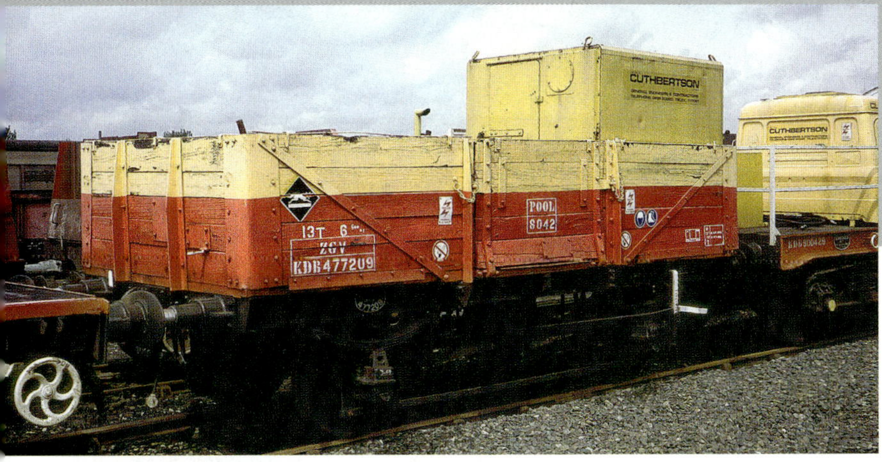

ABOVE &LEFT: **One of several specialist conversions for S&T use was Flatrol MDD KDB900429, which had been converted to a 'Mole' wagon, complete with a former lorry cab! The contraption was seen at Carlisle Currock in May 1990 after receiving Satlink colours. Two years later in June 1992 and at the same location, it had been joined in a supporting role by ZGV Highfit KDB477209.** David Ratcliffe

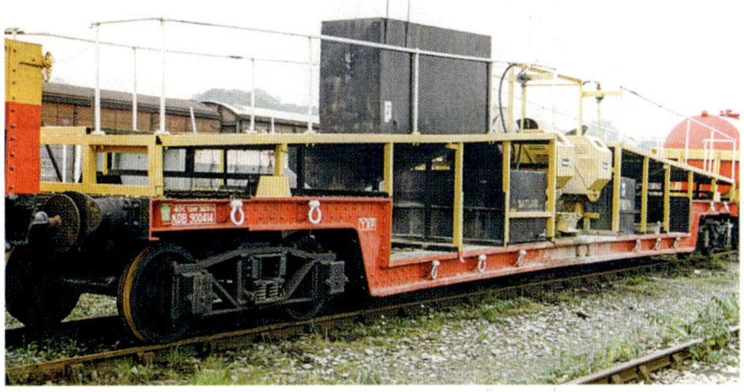

ABOVE: **Former Flatrol KDB900414 was the epitome of a specialist S&T wagon, having been converted to carry two cement mixers. When first modified some years prior to its Satlink repaint, it worked with four Plate wagons, two being marshalled on either side. Those nearest to the Flatrol formed a continuation of the sloping access ramps with safety handrails while the outer pair were used as access wagons and also carried supplies. When seen at Radyr Yard on October 13, 1991, these support wagons had been dispensed with. However, still accompanying the YXP was former GWR milk tank KDW2952, this also carrying Satlink livery as a water supply.** Hywel Thomas

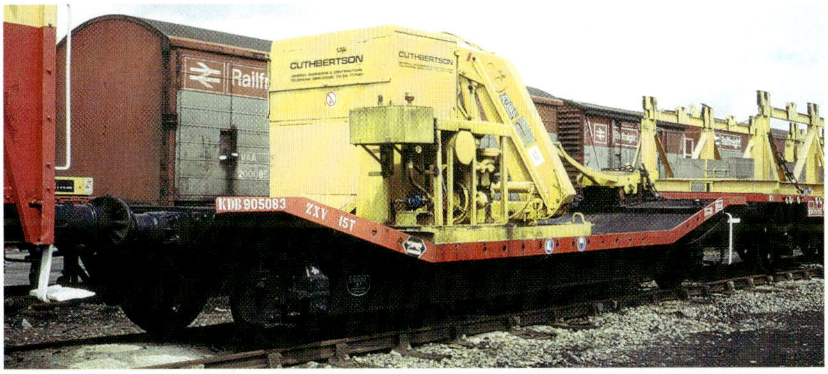

ABOVE: **Carrying the same Cuthbertson contractors lettering, KDB905083 was also to be found at Carlisle Currock in May 1992. This had begun life as a 15-ton Lowmac WV to diagram 2/248 before being fitted with an Atlas hydraulic arm and diesel engine. It is believed this was used as a trenching unit with what appears to be a manual roller also chained to the deck. To the right is a Conflat A that has been converted into a cable drum carrier with the addition of a substantial support framework.** David Ratcliffe

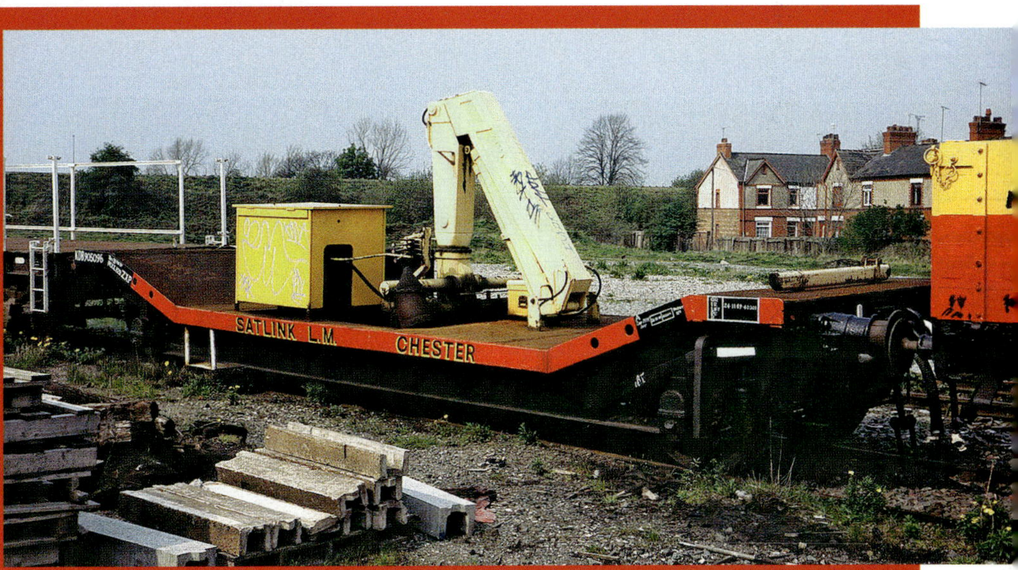

RIGHT: **The crane-fitted Lowmacs were useful for lifting bulky but comparatively light items, such as relay cabinets. For signal installation, a Civil Engineers' crane would be called upon. Part of the Satlink LM allocation, ZXP KDB905096 displays such a conversion at Chester S&T Sidings in April 1990.** David Ratcliffe

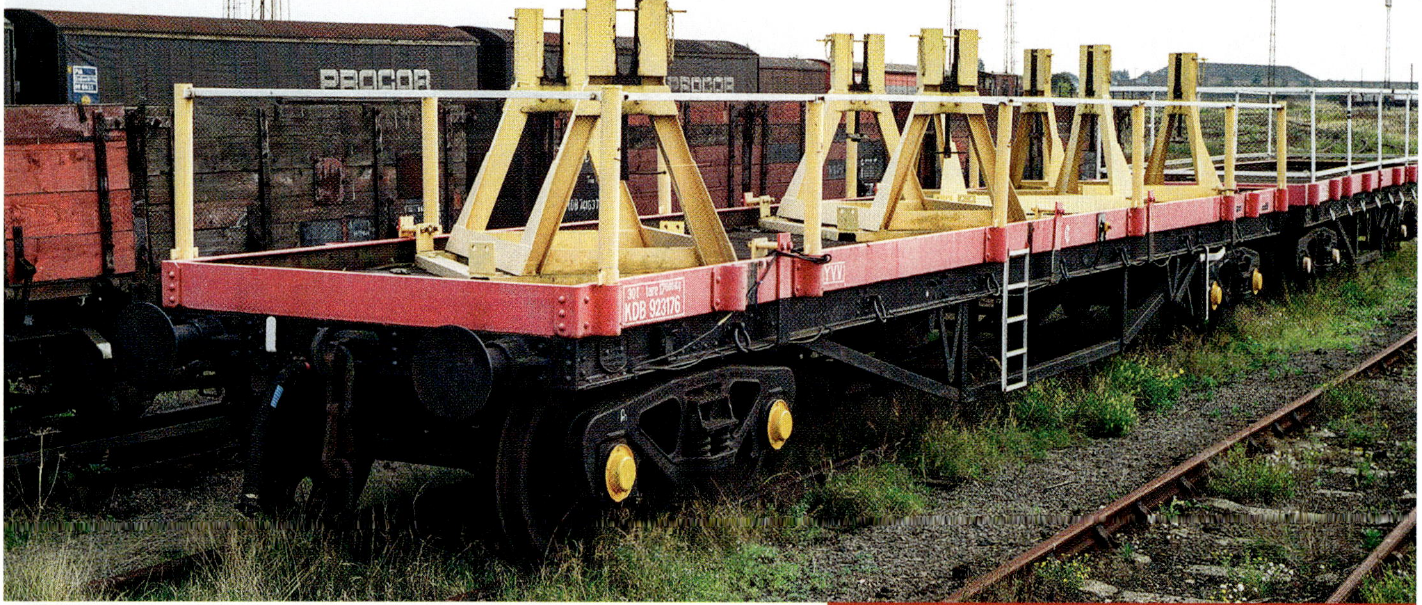

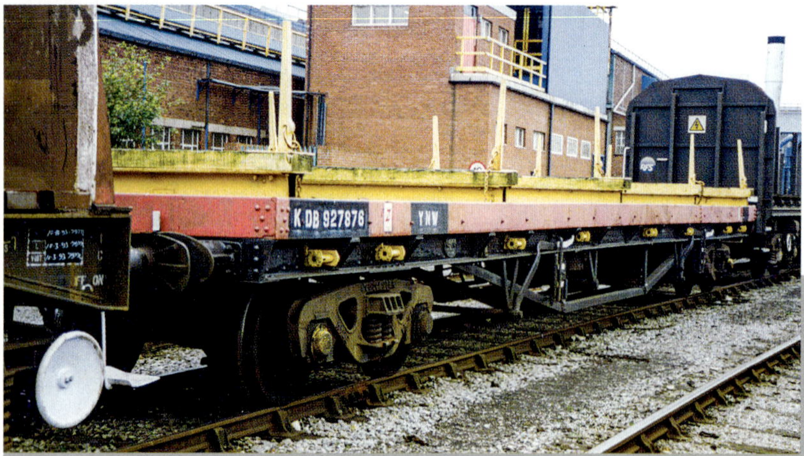

ABOVE: **Apart from the YVA cable drum carrier conversions of BDA bolster wagons, various vacuum-braked flat wagons were also modified for the same purpose. Typical of the breed is former Bogie Bolster C KDB923176, the YVV being recorded at Whitemoor Yard in September 1993. Also visible is YRW KDB923962, which was originally a Bogie Bolster E. This has been fitted all round with safety handrails for use as a mobile work platform, for example it could be positioned under signal gantries to improve access rather than staff having to work from ground level.** David Ratcliffe

LEFT: **Not all of the Bogie Bolster D wagons were converted to air brake and became BDAs, One such example was KDB927876, which was taken into S&T use for carrying assorted long loads, becoming a YNW. However, when seen at Allied Steel and Wire's Tremorfa Works in Cardiff on October 24, 1993, it was back in revenue-earning traffic but neither recoded nor repainted.** Hywel Thomas

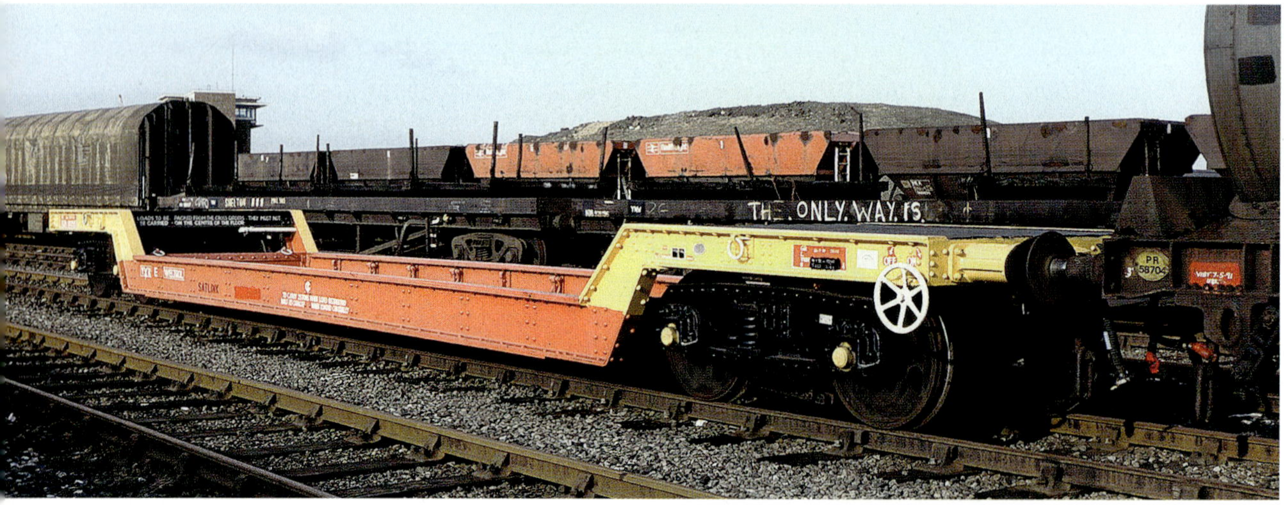

ABOVE & RIGHT: **The Weltrols were a useful addition to the S&T fleet, duties including carrying scrap material, such as signals, away from worksites while they could also be used to move portable buildings. When seen at Tees Yard in February 1992, dual-piped KDB900935 was sporting full Satlink livery while vacuum-piped sister KDB900937 was only in all-over signal red at Radyr in August 1991.** David Ratcliffe

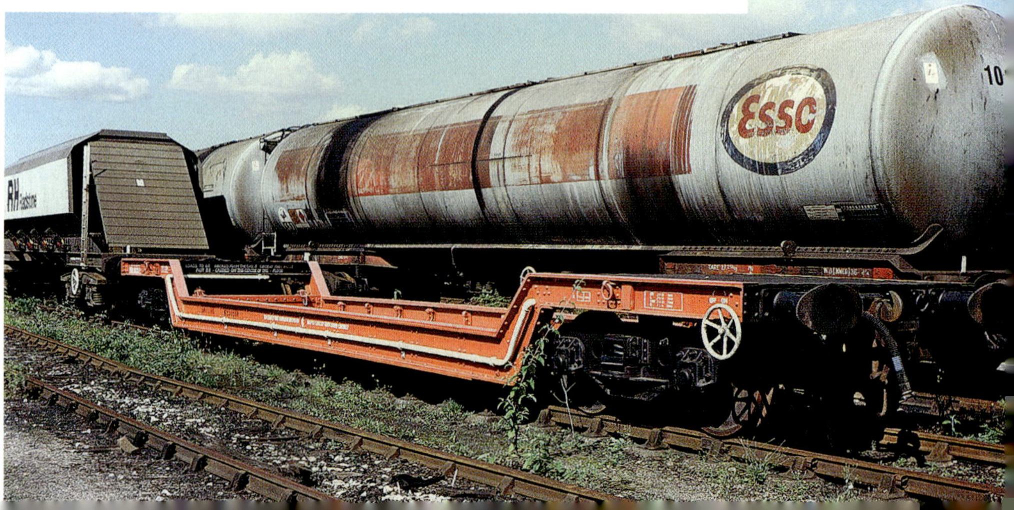

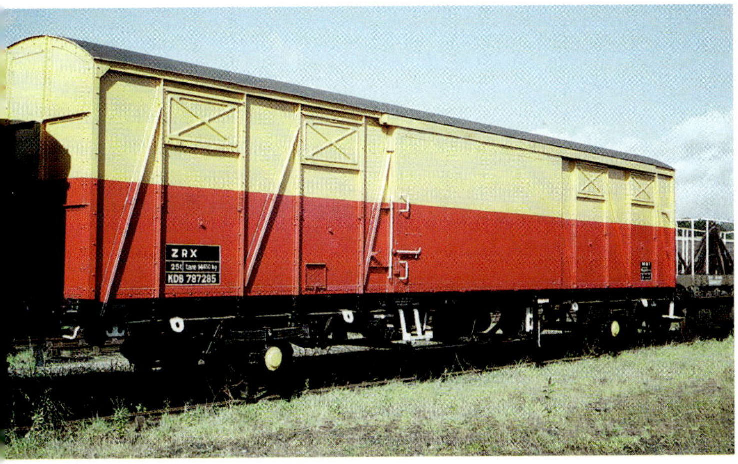

ABOVE: **Repainted in Satlink colours but otherwise unaltered, 20-ton ferry van KDB787285 was at Radyr during September 1991 and recoded as a ZRX. Like the former VDA vans, these were used to move stores to and from S&T depots, providing both weather protection and security.** David Ratcliffe

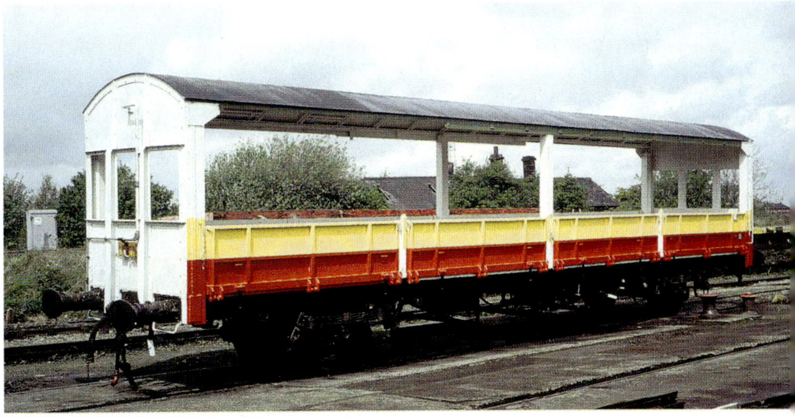

ABOVE: **As their stores use petered out in favour of road movements, some of the ferry vans were converted into ZDX general material carriers. These retained their ends, albeit modified, and roof but the sides were completely replaced by four drop doors. The wagons were also fitted with integral lighting. KDB787167 is seen part way through conversion at Carlisle Currock in May 1992 with its paintwork yet to be completed and lettering applied** David Ratcliffe

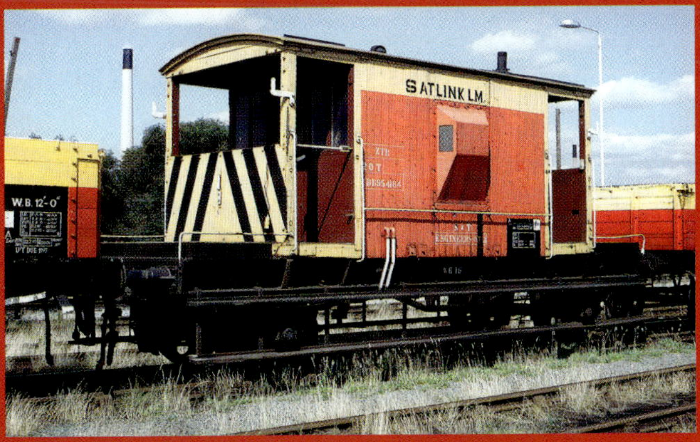

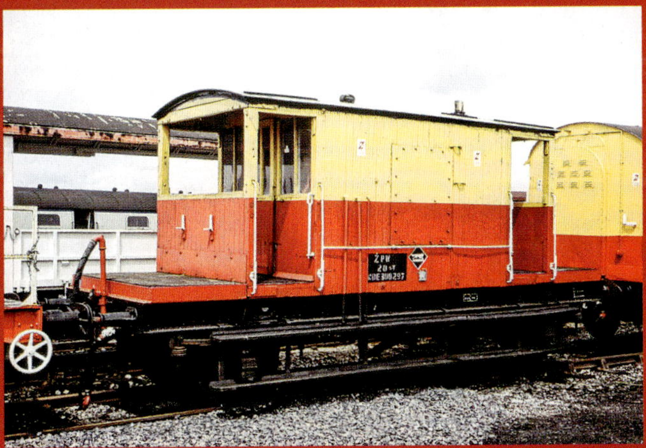

BOTH ABOVE: **The brake vans owned by the S&T Engineers were not used in their traditional role by this time, instead serving as personnel carriers. When seen at Ellesmere Port in July 1992, ZTR KDB954164 had received no obvious modifications for this role but its positioning within the middle of the rake of wagons confirms its new purpose. Veteran LNER brake van KDE300297 was more obviously altered at Carlisle Currock in September 1995, having seen its duckets removed and plated over. Also recoded as ZPW, it still retained tall vacuum pipes.** David Ratcliffe

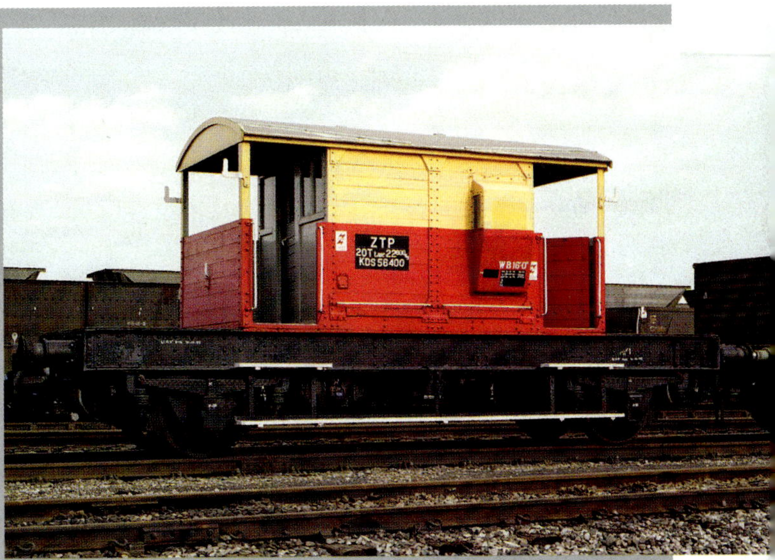

ABOVE & BELOW: **In much the same way, Southern-design brake vans were also retained for personnel transport. On former Southern metals, the two-axle Pillbox design was quite common as typified by ZTP KDS56400 at Hoo Junction on February 12, 1995. Over two years later, YTW Queen Mary KDS56305 is seen at Warrington Arpley during May 1997. Although now in EWS ownership, it had performed a similar role earlier in the decade.** Ian Cuthbertson/David Ratcliffe

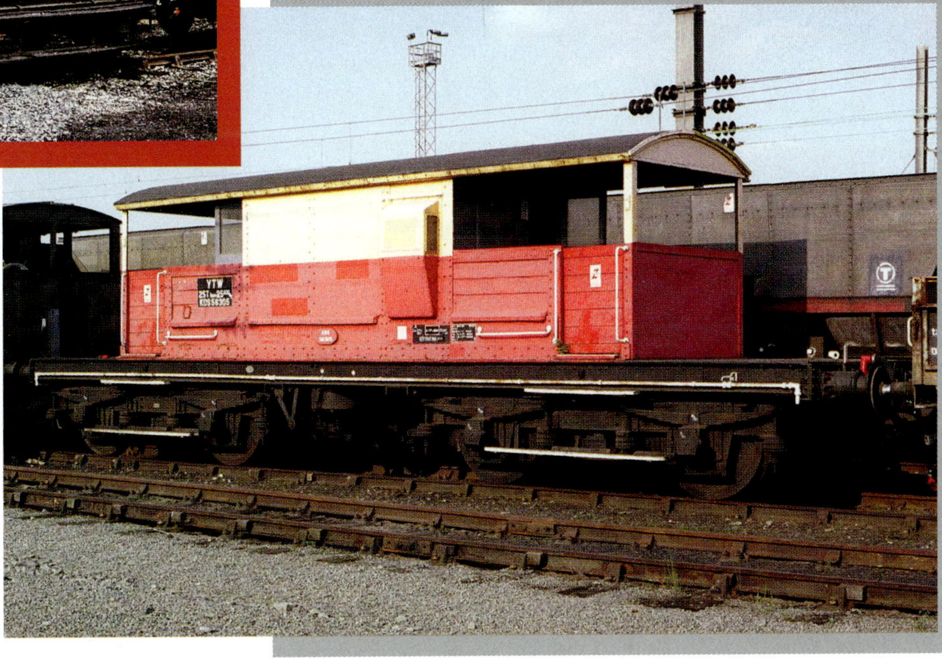

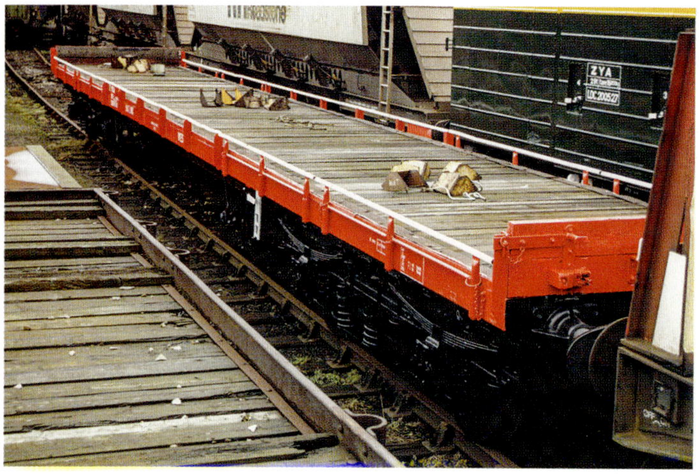

ABOVE: **Carflat KDB745138 seems an unlikely transfer to the S&T fleet but, freshly repainted in red, the YRW is seen at Radyr on January 20, 1991. Still carrying its vehicle chocks on the deck, it is unknown what role it performed but is lettered for Satlink Western.** Hywel Thomas

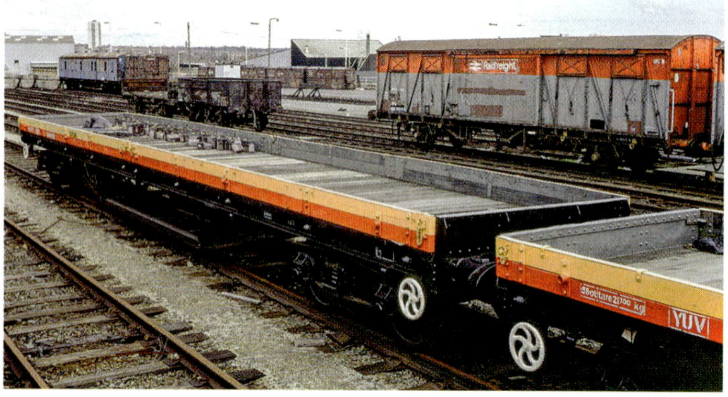

ABOVE: **The former vacuum-braked Boplate wagons tended to be used in the recovery of scrap materials from worksites or S&T depots. However, when recorded at Tyneside Central Freight Depot in March 1991, YUV KDB948059 was seemingly an odd choice of wagon to be carrying numerous scrap batteries recovered from lineside equipment.** David Ratcliffe

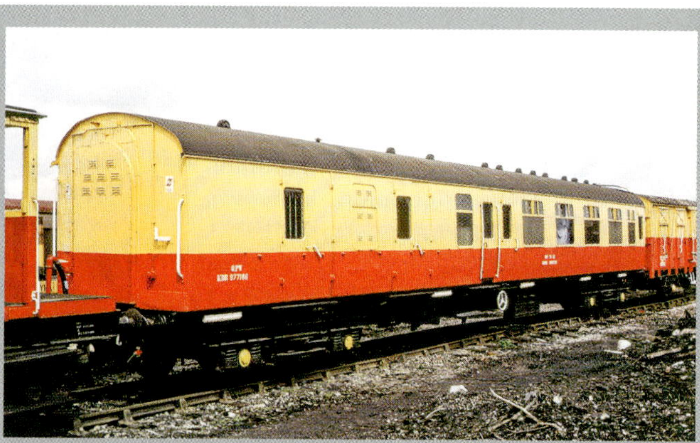

ABOVE & BELOW: **A small number of Mk1 and pressure-ventilated Mk2 staff coaches were given Satlink colours, the style of application typically varying depending on where the repaint was done. Originally converted for Project Mercury before joining the regular S&T fleet, KDB977168 was at Carlisle Currock in May 1992 with red and yellow ends. In contrast, KDB977143 had black ends upon outshopping from Cardiff Cathays in June 1991 along with anti-vandal mesh and Satlink Western branding.** David Ratcliffe/Hywel Thomas

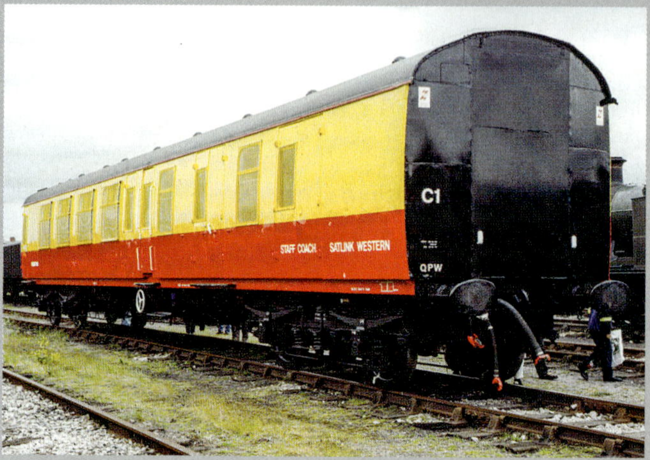

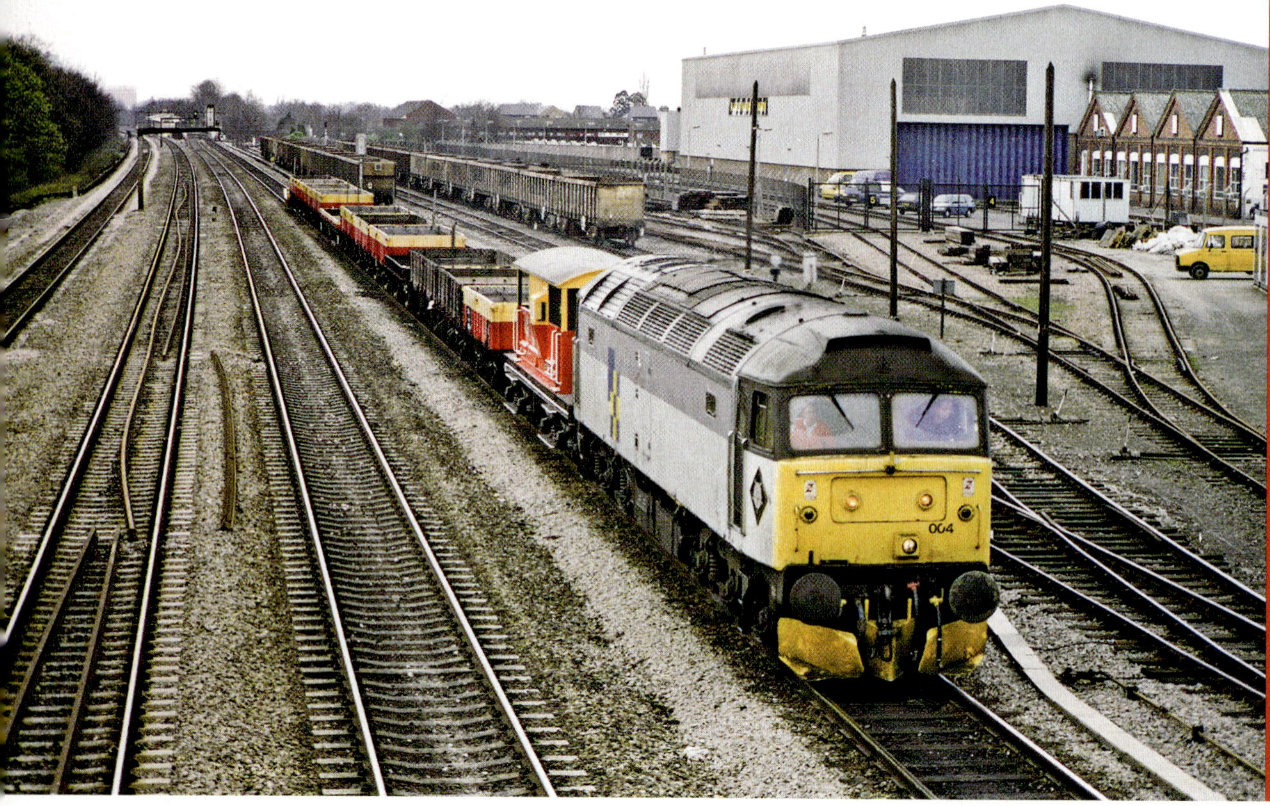

LEFT: **Railfreight Construction-liveried 47004, by then part of the InterCity-operated Great Western infrastructure fleet, ambles past the Plasser & Theurer works at West Ealing on March 18, 1993, with a mixed rake of vehicles. The majority are 12-ton Pipe wagons with a couple yet to be repainted and some carrying the wooden poles for lighting to be added to. Other types include a Queen Mary brake van showing its personnel carrier role, a Plate still in bauxite, a repainted Boplate and, just visible on the rear, a Satlink-liveried Lowmac.** Ian Cuthbertson

Satlink HAP crane wagon by Paul Wade

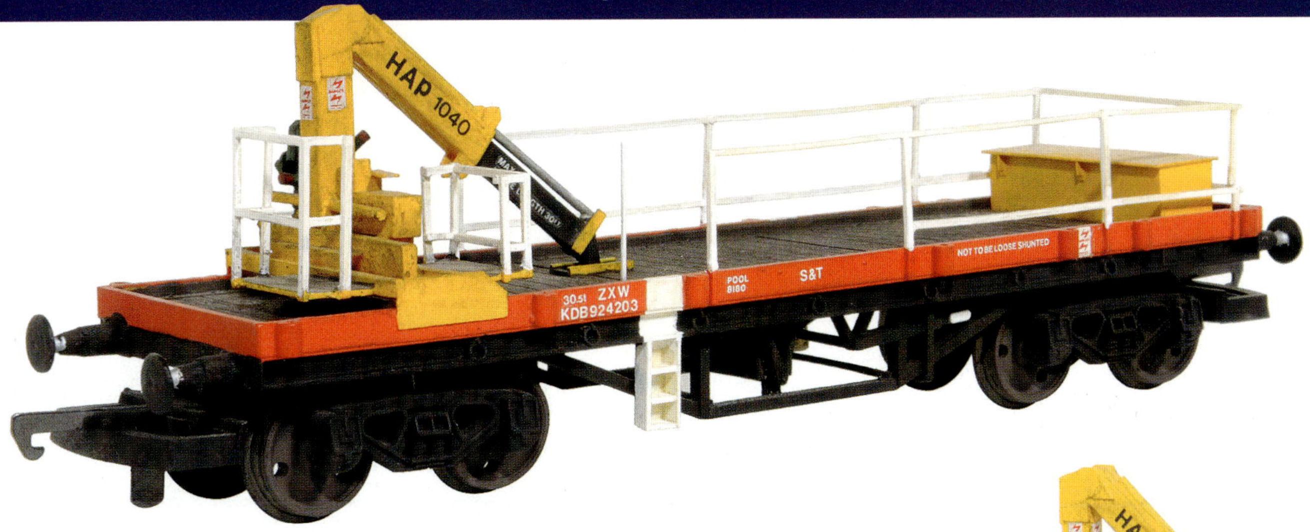

This wagon, KDB924203, was converted from a Bogie Bolster E but was incorrectly coded ZXW instead of receiving a 'Y' code from the bogie engineers' wagon grouping. It had a HAP 1040 extending arm crane to load and unload items from its wooden floor and is pictured in an earlier form on page 91. The wagon was provided with handrails for staff protection while in use on site, plus a tool box at the far end.

I used the Lima Bogie Bolster E wagon as the starting point, first removing the bolsters from the floor and then covering the slots left behind with lengths of styrene strip. The tool box was made from 20thou plasticard with a 10thou lid and small sections of strip used as hinges and floor mounts. The HAP crane, mounting frame and small engine were all completely scratchbuilt from plasticard and sections of various profiles. Luckily, I had many photos of this wagon, including looking down from the footbridge at Tonbridge West Yard. When the jib was stowed, it rested on a small frame on the floor, which was again made from plastic strip.

The handrails on the HAP crane and those around the sides of the wagon were made from 30thou by 30thou strip with the uprights fixed to the sides. While this is not that strong, care when handling helps plus any breakages are usually at joints that can be re-glued. Other additions included a handrail by the step on one side, made from a length of 0.5mm brass wire, while the steps themselves were fabricated from plastic strip on 10thou bases and then fitted to the solebars. Future jobs include replacing the incorrect Lima bogies with the Gloucester type from Cambrian while the vacuum and air pipes along with coupling hooks also need to go on.

The underframe has received some attention with the addition of cross bracing on the trussing. Painting encompassed red

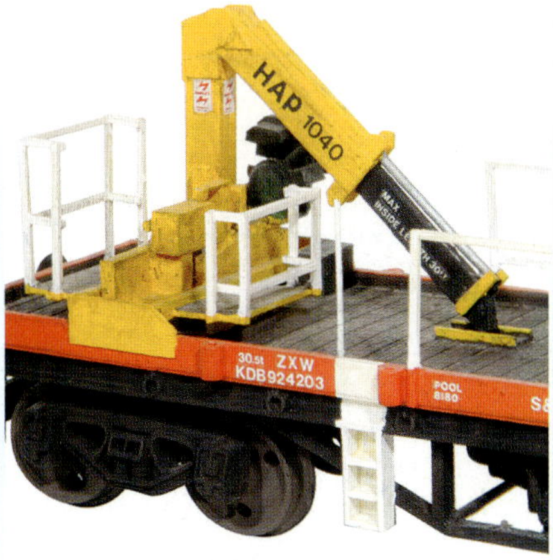

bodysides and ends, yellow tool box and crane, green engine, white handrails and steps, brown floor and black solebars, underframe and bogies. Transfers were from Woodhead with the HAP 1040 branding made with lettering and number sheets.

A HIAB Lowmac by Steve Farmer

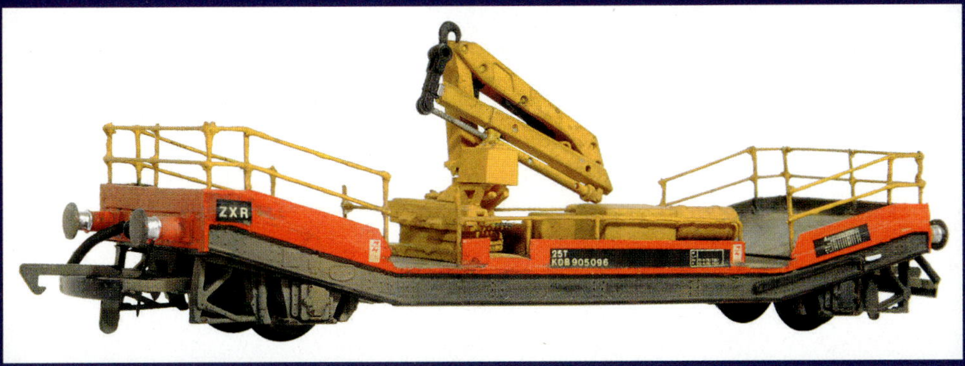

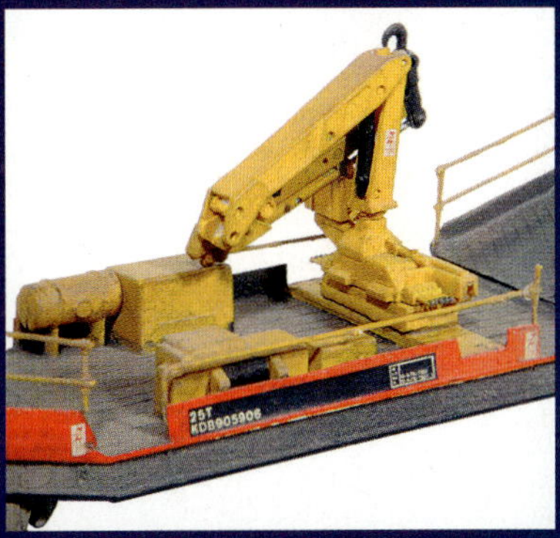

Numbered KDB905096, this was a former Lowmac fitted with a HIAB crane and coded ZXR. The prototype worked out of Chester delivering equipment to the lineside. This uses the former Airfix, now Hornby, ready-to-run model as a basis with the handrails round the sides and ends made from brass wire. At the base of the handrails, kickboards were made from plastic sheet, while the floor of the angled ends was covered in chequer plate, which was represented using embossed plasticard.

The HIAB crane came from Kibri and was mounted to a section of plasticard and fixed to the floor. In the well section, a plastic air tank was fitted to represent the fuel tank while a compressor from Southern Pride's EMU underframe set was placed on its side, this giving a good match to one of the boxes on the prototype. The other items were cobbled together from the scrap box.

The kickboards and ends were painted red with the crane, handrails, tank, and boxes in the well all in yellow. The floor was finished in brown and the chassis in black. The transfers were black panels onto which the numbers and lettering were applied using Fox Transfers individual character sheets, with the wagon then varnished and weathered.

Project Mercury

Installing the Mercury communications network during the 1980s and early 1990s brought much additional work for BR as the fibre optics were laid alongside its lines. This included providing a dedicated fleet of wagons in a fetching blue livery as David Ratcliffe explains.

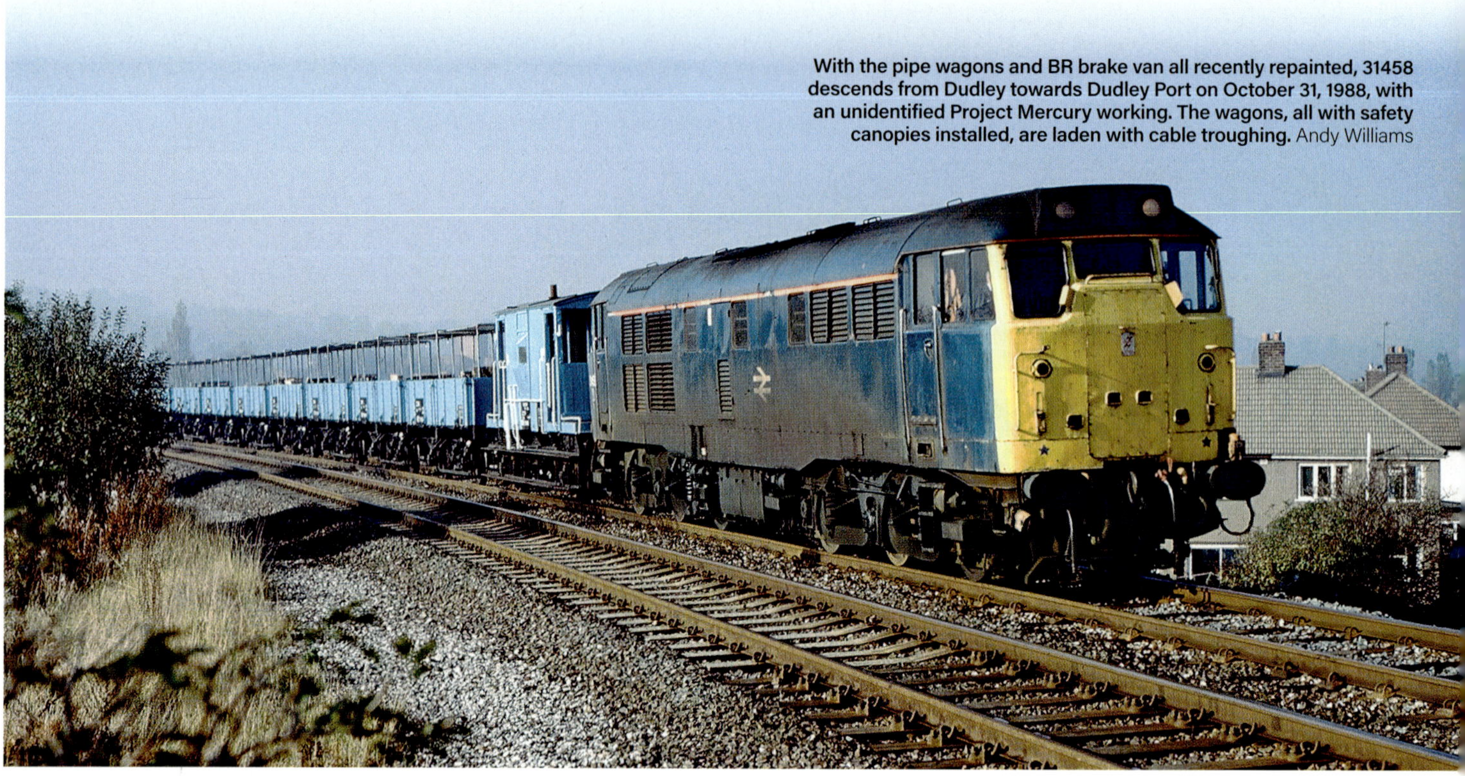

With the pipe wagons and BR brake van all recently repainted, 31458 descends from Dudley towards Dudley Port on October 31, 1988, with an unidentified Project Mercury working. The wagons, all with safety canopies installed, are laden with cable troughing. Andy Williams

In 1982, a consortium comprising Cable & Wireless, British Petroleum and Barclays Merchant Bank were granted a licence to construct a new digital fibre optic communications network in competition with British Telecom. Known as Mercury Communications, the network was in the form of a figure of eight centred on Birmingham, where Mercury established its national operations centre.

The fibre optic cables were laid along British Rail's right of way, with the northern loop running via Wolverhampton, Stafford, Stoke, Crewe and Warrington to Manchester, and then on to Leeds via Huddersfield before returning back south to Birmingham through Sheffield, Nottingham, Derby and Tamworth. The southern loop ran from Birmingham via Coventry, Rugby and Milton Keynes to London, before heading west through Reading and Swindon to Bristol. The loop then returned to Birmingham by way of Gloucester, Cheltenham and Worcester.

Several additional cable branches were also subsequently laid, such as those to Dover, Exeter, Liverpool, Newcastle and Southampton. Although the original plan had only envisaged serving large businesses, this changed in 1986 when the company invested heavily in order to offer access to smaller firms and residential customers, while 1987 saw the opening of the first Mercury public telephones at London Waterloo.

Dedicated fleet

BR allocated well over 100 wagons to the project, including pipe and tube wagons to carry the concrete troughing for the cable runs and modified Bogie Bolster C to convey

BELOW: **At first, the Project Mercury wagons retained their existing liveries, sometimes with additional 'Mercury' lettering. Pictured at Ardwick West, Manchester, in February 1986 are KDB732681, a 22-ton tube wagon, and 12-ton pipe wagon KDB740678. Both are coded ZDV and display the rudimentary lighting fitted to these vehicles, which was light bulbs suspended between wooden posts nailed to the wagons!** David Ratcliffe

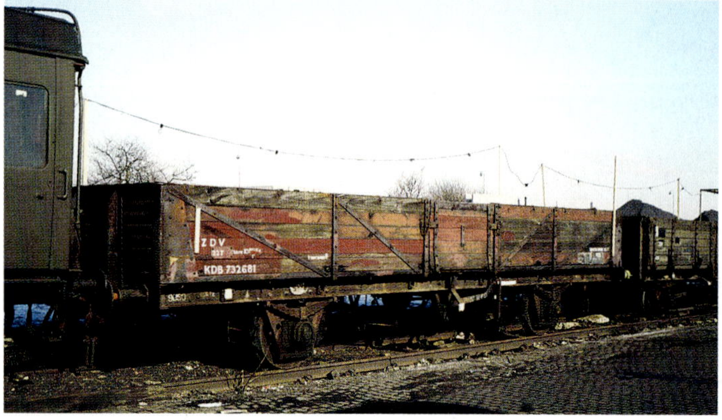

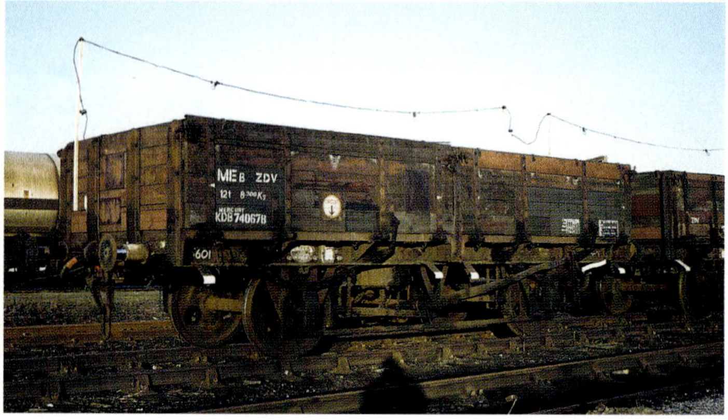

the large drums of cables. Each Mercury works train also included a coach that had been converted into a staff and generator vehicle. This provided mess facilities for the work crews as well as power for the rudimentary lighting which had been fitted to the wagons, given that most cable laying was undertaken at night.

At first, the various vehicles allocated to Project Mercury retained their existing bauxite or olive green liveries but from mid-1987, all the wagons were gradually repainted in an attractive light blue colour as well as being fitted with a through air pipe. In addition, from 1984 some of the wagons were fitted with a mesh canopy which provided staff protection when working beneath overhead wires.

As cable laying progressed during the 1980s, the work moved from area to area with the trains operating from several different bases including Ardwick, Chaddesden, Great Bridge, Normanton, Poole, Reading, Retford, Stafford, and Worcester.

BR Telecommunications

In 1992 and with rail privatisation on the horizon, BR Telecommunications Ltd (BRT) was created to manage and maintain the railway's own extensive telecom network and with many of the existing S&T and Mercury wagons now reaching the end of their life, authority was given to begin modifying redundant air-braked stock for future work.

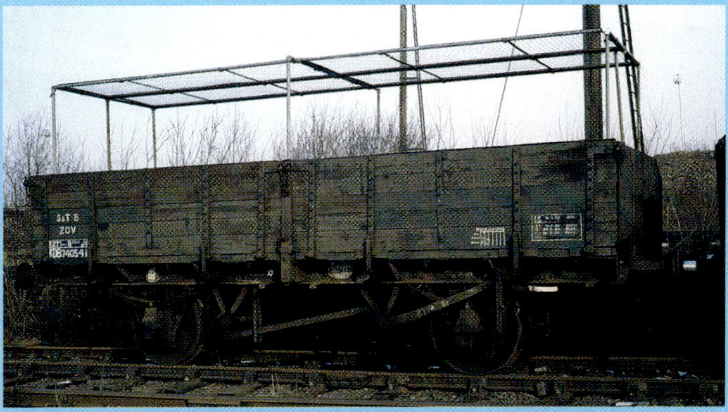

RIGHT: **By 1986, an increasing number of Project Mercury wagons were being fitted with a protective mesh canopy as seen on olive green ZDV KDB740541, this being a LNER-design pipe built by BR in 1949, which was recorded on a cold January 2, 1986, at Ardwick West.** David Ratcliffe

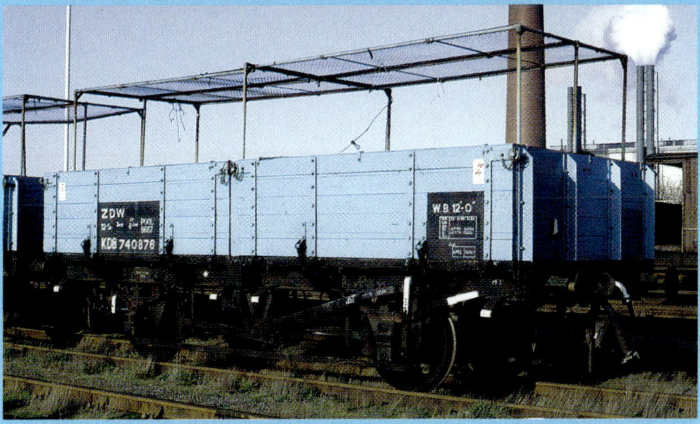

RIGHT: **The introduction of the light blue livery in 1987 transformed the Project Mercury fleet from drab anonymity to some of the most colourful on the network and ensured they are still remembered today. Twelve-ton pipe KDB740876 was at Ellesmere Port in December 1992.** David Ratcliffe

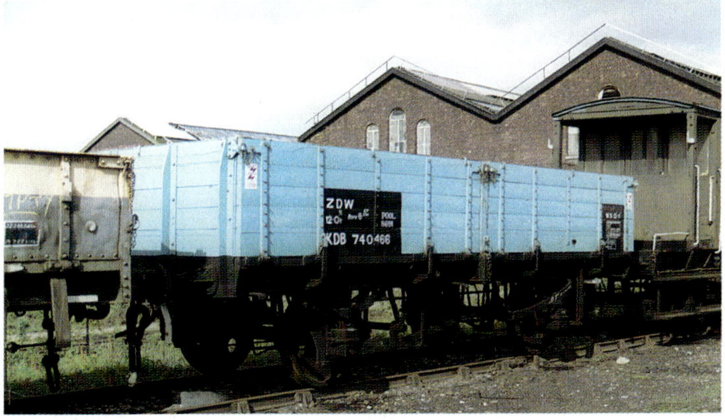

ABOVE: **Not all the pipe wagons received a canopy as illustrated by KDB740466, seen at Newton Heath Concrete Works, Manchester, in September 1990. Much of the troughing required for Project Mercury was produced here, but by this date the works was in decline, losing its rail connection in October 1992.** Colin Wright/David Ratcliffe Collection

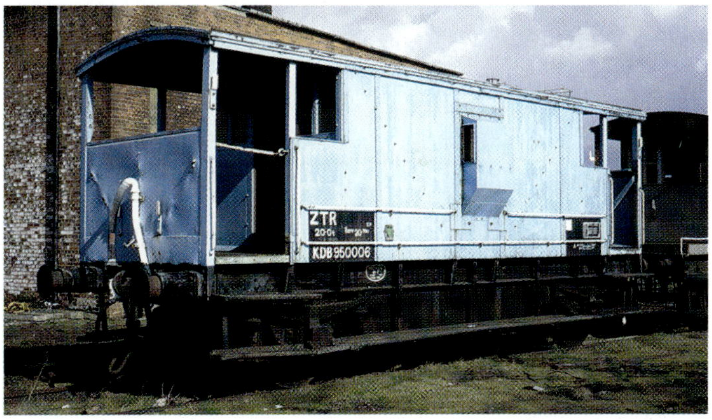

ABOVE: **Built in 1949, ZTR KDB950006 was the only LMS design brake van assigned to the project. At some point prior to its blue repaint, it had received a complete reskin, losing its planked bodywork in favour of patched plywood. It was withdrawn from the main line at the end of 1993 and when seen in March 1996, was in internal use at Ditton creosoting works.** David Ratcliffe

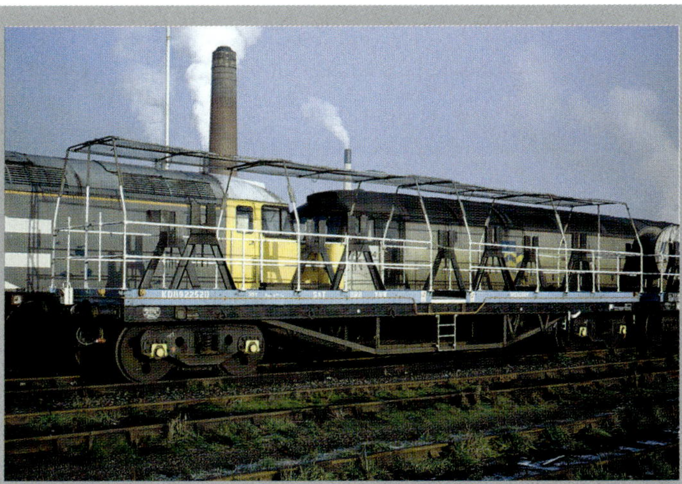

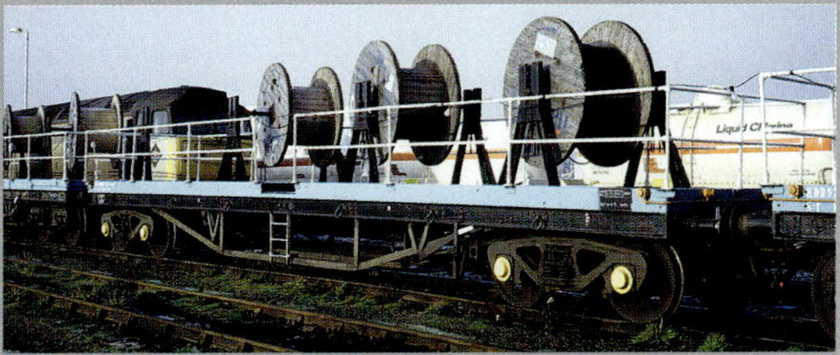

LEFT & ABOVE: **The modified 30-ton Bogie Bolster C used to carry the cable drums also received the light blue livery, although not all were fitted with mesh canopies. Conversely, some of those that did gain canopies were still finished in olive green. Seen at Ellesmere Port on December 20, 1992 and both coded YNW were KDB922520, this having the canopies, while KDB923293 was unmodified and still loaded with empty drums after a previous job.** David Ratcliffe

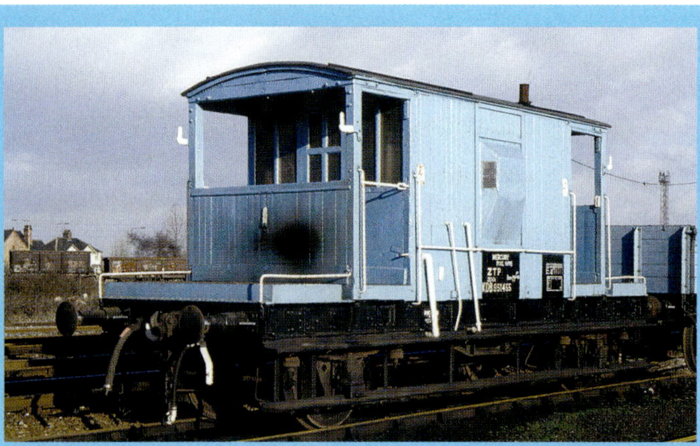

ABOVE: **It is believed that Project Mercury was only assigned five BR standard brake vans including ZTP KDB954155, which was often used to assist the propelling move required to access the concrete works at Newton Heath from Thorpes Bridge Junction, where the connecting link crossed the Red Bank line around a sharp reverse curve. However, in December 1988 it was to be found with a works train at Northwich Down Sidings.** Trevor Mann

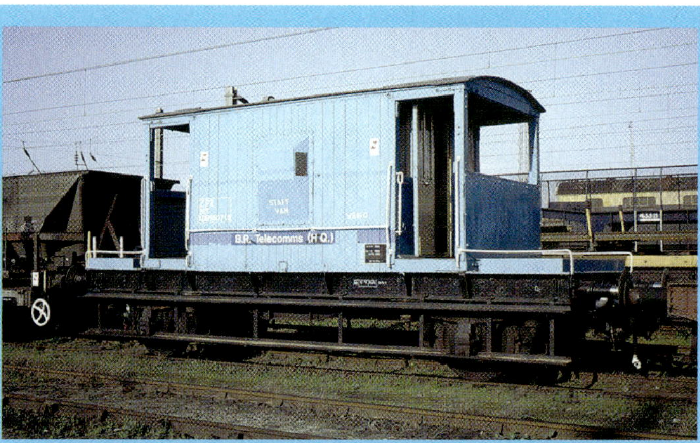

ABOVE: **Like a number of other brake vans assigned to the S&T Engineers, KDB950718 had been modified into a staff van for use by Project Mercury personnel when heading to and at worksites. Seen at Warrington Arpley in May 1992 and now coded ZPR, this also included a more elaborate livery with the addition of a dark blue band. By this date, BR Telecomms (HQ) branding had also been applied.** David Ratcliffe

This began with the conversion of BDA bogie bolsters into YVA cable drum carriers while five dual-braked BR ferry vans were rebuilt into ZDX general materials carriers. Then in 1994 some 16 VDA vans underwent a similar conversion into ZDAs while more YVAs were also authorised, all these rebuilt wagons then being allocated to a new BRT operations base at Stafford. The ZDA and ZDX were frequent seen in the engineers' sidings at Crewe Gresty Lane and Ditton, from where they would collect new concrete troughing, while the YVAs were loaded with cable at several locations, including Leeds Whitehall Road and Preston Dock Street.

Like the rebuilt ferry vans, the initial YVAs were painted in S&T red and yellow but the 1994 batch appeared in a pale grey livery with green BRT lettering as did the 16 ZDAs. This matched the look of the Class 20s that had also been assigned to the operation.

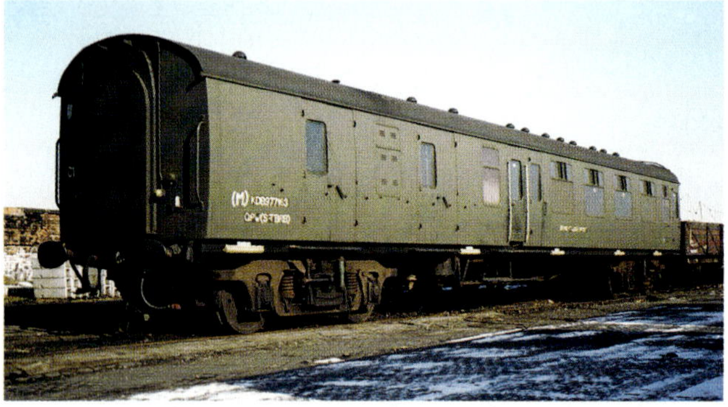

ABOVE: **To power the lighting, each Project Mercury train included a staff and generator coach such as QPW KDB977163 seen at Ardwick West in February 1986. Seven converted Mk.1 coaches, KDB977162-68, were allocated to the project and finished in olive green, although by 1991 at least one of the coaches had been repainted in Satlink red and yellow.** David Ratcliffe

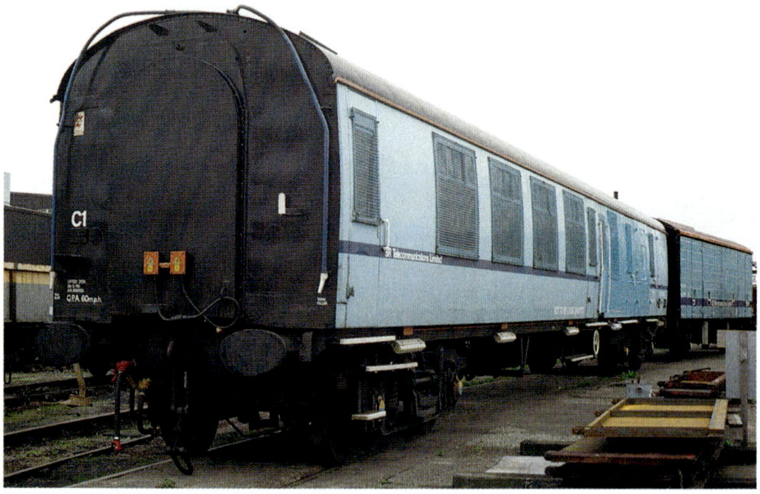

ABOVE: **Most of the Mk.1 staff and generator coaches would go on to receive the Project Mercury blue livery and then transfer to the BRT fleet. However, only three appear to have seen much further use with BDC977165/66/68 being supplemented by two generator vans converted from VDAs. Now coded QPA after conversion from vacuum to air brakes, BDC977166 (ex BSK 35419) is seen at Chester wagon repair depot on April 4, 1997 in the company of ZXA generator van BDC210382. BRT adopted the ownership prefix of 'B' for its rolling stock, hence 'BDC', but this was even used on the coaches when they should have become 'BDB'. The Mk.1 is also now fitted with anti-vandal mesh screens over all the windows.** David Ratcliffe

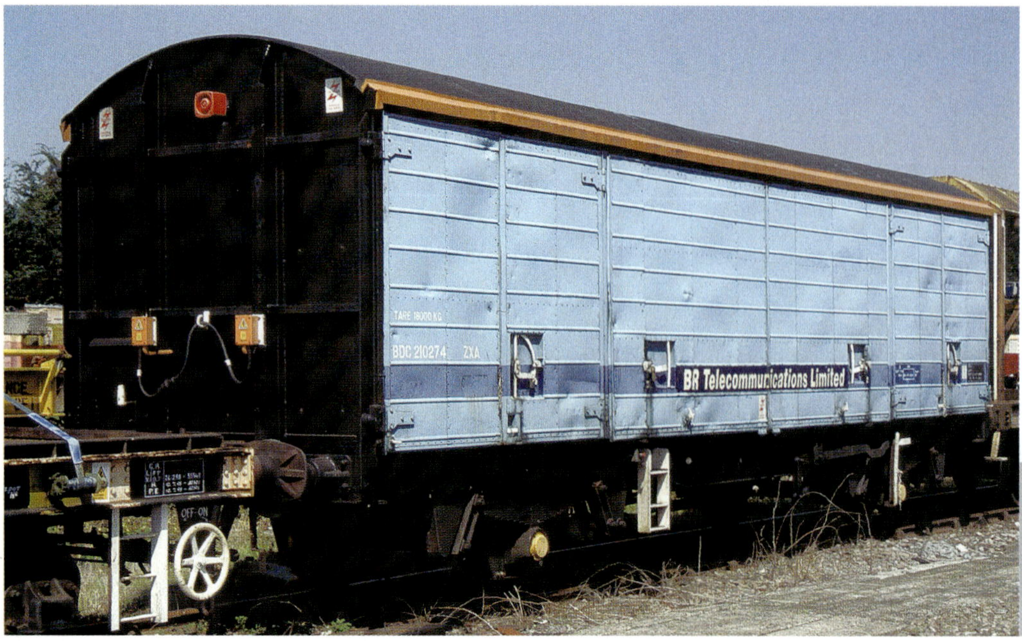

LEFT: **The other former VDA van converted into a ZXA generator vehicle was BDC210274, which is seen at Crewe Gresty Lane engineers' yard in August 1998.during its time in BRT ownership.** David Ratcliffe

Only the Mk.1 staff and generator van lets the side down in the corporate image stakes as 20128 *Guglielmo Marconi* and 20075 *Sir William Cooke* climb away from Ryecroft, near Walsall, with a 6L95 Bescot to Beeston working on May 13, 1996. The rest of the train is made up of 12 ZDA material carriers. By this date, BRT had been acquired by Racal and would be merged with another division the following year, leading to the sale of the Class 20s to Direct Rail Services. Andy Williams

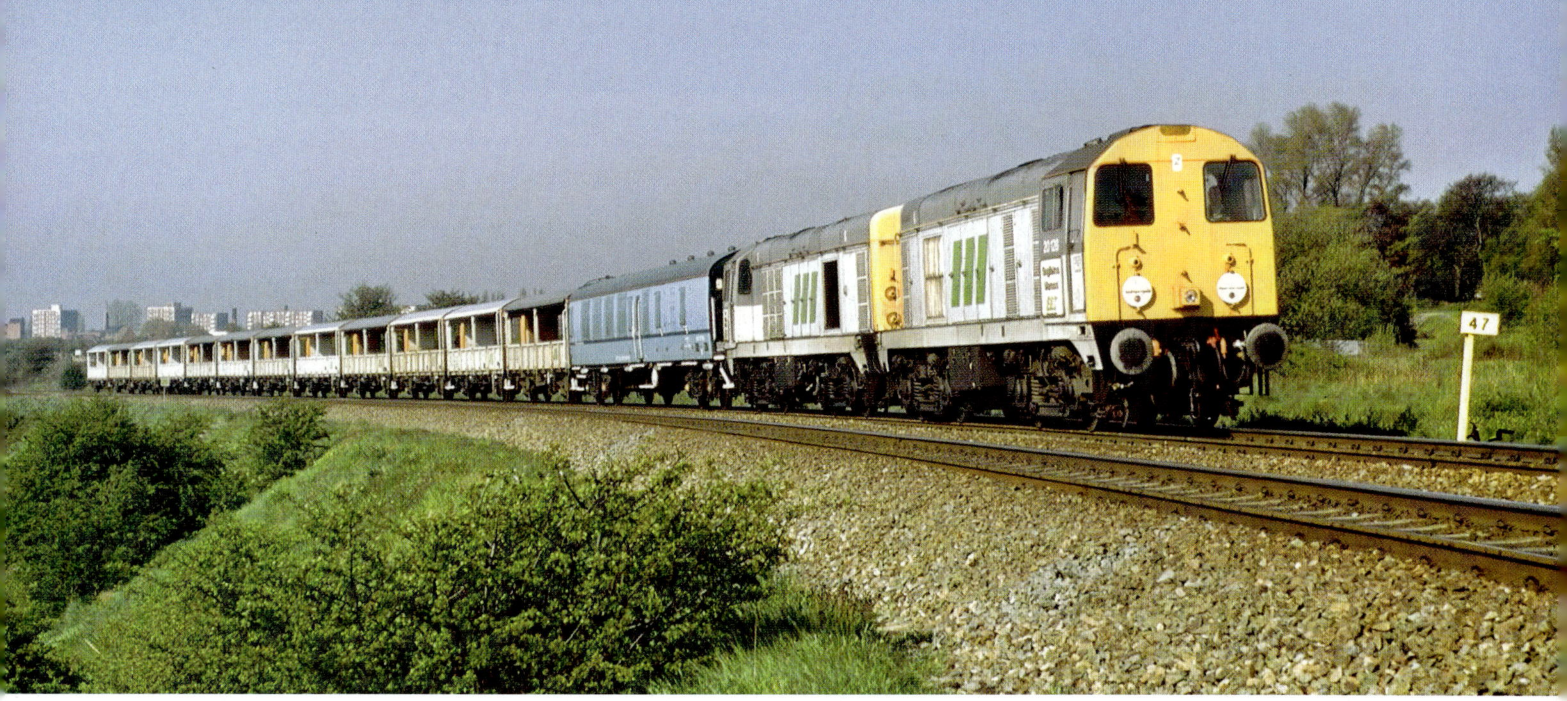

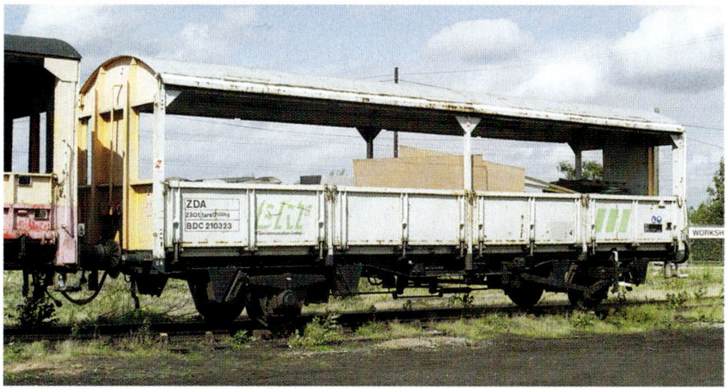

ABOVE: **Converted from a VDA van at Doncaster Works during 1994, ZDA BDC210323 was recorded at Ditton in August 1998 when carrying waste sheets of plywood and miscellaneous packaging material.** David Ratcliffe

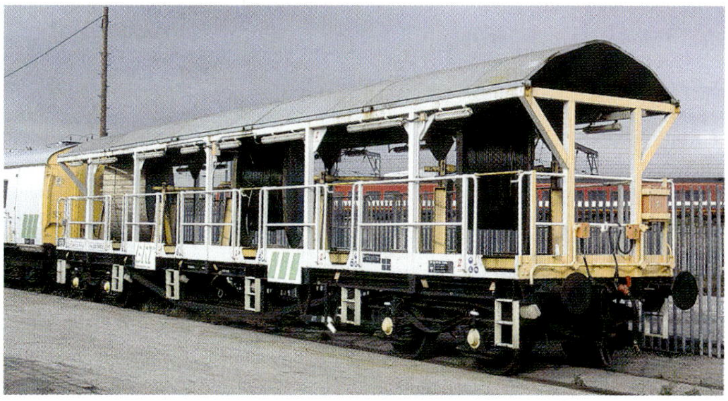

ABOVE: **The YVA cable drum carriers followed their S&T sisters in having an open framework to support electric lighting. Unlike these earlier examples, the BRT batch also gained a roof as demonstrated by BDC950210 at Leeds Whitehall Road in November 1996, this carrying drums of new cables.** David Ratcliffe

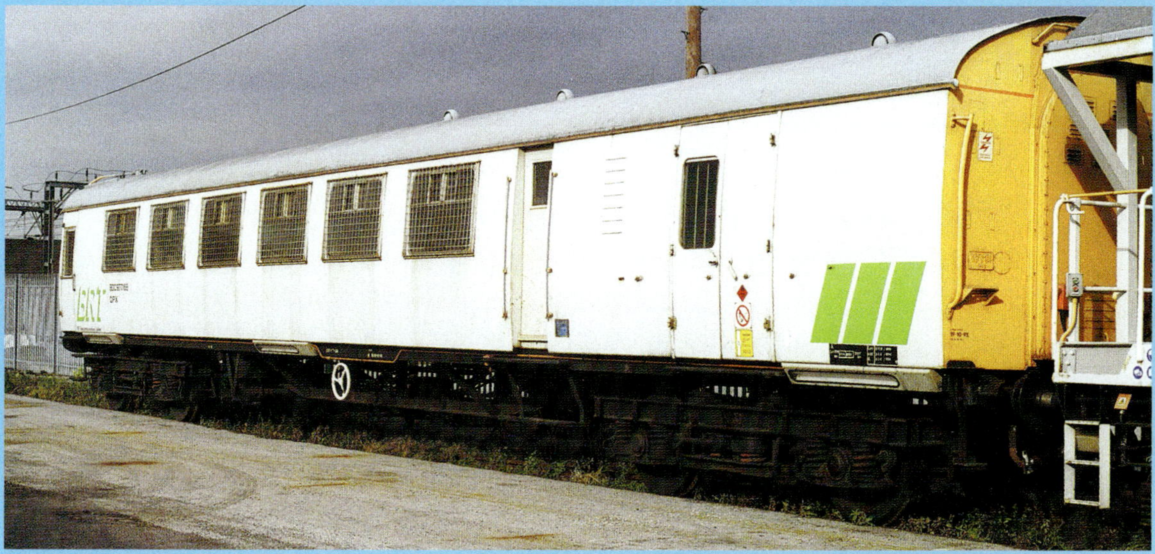

LEFT: **Also stabled with the YVA at Leeds on the same day was staff and generator coach BDC977168, the dual-braked QPX having also gained BRT colours. By the end of the decade, this coach along with BDC977166 were in use on the West Coast route modernisation project, being employed in the Multi-Purpose Vehicle (MPV) formations.** David Ratcliffe

Modelling Mercury by Mike Cubberley

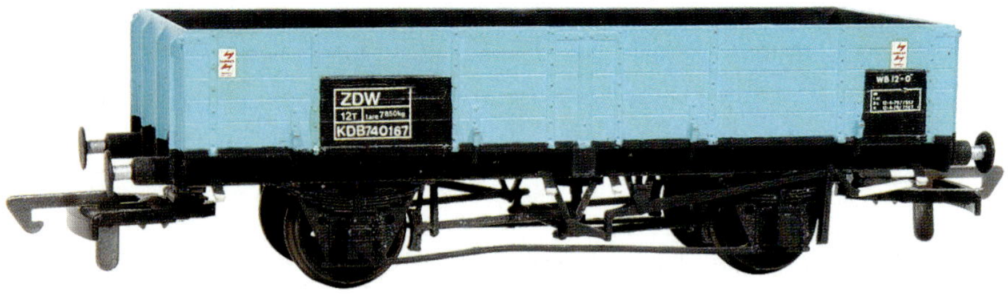

Despite the colourful livery, it is quite rare to see Project Mercury stock modelled, certainly in any quantity and going much beyond the pipe wagons. These three 4mm scale examples were actually built back in the mid-1990s and appeared on the Model Railway Club's New Annington layout. As such, they use the models of the day but the same methods can still be applied now to current generation offerings.

Beginning with the pipe wagon, these were used to carry concrete troughing and were the most common of the Project Mercury vehicles. The model pictured here is from the venerable Parkside kit (PC43), which is still available today. An alternative option is the ready-to-run 12-ton pipe now produced by Bachmann, which would require a repaint and is certainly a more expensive option if looking to produce a full train. The kit was built as per the instructions with the tension lock couplings mounted at the correct height on blocks of plasticard using superglue.

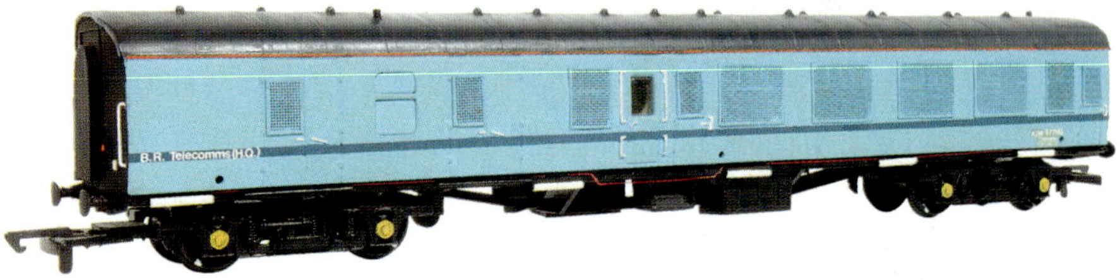

The BR brake van represents one of the staff riding vans used on the works trains and employs the even more vintage Airfix kit, as now produced by Dapol or easily found second-hand. Nowadays, the RTR model produced by Hornby is generally considered the most accurate of the various options and is relatively inexpensive. On this Airfix model, I carefully removed all of the moulded-on handrails using a small Xacto chisel blade and replaced them with 0.45mm brass wire fitted into 0.5mm holes drilled in the body with a pin vice. The horizontal bodyside handrail was soldered in situ to the adjacent vertical handrails with a quick swipe of a soldering iron; the plastic beneath being protected using wooden coffee stirring sticks. Careful painting using a self-mixed colour also produced a representative finish on the cast concrete end weights.

Coach conversion

The former Mk.1 BSK staff and generator coach conversion involved the most work and employed a Mainline model as the basis. This is still a valid choice today via the second-hand market, although the circular cut-outs in the body for the chassis fixings have always been a drawback. Alternative donors are the BSK offered by both Bachmann and Hornby. The corridor connections were carved off the ends and a representation of the blanking plate added to the smoothed-off ends using five thou plasticard, superglue being used to avoid any issues with 'solvent melt' to the thin sheet. The electrical conduit that runs around the plated corridor connections on the ends and also along the solebars on both sides was made using 0.5mm Slaters plastic rod. This can be bent as needed using a small set of straight nosed pliers and the solebar sections were painted very carefully in orange after they were applied. As part of the same task, the solebar lights were represented using plastic strip filed to shape and painted white.

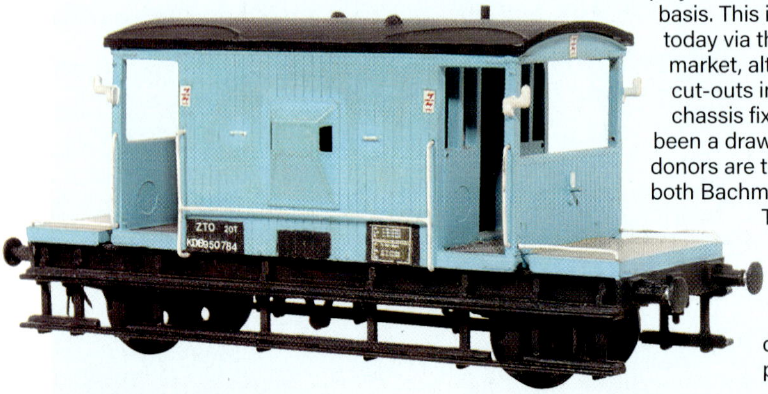

The anti-vandal mesh screens were made using some etched mesh from A1 Models with Microstrip added to create the framework. These were then carefully glued over each window, ensuring they were as straight as possible. All three models were painted using Railmatch Provincial light blue and coaching stock grey for the roofs. A little touch on the coach was to add the white tyre slip markings as these were prominent in photos.

The coach also received a Railmatch BR blue stripe along the lower bodysides and then the BR Telecomms (HQ) markings were added from individual Letraset rub-down dry print letters; those were the days! Other markings were a mixture of Replica, Cambrian and Fox with some being rub-down and others waterslide.

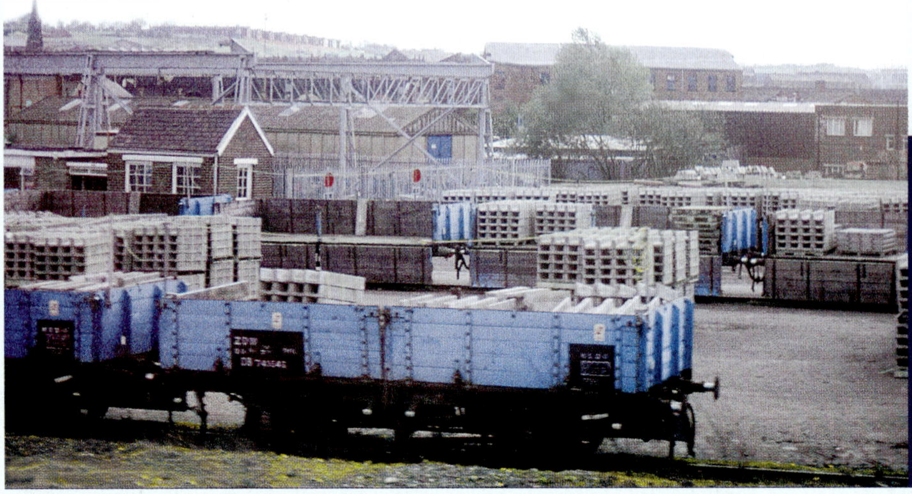

LEFT: **Although of indifferent quality, this image of Leeds Whitehall Road taken from a passing train in April 1993 shows Project Mercury in full swing and provides plenty of modelling interest. Numerous 12-ton pipe wagons are present and in the process of being filled with concrete troughing, these being loaded 16 to a pallet and secured with plastic strapping. The wagon on the far right also has a palletised load of troughing lids with approximately 40 stacked in an interlaced manner while the ZDW alongside has a stack of eight empty pallets as a partial load.** Simon Bendall Collection